EUROPEAN CITIES, PLANNING SYSTEMS AND PROPERTY MARKETS

EUROPEAN CITIES, PLANNING SYSTEMS AND PROPERTY MARKETS

Edited by

James Berry and Stanley McGreal
Real Estate Studies Unit, University of Ulster, UK

E & FN SPON
An Imprint of Chapman & Hall

London · Glasgow · Weinheim · New York · Tokyo · Melbourne · Madras

Published by
E & FN Spon, an imprint of Chapman & Hall, 2–6 Boundary Row,
London SE1 8HN, UK

Chapman & Hall, 2–6 Boundary Row, London SE1 8HN, UK

Blackie Academic & Professional, Wester Cleddens Road, Bishopbriggs, Glasgow G64 2NZ, UK

Chapman & Hall GmbH, Pappelallee 3, 69469 Weinheim, Germany

Chapman & Hall USA, One Penn Plaza, 41st Floor, New York NY 10119, USA

Chapman & Hall Japan, ITP-Japan, Kyowa Building, 3F, 2-2-1 Hirakawacho, Chiyoda-ku, Tokyo 102, Japan

Chapman & Hall Australia, Thomas Nelson Australia, 102 Dodds Street, South Melbourne, Victoria 3205, Australia

Chapman & Hall India, R. Seshadri, 32 Second Main Road, CIT East, Madras 600 035, India

First edition 1995

© 1995 E & FN Spon

Typeset by Best-set Typesetter Ltd., Hong Kong
Printed and bound in Great Britain by TJ Press (Padstow) Ltd, Cornwall

ISBN 0 419 18940 8

Contents

Contributors

Håkan Bejrum is Associate Professor in the Department of Real Estate and Construction Management at the Royal Institute of Technology, Stockholm. Professional interests include real property investment and management. Recent work has mainly focused on life-cycle economics and deregulation of the housing sector in Sweden.

Lorenzo Bellicini is Technical Director of CRESME in Rome. His research includes urban processes and non-urban transformation in contemporary society, with particular reference to the development process.

James Berry is a Lecturer in Estate Management at the University of Ulster and on the Board of the Real Estate Studies Unit. His main areas of research are economic development, urban regeneration and property investment. He is co-editor of *Urban Regeneration Property Investment and Development*.

Stuart Black is a Lecturer in the Department of Land Economy, University of Aberdeen. He specializes in policy evaluation and regional development, and was formerly a property research analyst with Hillier Parker Chartered Surveyors, London.

Jean-Claude Boyer is a Professor at the Institut Français d'Urbanisme (University Paris VIII). His research interests centre on the Benelux and the Paris regions. Publications include *La France: 22 régions de programme*, a study on the lle-de-France.

Guido De Brabander is Professor of Economic Geography, Urban and Regional Economics at the UFSIA University of Antwerp. He is currently Dean of the Faculty of Applied Economics. Research interests include economic development, urban decline and regeneration.

Göran Cars is Associate Professor in the Department of Regional Planning at the Royal Institute of Technology, Stockholm. His professional interests include the role of private and public actors in planning and urban development, and negotiation in the decision-making process.

Joseph Davis is Senior Lecturer in Urban and Regional Economics at the Dublin Institute of Technology. His research interests include demand forecasting, urban renewal, local and regional development.

Pavlos Delladetsima has worked as a planner and researcher at the National Technical University of Athens. He is currently a Human Capital Mobility Research Fellow (EC) at the Institut Fédératif de Recherche sur les Economies et les Sociétés Industrielles in Lille, France.

Hartmut Dieterich is Professor in the Department of Spatial Planning at the University of Dortmund and is a member of the University Senate. He has published extensively and was co-author of the recent text, *Urban Land and Property Markets in Germany*.

Egbert Dransfeld is in the Department of Spatial Planning at the University of Dortmund. He has researched into land and property markets in Western Europe and published on this theme, including co-authorship of *Urban Land and Property Markets in Germany*.

Charles France Fraser is currently Head of the Division of Planning within the School of Land Management and Urban Policy, South Bank University, London. He has conducted research on the housing development process in the United States and is currently engaged on an analysis of the impact on the planning system on the growth of owner-occupation in France.

Eamonn Judge is Professor at the Leeds Business School, Leeds Metropolitan University and a member of the university's Centre for Urban Development and Environmental Management. He has specialist research interests in Poland and has published extensively on the Polish planning system.

Thomas Kalbro is Associate Professor in the Department of Real Estate and Construction Management at the Royal Institute of Technology, Stockholm. He has published on the theme of urban and land development systems.

Olli Keinänen is a planner at the City Planning Department, Helsinki. He specializes in housing, strategic land-use planning and property development planning.

Geoffrey Keogh is Principal Lecturer and Head of the Unit for Property Research in the School of Urban and Regional Studies at Sheffield Hallam University and has been a Visiting Professor in the Universitat Autonoma de Barcelona. His research interests include the economic aspects of property markets and urban planning.

Seppo Laakso is Senior Actuary at the City of Helsinki Information Management Centre. Specialist interests include housing, the property market and population issues.

Kai Lemberg is an economist and town planner. Since 1986 he has been Professor at the Geographical Institute of Roskilde University, Denmark and was previously General Planning Director of the City of Copenhagen. His current research examines the relationship between transportation, planning and social economics.

Lila Leontidou is Senior Lecturer at the Department of Geography, King's College, University of London. She was formerly an Associate Professor at the National Technical University of Athens and has authored two books on the city of Athens.

Greg Lloyd is Professor of Planning Research at the University of Dundee. He is co-author of *Land Development and the Infrastructure Lottery* and *The Impact of Oil on the Aberdeen Economy* and is currently researching regional development agencies, land-use planning and property development.

Duncan Maclennan is the Mactaggart Professor of Land Economics and Finance, and Director of the Centre for Housing Research at the University of Glasgow. He has published widely in relation to housing market analysis, urban regeneration and the role of housing in national economies.

Stanley McGreal is Reader in Estate Management at the University of Ulster and on the Board of the Real Estate Studies Unit. His main areas of research include property market analysis, urban regeneration and housing. He is co-editor of *Urban Regeneration Property Investment and Development*.

Barrie Needham is Professor at the Department of Physical Planning, University of Nijmegen. He has published extensively and was co-author of *Urban Land and Property Markets in the Netherlands*. His research interests examine the relationship between town planning and the property market.

Ali R. Ghanbari Parsa is currently the Aubrey Orchard-Lisle Senior Research Fellow and Director of Property Research in the School of Land Management and Urban Policy, South Bank University, London. He has conducted research on the European property industry and is currently analysing UK and Japanese Environmental Planning and Policy.

Terry Prendergast is a Lecturer in Urban and Regional Planning at the Dublin Institute of Technology. She has worked with the UN Economic

Commission for Europe and her current research interests are in community planning and urban renewal.

Barry Redding is currently Professor and Head of Estate Management Division in the School of Land Management and Urban Policy, South Bank University, London. He is the Project Director of the Spare Space Project funded by the RICS and DoE, and Land Aid Charitable Trust.

Pere Riera is a Lecturer at the Autonomous University of Barcelona. He is an economist specializing in land-use issues and the valuation of environmental externalities in urban areas. He has published several books and is currently researching the economic impact of planning regulations in Spain.

Luděk Sýkora is a Lecturer in Urban Geography, Charles University of Prague. His research activities include contemporary urban restructuring with particular attention on revitalization processes and gentrification in the inner city of Prague, publishing widely on these themes.

Francesco Toso is responsible for Land and Property Information Systems at CRESME, Rome. His research involves the production of statistical information and analysis of the construction industry, a theme on which he has published a number of texts.

Johan van de Ven is a physical planner. He has worked at the Town Planning Agency of the Municipality of Amsterdam undertaking research into office policy and is now with Zadelhoff.

Ann Verhetsel is a Lecturer in Economic Geography and Spatial Economics at the UFSIA, University of Antwerp. Her research interests include the financial appraisal of enterprises and the analysis of property markets.

Preface

The increasing political and economic attention focusing on European integration has stimulated a growing interest in the investment markets of the major cities of Europe. International property investment criteria specify that a market must be accessible to overseas investors and that it must be relatively liquid in terms of the transactions that take place. In fulfilling these requirements planning systems have a significant effect in promoting or limiting development and investment opportunity. Throughout the market economies of Western Europe and the old command economies of Eastern Europe, the diversity of planning systems and practices and the relationship with institutional structures, cultures and economic opportunities is complex. However a common theme is the desire to combine local economic development objectives with those of the international investor. In this context the interaction between planning and other regulatory measures and land and property markets in both Western and Eastern European cities is of paramount importance.

Cities are, and will increasingly continue to be, major players in the overall development of regional, national and international economic systems. As centres of innovation cities are the driving force behind technological progress. The proliferation of new information technologies is leading to profound changes in which the traditional industrial city based on the production and manufacture of goods is being superseded by the new modern city labelled as the transactional city, the technology city and the informational city. The new information technologies are directly connected to fundamental economic change in which the city is bound ever more tightly into a single global market.

The structural trend towards the formation of the global economy will affect European cities through the internationalization of capital flows, labour markets, commodity markets, information, raw materials, management and organization. European cities will have to acknowledge their role in this new global economy by being competitive and capable of sustaining national and international development opportunities and investment. As cities jockey for new position in the emerging global economy those which intensify their dominance as a Eurocity will require international infrastructure, trade and communication flows, networking with other world cities, linkage into global investment markets and the resource base to attract key European institutions.

In this ongoing process European cities are beginning to adjust to the process of European Union based on the removal of barriers to international trade and including the harmonization of fiscal policies. Indeed if cities are to effectively meet the challenges following the ratification of the Maastricht Treaty, which came into force on 1 November 1993, managerial systems must support and in turn be supported by the efficient operation of land and property markets. Perhaps the most significant theme prevailing is that European business in its wider sense is seeking the means of consolidating operations on a cross-border basis. Despite the difficulties in the implementation of monetary union business pressures are shaping patterns of property demand. Ultimately this will incorporate both public- and private-sector interests, the fusion of which will be critical to optimizing returns and ensuring competitiveness between the major Eurocities.

To draw out these relationships within specific European cities we have called upon the expertise of academics and practitioners. Our purpose has been to bring together viewpoints from both town planning and real estates disciplines. Although several accounts have been published on planning, particularly in Western European countries, the interaction between planning systems and property markets at a city-wide level spanning both Western and Eastern Europe is a new area of research. One often repeated view of the European property market is that the volume and accessibility to rental and investment data is poor. Although this has undoubtedly been the case in the past, the situation is certainly changing. Data series now are being assembled by chartered surveying firms and other property consultants for most major European cities including those considered in this text, though it must be acknowledged that the quantity and quality of such data is highly variable between cities.

This text on *European Cities, Planning Systems and Property Markets* seeks to make a substantial contribution towards an understanding of how planning and property markets function under the different administrative regimes in comparative European cities. Drawing upon current research and property market data the book provides an insight into current practice and future direction; and is tailored to the needs of property professionals, investors, planning and development consultants, real-estate practitioners, academics and students reading in the disciplines of urban planning and real estate.

As editors we would like to thank our expert contributors for developing the linkages between the planning system and the property market in the chapters on respective European cities; and for the discourse this has generated among ourselves. We hope this book will help to contribute to the wider debate on planning and property issues and their spatial effects on cities in Europe.

1

European cities: the interaction of planning systems, property markets and real estate investment

James Berry and Stanley McGreal

The focus of this book is to explore the complementarity between planning systems and property markets in selected European cities. Currently many cities are experiencing a restructuring process and those which retain their economic dominance in the 1990s will require more effective planning systems in order to exploit different development and investment scenarios. For many the process of internationalization will necessitate a strategic vision to enhance identity, upgrade image and market services. The dynamics underlying this process will be considered with regard to efficient management and control structures, infrastructure provision, coherent land-use policies, flexible production technologies, environmental awareness, and the attraction of both individual and corporate investment.

1.1 CONTEXT

As the urban hierarchy adjusts to the emerging economic and political dynamics in Europe it is conceivable that a number of cities may emerge as continental capitals assuming roles similar to those performed by New York, Chicago and Los Angeles in North America. Assuming that a frontier-

European Cities, Planning Systems and Property Markets Edited by James Berry and Stanley McGreal. Published in 1995 by E & FN Spon. ISBN 0419 18940 8.

free Europe will emerge, capital will migrate to the area or centre of greatest competitive advantage (Jolliffe, 1993). In such an environment cities and regions will need to develop their inherent strengths and promote themselves in the competition for footloose capital. The completion of the single European market will also result in increasing competition among corporate identities. As Jolliffe points out the loss of historically protected home markets and the freeing up of public procurement practices is likely to stimulate new corporate structures which parallel those pertaining in America and Japan. This restructuring and rationalization will have a fundamental impact on property markets and real estate asset management practice.

In determining how cities might mature within the context of market evolution and in identifying the location and nature of future opportunities for international investment an appreciation of pan-European issues and trends is required. Assessing the competitiveness of cities in this context will depend upon their relative performance in three key areas. First, the strength and flexibility of the city's strategic planning machinery and its organizational capacity to formulate and deliver a strategy of long-term relevance to its inherent strengths and position in the European urban hierarchy. Second, the effectiveness of the city in the management of its assets and in co-ordinating a programme for long-term investment linked to the achievement of an overall vision and plan. Third, the vision for the city must be capable of translation into a coherent marketing strategy to enable the city to be sold and constantly resold to existing and potential investors.

In the European development market, planning policies will therefore become increasingly important in attracting or repelling commercial property investment activities (Sweby Cowan, 1989). Particularly in established cities where central area conservation and heritage policies are observed planning constraints will need to incorporate flexibility to ensure that commercial property markets remain buoyant. Within the rapidly changing political and economic climate of Europe the inter-relationships between planning systems and property markets will be fundamental in maximizing investment return and minimizing risk.

1.2   PLANNING AND THE MARKET

The restructuring of economies, institutions and politics which took place in the 1980s has had a fundamental effect in strengthening the relationship between planning systems and property markets throughout Europe. Several authors such as Boyer (1986), Healey *et al.* (1988) and Albrechts and Swyngedouw (1989) have commented upon this restructuring process. The interpretation most generally accepted is that the Fordist mode of economic development in the 1960s and 1970s, based on an international spatial division of labour in the industrial sector and on regulatory state intervention, has been superseded by a new, more competitive market based economy (Albrechts, 1991). With the emergence of economic liberalization Thornley (1991) argues that the role of the State has been re-orientated to support rather than supplement the market in dealing with externalities and in providing a framework for infrastructural development, legal support and public-sector financial provision. In the context of these changes the planning system has likewise become increasingly geared to the priorities of the market, and land and property as an investment more closely tied to the strategies of the financial sector (Healey, 1989).

The proliferation of initiatives designed to lever private investment has been a central plank of policy in recent years. In Britain the streamlining of bureaucratic constraints on the planning system through mechanisms such as enterprise zones and simplified planning zones have facilitated development and investment opportunities in inner-city localities (Brodtman and Johnston, 1993). The public sector, by effectively subsidizing development schemes to underwrite risk through urban development grant/city grant, has helped stimulate weak market areas and release private-sector investment (Berry and McGreal, 1992). Leverage planning is therefore designed specifically to generate market confidence in the commercial core and inner-city areas by providing infrastructural requirements to support the development process (Brindley *et al.*, 1989). This rationale, based on expected economic benefit, depends fundamentally upon shifting the priorities of the planning system to reflect market-based objectives. The central theme running through these various initiatives is the need for the planning system to be flexible to changes in market demand. However, the dominance of the market has been criticized in some circles due to the downgrading of social criteria, although the strategy pursued by most urban development corporations would contend that local community objectives are adhered to through economic spin-off and filtering down processes.

Whilst economic issues are likely to retain their importance, the planning system is nevertheless gradually shifting its focus towards a more integrated approach of promoting economic development, environmental quality and social integration within the context of urban regions. Indeed Mega (1992) argues that land-use management is highly linked to the economic efficiency and viability of a city, its social value system and its environmental aspirations. Land use is an investment-attracting factor and an urban added value generator but is also an indicator of social equity and environmental quality. Recreating the city's identity through the mix of land uses and functions is emerging as one of the important debates of the 1990s (European Foundation for the Improvement of Living and Working Conditions, 1992). Collaboration based on partnership between the state, the citizens and the market for the efficient and equitable functioning of urban land use is considered important for the sustainability of the urbanization process in Europe (Mega, 1992). This type of development partnership is characterized by EU efforts to assist economic regeneration in the old industrial regions (Objective 2 Regions) which are typically centred in urban areas (CEC, 1991).

In coping with the changing character of urban problems and solutions, Albrechts (1991) argues that new concepts for planning will emerge involving a shift from planning for capital to planning for society. Harvey (1989) on the same theme suggests a switch from the managerial approach to governance to one based upon urban entrepreneurialism. The four key competitive strategies engaged in urban entrepreneurialism entail competition over, first the international division of labour (attracting mobile investment and employment); second, the spatial division of consumption (tourism and consumerism); third, the acquisition of control and command functions in finance, government, information gathering and processing (securing high status activities, media and financial decision-makers); and finally, the redistribution of surpluses by central governments (transfer payments, health and education expenditure etc.).

This shift to urban entrepeneurialism implies some level of inter-urban competition in activating markets based on supply rather than demand side mechanisms. This encourages the development of activities which have the strongest localized capacity to enhance property values, the tax base, the circulation of revenue and employment growth. With the reduction in transport costs and barriers to movement of revenues, the locational characteristics offered by urban areas becomes increasingly important with regard to the inter-urban competition for development, investment and employment opportunity. The institutional, regulatory, physical and infrastructural framework offered by urban localities will determine the success or otherwise in attracting the free movement of capital (Albrechts, 1991).

Despite constraints, all European cities are becoming more entrepreneurial. Economic restructuring, political and administrative decentralization, changes in regional policies, and the urban regeneration of waterfront areas represent concerted efforts by cities to market themselves more successfully on an international scale (Parkinson et al., 1991). This entrepreneurial drive has also been stimulated by the decline in spending by national governments, together with the public spending constraints of the Exchange Rate Mechanism and the fears and opportunities of the Single Market. According to Parkinson et al. the cities with the greatest potential will be those with a diverse manufacturing and service economy concentrated in high value-added industries and aspects of production; an educated and skilled labour force with the ability to stimulate and exploit innovation; the research, design and educational infrastructure capable of supplying necessary skills; cultural and environmental assets that can attract and retain qualified and mobile labour; excellent communication links to key decision modes in the international urban network; innovative capacity and urban institutions capable of continuous improvement of policy and strategy.

Drewett *et al.* (1992), focusing specifically on science and technology in the future development of European cities, argue that the role of the city as centres of production is being superseded by knowledge-based activities. Thus cities are becoming more pro-active in initiating policies which inter-relate with global knowledge networks. It is contended that local economic development strategies have been too traditional, focusing on creating production jobs by improving physical infrastructure and land use rather than seeking to expand activities in the knowledge sector. The shift to knowledge-based development favours cities due to the concentration of resources and innovative activities. Drewett *et al.* argue that most cities in Europe are neither sufficiently geared to the knowledge-generation process nor do they fully appreciate the assets they possess. Consequently knowledge generated through research and development, product marketing and managerial innovation needs to be more effectively integrated into local economic planning strategies. A change in perception and in strategy at the urban level to reflect these new realities is therefore considered necessary.

In examining the spatial transformation of major European cities, Castells (1993) argues that the economic base of many cities is increasingly dependent on global processes. Cities used to be pre-eminent within their own region, but now that dominance is being challenged by global corporations and markets (Lambooy, 1993). Two decisive factors, money and knowledge, are becoming global resources, and some cities appear more likely than others to attract these assets. In Castells' opinion this will include those cities which develop into centres for the informational economy with a strong dependence on knowledge-related activities. These attributes will result in a strong growth of the producer services, offices, telecommunications and organizations, both governmental and non-governmental. In the new economy the productivity and competitiveness of cities and regions will be determined by their ability to combine three key values. These are the informational capacity, quality of life and connectivity to the network of major metropolitan centres at the national and international level (Castells, 1993).

However, one of the most important challenges for European cities is articulating the globally orientated economic functions of the city at the local level. There are a range of pressures for change to which Europe's diverse planning systems are responding (Healey and Williams, 1993). To some degree EC policy initiatives, and further measures which will stem from the European Union, are helping to shape local systems (CEC, 1990) including a strategic approach to the spatial dimension of economic development and property markets. However the institutional diversity of Europe's planning systems remains apparent with each system operating under different legal, political and administrative structures.

Healey (1992) in considering the challenges to market sensitive planning in the 1990s argues that the planning system needs to become involved in the negotiation process in which both the strategic justification and the detailed design of developments are considered on a project-by-project basis. In such circumstances, planning authorities will therefore need to understand clearly the dynamics of volatile land and property markets, and to facilitate market criteria without prejudicing other social and environmental objectives. Healey maintains that if more productive interaction between planning regulations and market conditions is to take place in the 1990s a greater knowledge of the workings of local land and property markets will be of paramount importance. Furthermore, with the renewed focus on development plans in the decision-making process in Britain more complex questions about the role of regulatory policies in shaping market opportunities can be expected, particularly in the light of the macroeconomic fluctuations which occurred in the 1980s (Adair *et al.*, 1993).

1.3   PROPERTY INVESTMENT

Investment in real estate by the major financial institutions, insurance companies and pension funds, has been a feature of investor strategy in the post-war period. The inclusion of property in portfolios has arisen from a number of attributes perceived as favourable including a hedge against inflation, diversification and the opportunity to capitalize upon information to the benefit of the investor (Brown, 1991). However property investment may have negative aspects including liquidity, depreciation, obsolescence and management costs. Furthermore the exact exposure of an institution to property varies through time. In illustrating this MacLeary (1988) notes that during the period 1983–7, in the United Kingdom, the proportion of institutional portfolio structure taken by property halved from 20% to 10%. This was seen to be largely attributable to a relatively low rate of inflation over this period and a shifting of comparative advantage from property to other forms of investment.

Property must therefore be considered as an asset class the relative attractiveness of which, as an investment, needs to be evaluated against the performance of other assets. Typically a diversified institutional portfolio consists of equities, bonds, gilts, cash and property. However in structuring a portfolio, McNamara (1993) argues that long-term financial institutions are not entirely free agents in terms of their investments and are restricted in their ability to take risks. Indeed Sieracki (1993) identifies four principal criteria underlying institutional investment policy: to match assets to liabilities; to be risk adverse; to have a diversified asset base and to obtain above average performance. Thus competitive levels of return are required. Property, through income flow and potential for capital growth, provides one media by which investment objectives can be fulfilled.

Property is also a means of diversifying the asset base through investment into direct real estate. Normally this is into different sectors of the commercial market viz offices, retail, industrial premises though in certain circumstances, mainly investment by private individuals or small companies rather than the institutions, residential property and land can form part of an investment portfolio. Diversification can also be achieved by investing internationally. Removal of barriers, increasing information flow allied with IT developments and liberalism in financial markets have collectively made it attractive to diversify internationally. Indeed as Vos (1993) argues a global investment strategy may target countries in different phases of the economic cycle. While property may not be perceived as a mobile commodity Healey et al. (1992) consider that removal of barriers to capital flow has resulted in a globalization of real-estate investment and property development. Hence the challenge to the property industry is not only to consider the merits of competing projects or investments nationally but also internationally.

In a European context the movement towards greater political integration post-Maastricht, the advent of the Single European Market and future expansion of the EU open up new opportunities for development and investment while at the same time posing threats to certain cities, particularly those in non-competitive locations. However, and in spite of these processes, a single European property market clearly does not exist. Parsa (1992) identifies a number of barriers constraining the emergence of a European property market namely taxation structures; land and property ownership; planning systems; social, cultural and political differences; divergence of property markets; sources of finance; reluctance to participate in cross-border activity; and the disparity of market data.

Concerning planning systems each European country operates different planning and development policies. Dieterich (1992) observes how the aim of physical planning differs within Europe. It is argued for example that within the UK and Germany use of space is at the core of physical planning; in Italy and France planning systems are more orientated to economic development while in Spain and Greece there is a strong link to sectoral planning. Furthermore the efficiency of planning systems differ, often with several tiers of responsibility. It is now widely accepted that to facilitate the development process planning systems need to be responsive to the market and create conditions conducive to the property industry. Indeed Parsa (1992) suggests that there is a direct link between the ease with which development is permitted and the value of property. While investment in property is frequently based upon transactions involving the existing stock rather than on new projects, it is the latter that creates the image of a vibrant city equipped for the needs of modern business activity. Thus it is the facilitating role of planning in creating a development/ investment ethos in an appropriate environment which is of such importance in projecting the image of the city. Whereas if market choice is limited due to restrictive planning policy or development control procedures the investor may avail of the freedom provided by capital movement and target alternative cities.

In considering the weighting of property in a portfolio, Sieracki (1993) has identified the need for 'above average performance' which, it is argued, can be obtained by having the correct weightings in each of the asset classes. Employing a similar argument Vos (1993) maintains that investors adopt a conservative policy, trying to combine the highest return with the lowest level of risk. For such strategies to be achieved information about market performance and expectation is necessary. This requires access to data of sufficient quality and quantity.

Yield and rental value are normally considered to be the most diagnostic indicators of investment performance, their measurement allowing the determination of expected return.

Essentially these parameters reflect demand and supply within the market. In the case of yields, demand is created from the level of institutional investment with yields falling as the amount of investment increases and capital values rise. Moreover Hetherington (1988) considers that movement of yields is a function of several other factors, namely how property is performing relative to other investments, investors' perception of rental growth, porfolio weighting, balancing of risk and return, and the desire to invest in a real asset. Institutional and corporate buying of property and the need to diversify portfolio structure has increasingly led investors to target opportunities internationally, particular city locations and specific market sectors within these centres. In this context the principles of Modern Portfolio Theory and analysis based upon the concept of the efficient frontier can be used to highlight the risk/return profile of property sectors within major urban centres (Vos, 1993).

Nowlan (1993) argues that a property-based investment strategy needs to consider lease arrangements, liquidity transparency and tenant demand coupled with a low-risk economy, identifiable CBDs and an established system of planning and development control. The linkage between investment and planning is complex but as identified by Nowlan can be critical in decision-making. For example, a city's planning system can portray positive or negative images to potential investors ranging from flexibility to bureaucratic inefficiency. The planning system needs to be responsive to development, facilitating the emergence of new investment opportunities. Yet at the same time regulation is required in that an over-supplied market will ultimately influence investment return. However over-regulation through tight planning controls may impose restraint upon the property investment market. Thus planning systems need to be both sophisticated and show an appreciation of market conditions.

Rental value is also influenced by demand-supply factors. Tenant demand is the driving influence, while the supply side is a function of rate of take-up and input through new development activity. The potentially long lead-in time in relation to development often influenced, among other factors, by the efficiency of the planning system frequently means that the phasing of supply can lag market demand. Thus the pattern emerges whereby the realization of certain development projects occurs after the peak of the property cycle. This raises the potential for over-supply in the market, ultimately impacting upon rental levels and yields as demand slackens. In most European cities this scenario has prevailed at some stage during the early 1990s, irrespective of the level of market maturity.

Performance statistics based upon rental growth and yields provide institutions with the core property information required for their assessment of risk and return. However attempting to evaluate the relative performance of cities on a European scale presents difficulties and raises issues concerning property valuation. As Sieracki (1992) points out property performance analysis while well established for the UK is virtually non-existent in mainland Europe. Whether the lead given by the UK with use of quantifiable indicators based on either market transactions or portfolio measurement can successfully be applied within other European countries is a matter of conjecture.

Essentially two problems arise in constructing comparable property indices for other European countries, namely information sources and use of valuation techniques. As discussed by Nabarro and Unsworth (1992) property data are expensive to assemble, large sample sizes are required with many sampling points and a rigorous methodology. It is argued that while investment markets are well developed in, for example, Paris, and for various Dutch and German cities, there are a number of substantial differences between European and UK practice. Nabarro and Unsworth refer to limited property trading due to high transaction costs; no general agreement on valuation methodology; property held explicitly for income security purposes with relatively little regard to capital value; insurance companies dominating institutional ownership and having less interest in performance research than pension funds; banks playing a major role in financing development; lower levels of speculative development and planning regimes which are less flexible. Thus the European market is less geared to investing in commercial property and constraints imposed by planning regulations may dissipate against the type of development scheme put together in the UK and frequently sold on to an institutional investor.

In those market situations where data are not plentiful due to a limited number of transactions, valuations can provide a surrogate for market price. However, problems arise due to the lack of standard valuation methods and variations in practice. It is argued by MacGregor and Nanthakumaran (1992) that implicit methods of valuation which fail to take explicit account of important factors such as expected rental growth, risk and depreciation exacerbate the problem. The need for some form of standardization throughout the EU is becoming increasingly apparent with ultimately a directive regarding a code of practice a likely outcome. In articulating this argument Wheatcroft (1992) draws attention to the fact that not one of the 279 EC directives (at that time) addressing the harmonization of pan-European services mentions property. Almost certainly this is due to the extremely complex legal, taxation and regulatory framework in which property is set, including planning.

1.4   THEMES

This book aims to inter-relate, for each of the cities considered, the operation of the planning system to the functioning of the property market. Arguably each of these core themes provide subjects worthy of investigation in their own respect. For example, the evaluation of planning systems, differences in development control and development plan policy, and how these relate to the distinctive environment within each city raise fundamental issues concerning the development of city space. In marrying the planning process to the property market the degree of mutual interaction and the responsiveness of the planning system, as a public-sector regulator, to private market inputs emerges as a dominant consideration.

Throughout Europe there are distinctive differences in planning systems varying initially on a national scale and secondly on how planning powers and functions are devolved to regional and city authorities (Wood and Williams, 1992; Dieterich, 1992). The particular thrust of this book lies at the urban/metropolitan level though to appreciate fully how planning systems operate it becomes necessary to consider the wider overlay as appropriate particularly the relationship, if any, between different tiers of administration. While differences are most sharply defined between Western cities and those of the former control economies of Eastern Europe, substantial differences do emerge, for example between the major cities of the EU. Likewise property markets vary in their degree of maturity and sophistication from the core cities to those in more peripheral locations notably in southern and Eastern Europe.

Contained within these central themes of planning and property markets a number of issues are highlighted in each chapter, depending upon the particular circumstances and characteristics of the city, the level of economic advancement, and the efficiency and reliability of statistical information. These issues include:

1. The efficiency of administrative and management structures in the planning and development process, including the respective roles of central and local government agencies and the relationship to the political-economic framework.
2. An evaluation of the extent to which the planning system possesses a strategic vision concerning, for example, the creation of a city identity, its ability to facilitate infrastructure provision and enhance environmental quality.
3. The planning process including an overview of the development plan and development control policies, impact upon urban development opportunities, the extent to which planning is contributing to the stimulation of commercial property markets and the attraction of property investment activities. Emphasis is placed upon the commercial sectors viz office, retail, industrial property but not to the total exclusion of the residential market.
4. The operation of property markets, including the role of key actors and agents, public–private partnerships, development mechanisms and investment incentives, the responsiveness of the planning system to the urban land market including demand-supply side factors.
5. The structure of the property investment market and the flow of investment funds, legislative controls, taxation and fiscal policy concerning property investment, the ratio of owner-occupiers to investors and the rate of change to the rental sector.
6. The performance of property markets over time including quantifiable factors such as the rate of development activity, rental and capital values, property investment yields, rates of return, rate of uptake of accommodation, degree of vacancy/dereliction.

1.5   ORGANIZATION OF THE BOOK

The underlying structure of the book reflects to a large measure the concept of core and peripheral centres, with the text sub-divided into four sections on a geographical basis. Part 1 is concerned with cities in the perceived mature heartland of Europe and their influence as major centres of economic and financial activity, and/or political power. Thus, this opening part of the book includes London which along with Tokyo and New York is one of the world's major financial powerhouses. In considering cities, London arguably performs a more global function rather than a European role and conceivably the continuing ambiguity of the UK towards European integration may continue to perpetuate this distinction for some considerable time. Also included within Part 1 are – Paris, possibly the largest continental competitor to London; Brussels, the political and administrative centre of the EU; Amsterdam, an emerging centre of financial influence, and Düsseldorf, a key centre in the western part of Germany, particularly with regard to industrial and office property.

In the following three parts of the book cities arguably in a more peripheral position relative to the core, in a locational context, are discussed. It should be stressed that each of these centres are established cities with long urban traditions and incorporating economic, financial, commercial and administrative functions. For example Part 2 of the text contains the Scandinavian capitals of Helsinki, Stockholm and Copenhagen, and two further examples from the British Isles, namely Edinburgh and Dublin. Concerning the latter two Edinburgh, although lacking certain political functions, has the status of a capital city within the UK and financial institutions second only to London. Likewise Dublin, although the most peripheral of all EU capitals, has emerged in recent years as a modern business centre with planning and taxation linked incentives, designed to stimulate its growth as an international financial centre.

Part 3 examines major cities in southern European countries, traditionally considered to be within the less economically developed part of the continent. However changing political and economic circumstances together with geographical influences has led to different developmental paths in recent years. Barcelona, for instance, has benefited from two major political influences over the past twenty years namely the democratization of Spain and entry into the EC. Also Barcelona's location as part of Europe's sunbelt has greatly enhanced investment interest. In contrast Athens burdened by a highly centralized planning system and legislative regulation has not experienced the same level of property investment by institutions and mobile funds in spite of similar political progress. Whereas for Rome complexity has been augmented by extensive unauthorized development. In particular the deficiencies of the planning system have been exposed by the growth of commercial development in the late 1980s.

In Part 4, cities in the former command economies of Eastern Europe are assessed including Budapest, Prague and Warsaw. Berlin is also included in this section though its unique history over the past fifty years and its formerly divided status sets Berlin apart in terms of the distinctive problems arising from unification. Arguably the most critical issue facing these cities is the question of title and land-ownership. While planning systems reflect the legacy of centralized political control, the challenge is to bridge lost opportunities of the past fifty years over the next decade. Clearly the opening up of Eastern European economies has produced investment possibilities but the risk factor acts as a potential deterrent to Western institutional investment, particularly on the part of UK based companies. However Hudson (1993) argues that the brakes on Western investment namely newness of the market, technical matters including planning, taxation, currency and title risks are not insurmountable and that while mature markets in the West stagnate, new horizons are emerging in Eastern Europe.

The final chapter of the book takes a wider perspective in terms of social and economic issues facing European cities. It seeks to articulate further those challenges which will be paramount for planning systems and property markets at city, national and European perspectives. In this context political progress in the EU and the expansion of the existing community to incorporate other states (and thus several of the cities considered in this book) poses substantial challenges to European structures. While the debate is seemingly far from resolved, European cities must be prepared to respond to increased competitiveness through networking, city marketing and improved economic and environmental infrastructures.

REFERENCES

Adair, A.S., Berry, J.N. and McGreal, W.S. (1993) The interaction between macroeconomic and housing policy in the UK, *Journal of Property Research*, **10**, 121–34.

Albrechts, L. (1991) Changing roles and positions of planners, *Urban Studies*, **28**(1), 123–37.

Albrechts, L. and Swyngedouw, E. (1989) The challenges for regional policy under a flexible regime of accumulation, in L. Albrechts, F. Moulaert, P. Roberts and E. Swyngedouw, *Regional Policy at the Crossroads: European Perspectives*, Jessica Kingsley, London, 67–89.

Berry, J.N. and McGreal, W.S. (1992) Urban development grant: funding the commercial revitalisation of Belfast, *Journal of Property Finance*, **3**(1), 59–65.

Boyer, R. (1986) *La théorie de la régulation*, La Decouverte, Paris.

Brindley, T., Rydin, Y. and Stoker, G. (1989) *Remaking Planning: The Politics of Urban Change in the Thatcher Years*, Unwin-Hyman, London.

Brodtman, M. and Johnston, R. (1993) Enterprise zones, property development and investment, in J. Berry, S. McGreal and W. Deddis, *Urban Regeneration, Property Investment and Development*, E & FN Spon, London, 240–53.

Brown, G.R. (1991) *Property Investment and the Capital Markets*, E & FN Spon, London.

Castells, M. (1993) European cities, the informational society, and the global economy, *Tijdschrift voor Economische en Sociale Geografie*, **84**(4), 247–57.

Commission of the European Communities (1990) *Green Paper on the Urban Environment*, COM (90) 218 final, Brussels.

Commission of the European Communities (1991) *Europe 2000: Outlook for the Development of the Community's Territory*, Brussels.

Dieterich, H. (1992) How planning practice varies across Europe, paper presented at conference. *European Property, a Briefing for Property Researchers*, Henry Stewart in association with Society of Property Researchers, November 1992, London.

Drewett, R., Knight, R. and Schubert, U. (1992) *The Future of European Cities: the Role of Science and Technology*, Commission of the European Community, DGXII Monitor.

European Foundation for the Improvement of Living and Working Conditions (1992) *Proceedings of European Workshop on Land Management and Environmental Improvement in Cities*, Lisbon, May 1992.

Harvey, D. (1989) From managerialism to entrepreneurialism: the transformation in urban governance in late capitalism, *Geographiska Annaler*, 713, 3–17.

Healey, P. (1989) Directions for change in the British planning system, *Town Planning Review*, **60**(2), April, 125–49.

Healey, P. (1992) The reorganisation of state and market in planning, *Urban Studies*, **29**(3/4), 411–34.

Healey, P., Davoudi, S., O'Toole, M., Tavsanoglu, S. and Usher, D. (1992) Rebuilding the City: Property-led urban regeneration, E & FN Spon, London.

Healey, P., McNamara, P.F., Elson, M.J. and Doak, A.J. (1988) *Land Use Planning and the Medication of Urban Change*, Cambridge University Press, Cambridge.

Healey, P. and Williams, R. (1993) European urban planning systems: diversity and convergence, *Urban Studies*, **30**(4/5), 701–20.

Hetherington, J.F. (1988) Forecasting of rents, in A.R. MacLeary and N. Nanthakumaran, *Property Investment Theory*, E & FN Spon, London, 97–109.

Hudson, P. (1993) Scope for and funding of urban regeneration in Eastern Europe, in J. Berry, S. McGreal and W. Deddis, *Urban Regeneration, Property Investment and Development*, E & FN Spon, London, 77–94.

Jolliffe, C. (1993) *Real Estate Investment in the Changing European Environment: Positioning for Long Term Performance*, occasional paper, British Council for Offices, Reading.

Lambooy, J.G. (1993) The European City: From Carrefour to organisational nexus, *Tijdschaift voor Economische en Sociale Geografie*, **84**(4), 258–68.

MacLeary, A.R. (1988) Property and investment, in A.R. MacLeary and N. Nanthakumaran (eds), *Property Investment Theory*, E & FN Spon, London, 1–12.

MacGregor, B.D.and Nanthakumaran, N. (1992) The allocation to property in the multi-asset portfolio: the evidence and theory reconsidered, *Journal of Property Research*, **9**, 5–32.

McNamara, P. (1993) Parameters for institutional investment in inner city commercial property markets, in J. Berry, S. McGreal and W. Deddis, *Urban Regeneration, Property Investment and Development*, E & FN Spon, London, 5–15.

Mega, V. (1992) Socio-environmental improvements and problems in the European city, the EC perspective, paper presented at a conference, *European Cities: Growth and Decline*, The Hague, April 1992.

Nabarro, R. and Unsworth, R. (1992) European Property Investment Performance Measurement, paper presented at conference, *European Property, a Briefing for Property Researchers*, Henry Stewart in association with Society of Property Researchers, November 1992, London.

Nowlan, W. (1993) Investor's perspective: comparative investment across Europe, paper presented at conference, *Property Investment in the 1990s*, University of Ulster in association with the Royal Institution of Chartered Surveyors.

Parkinson, M., Bianchini, F., Dawson, J., Evan, R. and Harding, A. (1991) *Urbanisation and the Functions of Cities in the European Community*, Commission of the European Community, DGXVI.

Parsa, A. (1992) The role of research – overcoming the barriers of an integrated property market in Europe, paper presented at conference, *European Property, a Briefing for Property Researchers*, Henry Stewart in association with Society of Property Researchers, November 1992, London.

Sieracki, K. (1992) UK institutional research requirements for European property, paper presented at conference, *European Property, a Briefing for Property Researchers*, Henry Stewart in association with Society of Property Researchers, November 1992, London.

Sieracki, K. (1993) The role of financial institutions in urban regeneration, paper presented at conference, *Urban Regeneration – Vision and Delivery*, University of Ulster, March 1993.

Sweby Cowan (1989) *The Guide to European Property Investment*, in conjunction with FIABCI, Waterlow Publishers, London.

Thornley, A. (1991) *Urban Planning under Thatcherism: the Challenge of the Market*, Routledge, London.

Vos, G. (1993) International real estate portfolios, in J. Berry, S. McGreal and W. Deddis, *Urban Regeneration, Property Investment and Development*, E & FN Spon, London, 16–31.

Wheatcroft, D. (1992) Valuation practice throughout Europe, paper presented at conference, *European Perspectives, a Briefing for Property Researchers*, Henry Stewart in association with Society of Property Researchers, November 1992.

Wood, B. and Williams, R. (1992) *Industrial Property Markets in Western Europe*, E & FN Spon, London.

PART ONE ————

EUROPEAN
HEARTLAND

2

London

Ali R. Ghanbari Parsa,
Barry Redding
and Charles France Fraser

London defies easy definition. Historically it has two cities at its core. The square mile of territory controlled by the ancient City Corporation is internationally recognized as 'the City'; historically the hub of Britain's trading, banking and financial services. The other, Westminster, is the location of the seat of government and is associated with the trappings of majesty, and parliament: historically the centre of political life and the capital of the United Kingdom (Hall, 1989). These form two major areas of investment and employment.

Beyond these core city areas, the name London has been used to refer to a far broader urban agglomeration which is the focus of several distinct geographical areas. First, the densely built-up areas developed during the nineteenth and early twentieth centuries and which comprised the old County of London. This administrative area, established in 1888 and governed by the London County Council (LCC), is usually referred to as inner London. The second area resulted from the frenzy of speculative building between 1918 and 1939 and extended the metropolis beyond the boundaries of the LCC area to create in effect a greater London. This larger area was formally recognized in 1965 by the abolition of the former LCC and the establishment of the Greater London Council (GLC) as the strategic local authority responsible for Greater London. This local government body lasted until its abolition in 1986. Presently the Greater London area is administered by 32 London boroughs and the Corporation of the City of London. Of these, 12 plus the city comprise inner London and the remaining 20 boroughs constitute outer London. The distinction between inner and outer London has ceased to have any administrative significance.

European Cities, Planning Systems and Property Markets Edited by James Berry and Stanley McGreal. Published in 1995 by E & FN Spon. ISBN 0419 18940 8.

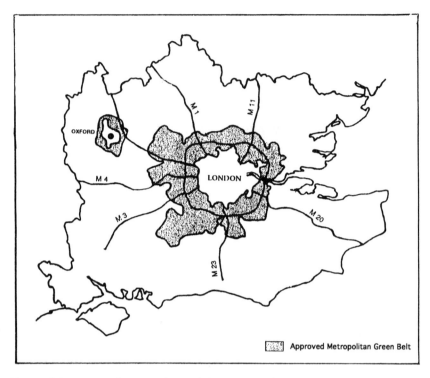

Figure 2.1   Metropolitan London and the Green Belt
Source: Green Belts and Regional Planning, adapted from DoE Government Statement on Strategic Plan for the South East, HMSO, London, 1978, 33. Drawn by Mahtab Akhavan Farshchi, South Bank University, SLMUP.

Broadly speaking there is some coincidence between the physical delineation of the built-up area and the administrative boundary of Greater London. This arises from the limitation to the outward physical growth of London, a consequence of the sophisticated and highly regulated system of land-use planning introduced in the UK during the late-1940s. Of particular importance in stemming the continued physical expansion of London was the designation, in a ring around the capital, of the Metropolitan Green Belt (Figure 2.1). However the London metropolis did not stop growing, rather development took place beyond the Green Belt in planned new and expanded towns, as well as in the older market towns (Rasmussen, 1983). The economic and social reality of a large metropolis was the establishment of patterns of settlement distant from central London jobs. While independent economic centres evolved within these outer metropolitan areas, the ebb and flow of daily journey to work commuting into London has become synonymous with the third and largest geographical area, the London Region.

London can be viewed at quite a different plane to other European cities. At a global level it jockeys with New York and Tokyo for leadership in financial transactions. London is in the fortunate geographical position of being able to take advantage of trans-world communications and trade 24 hours (Hall, 1993). Furthermore it has strong international linkages: currently (1993) it is estimated that London has 478 foreign banks (Paris has 277 and Frankfurt 247); 544 foreign listed companies (87 in New York, 119 in Tokyo, 223 in Paris and 310 in Frankfurt); as well as having the principal international markets in bonds, securities and foreign exchange. The capital has become the location for headquarters offices: 41% of *The Times* top 500 UK world transnational firms have their headquarters in London (SPR, 1992; LPAC, 1993). Indeed the service sector, which has long supplanted manufacturing as the economic base for London, can itself be differentiated into financial corporate control and decision-making functions operating in the interlocking global markets; business, professional and producer services which support the global sectors; and more general services support sectors including tourism (Hoggart and Green, 1992).

The significance of London's economy is difficult to deny. Its Gross Region Product, estimated by the Central Statistical Office to have amounted to US$78 billion in 1985, represents 17% of the UK GNP: the 25th largest economy among the world's 212 independent territories or nations (Hamilton, 1992).

2.1 THE STRUCTURE AND ORGANIZATION OF PLANNING IN LONDON

Prior to 1985 the GLC acted as a strategic planning body to guide and manage development in the capital through the Greater London Development Plan (GLDP). Under the umbrella of the GLDP each London borough prepared their own borough plan to meet the specific land-use needs of the local area. Borough plans varied widely in format, scope and content. Following the publication of the Government's White Paper *Streamlining the Cities* (1985), the Metropolitan Councils, including the GLC, were abolished creating a single tier of local government within these metropolitan areas. Thus the political geography of planning in London was changed, placing the responsibility on the existing London boroughs to prepare statutory plans in their respective areas.

The functions of the former GLC were reallocated broadly in three ways. Strategic planning and traffic management on main roads were placed within the remit of central government: in particular the enlarged London Regional Divisions of the Departments of the Environment and Transport. Some functions have been transferred to quangos (quasi-autonomous non-governmental organizations), for example English Heritage or the National Rivers Authority or the South Bank Board, or to the private sector. Most functions, however, are controlled and administered through joint committees of the London boroughs (Hebbert, 1992a).

As a planning document for London, the GLDP is out of date. Contemporary planning policy for the capital is to be derived from the 33 separate Unitary Development Plans (UDPs) which will contain elements of the structure plan and the local plan all rolled into one. The early UDPs were largely reworked versions of previous Borough Plans incorporating elements of the GLDP. Their preparation is well advanced; thus while by June 1993 only two have been adopted, 30 have reached deposit stage (i.e. final drafts available for public comment) and of these 23 have been subject to inquiry prior to the final stage of adoption (LPAC, 1993). By the end of 1994 London should for the first time have comprehensive coverage of up-to-date development plans thus enabling the capital to work within a plan-led development process as envisaged in the Town and Country Planning Act 1990 (as amended in 1991). In form, style and content the UDPs consist of a written review of borough problems with an analysis leading to the formulation of policies to guide the borough in its response to development pressures or the emergence of new demands on space, such as the need for areas of Nature Conservation or new recreational demands. Each contains a set of proposal maps which translate these policies into space specific proposals.

The UDPs are contained within a framework of advice and guidance provided by higher level government agencies. The first of these is the London Planning Advisory Committee (LPAC). A consultative committee of borough representatives with a central government presence, this small body is not politically independent. Technically its staff and premises are run by the London Borough of Havering as a service to the Capital. The Borough of Havering was chosen as the location for the organization because it is physically remote from the previous seats of metropolitan power in the core boroughs of Lambeth (the location of County Hall, the headquarters of the former GLC), Westminster and the City. The LPAC has a small staff of 15–20 people and its success in retaining the confidence of the London boroughs is that it has worked assiduously, under successive directors, to maintain an impartial posture on the competing claims of boroughs and to be an 'honest broker', as well as to drive forward policies in areas where borough co-operation can be assured. It has therefore attained a degree of respect and influence across the political spectrum and in every borough of London which the preceding (and highly politicized left or right) GLC never could.

Further co-ordination between boroughs within London is achieved by the operation of several voluntary bodies though not without the influence of party-political differences. Thus the Conservative controlled boroughs are represented by the London Boroughs Association (LBA) while the

Labour controlled boroughs by the Association of London Authorities (ALA). While overt political co-operation between the LBA and the ALA is the exception rather than the rule, they have achieved consensus on a growing number of issues, particularly in advocating London's needs to government. Linkages between chief officers such as the Association of London Borough Planning Officers are an important component of the network (Hebbert, 1992b).

The London boroughs are constituent members of the London and South-East Regional Planning Conference (SERPLAN) along with other local authorities at county and district level throughout the South-East of England. As with LPAC, SERPLAN depends on co-operation to enable it to function. It performs a research and statistical collection and analysis role, for example focusing on the impact of development proposals or the need for infrastructure or housing in the South-East. It does not prepare plans, but is influential in shaping government attitudes and proposals in the plan making process. Again the political skill of SERPLAN, in balancing the needs of the wider, largely rural and suburban, hinterland with those of the urban core of London, has earned it the respect of all authorities in the region.

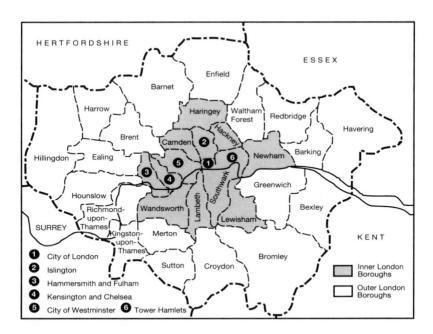

Figure 2.2   Greater London Boroughs
Source: City of London, Local Plan, p. 9, Dept. of Planning, Corporation of London. Drawn by Mahtab Akhavan Farshchi, South Bank University, SLMUP.

In the realm of planning central government treats London in most respects in the same way as any other British Metropolitan area. The government does not prepare plans for the capital or its region but seeks to guide the development plan process by the preparation of a series of Planning Policy Guidelines (PPGS). These cover subjects such as Nature Conservation, Affordable Housing, Retailing which are prepared by the Department of the Environment and administered by its London 'Regional' office responsible for the urban core of the 33 boroughs (Figure 2.2).

Regional Guidance for the South-East (PPG9) dates from 1980, 1984 and 1986. In March 1993 the Government published a new draft Regional Planning Guidance for the South-East. The aim of this policy document is to shape the region's environment and guide its development up to the year 2011, to provide a framework for structure plan reviews (by the county councils outside Greater London) and up-to-date strategic planning guidance for London. The draft guidance emphasizes the vital role of the South-East to the development of the UK economy, it embraces the principles of sustainable development, the need to co-ordinate land-use and transport planning policies, and restates the need for a balance to be struck between development in the west and the east of the region.

This regional guidance on the preparation and nature of plans is counterbalanced by the Department of the Environment's (DoE) checking of final implementation decisions through its role in the plan approval and the appeals process. Each UDP in turn must go through an inquiry process chaired by one of the Department's inspectors. At the end of this process in which the proposals are tested, not only against local opinion, internal borough policies and LPAC suggestions, but also against the Regional Guidance of the DoE itself, the UDP is formally adopted by the borough council. From then on this represents the definitive document against which development proposals are judged. The Government has made several statements stressing the importance of this document in a 'plan-led' system, but the important steps in plan implementation and enforcement also depend on consistent backing for the system. Here the Government's record is patchy because while the 'plan-led' approach may appear to reduce development control decisions to the level of building permits, the simultaneous insistence on deciding each case 'on its merits' means that the approved appeal and public inquiry processes retain their adversarial nature. This can lead to inconsistent decision-making and to the creation of a climate of uncertainty which is detrimental to both developer and planning officer alike, and tends to undermine confidence in the development plan as a robust statement of the future. While the Department of the Environment is the focus of the town planning system it is by no means the only government department which may make decisions concerning the development process in London: others for example include the

Departments of Transport, Trade and Industry, Employment and the Home Office. Also central government has established a Cabinet Committee for London and a Ministerial post for Transport in London though to date neither initiative has had any positive impact on the reality or perception of a co-ordinated government approach to London (*Property Week*, 1993).

2.1.1   East Thames Corridor

A significant characteristic of the capital's urban geography for many decades has been the imbalance in economic development and employment opportunities between east and west London. Proximity to Heathrow, Europe's busiest airport, and to the booming information economy of the M4 corridor has contributed to a sustained period of development pressure in the outer-London boroughs and county districts to the west of London. Among the strengths of this western corridor is the calibre of the companies already located there, many of them representing overseas investment and at the cutting edge of the development and application of new technologies. The existence of a highly skilled and sophisticated workforce emphasizes the locality's competitive edge over other London fringe locations.

In contrast, east London has experienced a stagnating economic base for much of the period since the Second World War. The traditional location for much of the capital's heavy and manufacturing industry, east London lost most of its industrial employment through periods of post-war reconstruction, rationalization of the docks and associated activities, and de-industrialization. The latter process, part of a general decline in manufacturing employment within the UK, contributed to a decline of manufacturing workers in Greater London from just over 1 million in 1971 to 445 000 in 1989 (LPAC, 1991). The bulk of the capital's vacant industrial land is located in east London; the prospects for much of it being redeveloped is limited by physical and infrastructural constrains, contaminated land and poor environmental quality. Furthermore the labour market is characterized by high unemployment and an outdated skill-base. The economic benefits arising from the redevelopment of parts of the London Docklands and the spillover of City-activity following the deregulation of financial services have had little effect and very localized impact upon the economic base of east London which remains largely static and underdeveloped.

The Government's draft Regional Guidance has emphasized the importance of promoting the opportunities for development of east London and the East Thames Corridor (ETC). LPAC supports this in its current draft advice on Strategic Planning Guidance for London not only in an effort to achieve a better east/west balance across the Capital, but also to counter the possibility of any renewed decentralization of activities beyond London (LPAC, 1993).

The quality of strategic accessibility and provision of transport infrastructure will be vital to the regeneration of east London. While improvements of infrastructure are being made there is doubt that it will be either adequate or soon enough to encourage significant private economic investment into the area. Furthermore the financing of infrastructure projects is a major problem. Hence the Government, struggling to balance the national budget, has sought private-sector funding for public infrastructure but the size and cost of such projects and the long lead times before a return can be expected are significant deterrents to private investment. Also, the public controversy associated with major schemes, there will always be businesses and residents adversely affected by any proposal, can bring an unwelcome image for a company considering the investment. Indeed London has witnessed a Catch-22 situation in recent years with the private sector unwilling to contribute significant proportions of development cost unless the Government commits itself to the particular projects and vice versa (the Jubilee Line, Cross Rail, Channel Tunnel Rail Link).

The Channel Tunnel Rail Link project illustrates further the dilemmas facing strategic transport and land-use planning (Judd, 1993). In economic cost-benefit terms the eastern route to Kings Cross in central London via Stratford may not be the most suitable but on environmental and political grounds it avoids the sensitive South London route to Waterloo favoured by British Rail. Moreover, the easterly route addresses the land-use and social-planning objectives of regenerating the ETC, the trade-off between these interests being determined within the political arena. The economic impact on the ETC of the Channel Link is dependent upon the location of the intermediate international passenger station which in turn will provide the focus for development activity. Two possible locations are under consideration, Stratford in east London, and close to the M25 crossing of the Thames. Meanwhile the international rail terminal at Waterloo opens in 1994 and will be the Central London terminal for cross-channel passenger rail traffic until well after the year 2000.

The Government is committed to preparing a strategic framework for the ETC and has established a DoE Task Force to effect this and encourage inward investment into east London. The DoE is now adopting a more flexible approach to the financing of schemes that have the potential to contribute towards urban regeneration, employment growth or substantial environmental improvement. Amendments have been made to designated 'assisted areas' of the UK (since July 1993) favouring Park Royal in West London, the Lea Valley in the north-east and the London end of the East Thames Corridor. In the latter, parts of Greenwich, Bexley, Havering, Newham, Barking and Dagenham have received 'intermediate area' status

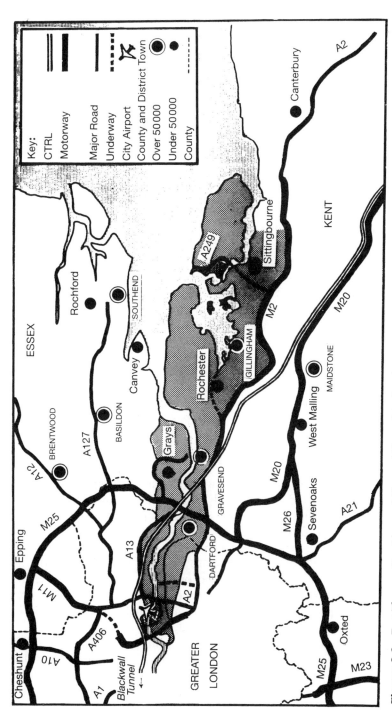

Figure 2.3 East Thames Corridor and Channel Tunnel Rail Link
Source: based on DoE SERO, 1992. Drawn by Mahtab Akhavan Farshchi, South Bank University, SLMUP.

and are able to take advantage of regional selective assistance to create or safeguard jobs and regional enterprise grants for investment by small companies.

The East Thames Corridor embraces land within London, the two adjoining counties, Kent and Essex, and at least 15 boroughs or districts in a wedge stretching from the London Docklands near Greenwich out to near Faversham in Kent and Stanford le Hope in Essex (Figure 2.3). It comprises an area of some 2000 ha, encompasses some of the region's most densely built-up areas, such as the Medway Towns, a number of major social housing projects, for example the Becontree Estate in Dagenham (built in the 1930s) and Thamesmead (1970s); and most of the largest medium- to long-term development sites in the region. The Llewellyn-Davies report identifies circa 3955 ha of development opportunity sites larger than 2 ha, but the Report cautions that serious contamination probably affects 19% of the area. A number of important ecological sites of special scientific interest exist in rural fringe areas around Greater London, for example Rainham Marshes, which have been safeguarded from urban development pressure by the restraining influence of the green-belt planning policies.

A major factor which will constrain development prospects in the ETC is its poor environmental quality, particularly contaminated land and air pollution. The former will add to the cost of redevelopment. However, a more immediate problem is air pollution, closely linked to the many power stations and sources of heavy industrial pollutants (including waste incineration) located along the banks of the Thames Estuary. This is exacerbated by pollutants from road traffic using the major arterial routes through the corridor to the M25 and London.

2.2   PLANNING AND PROPERTY DEVELOPMENT PROCESSES

The property market does not always operate effectively. Difficulties are encountered at the urban–rural fringe where outward development pressure conflicts with the restraint policies of planning authorities. Furthermore particular problems are apparent in inner urban locations. Over several decades government has taken direct action to stimulate both the supply of and the demand for land to facilitate economic growth and urban regeneration. However imperfections exist in the property market with supply–demand not equating in space or in time. The excess supply of office floor space in central London is an example of the oscillation of demand and supply functions during the late 1980s and early 1990s.

Supply of land for (re)development is primarily determined by the planning policies of central and local government. Demand for land and buildings depends largely on private-sector action, resulting from the interplay of decisions taken by individuals, companies, and other organizations that generate a demand for shelter or goods or services and which is translated into a demand for built facilities (Healey *et al.*, 1992). Some of this 'derived demand' for buildings and land will be satisfied through existing facilities, which may require minor modifications or improvement, demand will also lead to the adaptation of existing buildings to accommodate new uses viz redundant inner-city school buildings have been converted to high-tech industrial or business centres, factory sheds to sports halls or discount retail outlets. Intensification, change of use and refurbishment, and the redevelopment of urban sites are the characteristics of the development cycle in a metropolitan city like London whereas new development on 'greenfield' sites is an extremely small proportion of the total development activity in the Capital.

The policies of the local planning authorities seek to express the needs and demands for land use in spatial plans and programmes, but the identification and allocation of land as being suitable for development does not in itself lead to the implementation of the planned proposals. Property ownership is a critical component of the development process. Private owners may be unwilling to sell for a variety of reasons: they may be safeguarding their own future needs; perhaps they are unaware of the value of the market opportunity with an unrealistic high view of market value (a high element of hope value or the land has a high book value used as loan collateral); or perhaps its true potential has still to be determined (possibly by public investment in infrastructure). Arguably the objectives of large landowners have had significant impact: for example, in Central London the estate management policies of the major landed estates, balancing the continuation of residential use with demand for offices, have helped to shape the built environment of large areas of Chelsea, Victoria, St James, Mayfair, Maida Vale and Bloomsbury (Figure 2.4). The Corporation of London owns the freehold interest of much of the City and extensive urban and rural land elsewhere in Greater London, and has initiated major redevelopment schemes including a highly acclaimed residential and cultural development at the Barbican.

2.2.1   Measures affecting the supply of development land

The objectives and attitude of the landowner are important; however, the landowner, public or private, is but one 'agency' which operates within the urban land market. There is considerable interdependency between agencies in possession of different resources: for example, finance, land, labour, materials and professional skills. Which 'agency' actually does what in any given situation will be determined partly by the degree to which scope for action is prescribed by, for example, legislation, and partly by the interests of particular agencies and their attitudes towards risk. Roles are not static; many can be undertaken by more than one agency. Similarly,

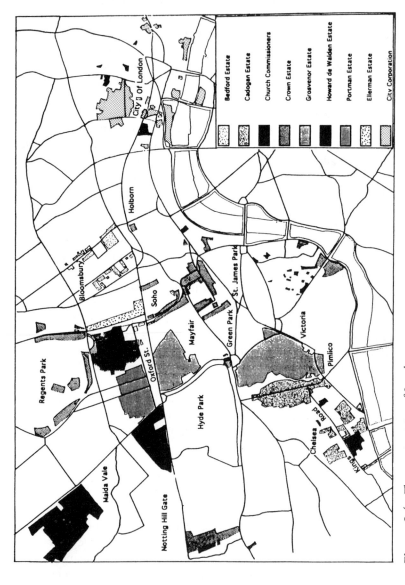

Figure 2.4 The great estates of London

Source: based on original map (Oliver Mariot) and modified by Philip Marshall. Drawn by Mahtab Akhavan Farshchi, South Bank University, SLMUP.

a single agency may perform more than one role within the development process.

The development function, traditionally entrepreneurial but increasingly focusing upon the strategic appraisal of development opportunities is provided by development companies (for example British Land, Hammerson, Land Securities and MEPC), the activities of financial institutions (for example Prudential and Norwich Union), and major retailers (for example Marks & Spencer, Tesco and Sainsburys). Development companies may hold completed schemes as part of an investment portfolio or refinance their operations by disposal. Financial institutions (pension funds, insurance companies and the banking sector) have been very influential in the London property market. Through their investment in property they are the prime source of finance. In 1992 insurance companies had estimated property holdings amounting to £35 billion in direct property investment and in shares in property companies whereas the estimated property holdings of the major pension funds for the same year is £20 billion. The largest single focus for this investment is the London office market.

The financial institutions fund, own and carry out development schemes. Major commercial companies, including large retailers, may adopt two or more functions in the process (Morgan, 1992). The local authority will be involved in all development schemes in one way or another exercising its various statutory functions, for example, as the planning authority or the highways authority. There are many examples of London boroughs owning land suitable for development and taking a positive approach towards a partnership with private developers and financial institutions to effect the development. The most recent town centre development scheme to be completed in London, and possibly the last of this scale, is The Glades in Bromley, a partnership development between the London Borough of Bromley, Capital and Counties and General Accident Assurance.

Measures which act on the supply side of the property market include the statutory development plan system and mechanisms to regulate and control development through the requirement to obtain planning permission from the relevant local planning authority. It also extends to measures to bring more land onto the market and to improve the potential of land for development. The London boroughs are required to make adequate provision in their Unitary Development Plans for different types of development, including the identification of areas for major development. There are also areas of planning restraint where authorities will resist development or redevelopment pressures or apply more demanding criteria in their decisions concerning proposed development. At the fringe of London these areas embrace good quality agricultural land, designated greenbelt, Areas of Outstanding Natural Beauty (AONB) and Sites of Special Scientific Interest (SSSI). Within the urban area sensitive areas include the

Thames riverside, designated conservation areas and the locality around 'listed' buildings of special architectural or historic interest.

The potential for tension between economic development and conservation is well illustrated in the local planning policies of the City. On the one hand the Corporation's ambition, following de-regulation is to promote new, more advanced office development so as to reinforce the City's position as the leading financial centre (Diamond, 1992). Yet the City comprises 23 conservation areas, with numerous listed buildings; such assets underpin policies to preserve the City's heritage and distinctive character through measures such as restrictions on building heights. The trade-off between development and conservation was very evident in the mid 1980s. Faced with competing locations, particularly the London Docklands which potentially could offer the amount and design of space being demanded by the changing financial sector, the Corporation's response was to amend its policies and actively encourage new development.

Sites identified in development plans as important to the implementation of the planning authority objectives are often the subject of planning or development briefs. Such a brief will provide detailed planning and design guidance for the development of the specific site and considerations of marketing and disposal, financial and future relationships depending upon the authority's legal interest in the site and their intention for it. In recent years central government policies have prompted a rationalization and closure of school properties by the London boroughs (as educating authorities) and hospital sites by the Regional Health Authorities. These sites, often of some size, offer significant development opportunities within otherwise highly built-up urban areas.

The planning system in the UK permits the exercise of considerable discretion by local planning authorities (London boroughs) in determining applications for planning permission. Negotiations between planning officer and applicant (developer) has been a feature of the system for several decades. This has evolved concurrently with widening interests of planners to embrace key social and economic concerns of the inner city; a greater public awareness of land value gains on receipt of planning permissions and associated pressure on local politicians and town planners to seek some tangible benefit for the local community. The increasing restraints applied by successive central governments on local government expenditure simply encouraged a more entrepreneurial approach to negotiation with developers seeking planning permission (Credit Fondiario, 1991).

In this context London planning authorities have utilized planning gain, for example to include a housing component in commercial schemes viz the proposed Kings Cross Development by London Regeneration Consortium (LRC); conveyance of housing units to the authority or granting them nomination rights; leisure facilities in office or retail development; contributions to the cost of off-site infrastructure works; construction of roads, footpaths, bridges, underpasses and realignment of junctions off-site; public access to private land; opening up riverside walks; dedication of private land for public use; and restoration of historic buildings. Many London UDPs give guidance on the type of planning gains that would normally be sought and in what circumstances (Edwards, 1992a). Indeed the 1993 draft strategic guidance from LPAC provides encouragement for this. Rather than rely simply on the grant of planning permission to secure such planning gain, planning authorities have increasingly employed the use of legal agreements. For example, usually the planning authority will withhold permission until such an agreement has been negotiated and signed. Since 1991 applicants for planning permission are able to include unilateral undertakings (obligations) in their submission to the authority.

2.3   PLANNING AND DEVELOPMENT INITIATIVES

Since the mid to late 1970s central government has targeted inner locations within the major urban areas of the United Kingdom, including London. Throughout this period up to the present (1993) a wide range of policy initiatives and financial support mechanisms (for example City Grant) have been employed in underpinning the planning and development process and the levering of private sector investment. For example Urban Development Corporations (UDCs) were launched to secure the regeneration of specific and designated inner city areas. The first UDC was established in London Docklands, the London Docklands Development Corporation (LDDC), under the Local Government, Planning and Land Act 1980, Part XVI. This Act gives the Secretary of State the power to designate areas in metropolitan districts or Inner London Boroughs as Urban Development Corporations (Thornley, 1992a). With the LDDC particular emphasis has been placed on land reclamation acquiring it, if appropriate, by compulsory purchase or through vesting orders. In order to facilitate speedy development the LDDC has planning powers but is not the statutory plan-making authority; this responsibility remains with the local authorities. Furthermore the designation of the Isle of Dogs Enterprise Zone (1981) provided taxation incentives and further relaxed administrative procedures.

The Urban Programme forms an umbrella structure for a range of government initiatives and as part of the Government's inner city policy there are 57 urban programme authorities, 13 of which are in London (Hall, 1990). The Urban Programme was designed to promote joint action between Government Departments, local authorities, the private sector and local agencies (DoE, 1987). The principal objectives of the Urban Programme include job creation and the appropriate education and training of local residents, utilization of land and buildings, encouragement of private-sector involvement, improved housing conditions; and encouragement of self-help and improvement of the social fabric.

In addition the DoE have set up City Action Teams in a number of urban areas including London in 1985, launched the Inner City Initiative in 1986, and the Action for Cities Initiative in 1988 (DoE, 1992). Each of these programmes have specific objectives such as skills training, education and reduction of unemployment. The Inner Cities Initiative is to 'concentrate joint Departmental action' in selected areas with severe unemployment whereas the overall aim of the Action for Cities Initiative is to bring together and give a new focus to the comprehensive range of programmes designed to promote regeneration in inner city areas (DoE, 1993a).

City Challenge was launched in May 1991 and as part of this initiative 15 Urban Priority Areas were invited to bid for resources in 1992/93. The aim of City Challenge is to transform specific run-down inner-city areas and significantly to improve the quality of life for local residents in Urban Priority Areas (DoE, 1993b). There have been two rounds of competition through bids invited by the DoE since 1992. In London in the first round, Lewisham and Tower Hamlets were successful in their bids and have begun implementing a detailed five-year programme running between 1992 and 1997. Five more London boroughs won City Challenge Partnerships commencing in April 1993. Each City Challenge Partnership receives £7.5 million a year for five years, based on the degree of the success of their stated targets and objectives.

The core of the City Challenge programme is based on partnership between local authorities with private-, public- and voluntary-sector bodies and the local community, to 'devise and compete for resources to implement comprehensive economic, social and environmental strategies for the regeneration of key areas of deprivation' (DoE, 1993a). City Challenge emphasizes 'co-operation' to break down the barriers between the various regeneration programmes and projects promoted by different organizations or interest groups; 'concentration' to achieve lasting success where people can see results; and 'competition' to shift away from the mechanical allocation of urban resources to encourage imaginative and innovative approaches to tackling inner-city problems. It is important to note that the City Challenge resources do not include new funds but comprise a reallocation from a range of existing government programmes operating in inner cities (Ghanbari Parsa and Lyons, 1992). The Government defends this policy stating that it should achieve a more effective use of resources by simplifying and streamlining grant procedures to enable project packages to be assembled. However the critics of the City Challenge Initiative point out the fact that this is a different name for existing inner-city policies and thus no new resources have been allocated.

The proposed Urban Regeneration Agency for England, initially forwarded in a consultation paper in July 1992 and provided for in the

Leasehold Reform, Housing and Urban Development Act 1993, has been renamed, English Partnership. The new agency was established on 4 November 1993 with the overall aims of providing a more unified approach to the regeneration of vacant and derelict land and to bring about renewal through partnership with local authorities, the private sector and other bodies involved in regeneration (DoE, 1993b and 1993c). English Partnership intends to build upon the success of existing programmes targeting resources more effectively, maximizing the leverage of resources and forging a new spirit of partnership.

The array of urban policy initiatives highlight the underlining value attached by the government to the role of the private sector in inner city and urban regeneration. Increasingly corporatism is having a profound impact on the economic and physical structure of the inner cities. The various instruments of state finance and legislation are being used to erode the influence and autonomy of local government. In this evolving context the different actors in the property development process, for example the State, the private developers, sources of private funds and property consultants, have been mobilized to help transform selected inner-city areas by means of physical regeneration through property-led urban regeneration. The establishment of the Enterprise Zone in the Isle of Dogs, the setting up of London Docklands Development Corporation and introduction of City Challenge Companies in five London boroughs all bear witness to the increased level of corporate influence. An analysis of the City Challenge bidding process reveals the degree of emphasis placed on the involvement of the private sector and local businesses. Provision of land for development has been identified as the most important element of the various urban initiatives. In this context English Partnership has the power to acquire land and buildings by agreement and to reclaim, service, develop and dispose of that land, and provide market information to the private sector.

This will enable the partnership to play a crucial role in land assembly, identifying sites in consultation with local developers and local authorities, and to dispose of any assets in the form of developed land and property.

2.4 CONTRADICTIONS AND CONSTRAINTS IN THE PLANNING PROCESS

The fragmentation of government agencies and the lack of co-ordination of their strategies parallels that of the many agencies in the landowning and development sector. Each government agency tends to plan within its own introverted development framework, often directed and driven by political agendas set by those in charge. At its most basic there are serious problems of co-operation within boroughs and between their internal departments. Such conflicts tend not to surface in the public domain, but lack of co-ordination between government departments can be frustrating and costly to the small developer. Furthermore in the late 1980s the constant cutting of public expenditure has meant more conflict between departments as they attempt to maintain their level of service at the expense of others. Deregulation and privatization also has consequences for the development of cohesive strategies (Ryser, 1991).

There are also serious problems concerning the co-ordination of policy and practice across boroughs. As well as the existence of different and rival authority associations there are clear differences of policy emphasis in any given area between adjacent boroughs. Where one may welcome and accommodate middle-class gentrification, another may use every means possible to resist it; where one is indifferent to the effects of heavy traffic on the local environment the next is actively proceeding with extensive traffic calming measures. While it is difficult to find a common set of policies which are applied throughout the London conurbation, there is growing evidence that the development of networks in the capital, aided and abetted by LPAC, is beginning to produce a sense of common interest among the elected and non-elected interest groups (Eversley, 1992).

On a different plane there are clear problems of policy co-ordination between central government departments which impinge on plan-making at the local level, thus affecting the decision-making process (Thornley, 1992b). The most obvious effect is the complete diaspora of organizations controlling the management of the city's transport network and the lack of links not only among themselves but also with the planning system. The transport network is run by British Rail, itself divided into Inter-City and Regional sub-networks, by London Underground, and London Buses as well as many deregulated bus companies (Pharoah, 1992). Each runs and plans its future routes and activity with little reference to the land-use planning system or overall strategy. Thus the Docklands has been developed ahead of any major infrastructure investment though the future of the Jubilee line extension to Canary Wharf is more certain following recent government announcements. Similarly major expansion has taken place at Heathrow and Stanstead airports prior to the completion of proper public transport links. Indeed British Rail is more likely to come into contact with the planning system as a developer of its extensive surplus land than in a scheme to co-ordinate land use and transport.

Separate from this again is the planning of the road network. The Department of Transport, which is responsible for road planning nationally and for major national roads in London, plans these almost entirely on traffic grounds. The constant attempts to push through schemes such as the Archway Road widening or the East London River Crossing in the face of extensive opposition from other agencies and the public testify to its insensitivity. It is equally insensitive to the cost of inner urban road construction. The effect of this is to spread 'blight' over considerable areas of the capital.

In housing too the situation has become highly decentralized, with housing associations now taking up the burden of social provision in conjunction with tenant co-operatives as the old local authority stock is sold off. In addition to this, the cutting of funding to these agencies has resulted in a growing polarization in the nature of the housing stock in the city. Some boroughs have gone along with the government's strategy and their action has encouraged gentrification of the areas of better stock and the 'getto-ization' of the major council estates. Thus certain boroughs go upmarket in their social group structure and become more attractive to further investment in new offices, particularly those using new technological skills as in Wandsworth, while other boroughs which have gained a reputation for social discord remain unattractive to the investor, for example Hackney. Thus despite the investment in Docklands the residential changes brought about in the East End are few and isolated. Indeed the area outside the LDDC area has remained stubbornly unaffected by the changes and the planning system is ineffectual in redressing this process of polarization, since there is no London strategy for housing.

The marketing of London has gathered pace in recent years judging by the number of new agencies established and the number of conferences and seminars on the topic. The focus of the marketing effort is primarily on 'promoting' the capital to various target markets, part of which is clearly directed internally towards government to ensure that London receives an appropriate share of public investment (Edwards, 1992b). In addition promotion will need to be targeted towards occupiers and investors, both existing and new. Among the recent bodies to be established are: London First, a private-led partnership intent on lobbying local and central government; London Forum which aims to promote London internationally to expand its role as a tourist and cultural centre, and retain and expand inward business investment; First Stop Shop, an initiative of the Corporation of London, the Westminster City Council and the LDDC to provide a single point of contact where companies interested in investing in London can get a full range of information on what the capital has to offer; and finally the Vision for London, a network of people and organizations working to promote a view of London. In addition many boroughs have promotion strategies designed to attract inward investment to their area, and the LDDC has operated a sophisticated marketing strategy since it was established (Ghanbari Parsa and Lyons, 1993).

2.5 INVESTMENT AND PROPERTY MARKETS

London's property market has undergone considerable change in recent years with a number of factors contributing to this process. These include government policy in relation to the deregulation of the financial sector, commonly referred to as the 'Big Bang', the streamlining of planning and development control systems and the globalization of property.

London's role as one of the major international financial centres, together with New York and Tokyo, therefore provides a natural focus for office and retail property investment. Diversification of capital from industry to real-estate investment provided the drive for the property boom in London in the mid 1980s, while more flexible planning and development control reflecting the prevailing political ideology played a major role in encouraging real-estate development. The 1986 'Big Bang' contributed to an unprecedented property boom with an influx of international financial institutions into the UK market. This was proceeded with a dramatic rise in demand for commercial property.

The Central London area accounts for some 60–70% of all London's office floor space (Diamond, 1992) and during the period of the 1984–8 property boom a total of 2.3 million sq m of office space was given planning permission. Rental levels in the City reached £650 per sq m in 1988 and £680 per sq m in the West End in 1989, making London one of the most expensive office locations in Europe. However, between 1989 and 1993 rental levels have declined, initially at a steady pace but over the 12-month period to December 1992 by 32.79% in the West End and 27.53% in the City of London (Healey and Baker, 1993). This has been attributed to an oversupply of property and lack of demand for office space during the economic recession of the early 1990s. There is now (1993) however the contradictory situation where much of the office property in Central London is overpriced in terms of rents, but proving particularly attractive in terms of yields. Consequently UK institutional investors are becoming increasingly active in the investment market and this has led to a signalling of the bottoming up of the London property market.

Foreign investment activity in the UK market declined significantly at the start of the 1990s. According to estimates by the Department of Trade and Industry and DTZ research, overseas investors purchased just over £3 billion of property during 1990, a drop of 5% from the 1989 total and in 1993 this had declined to just under $1 billion (DTZ, 1993). The most active of the foreign players had been Japanese and Swedish investors, accounting for 75% of purchases from overseas, and American companies. Swedish investors in particular scaled down their level of activity as some of their schemes were particularly affected by the market downturn. However with evidence of greater optimism starting to return to the London market in 1993 there is renewed interest, as confirmed by a number of major purchases by German property funds (Chandler, 1993).

Japanese investors have played a major role in the British property market especially in prime Central London locations. This has been mainly in the form of direct purchase of property though there has also been a number of joint ventures with British companies with mixed results. For example in 1989 Japanese investors accounted for 75% of the £1.55 billion of investment and development involving single properties of more than £100 million. At the same time 70% of all City purchases by insurance companies and pension funds were Japanese, attracted to UK property due to relatively high yields compared to Tokyo. Indeed of the 23 Japanese life companies several are represented in London including Nippon Life, Daichi Sumitomo, Asahi, Yasuda, Chiyoda and Toho. The first wave of Japanese property purchases in the UK represented 'trophy buildings' and involved some of the most prestigious property in Central London.

Institutional investors including pension funds, insurance companies and property companies are major players in London's property investment market. In terms of new investment in property, insurance companies accounted for 15% in 1980, about 10% in 1988 and 3% in 1992. During this period pension funds accounted for 14% of new investment in property in 1980, about 3% in 1988 and 7% in 1992 (DTZ, 1993). Such statistics highlight the fact that the property asset holding of institutional investors is only a fraction of their overall investment portfolio. Indeed a survey of the top 50 institutional fund managers by DTZ (1993) indicates that property accounts for just 5% of pension fund and 9% of insurance company assets, contrasting sharply with equity holdings of 55% in 1992 (38% in 1980). The estimated property holdings of the major pension funds is circa £22 billion and that of the insurance companies, including shares in property companies, topped £35 billion in 1992.

All of the top UK property companies have been involved in major developments in London throughout the 1980s (Figure 2.5) with flag-ship schemes including the London Docklands (case study 2.6.1) and Broadgate (case study 2.6.2). Such companies therefore experienced mixed fortunes in the property crash of the early 1990s, in particular those which financed large-scale speculative development with high borrowing requirements suffered most due to the diminishing demand for property and the falling value of their assets. Rather ironically with the erosion of rental levels, which are currently (1993) a fraction of their 1989 values, London in terms of occupational costs is now very competitive with other continental cities such as Paris.

Recent IPD calculations suggest that the decline in rental levels has slowed down and that the easing out of yields more than compensates for rental performance. Such trends reinforce the argument that during 1993 there has been a marked improvement in property returns, particularly in the office sector. In September 1993 yields for office property in the City of London and the West End stood at 6.5%, though a number of deals in the City suggest a new low yield of 7.2% (Lennox, 1993). Furthermore an increase in property financing and new planning applications received by the City of Westminster and the Corporations of London in the third

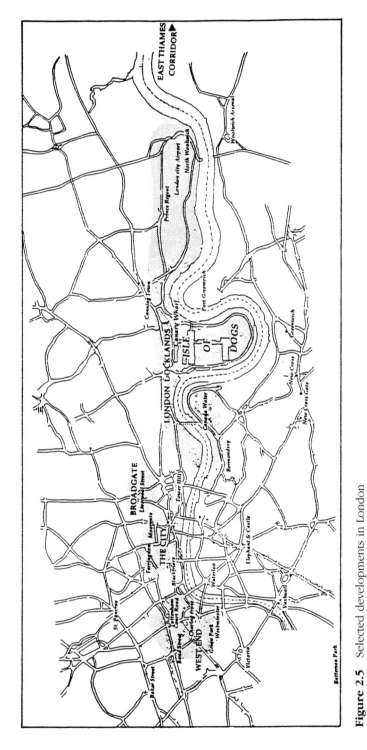

Figure 2.5 Selected developments in London
Source: based on Master Plan of London, Edition 6B (part revision), 1992, and Transport in Docklands, *London Docklands*, Nov. 1989, 4. Drawn by Mahtab Akhavan Farshchi, South Bank University, SLMUP.

quarter of 1993 also point to a reversal of fortune in the property investment market.

2.6   CASE STUDIES OF DEVELOPMENT AND INVESTMENT ACTIVITY

2.6.1   London Docklands development

London's Docklands stretches from London Bridge eastward along the Thames. The total area of the docks covers an area of some 2226 ha (22 sq km), the bulk of this being peripheral tracts of underused and derelict land. Docklands cover four zones namely: Wapping and Limehouse to the north of the river; the Isle of Dogs; the Royal Docks and Beckton; and Surrey Docks to the south of the river. Under the LDDC's strategy, each of these areas are treated as separate planning zones with their respective Area Team (Brindley *et al.*, 1989).

The collapse of the Dockland's economy first occurred in the 1960s and worsened rapidly throughout the 1970s. The establishment of LDDC in 1981 heralded a new era of leverage planning, namely the use of public investment to stimulate a weak or fledging private market in land and property development (Brindley *et al.*, 1989). With the deregulation of financial services and computerization of financial dealings the desire for a location in the City of London, the capital's business core, had diminished. The development of a new business district six kilometres to the east of the City of London with the potential to offer modern and cheap office accommodation was particularly attractive.

The election of a Conservative government in 1979 brought about a new era in town planning and development control not experienced previously. With the abolition of foreign exchange controls in 1979, office development permits and the Location of Offices Bureau the new government had sent a clear signal of deregulation and the type of changes to come. The beginning of 1980s saw rapid unemployment as a result of massive scaling down of the traditional heavy industries in different parts of the UK. In East London this resulted in the final shut-down of the dockyards and port facilities in the Docklands by 1981. Meanwhile Docklands had experienced loss of population of 24% between 1971 and 1981 and at the time of the establishment of LDDC it had a population of 39 700 and an unemployment rate of 18.6% (GLC, 1985). The establishment of LDDC which was to administer the Isle of Dogs Enterprise Zone, was intended to tackle these issues with private-sector involvement, especially the physical transformation of the area through property-led urban regeneration. The most well-known of all the major developments in the Docklands is Canary Wharf, a £4 billion scheme providing 400 000 sq m of office floor space, half of which is already let (Home, 1990).

In this context the role of the LDDC has been to overcome 'the perceived inability by local government to tackle the problem of urban regeneration effectively' (Carbonaro and D'Arcy, 1993). In order to do this, the LDDC was granted unprecedented powers to accomplish its stated aims and objectives. These included the power to purchase and sell land and property, grant planning permission and consider applications for grant and financial aid to developers. Thus according to Ambrose (1986), the DoE had directly instructed the LDDC 'to short circuit the planning procedure'. This reflected LDDC's own stated strategy to change the direction of the planning policies in the area (Thornley, 1992a). Such a strategy was to facilitate private developers by speeding up the process of development control through a flexible planning framework.

The creation of LDDC and the development of London Docklands has been subject to much debate among the professional and academic community. These have focused on different aspects of this development including; planning policy, economic strategy, urban regeneration and development, socio-economic impact, operation and involvement of the public and private sectors and increasingly transport and infrastructure. Much criticism has been made of the way LDDC ignored the needs of the local community and the resulting conflicts (Coupland, 1992). Its location and perceived distance from the City have bedevilled the future success of the Docklands from the outset. This has been compounded by the policy of a cautious demand-led approach to the provision of infrastructure based on staged development, firstly upgrading and secondly developing new major road and rail links. Carbonaro and D'Arcy (1993) criticize this on two counts: the higher cost of staged upgrading, and the lead time required for development of major transportation infrastructure. It is argued that the lead time for schemes of property development is shorter than the lead time for infrastructure development, thus posing the obvious risk that medium-term capacity infrastructure will be inadequate upon completion of a property scheme. There is serious under-capacity provided by the Docklands Light Railway the urban transit network built along the routes of existing railway track.

Undoubtedly the Docklands development has transformed the physical structure of the area fundamentally, however the goal of economic re-structuring has had more limited achievement (Punter, 1992). The stated objective in terms of employment in Docklands was 'potential end state employment for over 200 000 equivalent to two-thirds of the current estimate of jobs in the City of London' (LDDC, 1990). By 1987, 42 053 jobs were located in the urban development area against the total number of 27 213 in 1981. Population growth has been more substantial, reaching 73 800 in 1986 and forecast to reach 98 000 by 1996.

Against the stated criticism by a number of commentators the LDDC boasts the following achievements. Under the LDDC and with central government initiatives, in excess of £8 billion of private-sector investment has been attracted complementing the £803 million cumulative public investment generating an estimated private to public investment ratio of 10:1 (LDDC, 1990). The result has been the completion of some 1.2 million sq m of commercial and industrial space at end of March 1990. Furthermore with 1.6 million sq m under construction and another committed space of 0.8 million sq m and potential development of 2.57 million sq m creating a total of circa 6 million sq m of industrial and commercial space.

However in 1993 with continued economic recession, the future of Docklands Development looks bleak. The crash of the property market and difficulties faced by the Canary Wharf Development have marred the degree of achievement by the LDDC. A large proportion of completed developments both commercial and residential stand empty with ever decreasing capital values and rental incomes. This has been exacerbated by uncertainties arising from the lengthy negotiation between the government and private sector agents over contributions to funding and implementation of the Jubilee line extension.

2.6.2 Broadgate: innovative financing

One of the developments that changed the norm of commercial property development and investment in contemporary London has been unanimously recognized to be Broadgate by Rosehaugh Stanhope Developments (RSD) in partnership with British Rail Property Board. It is important to examine the development of Broadgate in the context of the rapid changes in London in the 1980s and to evaluate its impact on office development in the capital. Broadgate's development has followed an interesting path in terms of innovative financing, planning, design, implementation and marketing compared with previous office developments in London. Broadgate occupies the former site of Broad Street Station and land adjacent to Liverpool Street Station, a major transport interchange. British Rail owners of the land had plans for development of the site for some time in conjunction with a partnership between Taylor Woodrow and Wimpey, two British construction conglomerates. However, by 1983 due to lack of development, British Rail has decided to look for new partners and found these through a newly established Rosehaugh Stanhope Developments who succeeded in their bid to develop Broadgate in competition with ten other consortia.

Unlike any other major development previously, the Broadgate concept was very much based on the premise to 'satisfy the sophisticated space requirements of the City-based financial services organisations, and their professional advisors, that represent Britain's corner in the New York/Tokyo/London Golden Triangle' (Rosehaugh Stanhope Development,

1988). Such an objective was as a result of comprehensive research to determine the office space requirements of the potential tenants in a changing business environment particularly in the financial services sector. Research commissioned by RSD and conducted by DEGW a major firm of architects concluded that there has been widespread dissatisfaction with City of London office space available to financial services companies (Goobey, 1992). Client requirements were outlined as: prestige, large and flexible floor areas that would allow incorporation of technological changes specially in telecommunications. In fact development in information technology and increased use of computers had given rise to different design specification. Apart from such technological sophistication required of these buildings the new tenants demanded high-quality interiors, private and semi-public amenities and high-quality architecture and urban design externally that would be of international standards (Punter, 1992). RSD was able to respond to these requirements, to provide space that is custom-built to meet the physical, organizational and servicing strain imposed by 24-hour operation, within buildings that enhance the Cityscape as well as the separate corporate images of the tenant organization (Rosehaugh Stanhope Development, 1988).

Broadgate comprises 14 buildings implemented in different phases providing a total of 370 000 sq m of highly advanced office space and is the largest office development undertaken in London prior to 1985. The development of Broadgate was possible with the relaxation of development control as a result of the new City of London Local Plan in 1986 in response to the growing competition from Docklands. The new local plan allowed higher density development of plot ratio of 7.5:1 as against the maximum of 5.1 (Punter, 1992). The City of London Corporation had become particularly alarmed by the creation of LDDC and the granting of permission for development of 1 million sq m of office development at Canary Wharf (Diamond, 1992). The deregulation of financial services, the resulting property boom and increased competition from Dockland had pressurized the City to respond by redrafting the City of London Local Plan between 1984 and 1986. Among the key changes to the Local Plan was the decision not to bargain for section 52 agreements for planning gain.

The financing of Broadgate development merits closer examination. In November 1983 the RSD was formed owned 50/50 by the two companies, Rosehaugh and Stanhope. The initial equity investment in 1983 and 1984 was only £550 000 and the total reached £1 012 000 against a total development cost of around £2 billion. In terms of investment performance, Phases 1 and 2 of Broadgate were completed and let in 1987 with estimated construction cost of £174 million and valued at £258 million. The estimated value of Phases 1–4 and 6–7 was put at £1 billion by DTC, a major firm of property consultants in 1988 (Goobey, 1992).

2.7   CONCLUSION

London is in essence a city without a plan. The framework for decision-making is becoming more diffuse and impenetrable and therefore more uncertain for the millions of individuals, companies and other agencies in the private sector which have to operate in London. Needless to say this is translated into an absence of any physical or design coherence in what is built. The politics of anarchy are giving rise to the architecture of anarchy. However in recent years a new organization, Vision for London, has been created and this has begun to generate a debate to fill the vacuum which exists in strategic planning. In the business world other new agencies have emerged with the objectives of lobbying the Government on the quality of life in the capital as it sees London's pre-eminent position in this field being eroded in favour of other cities which plan strategically for the world of business and its participants. Together with the gentle cajoling from LPAC and SERPLAN they are beginning to shape the basis for a new structure of government with London-wide responsibilities but more detached from the local politics of it than the GLC. It is unlikely that the present central government will be disposed to establish any London-wide body of the sort needed. Until this emerges investors, businesses and developers must operate in an environment without a London-wide coherent strategy on planning for land use and infrastructure, the management of human, cultural and physical assets, and the capital's quality of life. However the recent City Pride initiative through which the local authorities and London First are being asked to come forward with a vision of the city over the next ten years may at least partly go towards redressing the balance.

Acknowledgement

The authors wish to acknowledge Mahtab Akhavan Farshchi for the production of the graphics used in this chapter.

REFERENCES

Ambrose, P. (1986) *Whatever Happened to Planning?*, Methuen & Co., London.

Brindley, T., Rydin, Y. and Stoker, G. (1989) *Remaking Planning: The Politics of Urban Change in the Thatcher Years*, Unwin Hyman, London.

Carbonaro, G. and D'Arcy, E. (1993) Key issues in property-led urban restructuring: a European perspective, paper presented at the European Real Estate Conference: *An Agenda for Research*, Faculty of Urban & Regional Studies, University of Reading, 15–16 July 1993.

Chandler, M. (1993) Funds flee from City offices, *Estates Times Review*, 19 November 1993.

Coupland, A. (1992) Docklands: dream or disaster?, in A. Thornley (ed.), *The Crisis of London*, Routledge, London, 149–63.

Credito Fondiario SPA (1991) *La Costruzione Della Citta Europa Negli Anni '80*, Roma.

Department of the Environment (1987) *Action for Cities: Building on Initiative*.

Department of the Environment (1992) *The Urban Regeneration Agency: A Consultation Paper*.

Department of the Environment (1993a) *The Government's Action for Cities Initiative*.

Department of the Environment (1993b) *Urban Regeneration Agency: Draft Guidance*, August.

Department of the Environment (1993c) *English Partnerships: News Release*, 10 November.

DTZ (1993) *Money into Property*. Annual Report, DTZ Debenham Thorp Ltd.

Diamond, D.R. (1992) The City, the 'Big bang' and office development, in K. Hoggart and D.R. Green (eds), *London: A New Metropolitan Geography*, Edward Arnold, Sevenoaks, 79–94.

Edwards, M. (1992a) A microcosm: redevelopment proposals at King's Cross, in A. Thornley (ed.), *The Crisis of London*, Routledge, London, 163–85.

Edwards, M. (1992b) London: world city and citizen's city: problems and possibilities. *Regenerating Cities*, May 1992.

Eversley, D. (1992) Comparisons: urban goals, procedures, politicians and developers, in J. Ryser (ed.), *Germany in Transition: New Strategies of Urban Development, Berlin–London*, Goethe Institute & Citystate Publishing, London, 26–8.

Ghanbari Parsa, A.R. and Lyons, M. (1992) Gentrification and change in South East London, paper presented at *Conference on European Cities: Growth & Decline*, The Hague, April 1992.

Ghanbari Parsa, A.R. and Lyons, M. (1993) Marketing the inner city: locality and competition, forthcoming.

GLC (1985) Monitoring the London Docklands Strategic Plan 1976: land availability, unpublished report, Docks 354.

Goobey, A.R. (1992) *Bricks and Mortals: The Dream of the 80s and the Nightmare of the 90s: The Inside Story of the Property World*, Century Business, London.

Hall, J.M. (1990) *Update – Metropolis Now: London and its Region*, Cambridge University Press, Cambridge.

Hall, P. (1989) *London 2001*, Unwin Hyman, London.

Hall, P. (1993) Forces shaping urban Europe, *Urban Studies*, **30**(6), 883–98.

Hamilton, F.E.I. (1992) A new geography of London's manufacturing, in K. Hoggart and D.R. Green (eds), *London: A New Metropolitan Geography*, Edward Arnold, Sevenoaks, 51–78.

Healey, P., Davoudi, S., O'Toole, M., Tavsanoglu, S. and Usher, D. (1992) *Rebuilding the City: Property-Led Urban Regeneration*, Spon, London.

Healey & Baker (1993) *International Office Markets – A Guide to International Office Rent*, Healey & Baker, London.

Hebbert, M. (1992a) The borough effect in London's geography, in K. Hoggart and D.R. Green (eds), *London: A New Metropolitan Geography*, Edward Arnold, Sevenoaks, 191–206.

Hebbert, M. (1992b) Governing the capital, in A. Thornley (ed.), *The Crisis of London*, Routledge, London, 134–49.

Hoggart, K. and Green, D.R. (1992) *London: A New Metropolitan Geography*, Edward Arnold, Sevenoaks.

Home, R. (1990) *Planning around London's Mega-projects: Canary Wharf and the Isle of Dogs*, unpublished occasional paper, Department of Estate Management, Polytechnic of East London.

Judd, M. (1993) A safety valve for the South East, *Estates Times*, 2 April.

Lennox, K. (1993) Playing the yield game, *The Estates Gazette*, Issue 9347, 27 November, 113–15.

LDDC (1990) *LDDC Key Facts and Figures to the 31st March 1990*, LLDC, London.

LPAC (1991) *Annual Review of Strategic Trends and Policy*, London Planning Advisory Committee, London.

LPAC (1993) *Draft 1993 Advice on Strategic Planning Guidance for London*, London Planning Advisory Committee, London.

Morgan, B.S. (1992) The emerging retail structure, in K. Hoggart and D.R. Green (eds), *London: A New Metropolitan Geography*, Edward Arnold, Sevenoaks, 123–40.

Pharoah, T. (1992) Transport: How much can London take?, in K. Hoggart and D.R. Green (eds), *London: A New Metropolitan Geography*, Edward Arnold, Sevenoaks, 141–55.

Property Week (1993) Selling London, *Chartered Surveyor Weekly*, 15 April 1993.

Punter, J. (1992) Classic carbuncles and mean streets: contemporary urban design and architecture in Central London, in A. Thornley (ed.), *The Crisis of London*, Routledge, London, 69–103.

Rasmussen, S.E. (1983) *London: the Unique City*, The MIT Press, London.

Ryser, J. (1991) *Germany in Transition: New Strategies of Urban Development Berlin–London*. Goethe Institute & Citystate Publishing, London.

Rosehaugh Stanhope Development (1988) *Broadgate: A Tenant's Guide*,

RSD, London.

Society of Property Researchers (1992) *London as a Business Location*, SPR, London.

Thornley, A. (1992a) *Urban Planning Under Thatcherism: The Challenge of the Market*, Routledge, London.

Thornley, A. (1992b) *The Crisis of London*, Routledge, London.

3

Amsterdam

Barrie Needham
and Johan van de Ven

The aim of this chapter is to explain the relationship between the planning system and the property market in the Netherlands in general, in Amsterdam in particular, and to describe how that relationship affects the physical development of the city. In the Netherlands there is general agreement that development should be initiated by the public sector and should take place along lines specified by that sector. The 'shape of Amsterdam' has therefore been determined by public planning. However, as most building is undertaken by the private sector, planning can exert its influence only by steering the private sector.

Enterprise and development are inherent characteristics of Dutch culture. On the monument commemorating the enclosure of the Zuiderzee is inscribed, 'A nation that lives, builds for its future.' Building, both residential and commercial, is stimulated by public administration. The private sector has responded to the generous opportunities offered to it to an extent which is, perhaps, not in its best interests, leading to a surplus of some types of commercial property and low prices.

In this chapter the rationale in support of this argument is presented. First, the institutional framework within which the property market operates is described; a context set by the planning culture, public administration, the planning process and the markets for property development and investment. Second, changes in the physical structure of Amsterdam over the last ten years are considered. These changes are the result of economic pressures interacting with public policies within the institutional context. Third, the performance of the property markets in Amsterdam is analysed by presenting the volume and location of new

European Cities, Planning Systems and Property Markets Edited by James Berry and Stanley McGreal. Published in 1995 by E & FN Spon. ISBN 0419 18940 8.

construction, take-up and vacancy rates, prices and yields. Finally an explanation of property market performance is given in terms of the interaction between the property market and the planning system.

3.1   THE INSTITUTIONAL CONTEXT

In the planning culture of the Netherlands, two national characteristics are of prime importance, first the desire for pleasant physical surroundings and second the preference for compromise over conflict.

Considering the first issue, the wish for a pleasant, well-ordered, predictable physical environment has led to public bodies taking a very active part in creating, maintaining and changing that environment. There is little political disagreement about this. The initiative for physical development often comes from a public body, which then approaches a private body such as a developer, in order to stimulate interest in a joint project. In all cases, development takes place only in accordance with a physical plan. The emphasis on the public administration determining the type, location, quality and timing of physical development is so great that public authorities are not entirely satisfied with the limited steering powers available to them under 'statutory physical planning', thus they employ other regulatory means.

Part of the physical surroundings which the Dutch consider to be so important is the natural environment. Policy for the quality of air and water, soil contamination, noise nuisance, natural resources, flora and fauna grew rapidly in the 1980s, but separate from physical planning. Recently however it has been realized that good and healthy physical surroundings require an integration between environmental policy and physical planning.

The second national characteristic that strongly affects physical planning is the preference for compromise over conflict, which Lijphart (1968) referred to as 'the politics of accommodation'. Hence there is great reluctance to use superior powers to impose a decision where there is a difference of opinion. For example, if the city of Amsterdam should want to pursue a planning policy with which the province or central government disagrees, then both of the latter are empowered to impose a 'directive' on the municipality, but rather than pursue this course of action consensus is sought, often taking months or even years (Dekker *et al.*, 1992). This applies to the making of plans at all levels. The consequence is that plan-making takes a considerable length of time, but the plan, once approved, has the commitment of those whose co-operation is necessary for its realization. As a result, development is relatively troublefree: it is not continually interrupted by aggrieved parties either boycotting it or requesting modifications.

The Netherlands' public administration is based on a decentralized, unitary state. The contradiction this implies has the potential for continuous tension, but the 'politics of accommodation' is followed and accepted by most parties. Under this system, the municipalities have a large degree of freedom. Financially, the central and the municipal levels are the 'spending agencies', with the provinces acting as intermediaries.

The mechanics of this are apparent in physical planning. Central government makes and adopts 'national physical planning key decisions'; provincial government makes and adopts regional plans (*streekplannen*), which have to be recognized by central government; municipal government makes and adopts structure plans and local plans (*bestemmingsplannen*), which in turn are approved by provincial government. Both central and provincial government may issue directives to municipal government specifying the content of the local plan. However, in practice the hierarchy is not imposed. Instead there is constant negotiation, with all levels influencing each other's policies for physical development. The outcome is that central government sets very broad outlines and municipal government has considerable freedom to determine its own planning policy within those guidelines, with provincial government playing a mediating role.

When a public authority wishes to influence physical development, the planning process usually has several means at its disposal. One way is by development control. In the Netherlands, all building works require a building permit. This is sought from the municipality, which checks the application against the adopted policies. First, building regulations which concern technical aspects, but also the appearance of the building, can be applied to control some types of use change. Second, the application for a building permit has to be in conformity with the local plan. Finally if the application affects a listed building or is covered by an urban renewal plan, then other checks have to be carried out.

If an application satisfies all of these conditions, permission must be granted; however, should the application fail on one or more of these conditions, then it must be refused. A local plan is deemed to be 'legally binding' and consequently no development can take place which is not in conformity with the plan. For example, should a private body make an application which contradicts the local plan and the municipality supports the application, the municipality must nevertheless withhold a permit until the plan has been changed, or a commencement made to change the plan. The same circumstances apply even if the central or provincial government wish a development to proceed.

The local plan is the only physical plan which is legally binding, the other plans (structure plan, regional plan, national key decisions) have an indicative status. These latter plans affect the process of development in so far as they influence the content of the local plan. That is, a local plan has to be approved by the province, which checks it against its own regional plan. Consequently, development control powers give the municipality direct influence over what is built, and to provincial and central government indirect influence. However the latter tiers of government have other functions including constant consultation and the power to turn the 'subsidy tap' on or off.

Another way of influencing development is through the legislation for environmental policy. Current requirements for construction and change of use usually necessitates one or more 'environmental permits'. These can be used to regulate noise nuisance, emissions into the air and water courses, waste disposal, and soil contamination. Since the beginning of March 1993 a number of these separate permits have been combined under a new Act (*Wet Milieubeheer*). The specifications under environmental impact assessment often require additional stringent testing.

Influencing physical development by means of development control and environmental permits is obligatory on local government. However, most municipal governments are not content to leave it at that, rather they want to exercise more influence than is possible through statutory obligations to issue or withhold permits. The latter is considered to be passive, whereas municipalities want to take a more active role. In consequence, they assume the function of 'land developer', acquiring land and servicing it in order to supply the 'building developer'. The practice in the Netherlands that most building takes place on land supplied by municipalities means that a municipality can regulate desired development through the provision of building land, while at the same time exercising control over the details and the quality of the development. It must be emphasized that while municipalities are not obliged to do this, they nevertheless choose to, and moreover provincial and central governments expect them to do so.

It is practice for the development process to be divided into two stages, except in those cases in which just one or two plots are involved. The first stage of 'land development' covers the change from land in existing use, with or without buildings on it, to the land parcelled into building plots ready for the new use, fully serviced and connected to the necessary infrastructure. The second stage, the 'building development', covers the change from serviced building plots with planning permission for their new use, to developed land. The fact that this distinction can be made so sharply is because different actors carry out the different stages. Land development is mostly carried out by municipalities, and building development by private developers and housing associations. The private sector does not wish to change this division, indeed building developers are content to buy serviced land 'off the shelf', without the problem of land assembly and the uncertainty of development control and infrastructure provision.

Whenever the property is for industrial use, most of the building development is undertaken by the users themselves (Needham and Kruijt, 1992). There is, however, little development for rent, mostly small units or combined production/office space (business parks). If the property is for retailing, seldom does the retailer commission it. Instead a property development company will normally build and then sell the completed shopping centre to an investor. Regarding offices, these are built both by the end users and by property companies, the latter selling both to end users and to investors.

In essence, as land development is a task for municipalities and the building development the responsibility of the private sector this means that the costs, risks and returns associated with property development are divided between both sectors. The municipality invests very heavily in buying and servicing land; the latter is often costly and might include soil decontamination and new transport infrastructure. The municipality hopes to recoup that expenditure, possibly with a profit, when it disposes of the land to building developers. However, this may take place several years later, with interest charges in the interim mounting up and no guarantee that a building developer will want the land or any certainty about the price at which it will sell. Furthermore, once the land has been sold, the municipality has the recurring costs of maintaining the public spaces but enjoys no benefit from subsequent rises in property values. The building developer is spared the costs and risks of land development, but has no opportunity to influence the content of the plan, as serviced land is offered under detailed planning and construction conditions on the basis of 'take it or leave it'. Another cause of dissatisfaction with the customary division of labour is that, when applied to urban re-development, it often leads to schemes where the land development must be subsidized. Yet money available for subsidies is becoming scarce.

Investment in commercial property comes from three main sources: institutional investors, general investment funds, and those funds investing exclusively in property. The interaction between investor/landlord and occupier/tenant is influenced by a rental contract. In the case of shops, special legislation gives the tenant strong security of tenure, but for offices and industrial premises contracts are short, usually for five years though with a possible extension for a further five years. The outcome is that final users of new shops are nearly always tenants; whereas new offices are divided between owners and tenants; and new industrial space is normally owner occupied. Hence the investment market in industrial property is small.

In the development of the retail structure, new building is tightly controlled and the supply thereby restricted. Rents, however, are not high when compared internationally. The supply of new offices, on the other hand, is stimulated by the public authorities. Developers have been able to sell their projects to investors, and have taken up the opportunities offered by the public sector in its role as 'land developers'. A consequence of the high land supply for offices has been low rental levels.

Shops and offices are built only in accordance with public plans, and consequently the market is fairly predictable. Investment in commercial property was, therefore, regarded as low risk and the investors were prepared to accept lower returns. For offices, the combination of low rents and low returns led to high capital values. This encouraged developers to continue construction projects, and the possibility of high land values and new workplaces encouraged municipalities to continue supplying office land to the private sector. Inevitably this led to an over-supply of office space and, in a period of low economic growth such as the early 1990s, high vacancy rates in most parts of the Netherlands.

An agency which is very important in the office market is the national agency for public buildings (RGD), which both commissions and acquires buildings for rental to public bodies. The RGD is active in The Hague, the seat of government, and in Amsterdam owns a considerable stock of property. Policy is increasingly geared to leasing rather than to owning (Needham *et al.*, 1993).

The practice of the municipal government playing a leading role in property development started in Amsterdam around 1850 (although the city was actively involved in supplying building land for urban expansion as early as 1585). Initially central government had created very few planning powers. The city, wanting nevertheless to act, made inventive use of building regulations, public nuisance ordinances and took an active involvement in the local land market, in order to steer urban growth. In pioneering the use of land policy, the city rather than disposing of building land has retained its legal interest through the issuing of long leases. Consequently the city owns most of the land (circa 80%) within its boundaries.

However the division of public responsibilities is more complicated in Amsterdam than in most other parts of the country, due to two additional levels of government. In 1990 16 neighbourhood councils were set up. Each of these has responsibility for preparing and implementing local land-use plans while the central city's authority lies with the structure plan and local land-use plans for projects with a city-wide significance. Furthermore in 1992 the municipality of Amsterdam and 15 other municipalities agreed to work together formally in a regional administration (ROA – Regional Organ Amsterdam) to ensure a better co-ordination on such matters such as public transport and infrastructure and addressing the competitiveness of Amsterdam in the new European Market.

3.2   THE PHYSICAL DEVELOPMENT OF AMSTERDAM

3.2.1   Economic context

Amsterdam is the economic capital of the Netherlands. Many national head offices together with the offices of foreign-based companies are situated there, even though government services are concentrated in the Hague. The leading sector is financial, viz business services, with the Dutch central bank and the stock exchange based in Amsterdam. Enormous growth of employment in the tertiary sector during the last few decades has necessitated the need for new office space. Although Amsterdam's share of the total office stock of the Netherlands has declined in relative terms, the city is still a dominant market regarding size and rents.

Concerning the manufacturing sector, Amsterdam is losing employment at a faster rate than other parts of the country. On the other hand, Amsterdam, and indeed the Netherlands as a whole, is increasingly becoming a distribution centre. In this context, the proximity of Schiphol airport (Figure 3.1) and the harbour (Westpoort) is of crucial importance (Jobse and Needham, 1988).

The three most important locations for economic growth are first, the city centre, the cultural focus of Amsterdam, with many historical sites and earning significant income from national and international tourism; second, Schiphol Airport, where the volume of cargo and passengers is growing rapidly; and third, the harbour Westpoort, which although having extensive sites, is considerably smaller than Europort at Rotterdam.

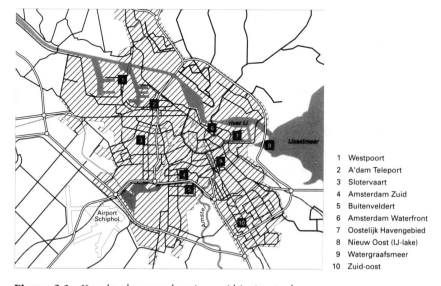

1   Westpoort
2   A'dam Teleport
3   Slotervaart
4   Amsterdam Zuid
5   Buitenveldert
6   Amsterdam Waterfront
7   Oostelijk Havengebied
8   Nieuw Oost (IJ-lake)
9   Watergraafsmeer
10 Zuid-oost

Figure 3.1   Key development locations within Amsterdam

3.2.2 Public policy context

Planning policy for Amsterdam in the 1970s was dominated by the renewal of the older housing areas through either the rebuilding or the rehabilitation of existing dwellings. The outcome was improvements to the stock of cheaper rented dwellings, at the expense of other types of housing and of other uses such as small firms. At the same time central government was pursuing the policy of growth centres, which encouraged the out-migration of the higher income groups. However this process started to change around 1985 with the introduction nationally, and strongly supported by Amsterdam, of the policy of the compact city. This was followed by a change in national housing policy, with the heavy subsidization of housing improvements being phased out, subsidies for rented housing being reduced, and unsubsidized housing both for rent and sale being encouraged. The combination of these policies in the early-mid 1990s is leading to more private housing being built within the city of Amsterdam.

Arising from the fact that a considerable proportion of commercial development has taken place outside the city centre, the core area is losing its role as the employment centre. In seeking to address this issue the municipal government wants to proceed with a major project on the southern banks of the river IJ. The proposed scheme is planned to include between 300 000 and 500 000 sq m of office space, together with housing, cultural and community facilities amounting to circa 1 250 000 sq m (Witbraad and Jorna, 1993).

A further policy likely to have a major impact on the physical development of Amsterdam is the 'location policy' (introduced by central government in 1988) whereby new offices and other development, generating large numbers of visitors and employees, may only be built near railway stations. The aim is to restrict the use of private transport, to keep town centres accessible and to restrict pollution. The proposed project on the IJ-banks fits in with this location policy.

3.2.3 Property development context

Concerning office space, the city centre is traditionally the most important location within the municipality. However in the 1970s this situation began to change and with many of Amsterdam's historic buildings and sites subject to a great number of restrictive by-laws, the city centre could not provide sufficient space for the rapidly expanding demand. As a result, a policy for 'subsidiary centres' within the municipal boundaries was introduced in 1981 whereby the municipality promoted the building of offices in those peripheral locations highly accessible to public transport and motorways. Among these Amsterdam Zuidoost and Amsterdam Teleport became popular subsidiary centres.

Table 3.1 Office space in Amsterdam (sq m gross): municipality and agglomeration (which includes Diemen, Amstelveen, Badhoevedorp, Ouder-Amstel)

Year	Amsterdam	Agglomeration
January 1983	3 600 000	4 100 000
January 1984	3 681 000	4 186 000
January 1985	3 732 000	4 238 000
January 1986	3 776 000	4 305 000
January 1987	3 779 000	4 330 000
January 1988	3 910 000	4 489 000
January 1989	3 999 000	4 654 000
January 1990	4 151 000	4 858 000
January 1991	4 316 000	5 181 000
January 1992	4 510 000	5 378 000
January 1993	4 678 000	5 611 000

Source: *Dienst Ruimtelijke Ordening*, Municipality of Amsterdam, 1993.

The result of the policy was a widespread development of offices in the sub-centres as many companies relocated from the city centre. Consequently the latter, although still having the most office floor space, is losing its relative position rapidly (Table 3.1).

There is little locational variation in rental levels as all the subsidiary centres offer more or less similar quality, although the highest price for office space in Amsterdam (and the Netherlands) is in Amsterdam South. However, further growth of supply in this locality is the subject of political argument with the city government's desire to develop the south banks of the river IJ with offices designed to the same quality standard as found in Amsterdam South.

Statistics concerning the amount of industrial space in Amsterdam are more problematic as almost all industrial premises are owner-occupied. Therefore there is little market evidence concerning rental transactions. Furthermore manufacturing industry in Amsterdam has declined during the last two decades, with physical planning contributing to this process as relatively little land was zoned for industrial development. Heavy industry is allowed to locate only in the harbour area of Westpoort while many former industrial areas within the city have been redeveloped and made suitable for other uses such as housing. The only industrial activities that are expanding are in the distributive (transport and warehousing) and high-tech sections, with Schiphol attracting airport-related activities and a policy of encouraging high-grade non-polluting employment.

Regarding the Amsterdam retail sector, there were 7200 shops with over 800 000 m² (net) of selling space (1992 data). Since 1987 the total

Table 3.2 Population and housing statistics, Amsterdam

Population at start of period	Year	Housing stock (mean figure)	Composition by sector (mean figures)
831 426	1970/74	291 400	67.8/27.6/4.6
758 155	1975/79	300 745	60.2/33.0/6.8
716 466	1980/84	307 912	88.6/8.9/2.5
675 152	1985/89	331 637	74.2/16.1/9.7
713 407	1990/91	343 001	61.3/33.1/5.6

Note: the composition of the housing stock is given for socially rented/lightly subsidized (rent and sale)/unsubsidized (rent and sale).
Source: *Dienst Ruimtelijke Ordening*, Municipality of Amsterdam, 1993.

number of shops has declined by 4% although selling space has grown by 2%. The city centre still remains the most important shopping area and in order to maintain this status, planning policy does not permit out-of-town development apart from schemes in suburban residential areas. However in some industrial estates, discount stores and furniture outlets are allowed.

Concerning population and housing, in the 1970s there was a huge outward migration from Amsterdam, but at the same time there was an inflow of people from outside the country with Amsterdam receiving 20% of all the foreign migration into the Netherlands. Consequently demand was for low cost rented housing and currently (1993) only 7.5% of the housing is owner occupied (Table 3.2). In terms of the development programme sites are being sought for 70 000 new houses by the year 2000. Thereafter sites on reclaimed land (Nieuw Oost) in the IJ-lake should help resolve the demand-supply imbalance.

In considering the future physical development of Amsterdam, key areas of policy for the next 15 years include development at higher densities; greater sensitivity to environmental issues; and a focus on economic activity to retain the leading position of Amsterdam as a business centre. The latter is of particular significance as in the emerging European framework competition is likely to be between cities and their regions rather than at national level. Therefore an integrated policy for the Amsterdam region as a whole is required, especially in relation to infrastructure and housing.

3.3   THE PERFORMANCE OF PROPERTY MARKETS IN AMSTERDAM

The Amsterdam office market received considerable impetus in 1987 spurred by the decision of companies to move following a period of economic recession. Frequently these office users occupied significantly

THE PERFORMANCE OF PROPERTY MARKETS IN AMSTERDAM 59

Table 3.3 Statistics of the performance of the Amsterdam office market (data in 1000 sq m gross floorspace)

Year	Construction (a)	Change of function (b)	Net change stock (c)	Net growth of office use (d)	Change of vacancy (e)	Vacancy absolute (f)
1983	126	−45	81	−43	124	293
1984	101	−50	51	97	−46	247
1985	114	−70	44	34	10	257
1986	33	−30	3	58	−55	202
1987	181	−50	131	120	11	213
1988	124	−35	89	44	45	258
1989	207	−55	152	216	−64	194
1990	185	−20	165	70	95	289
1991	204	−10	194	63	131	420
1992	187	−20	168	68	100	520
Total	1462	−385	1078	727		

Note: $c = a + b$; $e = c - d$; $f_{(t)} = f_{(t-1)} + e$.
Source: *Dienst Ruimtelijke Ordening*, Municipality of Amsterdam.

Table 3.4 Take-up of office space in Amsterdam (sq m net, average per year)

	1984–87	1987–91	1991	1992
Amsterdam	162 500	245 700	175 300	201 800

Source: *Dienst Ruimtelijke Ordening*, Municipality of Amsterdam, 1993.

more space than they left behind. Furthermore, the change in the national economy resulted in a major phase of construction activity with many developers continuing to build without pre-lets. Despite a slackening of demand, the rate of construction activity for offices continued at a high pitch (Table 3.3) with the result that the vacancy level climbed by early 1993 to 11% of total stock.

Although the net growth of office use has fallen back from the peak achieved in 1989, annual take-up remains high (Table 3.4) equating to approximately 5% of total stock. However, the average size of transaction has declined from circa 2358 m^2 in 1990 to 1673 m^2 in 1992.

The volume of new office floorspace (Table 3.5) being brought on to the market, together with low inflation has resulted in low rates of rental growth. The average rental price rose from 220 HFL per M^2 per annum in 1984 to 260 HFL per M^2 per annum in 1992. Highest office rents are in Amsterdam South (Amsterdam Zuid) varying between 300 HFL and 450 HFL per m^2 per annum (1993 figures). Initial yields for the Randstad

Table 3.5 Construction of office space (sq m gross) by location

	1983–87	1987–91	1991–93
City centre	8 500	101 500	27 600
Amsterdam south	72 800	57 700	39 400
Buitenveldert	1 800	20 700	10 000
Tuinsteden west (incl. Slotervaart)	5 600	59 800	40 400
Amsterdam Teleport	0	48 600	75 500
elsewhere Westpoort	7 700	18 800	45 800
Watergraafsmeer	47 000	2 000	41 000
Zuidoost	216 900	348 100	90 200
elsewhere Amsterdam	14 300	40 100	21 500
Amsterdam	374 600	697 300	391 400

Source: *Dienst Ruimtelijke Ordening*, Municipality of Amsterdam, 1993.

Table 3.6 Office construction (sq m gross) in Amsterdam by year of expected completion, 1993–7

		1993	1994	1995	1996	1997
For rental	In preparation	—	21 000	53 000	35 000	48 000
	Under construction	60 000	8 000	30 000	—	—
For owner	In preparation	—	17 000	6 000	50 000	75 000
occupation	Under construction	120 000	3 000	—	—	—

Source: *Dienst Ruimtelijke Ordening*, Municipality of Amsterdam, 1993.

as a whole range from circa 7.4% in prime locations to 9.25% for other locations (Zadelhoff Makelaars, 1992). Yields have risen slightly in recent years with the result that capital values have not been increasing, reflecting the high supply-side input of construction activity. This is expected to continue as data for Amsterdam indicates only a small decline in construction over the period 1993–7 (Table 3.6).

Less information is available about the performance of the retail market in Amsterdam. Prices remain highest in the city centre, with top rents of 1400 HFL to 1600 HFL per M^2 per annum in Kalverstraat, Leidsestraat and Hooftstraat. Initial yields for the Randstad as a whole are between 7.25% for the best locations and 9.5% for other locations. Again yields for shops, as for offices, have risen somewhat in the early 1990s (Zadelhoff Makelaars, 1992). The expected construction of new shops and their distribution within Amsterdam between 1992 and 2005 (Table 3.7) indicates an expanding retail base which, due to the requirements of planning policy, will be within the existing built-up area.

Table 3.7 Expected retail construction (gross floor-space in sq m) between 1992 and 2005

City centre	34 000
IJ banks south	33 000
North of the river	5 000
OHG – New East	20 000
Amsterdam Teleport and surroundings	3 000
Westpoort, Geuzenveld-Slotenmeer	9 000
Slotervaart-Osdorp	22 000
South-Buitenveldert	10 000
Watergraafsmeer	2 000
Zuidoost	14 000
Total	152 000

Source: *Programma voor de ruimtelijke vernieuwing*, Municipality of Amsterdam, 1992.

It is difficult to assess the performance of the market for industrial property as only a small proportion of this space is for rental. Nevertheless, as an indicator of performance, initial yields in the Randstad (1992) are between 9.25% and 12%.

3.4 THE IJ EMBANKMENT

This proposed project provides an insight into the key role being played by the municipality operating in conjunction with the private sector. Indeed the scheme illustrates the interaction between planning, development and market processes, in an effort by the city government to revive the central core.

The municipality's usual procedure in implementing such a plan involves buying, servicing and disposing of land to building developers. However in this specific scheme both costs and projected returns will be exceptionally high, for example, some of the development land will involve reclamation. In order to share the risk a public/private partnership, the Amsterdam Waterfront Financing Company was established in 1991 (Witbraad and Jorna, 1993). The scheme will include a high proportion of remunerative elements (high-quality office and retail floor space) to maximize development gain and achieve financial viability.

However, as discussed earlier, Amsterdam has high vacancy rates for offices and moreover, most users prefer a location in the southern part of the city. Consequently the private partners considered the financial risks to be unacceptably high. Furthermore the public sector was not prepared to underwrite these risks leading to the withdrawal of private investment. Nevertheless, this does not necessarily mean the end of the scheme as the city intends to proceed.

Indeed, even under the present circumstances, central government has promised substantial grants especially to the redevelopment around Central Station. The withdrawal of the private partners does however mean that the scheme will now be more piecemeal than before, and the financial viability of the project is still in doubt. In order to cover the costs of land development, the municipality has incorporated yet more high-quality office space in the plan, despite current expectations that demand may be substantially lower.

This case-study illustrates the strengths and weaknesses of the functioning of the property market in Amsterdam. The city government may provide encouragement, infrastructure and land, but is not specifically involved in the realization of the buildings. Rather, implementation is dependent upon the co-operation of private developers. In the past, the city has assumed an input from the latter however with the market currently over-supplied (1993), rental returns are low. Moreover, the municipality has permitted office complexes in the sub-centres of the city to the extent that the market now prefers high quality developments in Amsterdam-South. This is a further factor in the property industry's reluctance to work with the municipality in creating an alternative and potentially competing complex along the IJ banks.

3.5 CONCLUSION

The property market in the Netherlands in general and in Amsterdam in particular can only be understood by reference to the crucial role of local government. Indeed the latter provides (almost) all of the land for development and redevelopment purposes.

Potentially the local government could use this position to curtail market activity. However it wants to do precisely the opposite, although there are limits to what the city authorities can achieve in terms of the development activity. The crux of the problem is that the local government is the 'land developer' whereas the private sector is the 'building developer'. Local government must try, therefore, to anticipate the market. When the decision is taken to supply building land the local authority has to forecast what the demand from private developers will be several years into the future. If the municipality underestimates the shortage of building land it may become a political issue. Consequently the tendency is to overestimate, a situation that has obvious appeal to developers.

This practice emerged initially in the residential sector and was extended to the supply of land for office development. However for the latter the municipality could make a substantial profit by supplying office land, thus there was a tendency to over-supply. This causes problems in those circumstances where too much land has been designated in the land-use plan as it is not possible afterwards to refuse to issue a building permit. Also the demand for offices is more difficult to forecast than for housing with the result that an oversupply of office floor space tends to be dispersed over several locations.

The situation is different again for shopping. For many years planning policy has been to protect the position of the city centre as the main shopping location, to allow district centres to grow but not threaten the position of the former and to prevent out-of-town centres. Consequently the impact of policy has resulted in very few vacant premises and relatively high rents though in comparison with other Western European countries shop rentals are modest.

Concerning collaboration between the private property market and the public planning system, interaction in the past has operated reasonably satisfactorily (Kohnstamm, 1993). However two factors are now making change necessary. First, the increasing cost and complexity of many redevelopment schemes means that the task of land development is becoming increasingly difficult for a municipality to undertake on its own. Second, the high rate of social and economic change increases the risk that a municipality runs when investing in expensive land development, and restricts its freedom to adapt to the future.

REFERENCES

Dekker, A., Goverde, H., Markowski, T. and Ptaszynska-Woloczkowisc, M. (1992) *Conflict in Urban Development*, Ashgate, Aldershot.

Jobse, R.B. and Needham, B. (1988) The economic future of the Randstad, *Urban Studies*, **25**(4), 283–96.

Kohnstamm, P.P. (1993) Urban renewal and public-private partnership in the Netherlands, in J.N. Berry, W.S. McGreal and W.G. Deddis (eds), *Urban Regeneration, Property Investment and Development*, E & FN Spon, London, 220–29.

Lijphart, A. (1968) *The Politics of Accommodation*, University of California Press, Berkeley.

Needham, B., Koeners, P. and Kruijt, B. (1993) *Urban Land and Property Markets in the Netherlands*, University College of London Press, London.

Needham, B. and Kruijt, B. (1992) The Netherlands, in B. Wood and R. Williams (eds), *Industrial Property Markets in Western Europe*, E & FN Spon, London, 155–192.

Witbraad, F. and Jorna, P. (1993) Waterfront regeneration: the IJ Embankments project on Amsterdam, in J.N. Berry, W.S. McGreal and W.G. Deddis (eds), *Urban Regeneration, Property Investment and Development*, E & FN Spon, London, 230–9.

Zadelhoff Makelaars (1992) *Visie achter de feiten 1991–92: de neder-landse markt voor commercieel vastgoed* (with a summary in English), Utrecht.

4

Brussels

*Guido De Brabander
and Ann Verhetsel*

Brussels is a city of differing perspectives. From an internal Belgian perception the city has a disputed status while its external appearance is that
of an international city and, as the headquarters of the EU, the *de facto*
capital of Europe. The complexity which characterizes Brussels is illustrated by its administrative structure and corresponding urban planning
system. Consequently, it is necessary to appreciate the institutional structure of Brussels, before discussing planning issues and the property market.

4.1 THE REGIONAL AND NATIONAL CONTEXT

The revision of the Belgian constitution in 1993 was the finale in a long
process of federalization. Although partial revisions date back to the beginning of the 1970s the real origins of this process lie in the cultural
oppression of the Dutch-speaking part of the population in the nineteenth
century, and the economic decay of the most important Walloon mining
and steel centres in the twentieth century.

The federal structure embodies a twofold division. First for territorial
matters, including the planning system, the country is divided into three
parts: the Flemish, Walloon and Brussels regions. Second, for personal
and other matters, such as culture and education, division is based
upon language. Concerning the latter, three language communities are distinguished: the Dutch-speaking community (Flanders and in part Brussels),
the French-speaking community (Wallonia and in part Brussels) and the
(very small) German-speaking community. Thus, the population of the
Brussels region is divided into two communities, making implementation
of a consistent policy much more difficult.

European Cities, Planning Systems and Property Markets Edited by James Berry and Stanley
McGreal. Published in 1995 by E & FN Spon. ISBN 0419 18940 8.

The Brussels region contains 19 municipalities, with a total population of about 950 000 inhabitants, of which the municipality of Brussels counts for about 130 000. In a European and indeed in a world context such population figures are very moderate (total population of Belgium is little more than 10 million inhabitants). However the functional urban region of Brussels is much larger. If the traditional commutation criteria are used as a delimiting standard, this region can be considered to stretch from the south-east of East-Flanders and the north-east of Hainaut in the west, to the borders of Limburg in the east. The larger regional unit has a population of almost 2.5 million.

The distribution of population is the result of the concentration of employment on the one hand and the depopulation of the municipalities on the other. Indeed the volume of commuting to the Brussels region is estimated to be about 340 000, equivalent to about half the total employment in the area. The twin issues of growth of employment, especially in public and private services, together with decentralization has encouraged this trend. Depopulation stems from the relatively high average age of the population and a systematic process of net out-migration. The latter is the result of selective attraction: viz in-migration was 68 822 in 1992 but out-migration reached 80 974, resulting in a net loss of 12 152.

As the functional region is much larger than the administrative region, it is difficult for the Brussels decision-makers to develop and implement policies that maximize impact in their territory. This is particularly so in the case of physical planning, housing, industrial estates, environmental and economic matters as well as traffic policies. There is thus a need for strong interaction with the surrounding Flemish and Walloon Regions, however the co-ordination between the policies of the three regions is weak and instruments may be used in a conflicting manner, particularly if divisions between politicians are to the forefront. Furthermore falling rents and rising incomes, stimulated the suburbanization process particularly from 1987 onwards (Cabus, 1991; van der Haegen, 1991; Lagrou, 1993).

The distribution of economic activity may be regarded as part of the de-industrialization of urban employment which is taking place all over Western Europe. However opportunities for development in the secondary sector, for example in the neighbourhood of the Port of Brussels (the so-called Canal Zone) were not used, rather suburban municipalities established industrial estates. In this context the municipalities east of Brussels were highly successful in this operation and a spatial shift of employment in favour of these municipalities has materialized.

In addition, the general structure of economic activity was affected by this process, most notably the share of the secondary sector shrunk while tertiary sector performed very well. Expansion was particularly large in banking, insurance, producer services and commerce. Moreover, employment of civil servants also rose dramatically, not only because of the growth of national, regional and local administrations, but also from the impact of the location of international and especially European administrations. These institutions were at the same time an attractive element for the location of all kinds of internationally oriented private and public institutions (viz headquarters and embassies). Hence the demand for office space rose and the central area of the Brussels region changed quite fundamentally. This was achieved not only by the building of new high-rise offices, but also by the conversion of residential property into smaller offices.

The impact upon Brussels as the capital of the EC has not been restricted to the office market, wider effects include the communication infrastructure and the housing market. Likewise the presence of NATO, the requirements of domestic administration, and the terminal for the high-speed train (TGV) all give impulses in the same direction. These pressures seem destined to increase as the modern urban management style implies open and often hard competition for political and economic decision centres throughout Europe. These centres inevitably demand space and infrastructure, and thus put pressure on the adjacent region (EIVA, 1992).

Kesteloot (1990) in this respect sees a new urbanity in which flexibility is the key word. Flexibility is not only essential in modern administration, but also in changing methods of production, in new patterns of consumption, in the organization of employment, and in the use of urban space. Typical of this process are the technology-intensive, clean industries with strong relations to the scientific world, with high demand for international communications and qualified staff. Normally these are located in research parks with strong linkages to the university sector.

The new urbanity and the influx of foreign staff has raised both local spending power and the price of housing. Middle and high-class income groups are being attracted into the inner city through the renovation of older property particularly the architecturally attractive buildings found in and around the centre and in the nineteenth-century belt, east of the canal. Often these properties are purchased, renovated with the help of grants and through higher rental demands the original tenants are often priced out of the market. Thus a process of gentrification is taking place in the private sector and indeed is also augmented by some of the social housing programmes of the local authority.

The attraction of Brussels is not limited to residents, public and private companies but also extends to tourists and congress participants leading to a dramatic increase in hotel facilities. Likewise renewed interest in opera and theatre, the prestigious exhibition in many museums, art festivals, international sporting events and the supply of cultural goods adds to the new urbanity. Furthermore fun shopping and the demand for night life stimulate the changing use of the urban space.

4.2   THE PLANNING SYSTEM

In Belgium, the legal basis for spatial planning is the law of 29 March 1962. Although a number of planning levels are contained within this law, only two of them are frequently used and indeed only one has been developed for the whole country. The Gewestplan (regional plan) confers to more than 40 subregions responsibility for the use of land in areas such as housing, agriculture, manufacturing, recreation, roads. In contrast the Bijzondere Plannen van Aanleg (special lay-out plans) are prepared at a sub-municipal level, and are used to detail the Gewestplan, sometimes even for individual building blocks.

The Gewestplan for Brussels was produced for the region containing the 19 municipalities and was approved by Royal Decree on 5 November 1979. According to the official concept this plan should provide for the following: the safeguarding of open space as a green or agricultural area; housing zones immediately linked to existing urban and municipal centres; housing and industrial estates in proportion to the development opportunities of the region, and the limitation of scattered buildings. While the objectives of the plan are valid the gap between these goals and the practice of the politicial administration is very wide.

The impact of spatial planning has lead to a reduction of urbanization in the first belt around Brussels, but at the same time an increase in (sub)urbanization in a second and much wider, belt (Cabus, 1991). Thus growth of the built-up area around Brussels was not hindered or limited by the planning process in spite of the fact that the Gewestplans for the surrounding regions were not co-ordinated. This lack of co-ordination may be resolved as a new general plan for Flanders is currently being prepared (1993) and particular attention is to be given to the area surrounding Brussels.

As spatial and physical planning is one of the responsibilities delegated to the regions, the Brussels region is therefore required to organize planning for the 19 municipalities. Furthermore the ordinance of 29 August 1991 provides for a reorganization of planning. At the regional level, a development plan and a zoning plan are envisaged while at the local level municipal development plans and special zoning schemes are necessary. The central goal being to combine social and economic development with quality of life and an economical management of space. Hence the plans may include limitations in the use of property, including prohibitions on construction.

Until recently, restrictions have been placed upon the expansion of offices in Brussels. However, the new or expanding European institutions as well as the TGV terminal are creating new demands. For example the neighbourhoods around Leopold and the North and South Railway Stations are key sites for large-scale office development.

4.3   THE PROPERTY MARKET

The European dynamic underlying Brussels is giving rise to important changes in the property market, a process which is not yet finished. Indeed the Belgian Business Association (VBO) estimates that an additional 4000 enterprises will come to Brussels in the period 1992–7, creating about 90 000 new jobs. This implies a continuing rise in demand for more offices, and also for new or renovated houses.

Concerning investment sources, Belgian and Dutch insurance companies and pension funds have been very active in the Brussels market and while Swedish groups took a substantial market share for a period in the late 1980s more recently French and German interests have been dominant. However information about the Brussels property market is not abundant with reliance placed upon two sources namely real estate agents and the public sector administration for the Brussels region. Both of these are of course parties directly involved in the development process and by the (selective) use of information may present a different scenario.

4.3.1   Industrial

The ring motorway around Brussels is characterized by a concentration of industrial estates. Optimal accessibility and abundant parking space are the key factors underlying these locations though increasing traffic has now lowered relative accessibility and added to congestion problems at peak hours.

Most of the industrial estates and research parks are managed by the regional development agencies (GOM or SDR), hence there are Brussels, Flemish and Walloon organizations. These agencies nevertheless act in a similar manner using relatively strict selection criteria in terms of those sectors admitted on to these estates and imposing rather rigid requirements concerning the creation of employment. However regarding future expansion the regional development agencies are not planning any new industrial estates along or in the neighbourhood of the ring motorway before the year 2002, rather new estates are to be developed about 10 to 15 km from Brussels. By employing such a strategy these agencies operate independently from the real estate practices which operate in and around the city of Brussels and so avoid to a large extent any element of speculation.

The commercial estate agency sector generally is orientated to the building stock constructed after 1970, except for totally renovated older buildings suitable for a diversity of users. Apart from offices, usually, three types of building are distinguished:

- semi-industrial buildings, suited for warehousing and distribution and including some office space;

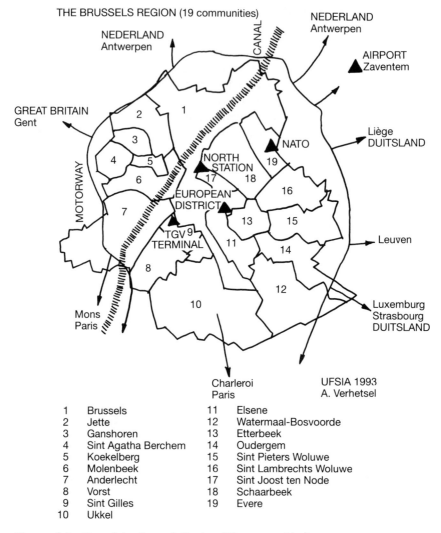

Figure 4.1   Map of the Brussels Region (19 communities)

THE BRUSSELS REGION (19 communities)

1	Brussels
2	Jette
3	Ganshoren
4	Sint Agatha Berchem
5	Koekelberg
6	Molenbeek
7	Anderlecht
8	Vorst
9	Sint Gilles
10	Ukkel
11	Elsene
12	Watermaal-Bosvoorde
13	Etterbeek
14	Oudergem
15	Sint Pieters Woluwe
16	Sint Lambrechts Woluwe
17	Sint Joost ten Node
18	Schaarbeek
19	Evere

UFSIA 1993
A. Verhetsel

- high-tech buildings, with more than 50% offices and the rest polyvalent (flexible) space;
- business buildings, with at least 80% offices.

Floorspace analysis for these sectors in six zones of Brussels (Figure 4.1) provide an indicator of the scale of this development (Table 4.1). However with increasing supply there is evidence of vacancy and in the more peripheral zones levels have risen to about 8 or 9%. This is likely to result in a fall in rents following the pattern set by high quality offices which dropped their prices by 10 to 12.5% during 1992.

Table 4.1 Total area of three types of industrial building in m² (March 1993)

Zone	Business	High tech	Semi industrial	Total
A	43 040	25 595	195 963	264 598
B	35 452	22 205	98 011	155 668
C	38 378	1 950	22 250	62 578
D	16 418	—	210 564	226 982
E	227 185	52 170	132 540	411 895
F	98 630	66 508	358 705	523 843
Total	459 103	168 428	1 018 033	1 645 564

A: Anderlecht/Vorst; B: Groot-Bijgaarden/St Agatha Berchem/Relegem/Zellik; C: Wemmel/Strombeek-Bever; D: Machelen/Vilvoorde; E: Diegem/Keiberg; F: Leuvensesteenweg/Zaventem.
Source: King & Co (1993).

Table 4.2 Rents per sq m in three zones around Brussels in BEF

Type	Anderlecht	Airport/Keiberg	Zaventem
Business	4500–5250	5000–5750	4750–5250
High-tech offices	4500–5000	4500–5250	4000–5000
High-tech mixed surface	3250–3750	3250–4000	3000–3750
Semi-industrial offices	3750–4250	4250–4500	4000–4500
Semi-industrial warehouses	2000–2100	2400–2750	2200–2500

£1 ≅ 53 BEF, 1$ ≅ 35 BEF
Source: King & Co (1993).

Concerning rents the range of values for three zones around Brussels are illustrated in Table 4.2 while for the city of Brussels average prices are 5750 BEF/m² for high-tech buildings, and 2750 BEF/m² and 2250 BEF/m² for small (500 m²), and larger (2000 m²) warehouses respectively (Healey and Baker, 1993a) though there is some evidence that the rents have declined during the first half of 1993.

Industrial estates in the traditional sense are not part of the Brussels market. As the price of land outside of the Brussels region is much lower, frequently by as much as 30 or 40%, warehousing and distribution services are relocating more and more to those surrounding municipalities with good access to motorways namely Ternat, Mechelen and Leuven. Unlike Brussels these locations can offer rents that guarantee a normal profitability on the investment.

The supply of semi-industrial buildings in the Brussels region seems to be in equilibrium with demand. According to a survey by the regional development agency there are some 680 buildings, with a total surface of about 820 000 m², half of which is to be found in Anderlecht, Laken and Molenbeek. Average selling prices were 15 573 BEF/m² in 1992. The same survey indicates that high-tech buildings have a relatively small share of the market, the estimated total floorspace being 88 000 m². Furthermore prices are relatively unstable with the periphery of Brussels showing a supply exceeding demand, due to stagnation in the computer sector. Consequently a lot of the polyvalent high-tech buildings have been transformed into 100% office buildings, especially in the Keiberg zone, near the airport. In this location about 90% of the supply is owned by investors, with rental levels in the range of 4500 to 6000 BEF/m². Although these prices are low in comparison with the London and Paris market, for Belgium such rents are relatively high.

4.3.2   Offices

The most important influences upon the office market stem from the growth of the European institutions. The so-called European quarter (or Leopold quarter), concentrated around Schumann Square, has impacted upon other parts of Brussels, for example the relocation of Belgian government departments from the European Quarter to the zone adjacent to the North Station. This serves to underline the fact that the market is characterized by a high degree of interdependence between different zones within the city.

The administrative authority of the Brussels region monitor changes in office activity throughout the 19 municipalities (Brat, 1992). In defining offices only those relating to private-sector functions are considered, thus offices associated with manufacturing industry or public-sector administration are excluded. Calculation of stock is based upon gross floor area exclusive of basements or space beneath ground floor. On the basis of this definition, there were 992 office buildings with a total surface of 6 659 000 m² in 1992. At the same time, 71 new buildings were in construction, adding a total of 1 095 000 m² to the Brussels office stock and resulting in a total volume of 7 754 000 m² by the end of 1994. Thus according to the Brussels administration, no shortages of office space will exist in the short to medium time period, with the exception of small, cheaper offices the demand for which should be satisfied by the adaptation of residential property. Furthermore existing plans for offices will add an extra capacity of 1 300 000 m² and draft plans imply an additional input of 835 000 m² which if realized will yield a total capacity of almost 10 million sq m.

The outcome will be a relatively high spatial concentration as almost 60% of the planned offices are either within the centre, in the European

District or in the neighbourhood of the North Station. Clearly the 'Manhattanization' of Brussels risks going far beyond what a historical city may support. Also, the regional administration insists that other economic and social activities in the region must not be hindered by the expansion of the office sector. Thus the public authorities are applying the Gewestplan (regional plan) very strictly, stressing the protection of the housing function and suppressing clandestine offices in houses and flats. The plan pays particular attention to mixed poles of development and in addition to a mixture of private and public initiatives, the regional authorities also want to realize a functional mixture of housing, working and recreation. This is achieved by a combination of conditions including building permission, and the need to take into account accessibility by public transport, particularly in the case of office development.

Demand for office space is evenly spread between the public and the private sectors. The latter accounts for 55% with banks and insurance companies relatively dominant (20% of the total). The public-sector share includes activities related to the EU, NATO, Belgian and regional public authorities.

Occupancy of offices is dominated by a relatively small number of institutions and companies. Normally complete buildings are taken by a single user, and thus small and middle-sized companies have some difficulty in acquiring suitable accommodation. Hence the practice to date has been for some companies to use the older (often former middle-class) houses along certain avenues; however, the ordinance which prohibits turning houses into offices will lead to even more difficulties for some of these companies.

While the image portrayed by Brussels is one of ready availability of office space, this perception is criticized by certain real estate agencies. It is pointed out that over half of the 1.1 million m^2 under construction is already sold or rented. However this claim should be qualified as over 50% of this floorspace is to be rented by the European Parliament. Also the economic recession affecting Europe has increased the level of vacancy in the existing stock. Thus in early 1993 Knight Frank & Rutley estimated that vacancies in the Brussels market were of the magnitude of about 6.7%. For Brussels, this is an unusually high figure, though low compared to the international situation. Nonetheless, it is expected that prices will rise from the end of 1994 onwards, as economic recovery materializes and additional supply will be low until the end of 1996.

Price indications differ between the various estimates, for example Ceusters (1993) quotes average rental values of 3000–8500 BEF/m^2 for the centre of Brussels in 1992 and between 2800 and 6000 BEF for more peripheral locations. However according to Knight Frank & Rutley (1993), average prices in 1993 are about 9500 BEF/m^2 while Healey and Baker (1993b) place rentals for high-quality offices in the range from 6000 to 9250 BEF/m². Similar statistics from Jones Lang Wootton (1993) stressed that 9000 to 10 000 BEF/m² is an absolute maximum in the centre.

Such rental estimates places Brussels in about nineteenth position of world office rents and due to its growing political role as European capital, estate agents stress the existing opportunities to locate within Brussels.

4.3.3   Hotels

The increasing function of Brussels as a political and economic decision-making centre has boosted the number of business-related visits dramatically. Consequently a number of international hotel chains have invested in Brussels. Moreover historical cities are becoming important destinations for recreational tourism, indeed city trips are one of the market segments with the fastest growth rate in the tourist industry opening up a number of opportunities for the hotel market. Economists and policy-makers alike stress the economic impact of tourism in particular revenue transactions and employment gain. According to estimates, the direct and indirect impact of tourism in Brussels exceeded 32 000 jobs in 1990, a growth of 24% in comparison with the 1980 figures.

The profile of the hotel guests in Brussels is dominated by visitors to Belgium, two-thirds of whom are of European origin and about 80% are on a business trip. The growing importance of the Brussels region as a destination is reflected in the increase in the number of beds. In 1981 this amouted to about 14 000, and by 1989 had risen to 18 700. The growth process continued, and in 1992 the total was more than 23 100. Development has been concentrated in the city of Brussels, although municipalities like Sint-Gillis, Sint-Joost-ten-Node, Elsene and Etterbeek, close to the city centre or the European Quarter also have benefited, as indeed has Evere due to its proximity to the airport.

Despite the rise in capacity, the number of hotels has dropped sharply from 214 in 1980 to 166 in 1990. The fall by about one-quarter over a ten-year period is the result of the closure of several small family hotels which were unable to respond to the higher quality levels demanded by customers. Thus the growth in the capacity is the result of new investments by large hotel chains. However, demand levels have not kept pace with the increase in capacity and average occupation rates in the region are about 60%, with the exception of Brussels and Sint-Joost-ten-Node where occupancy is about 70%. Consequently, tariffs are relatively high.

In accounting for this over-capacity the planning system is partly responsible. The regional plan permits the construction of hotels in residential areas as well as in mixed zones, thus no real limitations on the construction of new hotels exist. This set of circumstances applied until February 1992, at which point the high demand of investors for the construction of new hotels was countered by a complete stop on devel-

opment. In essence no new hotels were allowed to commence construction until the beginning of August 1992, corresponding with new regulations about the integration of hotels into the urban fabric. Since then,
every application has been controlled by the municipal authorities, especially in respect to environmental aspects, and is appraised with regard to
whether the project is suitable for the quarter in which the development
is proposed and the degree of hotel accommodation already available in
the neighbourhood. Issues such as the morphology of the city, the protection of green and open space and the conservation of the old city centre
are now important criteria in evaluating applications.

The new planning prescriptions of the regional authorities, the relatively
high price of land, and the attraction of industrial areas on the fringe of the
agglomeration may result in a deconcentration of supply in the near
future. Furthermore the overcapacity of high quality hotels might also lead
to a growth of middle ranked supply. However an alternative scenario is
that high-class hotels may apply tourist prices during the weekends and
over the summer to attract clients that normally would go to middle-class
hotels. It is also argued that suburbanization of economic activities relates
largely to production, warehousing and distribution while the activities
resulting in a high need for personal contacts remain in or close to the
existing centres of gravity in the region. Both arguments appear to have a
certain validity; however, it is clear that some uncertainty about the future
of the hotel market exists (Hamaide, 1992).

4.3.4   Retail

Retail outlets in or near commercial axes are attracting increased interest
from investors as well as policy-makers. These locations are regarded as
one of the best opportunities to create a lively city, hence pedestrian
zones have become very popular and add to the concept of the 'new
urbanity'. Investment interest has promoted an increase in property values
though this is not a continuous process. During the 1980s, peaks were
noted in 1984–5, 1987 and 1989. The overall trend, however, is of a rapid
rate of increase with prices in 1989 three times those of 1982. However,
1990–1 was a period of weak performance though in 1992 prices rose
again, but only by 4% (ANHYP, 1993).

Interest in commercial real estate in Brussels comes from a wide variety
of sources, in addition to internal Belgian investors, Dutch and French
companies have been active in retail investment. Again considerable variation in the price levels arises according to the location. Agency reports
for 1992 quote 51 000–53 000 BEF/m^2 for prime shops in the Nieuwstraat
(Rue Neuve) thereby placing it ninth in the world ranking of shopping
streets (Healey and Baker, 1993c). Another top location is the Louisalaan,
where prices are in the range 40 000–43 500 BEF/m^2.

4.3.5   Housing

The Brussels housing market differs significantly from that found in the rest of Belgium. Structural differences are primarily apparent in the level of ownership, 31% in the Brussels region compared to over 61% for the country as a whole. In considering the residential sector, social policy considerations are to the forefront though in reality only a small share of housing (8.3%) belongs to the non-profit sector (Goossens, 1991).

The price of residential property rose by 25% in Belgium over the period 1980–90 with existing property rising at a faster rate than the costs of new building. However recessionary conditions have forced a downward trend of prices since 1990; moreover, the raising of property tax, new regulations on renting and the increase of VAT on construction seems likely to exacerbate this trend. In addition the 12.5% registration tax on transactions presents a major impediment in the housing market in comparison to other countries. Furthermore, investment companies and project developers have a relatively small share of the housing market.

Concerning the long-term performance of the housing market 1981–2 represents the bottom point; the overall picture is of very steep growth from 1985 to 1988 with other years of the decade characterized by very slow or even negative growth rates (Figure 4.2). The apartment sector is the only component of the residential market remaining permanently below the average growth rate, with the increase in supply clearly hin-

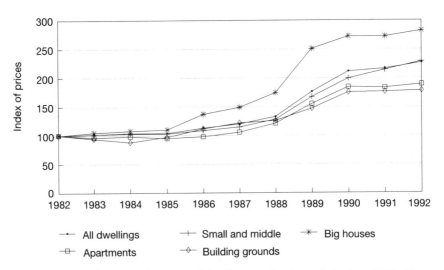

Figure 4.2   Evolution of the price of dwellings in the Brussels Region, 1982–92

dering the level of price performance. Furthermore investors in apartments have been interested almost exclusively in sales of complete blocks as this allows for more efficient management practices.

The pattern of price levels within the apartment sector shows important differences, with peaks occurring in the south-east of Brussels, a high demand location for EC-civil servants (average prices of 3.2 million BEF in 1989), while the lowest prices are recorded in Anderlecht (1.35 million BEF). A similar price distribution is apparent for single houses and villas; for example, relatively low-priced municipalities are to the north and west of the centre viz Sint-Jans-Molenbeek, Koekelberg, Anderlecht, Schaarbeek and Sint-Joost-ten-Noode, while Elsene and Etherbeek are located in the high-priced south-east. Prices of course reflect not only location but the quality of the construction, and the size of the building and the plot. Currently (1993) middle-sized houses, especially of the bel-eatage type (entrance and garage on the ground floor, living and kitchen on the first floor), are very much in demand costing between 2.5 to 3 million BEF. However large houses are in less demand and investor interest has dropped dramatically.

Regarding differences with the rest of Belgium ANHYP (1993) points out that the average increase of prices in Brussels was 5.3% in the period 1966–92 relative to 6.50% for the rest of the country. It is only if the prices of large properties or land are taken separately that significant positive differences with the national trends become apparent. However the relatively small number of such properties substantially reduces their impact on the general figures, but at the same time causes relatively modest rises in demand to have a dramatic impact on their price level. Hence attributing price inflation to the increasing demand of European civil servants and the employees of multinationals clearly is an over-simplification. Naturally these groups contribute to the price level, but this is limited to the houses and apartments at the upper end of the market, not only in the Brussels region but also in the municipalities to the south-east.

The expansion of EU services through its indirect and induced impacts could, according to expectations, create a demand for 30 000 new houses. This of course offers new perspectives on future price rises and sharpens the need for both urban renewal and the creation of social housing. Moreover, development of large-scale office projects leads to the demolition of houses to make way for such schemes thereby creating an additional need for further housing. Furthermore traffic increase and congestion may lower the quality of life in adjacent districts and so adversely affect residential neighbourhoods. Clearly, the need for spatial development planning is paramount under such conditions.

4.4   THE EUROPEAN DISTRICT

Concerning the impact of the EU administration on the Brussels property market, the most direct effect has been in the office sector. Currently the EU rents 850 000 m² or 13% of the total office area, additional to this a number of other European institutions have followed the EU administration. Moreover, international business and lobby groups are attracted in the same direction, accounting for a further 12% of office space. Such demand cannot be met by low-quality office accommodation. However impact is largely concentrated in the European district, consisting of the Leopold and the Schuman quarters, where about 1 720 000 m² of offices is accommodated for in existing buildings. The most famous is the Berlaymont building, of which 110 000 m² is presently being renovated, and an additional 300 000 m² of offices is under construction.

The office stock is of recent origin with only 11% built before 1960. Indeed considerable development activity occurred in the 1960s and 1970s, and, following the boom in economic conditions in the mid to late 1980s, further large-scale plans were forwarded. These developments are being realized in the first half of the 1990s, and it appears inevitable that the period 1990–5 will add a significant volume to the existing office stock. The most important new building projects are the offices of the European Council of Ministers, the International Congress Centre which will be used by the European Parliament with additional administration and meeting facilities, and the Borschette Centre which will become the conference centre of the European Commission. These new developments are likely to place high demands on accessibility and clearly improvements to the road infrastructure are needed. The most important new element of which is the Kortenberg tunnel providing a direct link to the ring motorway and the hinterland (Rijdams, 1992).

Approximately two-thirds of the users of these new buildings will be the European, international and national public administrations while the other third will be used by the private sector, in particular banking and insurance companies. Future demand is expected to be dominated by the EU and other international and foreign authorities, with the private sector as well as the Belgian public sector expected to take a lower share.

4.5   IMPACT OF TGV

In addition to the expansion of the administration of the European Communities, the TGV terminal is expected to impact significantly upon the Brussels property market. The basic decision for this development was taken in November 1989, when the ministers of transport of Belgium and its neighbouring countries met in the Hague to agree the organization and timing of the TGV network. The decisions reached include the acceptance of Brussels as the final destination for the train from London (originally planned for 1993) and as a stop on the lines from Paris to Amsterdam (1998) and Paris to Cologne (1998). Even if the timing has proved to be a little too optimistic the network and stop decisions will not be affected. However terminal facilities need to be upgraded in Brussels to cope with the envisaged traffic volume (9 million passengers from 1999) and in this respect the South station was selected, adaptation of which will be completed in 1997. The district around South station is to become a new development zone, essentially a business district, and as the Brussels region wants it to be a model project for public–private partnership a directive plan has been adopted. However, neighbourhoods around the South station are of very poor quality and until recently have been areas of concentration of disadvantaged population groups and numerous small businesses. It now seems likely that the changing functions of this quarter will probably crowd such activities out. How serious the social damage will be remains unclear because a 'spatial battle' between the national railway company NMBS, the regional authorities and the developers is currently going on. The outcome is still uncertain, a factor which has adversely influenced the realization of the plan.

While a fundamental renovation of the station would suffice the NMBS in 1990 presented a plan for the development of the whole neighbourhood incorporating an area of $350\,000\,m^2$, into which hotels, offices and shops would be integrated. However financial difficulties of the NMBS and the national government made it impossible to realize this plan, requiring an alternative means to be found. This involved the creation of Eurostation Ltd, a development company, aimed at maximizing the external effects provided by the TGV-stop. It was at this point that conflict arose with the Brussels region which did not agree with the ideas of the NMBS, since these were contrary to the directive plan which gives priority to the (amelioration of the) housing function. Provisional agreement between the parties is encompassed in the South Station Development Scheme which envisages $160\,000\,m^2$ west of the station for the hotel and office project of NMBS, while to the east of the station the region plans $300\,000\,m^2$ of new buildings, equally divided between offices, housing, commerce and hotels. The realization of the latter will be the function of a limited company, 'Brussels South', which will be required to provide alternative funding sources.

The provision of funding means cooperation with property investors and developers. In autumn 1991 specialized publications appeared about the creation of Expace Midi Ltd, a grouping of the most important developers who succeeded in raising the prices in this neighbourhood, thus making the process of expropriation expensive and slow. Such speculation is forcing up the price of land which may ultimately mean the more intensive use of the site in the form of office development. As yet the matter is unresolved (mid 1993) so adding to the level of uncertainty.

4.6   CONCLUSION

Urban planning and spatial policy are not the strongest instruments in Belgian policy-making, particularly in the case of the Brussels region. Complexities are imposed by the federal system though newly prepared general plans for the Brussels region and for Flanders are likely to bring about future change. In the meanwhile, Brussels has been the scene for large-scale projects that produce good returns namely offices, hotels and industrial property. Concerning future development activity mixed projects are likely to be in the forefront. In particular smaller business units and offices can be offered in both new and in renovated buildings and can be integrated more easily into an environment in which housing and green areas create a pleasant urban setting. This could provide an additional asset for the attraction of investment and further enhance the image of the Brussels region.

REFERENCES

ANHYP (1983–1993) *Waarde der onroerende goederen*, Antwerpen, ANHYP NV, departement Immobiliën Brussel.
Brat (1992) Review of office property, *Quarterly Report of the Brussels Capital Region*.
Cabus, P. (1991) De stedelijke ontwikkeling in Vlaanderen en Brussel tussen 1947 en 1988, in H. Van Der Haegen, Brussel een hoofdstad in beweging, *Leuvense Geografische Papers*, **3**, 1–33.
Ceusters (1993) *De vlaamse en Brusselse vastgoedmarkt, jaarrapport 1992*, Brussels, Immobilien Hugo Ceusters.
EIVA (1992) *Urbanisation and the Functions of Cities in the European Community*, Brussels-Luxembourg, Commission for the European Communities.
Goossens, L. (1991) *Wrikken aan wonen*, Brussels, Koning Boudewijnstichting.
Hamaide, C. (1992) La problématique des hôtels à Bruxelles, in *BRES-dossiers*, Brussels, IRIS-éditions, 8.
Healey & Baker (1993a) *International Industrial Real Estate*: London, European Research Services.
Healey & Baker (1993b) *International Office Markets: A Guide to International Office Rents*, London, European Research Services.
Healey & Baker (1993c) *Main Streets across the World: A Guide to International Retail Rents*, London, European Research Services.
Jones Lang Wootton (1993) *Quarterly Investment Report*, The European Property Market, London.
Kesteloot, C. (1990) Iedereen op zijin plaats: ruimtelijke en sociale breuklijnen in de stad, in Mort Subite, *Barsten in België*, Antwerpen, EPO, 141–78.

King & Co. (1993) *De immobilienmarkt rond de Brusselse Ring*, Brussels.

Knight Frank & Rutley (1993) *De Brusselse Kantoormarkt*, Brussels.

Lagrou, E. (1993) De nieuwe stedebouw- en monumenten-ordonantie, *Planologisch Nieuws*, **1**, 6–16.

Rijdams, M. (1992) Brussel bouwt voor Europa, in *Planologisch Nieuws*, **2**, 111–28.

van der Haegen, H. (1991) Brussel een hoofdstad in beweging, *Leuvense Geografische Papers*, **3**.

5

Düsseldorf

Hartmut Dieterich
and Egbert Dransfeld

As the capital of the most populated federal state within Germany, North Rhine Westphalia (17 million inhabitants), the city of Düsseldorf enjoys special status (Figure 5.1). Geographically Düsseldorf occupies a total land area of 217 sq km with a population of circa 600 000 inhabitants, and in addition is encircled by highly populated agglomerations. To the south and the west there is the so-called 'Rheinschiene' (Rhine Agglomeration) including the Cologne/Bonn area and the city of Leverkusen, and also to the west the cities of the Lower Rhine, Mönchengladbach and Krefeld. In the north there is the agglomeration of Ruhrgebiet containing the cities of Duisburg, Mühlheim, Essen, Bochum and Dortmund, and to the east are the large hill towns of Wuppertal, Solingen and Remscheid. This economic/geographical position also gives Düsseldorf a special status in a European context. The Ruhrgebiet and the Rheinschiene agglomeration is one of the biggest in Europe with about 10 million people living in a radius of circa 50 to 60 km.

The city of Düsseldorf is no longer the Schreibtisch des Ruhrgebietes (desk of the Ruhrgebiet), as Düsseldorf used to be known, fulfilling its role as the administrative and service centre for the production industries (the coal-mining and steel-industry) of the Ruhrgebiet. After the Second World War the city developed into an international trade and service centre, with a resulting shift in the labour market from production to the service sector. The market share of the service sector has increased to more than 70%.

Within Düsseldorf there are 90 000 German companies and more than 4000 foreign companies. On the one hand the traditional trading partners viz USA, Netherlands, Great Britain and France are represented, while on

European Cities, Planning Systems and Property Markets Edited by James Berry and Stanley McGreal. Published in 1995 by E & FN Spon. ISBN 0419 18940 8.

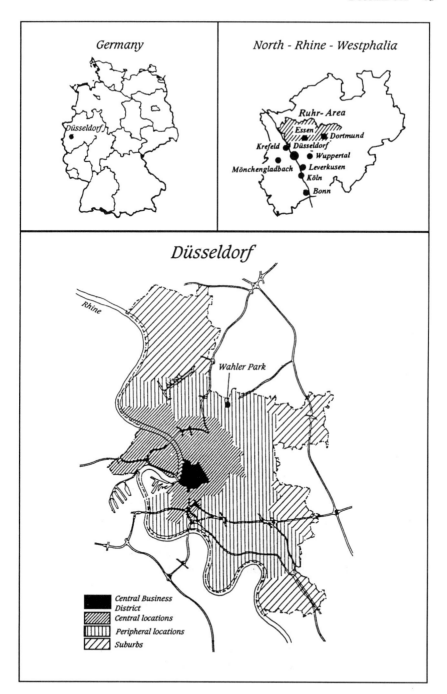

Figure 5.1 Location map Düsseldorf, metropolitan and regional setting
Source: Valuation Committee Düsseldorf (1992) *Jahresbericht zum Düsseldorfer Grundstücksmarkt*, Düsseldorf.

the other hand about 320 Japanese companies with more than 7000 people have settled. So, competing with London, Düsseldorf constitutes the continental European control centre for Japanese economic activities in Europe. Other East Asiatic growth nations such as Korea and Taiwan are also represented. Furthermore with respect to the East–West trading connections, which are, due to the changes in Eastern Europe, going to be of increasing importance, Düsseldorf is playing a leading part.

5.1   ECONOMIC CONTEXT

In establishing itself as an international business-centre the city of Düsseldorf is setting-up an 'international infrastructure'. The area around Düsseldorf provides excellent transport connections; all the European business centres are accessible within a short journey time. The Rhein-Ruhr-Flughafen is the second largest commercial airport in Germany with connections to 150 cities worldwide and is also an attractive location for different industrial uses.

Above all it is Düsseldorf's position in this area that makes its industrial location very attractive for domestic and foreign companies. The neighbouring municipalities can profit from their favourable position adjacent to the metropolis of Düsseldorf, one of the top business locations in the EC. For this reason the neighbouring municipalities cooperate with the city of Düsseldorf and in the course of the publicity campaign Düsseldorf & Partners the whole region Düsseldorf/Middle Lower Rhine is being promoted as a business location with a promising future. Nevertheless with regard to settlement activities there is strong competition between the city of Düsseldorf and its smaller surrounding cities (in the sense of a functional urban region), as each city is allowed to formulate its own land policy and can therefore profit by capturing companies.

The situation has now been reached where the city of Düsseldorf is unable to offer suitable plots for firms, contributing factors being the relatively small size of the town, a strong open-space policy (green belt policy) operated by the regional planning authority and a preparatory land use plan (*Flächennutzungsplan*). As a consequence more and more firms are locating in the surrounding countryside with the neighbouring municipalities providing the industrial land that Düsseldorf lacks.

In the new preparatory land use plan 210 ha of industrial land have been identified for release, with contaminated land not accounted for. Against this the predicted demand is in the order of at least 280 ha for the period up to the year 2000. However in reality only 85 ha of industrial land can be developed up until the year 2000 equating to approximately a two-year land supply.

Subsidies or grants are unnecessary for the Düsseldorf region for several reasons. Düsseldorf does not belong to a region of Germany or Europe entitled to structural aid. In addition, subsidies or incentives for development from the municipality are not necessary due to existing high demand. This also applies to the supply of industrial land and development on the sites of former industrial plants. The municipality of Düsseldorf does not need to act as an intermediate owner carrying out the decontamination of soil in order to create a supply of high-quality industrial land as in the case of certain other cities in the old industrialized Ruhrgebiet. The Düsseldorf industrial land market enjoys such strong attraction and demand, that high purchase prices for sites can be obtained, which still need to be cleared, i.e. the sanitation of contaminated soil is borne by the original owner in form of a reduced price.

The small physical size of Düsseldorf, high land prices and the open-space policy mean that multiple dwellings dominate the housing sector. About 80% of all new housing constructions are high-density multiple dwellings and only 20% are detached, semi-detached or terraced houses. The majority of individual houses are constructed in the surrounding countryside with the result that in the last decade Düsseldorf has become a typical commuting city like many other bigger towns in Germany.

Today there are nearly 300 000 flats in Düsseldorf, with a ratio of about two persons per flat and an average floor space of about 35 sq m per flat. The average floor area ratio for the whole town is about 0.51; although the density in the dominant multiple-dwelling areas is much higher circa 0.95. In the new preparatory land-use plan about 370 ha of new unbuilt land for housing has been zoned, so that with the already existing reserves nearly 440 ha are zoned for development to the year 2000. However the zoned building land is not always disposable for development; indeed landowners may not be interested in selling their land or possibly the municipality may have carried out new detailed local plans (*Bebauungsplan*).

5.2 THE PLANNING SYSTEM

Germany is a federal state, its constitution distinguishes three tiers of government:

- the national level or federal administration;
- the Länder, the states forming the federation with responsibilities of their own;
- the local authorities, the Gemeinden (towns and villages) and, less important, the Kreise (counties and districts).

The constitution defines exactly whether the federation or the individual states of the federation have the legislative power for given matters. Furthermore, the constitution grants self-government to the municipalities. The laws of the federation, as well as of the states, define strictly how far the competencies of the municipalities reach (Dieterich *et al.*, 1993).

The federal government holds the legislative power for the economy, land law, housing and planning, however, it has little influence in the preparation of development plans. Concerning spatial policy (*Raumordnung*) the federation can only set up a federal programme for spatial policy, the *Bundesraumordnungsprogramm*, which is a rather weak instrument. It is up to the Länder to formulate aims for the whole area or for parts of it (*Landesplanung* and *Regionalplanung*) while the responsibility for detailed land-use planning rests with the municipalities.

The federal government enacted the Baugesetzbuch (BauGB – Planning Code) in 1986 and in force since 1987, this governs detailed land-use planning (Battis, 1987; Braam, 1987). Essentially the BauGB was a consolidating act, incorporating in one statute the former legislation on town and country planning, urban renewal and urban development. This has been supplemented by the *Baunutzungsverordnung* (BauNVO, 1990 – Land Use Ordinance) which is based on the *Baugesetzbuch* as well as the *Planzeichenverordnung* (Notation Symbol Ordinance – PlanzV, 1990) and the *Wertermittlungsverordnung* (WertV, 1988 – Valuation Ordinance).

The *Baugesetzbuch* allows the municipalities to determine in a local plan the land use, density and form of development permitted on a site. However the municipality is bound to the specifications of the *Baunutzungsverordnung* which defines the kind of land-use zones (*Baugebiete*) that can be permitted, as well as the density of buildings within these zones. Furthermore, in 1990, due to a shortage of building land all over Germany, the *Wohnungsbauerleichterungsgesetz* (WoBauErlG – Act for facilitating the construction of housing) was added to the BauGB. In 1993 with the *Investitionserleichterungs- und Wohnbaulandgesetz* Act (to facilitate investment and to provide land for construction of housing) the BauGB and the WoBauErlG were amended by rules to allow for greater flexibility. In the New Länder in the east of the federation only a few special rules which have to be taken into account are still in force.

5.2.1 The legal framework for land-use planning

The Federal government has the objective of creating living conditions in the whole country which are, if not equal, at least of the same value. This principle is enacted in the *Bundesraumordnungsgesetz* (ROG, 1991 – Federal Act on Spatial Policy). The act is also binding on the Länder. In the *Bundesraumordnungsprogramm* (Programme for Spatial Policy) the necessity for a supply of jobs and housing throughout the country is emphasized. However it is up to the Länder to formulate the aims and objectives for certain regions and areas. *Landesentwicklungspläne* or *Landesentwicklungsprogramm* (plans or programmes for the development of the state) have also been established. These present the objectives for all sectors of land-use and environmental planning and determine, for example, which areas should be kept for recreational purposes or where industrial development should be fostered. The plans for part of the land (*Regionalplan* or *Gebietsentwicklungsplan*) may even contain explicit rules concerning its use. *Landesentwicklungspläne* as well as *Gebietsentwicklungspläne* are more than a statement on the planning policy of the land or the region, they are part of the legal framework and the municipalities have to comply with the content of these plans.

The competence as well as the obligation for binding land-use planning belongs to the *Gemeinden* (municipalities). For every *Gemeinde* a *Flächennutzungsplan* has to be set up. The *Flächennutzungsplan* outlines the essentials of the intended land use for the whole area of the municipality and is binding on those other public planning authorities involved in the process of setting up the plan. The main purpose of the *Flächennutzungsplan* is to provide a basis on which *Bebauungspläne* (local plans) can be prepared. *Bebauungspläne* are binding on everybody, having the status of a *Satzung*, a local law of the municipality. A *Bebauungsplan* must be developed on the basis of the *Flächennutzungsplan* and must not depart from it. Land use permitted in a *Bebauungsplan* can be carried out by anyone, whereas land use in contradiction to the *Bebauungsplan* is not allowed. There is no discretionary power of the planning authorities once a *Bebauungsplan* is set up. Everybody can read the plan and establish exactly the kind of land use and the density which will be allowed. Uncertainties may only arise from environmental law, which has to be taken into account and in some circumstances compensation may be required for environmental damage caused by development. The *Investitionserleichterungs- und Wohnbaulandgesetz* harmonized planning law and environmental law (*Bundesnaturschutzgesetz* – Federal Act on the Protection of Nature). The setting up of each *Bebauungsplan* is governed by the principle of weighing all conflicting interests concerning the use of the land within the area of the plan fairly and correctly. This is demanded by the BauGB and is strictly enforced by the courts.

5.2.2 Development control

Planning permission is necessary in Germany for all proposed development, involving construction and renovation of buildings as well as the change of use of buildings. This is laid down in the BauGB. Under the laws of the Länder building permission is also required. However both permissions are granted together in one act of the building administration, the *Baugenehmigung* (permission to construct).

Applications for the *Baugenehmigung* are submitted to the municipality, and in turn are passed on to the building authority which works in close contact with the planning office. If the application is made for development within the area of a *Bebauungsplan*, there is no discussion concerning the legality of the development, provided it complies with the *Bebauungsplan* it must be permitted. It must also be guaranteed that the area is serviced if the application is to be favourably determined. In those cases where the proposed development departs from the *Bebauungsplan* only in a minor degree, exceptions or dispensations from some rules contained in the plan may be asked for. These may be granted, if the dispensation is also for the public benefit, and provided neighbours are not affected. If the city council has decided to set up a *Bebauungsplan* but the procedure is not yet complete, it is possible to grant the *Baugenehmigung* provided the application is in compliance with the future *Bebauungsplan*.

In areas which are built up with a continuity of buildings but where a *Bebauungsplan* does not exist, proposed development may be allowed if the building fits into the existing environment, a matter which is judged by the land use in the surroundings and by the density of the neighbourhood (section 34 Ban6B). In other areas, where no *Bebauungsplan* is in existence and without a continuity of buildings, development is not altogether impossible, but usually permissions are only granted for certain types of use viz for agricultural buildings, or development which cannot be constructed in areas where people live (e.g. an electricity plant) because the development would disturb the neighbourhood. In Düsseldorf, in 1992, nearly 40% of all applications for the *Baugenehmigung* were in accordance with a *Bebauungsplan* while about 56% were in accordance with section 34 BauGB. Normally less than 10% of all applications are in the *Außenbereich* (outlying district).

Since 1993 a further possibility exists to grant a *Baugenehmigung*. Initially used in the New Länder, but now also an opportunity in the old Länder of Germany, is the *Vorhaben- und Erschließungsplan* (plan for development and servicing). Under this planning permission may be granted without a local plan if the developer commits to prepare a plan and to carry out and finance the servicing of the development. The municipality has to decide on the plan of the developer by using the same criteria employed in a local plan. The new instrument provides a possible solution to the very lengthy procedure of setting up local plans and enforces private activities in the land development process. In circumstances where planning permission is denied the applicant may raise objections. Furthermore where the decision of the authority is not changed the applicant may appeal to the administrative courts.

5.2.3   Land assembly

The *Baugesetzbuch* offers some instruments to the municipality in order to enable them to carry out their plans. Most important is the purchase or the assembly of land. For land used publicly the BauGB offers a right of pre-emption. The process of re-plotting of land is regulated in the BauGB and is often implemented (Dieterich, 1990). There are special rules for areas of comprehensive redevelopment as well as for the development of bigger industrial or housing areas on green field sites by *Sanierungs-und Entwicklungsmaßnahmen* (measures for urban rehabilitation and for urban development). Expropriation is only the very last resort (Erbguth, 1989).

5.3 PLANNING AND BUILDING ADMINISTRATION

If a city is to retain its prosperity, given that competition is taking place on a European rather than the national level, there must be a favourable economic climate within the city. While it is the responsibility of the *Wirtschaftsförderungsamt* (economic assistance board) to help achieve this goal, there is also a challenge for the planning and building authority. In particular the contribution of planning is very important in designating space for development. In Düsseldorf many parts of the city consist of water or woodland and cannot be changed in their use while other spaces are not at the disposal of the city, since the *Land Nordrhein-Westfalen* determined their use in plans of the state or in the *Gebietsentwicklungsplan*. Consequently it is becoming more difficult to carry out development in the city although some opportunities still do exist.

5.3.1 The planning and building department

The planning and building department of the city of Düsseldorf consists of eight separate offices. There is, first, the *Bauverwaltungsamt* (administrative office for the building department) which deals not only with all administrative matters for the department, but also with basic problems of organization. It has also responsibilities in the financial field and collects the fees for public amenities, and administers the money given by the federal and the state government for urban renewal and for other matters where subsidies can be expected. Second, there is the planning office which is responsible for the *Flächennutzungsplan* (preparatory land-use plan) and also for its continuation. In close connection to the *Flächennutzungsplan* there is the work on basic planning problems for the whole city. The *Flächennutzungsplan* for Düsseldorf is composed of the following elements:

areas for housing and offices	5 288 ha
areas for industry and trade	2 172 ha
infrastructure (social infrastructure, streets, railways, airport, harbour)	2 805 ha

green space and water	4 069 ha
areas for agriculture and forestry	7 374 ha
	21 708 ha

The city of Düsseldorf has about 3000 Bebauungspläne (detailed local plans), which covers nearly 50% of the total built-up area of the town (280 more local plans are currently being prepared). Subdivisions of the planning office specialize on planning law and urban renewal. The *Vermessungs- und Katasteramt* (Office for Surveying and the Cadastre) is responsible for all surveying work, for the continuation of the cadastre and prepares all maps which are necessary for the city. The functioning of the planning office depends on the data and maps produced by the *Vermessungs- und Katasteramt*.

The *Bauaufsichtsamt* (Building Inspection Office) has to examine all applications for development under the aspect of planning law as well as the building code and is responsible for the processing of all applications, whether the permission is given or rejected. The construction board is responsible for the construction and development of the city of Düsseldorf. It provides, once the city councillors have decided, much of the infrastructure for the city, especially new schools, facilities for sport, for the youth and for the cultural life, and is also responsible for conservation. The construction board's responsibilities extend to constructing the streets and roads in Düsseldorf as well as other traffic facilities. The functioning of traffic is therefore dependent on the work of this board together with any traffic restrictions which are carried out to enhance the environment. The *Kanal- und Wasserbauamt* (Sewer and Water Construction Board) constructs and maintains the sewer network in Düsseldorf, whereas the *U-Bahn Amt* (Office for the Subway) deals with the planning and construction of subways in Düsseldorf.

5.3.2 Management of the planning and building department

The work of the planning and building department is managed by a town councillor who is sensitive to the economic well-being of the city and to the need to offer sites for all kinds of development activity. As Düsseldorf occupies a small area it is necessary to co-operate with towns in the surrounding locality. One common point of interest is traffic. The development of trade and industry however is not easy to co-ordinate, since every municipality has to plan for its own needs (the finance of municipalities in Germany depends heavily on the *Gewerbesteuer* or business rate) (Dieterich and Dransfeld, 1992). Consequently, there is competition between the city and the towns adjacent to Düsseldorf. It is also difficult to convince the neighbourhood to accept the overspill population of

Düsseldorf and to build social housing for people in the outlying towns. However, high land prices in the city compared to the country restrict those wishing to build a (one-family) house in Düsseldorf, and alternatively are forced to look for sites within commuting distance of the city.

Relations with the state authorities and to the provincial administrative district work satisfactorily. However on matters where, in the field of planning and building, the state authorities had some reservation of rights these have become less numerous since 1993, thus less friction can be expected in the future. Concerning the relationship to the government of the state of North-Rhine-Westphalia, of which Düsseldorf is the capital city, again these operate effectively although there is one matter on which Düsseldorf is not satisfied with the state administration. The municipalities have to follow the lines of the regional development plan, put forward by the region, for their land-use planning. This plan acknowledges the central importance of Düsseldorf to the economy, especially for the tertiary sector and that the city has to compete not only with other German cities, but also with other European cities. Thus the city has to offer space for new development but one of the main goals of the regional plan is to preserve open space and to limit new development. Indeed the plan will only offer opportunities for new development if the necessary open-space provision can be guaranteed.

However potential exists with regard to the use of derelict land. Although many factories have ceased production or moved to smaller premises, most of the derelict sites are well serviced and often located at favourable distances to the city centre. Often these sites are suitable for office development, and thus Düsseldorf has become the first city in Germany to provide industrial and business parks (e.g. Wahler Park), the office proportion of which continues to expand.

The city administration, particularly the Planning and Building Department, need to maintain good relations with the politicans who are responsible for the city or for parts of it including a good working relationship with the *Bezirksvertretungen* which consists of representatives from the small districts of the city. In spite of the shortage of building land in Düsseldorf there is no great pressure placed on the land market which in consequence causes few problems for the planning department. The land market does, however, follow the directives laid down in plans with the result that planning as a process facilitates the expectations of the market.

5.4   THE LAND AND PROPERTY MARKET IN DÜSSELDORF

In Germany it is necessary to differentiate between the independent land market and the ensuing property market (Dieterich and Dransfeld, 1992). Arising from the legally binding planning system each land type obtains its own market value, irrespective of whether the land is developed or undeveloped. Normally the contents of valid urban plans with regard to whether land is zoned or not zoned, or the scale of development in terms of floor and ground-area ratio determine the land price. A derived land value for a development project is unusual. Indeed there are no statutory rules concerning a residual valuation or its methodology, although there are many regulations for property valuation in the *Baugesetzbuch*. This fact, to some extent, explains the lack of a widespread investment market in Germany and the need for standardized valuation procedure.

The local *Gutachterausschüsse* (valuation committees) and also some private companies (real estate associations, research institutions) normally provide and distribute information concerning land and property. In particular the *Gutachterausschüsse* collect information in the form of indices of land prices, the rate of return for certain land uses on the local market and coefficients of conversion for prices between different land uses. The published material and figures from the valuation committees are generally reliable, since all freehold, long-leasehold and inheritance contracts must be sent to the committee (duty of the notaries). It is therefore advisable to use this source of information at least for a preliminary investigation of the land and property prices. The importance of the land market is apparent in the annual *Bodenrichtwertkarten*, special maps of actual land values, which cover the whole area of a town. These provide an excellent source of information including land values in special locations.

5.4.1   The land market

Land prices in Düsseldorf vary spatially. In the Central Business District (Figure 5.1), an area with an average floor-area ratio of 3.0 to 5.5, the average prices in 1992 ranged between 3000 DM to 6000 DM per sq m. These prices are inclusive of servicing cost. However, in the Königsallee, the main shopping street and the prime location for retail and office space, the price increases to 25 000 DM per sq m. In the central locations mainly areas of mixed housing, retail and office use – the average land prices are between 100 DM to 2000 DM per sq m while in peripheral locations and typical suburbs the prices for housing land varies between 400 DM and 900 DM per sq m. There is no significant price difference between land prices for detached/semi-detached houses or multiple dwelling houses.

In 1992 land for industrial use cost between 250 DM to 500 DM per sq m. Industrial land is therefore on average cheaper than housing land, a phenomenon which is typical in most parts of Germany. Frequently the price, even in agglomerations, is below 100 DM per sq m, the reasons for this being that the municipality acts itself as an intermediate land supplier, buying up undeveloped land and selling off developed land. However the selling price is normally a subsidized price as the municipality wishes to profit from the new *Gewerbesteuern* (business rates) or from the creation of more (new) jobs.

Land prices in the housing sector in Düsseldorf are considered to be relatively high. The share of land cost to the total house price is circa 50% to 60%, so accessibility to the market can be difficult for the majority of income groups. Consequently many households need to move into the cheaper surrounding countryside, if they wish to become an owner oc-cupier. Although in certain cities, for example Berlin, Munich, Stuttgart or Frankfurt the prices are even higher (above 1000 DM per sq m on average for housing land) normally the land prices in Germany are much lower. In Dortmund, a city with a similar population and only about 60 km east of Düsseldorf, the average land price in the housing sector in 1992 was only 250–300 DM per sq m. Indeed the national average price for housing land in 1992 was circa 130 DM per sq m (Bundesministerium für Raumordnung, 1993).

Land prices in Düsseldorf have increased continuously over the past decades, only in the mid-1970s and mid-1980s has a price reduction been registered. Indeed the rate of increase in values has been above the cost of living index and the buying of building land has been an attractive investment without great risk. Underlying the growth in land values and a contributory factor to this process, is the binding character of the German planning system.

5.4.2   The property market

House prices differ according to location and quality. The differences with regard to location are an effect of the land price structure. For example in 1992 a detached house of medium quality cost on average about 570 000 DM, the price including all servicing and land cost; terraced houses 375 000 DM, and condominiums about 3500 DM per sq m. The house prices are above the national average prices; however, in other German cities (e.g. Berlin, Frankfurt, Munich, Stuttgart) the prices are higher.

Due to the high price of private housing (equivalent of ten years income for an average industrial worker) renting remains the dominant form of tenure in Düsseldorf. Rents in the free market sector for flats vary between 12–15 DM per sq m per month (without heating, electricity and water costs), while rents for new flats are about 17–20 DM per sq m. Rents in the social housing sector are normally below 10 DM per sq m per month.

In general rents for office space increased significantly in the 1980s (Figure 5.2) with top quality accommodation showing the strongest increase. In 1992 the rent per sq m per month for secondary locations was 19 DM, in good locations 35 DM and in prime locations the rents jumped up to 50 DM (Aengevelt, 1993). During the early 1990s demand con-

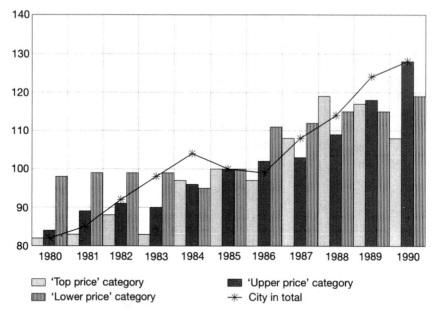

Figure 5.2   Indices for office rents in Düsseldorf, 1980–90 (1985 = 100)
Source: Aengevelt-Research (1992/93) Marktbericht, *Investitionsobjekte*, Düsseldorf.

siderably exceeded the supply by up to 50% and although there is currently (1993) no significant amount of empty office space, there remains
the prospect of over-supply if the German recession continues. In the
retail sector rents vary on average between 40 DM to 90 DM per sq m per
month. However in top locations (shopping malls and pedestrian streets)
can range from 185 DM up to 275 DM/sq m/month.

Returns are normally differentiated by market sector and location. In
prime locations in the CBD, the return for office and retail/housing are on
average around 3%. However in secondary and tertiary locations with a
greater investment risk the returns are above 7.5% for office and retail/
housing. Each year the *Gutachterausschuß* (local valuation committee)
publishes the current average returns for the whole city. For the city of
Düsseldorf the 1992 returns for buildings constructed after 1949 and
differentiated by market sector are as follows:

- detached/semi-detached house   3.0%
- three-family house   4.0%
- multiple dwelling house
  (commercial share below 20%)   5.5%
- rented houses (subsidized)   7.0%

Total number of transactions

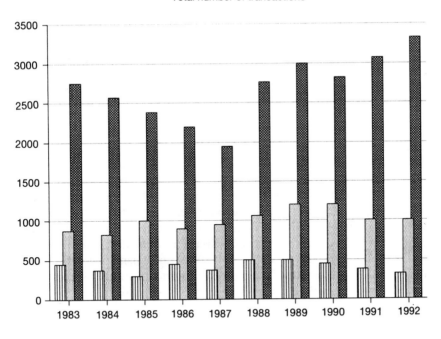

Turnover in million DM

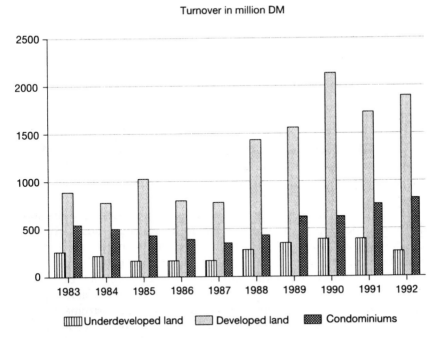

▓▓▓ Underdeveloped land   ▒▒▒ Developed land   ▓▓▓ Condominiums

Figure 5.3 Land and property market transactions and turnover in Düsseldorf, 1983–92
Source: Valuation Committee Düsseldorf (1992) *Jahresbericht zum Düseldorfer Grundstücksmarkt*, Düsseldorf.

- mixed-use house
  (commercial share above 20%)   6.5%
- office buildings   5.5–7.0%
- business parks   6.5–7.5%

5.4.3 Turnover

Concerning property turnover in Düsseldorf, in 1992 there was a total of
4500 transactions accounting for nearly 3000 million DM or about 78
transactions per 10 000 inhabitants (Figure 5.3). The market share of
undeveloped land transactions compared with other kinds of property
(e.g. developed land or condominiums) is relatively small. For example in
1992 only 5 transactions of undeveloped land per 10 000 inhabitants
accrued while in the same year 17 transactions with developed land and
56 transactions for condominiums per 10 000 inhabitants were registered
(Table 5.1). The latter clearly dominate in terms of market share (more
than 50% of transactions); however, in terms of value, developed land
remains predominant.

5.5 INDUSTRIAL PARKS CASE STUDY: WAHLER PARK

The Wahler Park is representative of the industrial property investment
market. It is selected as a case study example due to the dense concentration of business and industrial parks specifically in Düsseldorf and its
surroundings, and because of the growing influence of the property
investment market throughout Germany generally. Such investment activity
is particularly apparent in locations where economic efficiency seems to
be most secure (viz Frankfurt/Main, Munich, Hamburg, Düsseldorf) and
where an independent industrial property investment market has developed
through the initiative of private project developers. Essentially the aim is
to invest capital in industrial properties with expected returns from selling
or leasing.

   A distinctive characteristic of several new business parks in Düsseldorf
which have developed in recent years is the excellent quality of such
developments and their proximity to the inner city. Generally there are no
green field developments, due primarily to a shortage of sites, which
could be developed for industrial parks. However private developers
could benefit from shorter planning permission procedures, although this
depends on the decision of the municipality. One legal instrument which
is accelerating the realization of industrial parks in an inner-area location is
permission granted under section 34 BauGB (admissibility of projects
within inner area locations), which avoids a lengthy Bebauungsplan
(building plan) procedure. In this connection, the case study of the Wahler

Table 5.1 Total transactions and transactions differentiated between buyer and seller by property type

Kind of property	Total transactions					Transactions differentiated between buyer and seller							
	Number		Turnover	Expanse		Natural/juristic person		Housing company		City of Düsseldorf		Other public institutions	
	Total	per 10000 inhabitants	in mill. DM	in sqm (ths)	in % of total city area	Seller	Buyer	Seller	Buyer	Seller	Buyer	Seller	Buyer
Undeveloped land:													
• zoned by a local plan or inner urban areas (§ 34 BauGB)	293	5.0	267	523	2.4	163	198	16	42	89	45	25	8
	253	4.3	262	351	1.6	133	178	16	41	86	29	18	5
• outside from local plans or inner urban areas (§ 34 BauGB)	40	0.7	5	165	0.8	30	20	—	1	3	16	7	3
Developed land:													
• single family houses	1003	17.1	1863	853	4.0	847	895	141	94	5	4	10	10
	482	8.2	268	233	1.1	400	465	76	13	3	2	3	2
• multiple dwelling, business house or office building	473	8.1	1380	331	1.5	411	387	54	79	2	—	6	7
• production buildings (trade/industry)	48	0.8	215	288	1.3	36	43	11	2	—	2	1	1
Condominiums	3247	56.0	819	—	—	2521	3238	725	6	—	—	1	3
Hereditary leasehold	27	0.5	12	44	0.2	14	25	—	—	11	1	2	1
Total	4570	78.0	2961	1420	6.5	3545	4356	882	142	105	50	38	22

Source: Valuation Committee Düsseldorf (1992) *Jahresbericht zum Düsseldorfer Grundstücksmarkt*, Düsseldorf.

Park is a representative example of the new generation of industrial property development.

The Wahler Park has been a pattern for similar development in other growth areas. Until recently it has been the public sector, and usually the community, which decisively influences the industrial property market. Through planning instruments and massive assistance with finance, organization and advice, the municipality tries to attract firms and enlarge the supply of industrial property by providing cheap building land (reduced below market value) and infrastructure in advance. Renting in the industrial market sector is unusual and owner occupiers are predominant.

The site of the industrial park is located in the municipal subdistrict Rath less than 6 km from the centre of Düsseldorf, in the north-east of the city. In 1986 the developer Calliston bought 48 000 sq m of the site and at the same time produced their planning concept for the whole area. The new buildings were completed with a net usable internal area of 33 000 sq m in two–three storeys. The share of the office space is about 40%, while the share of the depot space is approximately 60%.

The unique method of construction with prefabricated elements (flexible buildings) was not standard for the German market at that stage, but it enabled the Calliston management company to adapt the office- and depot-space to the particular requirements of the potential tenants. Furthermore variations can be made for tenants' changing floor-space requirements, or in respect to a change of tenants. Calliston is able to react to the requirements of the new tenant, securing the long-term profitability of the buildings and having the option of increasing the rental prices. From the end users' point of view lease contracts negotiated with Calliston will include any special requirement of the tenant.

Exclusive façades create a representative and inviting effect. The varied landscape design satisfy tenants' demands for a quality image and a pleasant environment, and at the same time uplifts the value of the site. The share of green space is around 25%; the developed space is nearly 50% with 25% reserved for traffic space. The realized ground area ratio of 0.54–0.55 and floor area ratio of about 0.7 are further indicators of generally low density. Altogether 22 companies in the high-tech sector (mainly electrical) are located in the Wahler Park. The average size per company amounts to 1300 sq m and a total of 800 jobs have been created.

The buildings are rented to the companies at a price of 15 to 16 DM/sq m/month for office space and 8.50 to 10.50 DM/sq m/month for depot space. With lease contracts of five years, the project is planned with the expectation of multiple lettings of the buildings. Profits are not generated speculatively, but are nevertheless expected to be created over the long-term perspective through rising rental values.

The plan for the Wahler Park was submitted to the municipality of Düsseldorf for a building permit just after the area had been bought. In order to accelerate the granting of the building permission, Calliston insisted on calling all the private and public actors involved in the planning process to a 'round-table' meeting to discuss the *Bauvoranfrage* (first preliminary application) for a building permit, and within several weeks Calliston received the municipality's comment and the planning permission in accordance with section 34 BauGB (Klose and Kraushaar, 1989). Usually this period runs for at least six to ten weeks and the permission under section 34 BauGB, instead of a *Bebauungsplan* procedure, accelerated the project. Calliston as the owner of the Wahler Park, controls the buildings and streets, which gives the company a flexibility regarding utilization of the site. Development of the first office- and warehouse-building started in 1987, one year after the first planning concept and by 1990 the business park had been constructed and rented.

5.5.1   The development process – actors and their instruments

The private sector has been the decisive actor in the realization of the Wahler Park project. Calliston, the project developer and exclusive owner, holds the key position. The transformation of this former under-used inner city location to an attractive industrial park for high-tech firms has been exclusively carried out on the developer's own account. However, by setting up the plan, the private developer used the experience that the company, in comparison to the planning authority, had already gained from other industrial park projects together with a well-targeted market research exercise (Dieterich and Dransfeld, 1992). As the only investor and the exclusive owner of the Wahler Park it was important for Calliston to develop a project which would secure long-term profitability of the buildings.

It is important to emphasize Calliston's role as exclusive investor in the project, which was self-financed, a procedure that is generally not common for the German investment market. More usually financing is undertaken through open and closed property funds. Consequently the project developer had to press for planning certainty and for an acceleration of bureaucratic procedure, to enable lease negotiations with the potential tenants to begin. For this purpose a real estate agency was commissioned and during the course of the project the agency frequently acted as a negotiator between the developer and the city administration.

The municipality of Düsseldorf, while not directly involved in the project, made an important contribution concerning the acceleration of permission procedure. The regular dialogue between the private developer and the municipality permitted an extraordinarily fast realization of the project. The attractiveness of the locality for private-sector development potential in the context of the Düsseldorf industrial land market means that the municipality can only support private initiatives, not by means of

grants, but by assistance in the form of planning and by helping to overcome bureaucratic and statutory hurdles. In this way economic development can be facilitated by municipal help.

5.6   CONCLUSION

The German land and property markets are still heavily influenced by the
public-sector plan-led-systems in comparison with some other European
countries, such as the market-led-system in Great Britain. One significant
influence on German land and property markets is the strong binding
character of the planning system and the rather independent position of
the municipalities as a result of the federal character of the German
administration system.

The German municipalities influence spatial development through legally
binding plans. With regard to this planning/building permission is normally
only an administrative act of testing conformity with the plans. The planning system is hardly discretionary; negotiations for planning obligations
are almost unknown. The supply of developable land is decisively limited
by the preparatory land-use plans (*Flächennutzungsplan*) and the detailed
local plans (*Bebauungsplan*), which are set up by the local municipalities.
Therefore in Germany the municipalities are responsible for ensuring a
sufficient supply of developable land and their role in the development
process is regarded as active. However it is much more difficult to react
flexibly to changing demands for land and flats; although investors are, in
general, relatively secure with the result that intended development can
take place. Furthermore in Germany the development process needs time
because a lot of planning stages have to be followed.

As a consequence of the strong influence of the public sector in the
supply of building land in Germany there is a strong differentiation between
an independent market for land and a market for developed properties.
Land is seen as a 'good in its own right' which gives rise to self-propelling
expectations of profit derived from owning land; this tends to exert
an effect of driving prices up but without the tendency of cyclical
developments.

Interrelationships between the German planning system and the land/
property market can be found in the majority of German municipalities.
However since the mid 1980s in those regions and agglomerations,
where economic efficiency seems to be secure such as Düsseldorf, private
developers are becoming more and more active in the property investment
market. Very often they take over the duties of the municipalities such as
land assembly, re-plotting and servicing. In 1993 the government reacted
to this scenario by introducing legislation which supports in general terms
the private sector's role in the development process. Thus it could be that
in future Germany will have a more mixed system of private and public

elements. However, if public money becomes less available the private sector will increasingly dominate the property and investment markets.

REFERENCES

Aengevelt (1993) *Market Report Indices for Office Rents, the Market for Offices and Industrial Space*, Düsseldorf.

Battis, U. (1987) *Öffentliches Baurecht und Raumordnungsrecht*, 2nd edn, Kohlhammer Verlag, Stuttgart.

Braam, W. (1987) *Städteplanung: Aufgabenbereiche, Planungsmethodik, Rechtsgrundlagen*, Werner Verlag, Düsseldorf.

Bundesministerium für Raumordnung (1993) Bauwesen und Städtebau (eds), *Baulandberichte*, Bonn.

Dieterich, H. (1990) *Baulandumlegung*, 2nd edn, Beck Verlag, München.

Dieterich, H. and Dransfeld, E. (1992) Germany, in B. Wood and R. Williams R. (eds), *Industrial Property Markets in Western Europe*, E & FN Spon London, 27–60.

Dieterich, H., Dransfeld, E. and Voss, W. (1993) *Urban land and property markets in Germany*, Vol. 2 (eds R.H. Williams, B. Wood and H. Dieterich), UCL Press, London.

Erbguth, W. (1989) *Bauplanungsrecht*, Beck Verlag, München.

Klose, S. and Kraushaar, T. (1989) *Gewerbeparks – Das Beispiel des Grossraumers Düsseldorf*, University of Dortmund, 70.

6

Paris

Jean-Claude Boyer

Paris, like most metropolitan areas, is confronted with serious planning problems compounded by high land and property prices. The conurbation is characterized by a complex decision-making process with powers, including control measures over the land market, shared between central government and local authorities. Such fragmentation can be detrimental to the system as a whole, particularly when political divergences arise.

Initially, to clarify matters, it is useful to consider some of the terms used in this chapter. In particular it is important to appreciate that 'Paris' refers solely to the central part of the conurbation. Administratively speaking, it is both a commune and a department, with a population slightly over 2 million. The suburbs (*banlieue*) are the outlying urbanized areas of Paris, with a first 'inner ring' made up of the Hauts-de-Seine, Val-de-Marne and Seine-Saint-Denis departments (Figure 6.1).

Statistics derived from the 1990 census highlight the size of the conurbation with 9.3 million inhabitants living in 'the Paris conurbation' which, in spite of its size, is an area lacking a unified administrative structure. However the more extensive Paris region, Ile-de-France (population: 10.7 million), is a local authority endowed with an elected council. Until the 1970s, planning within the region was a relatively simple matter with central government taking decisions following those consultations deemed to be relevant. Subsequently matters have become more complex.

6.1 PLANNING POLICY AND DECENTRALIZATION

6.1.1 From Napoleon III to General de Gaulle

The real pioneer of urban renewal in Paris was undoubtedly Baron Haussmann who changed the physiognomy of the capital by laying out

European Cities, Planning Systems and Property Markets Edited by James Berry and Stanley McGreal. Published in 1995 by E & FN Spon. ISBN 0419 18940 8.

new avenues and rebuilding whole districts during the period of the Second Empire (1851–71). Acquisition of land presented few difficulties, compulsory purchase orders with proper compensation enabled Haussmann to make a clean sweep of old buildings and at the same time reshaped the configuration of plots of land. During the 3rd and 4th Republics (1871–1958) architectural design and city planning were to prove more problematic, by which stage counter-powers had begun to emerge with the rise of communes and departments. Although plans existed in certain sectors, particularly for the completion of major infrastructure projects (viz the underground 1900–14), urbanization was an erratic process dependent upon land availability and private-sector enterprise.

Urban plans for the Paris area, which date back to 1934, had little impact on the course of events and the first Master Plan drawn up in 1965, only gained official approval (in a slightly amended form) in 1976, yet by that stage the economic and demographic context had already changed appreciably. Indeed this plan is still (early-mid 1990s) expected to regulate the region's development.

The coming to power of General de Gaulle ushered in a much more interventionist period. In 1961 the Paris Region District ('District de la région parisienne') was established. Initially administered by a high-ranking civil servant, this position was later (1966) to become a 'regional prefect' but subject to government appointment. The 1960s were a period of large-scale projects characterized by the creation of Public Establishments for Development ('EPAs') with powers to issue compulsory purchase orders. Their activities enabled the creation of a new business district (La Défense) and five new towns which ultimately were to attract much of the conurbation's subsequent sprawl. Similarly transport provided another domain where state intervention was dominant viz the building of a motorway network, a ring road (around Paris), the regional rail rapid transit system (RER), and the extension of several underground lines into the suburbs.

6.1.2 Decentralization and reappraisal of the Master Plan

The State's omnipotence began to be seriously challenged from the 1970s onwards. Whilst the 1966 reorganization of departments had few short-term consequences, the application of statutory law to the Paris commune (1977) significantly altered the relations of the town with the State, particularly as the first elected mayor Jacques Chirac, head of the Gaullist Party (RPR), was a potential contender for the presidential elections. The process of decentralization (Defferre Acts, 1982–3) started by the socialists, who came to power in 1981, not only strengthened the position of Chirac but brought other protagonists into the limelight. For example, regional authorities, while not prone to meddle with Parisian affairs, wished to exercise control within the suburbs. Furthermore, a substantial power

Figure 6.1 Paris and its suburbs
Source: Baleste, M., Boyer, J.C., Gras, J., Montagné-Villettes, S. and Vareille, C. (1993) *La France: 22 régions de programme*, Masson, Paris.

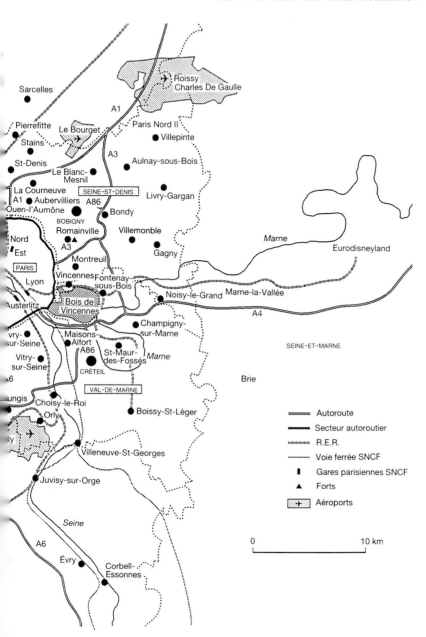

Figure 6.1 *Continued*

base emerged in these suburbs in the form of the Departmental Councils, not only in those run by the communists (Seine-Saint-Denis, Val-de-Marne), but also in some of those controlled by right-wing parties (Hauts-de-Seine). In addition suburban municipalities have come to realize that by availing themselves of the powers which decentralization has granted they can implement policies to exert more control over communal land.

Furthermore the State has, in some aspects, created a dilemma: it could not deprive the Paris region of the windfall of decentralization nor has it renounced exerting control over development given the national and international issues at stake. Thus conflicts have been numerous within the Paris municipality concerning for example 'the President's major projects', particularly as François Mitterrand has taken over the Gaullist tradition of initiating prestigious programmes (Cité des sciences de la Villette, Grand Louvre, Bibliothèque de France). The latest victim of this tug-of-war was the proposed International Congress Centre to be erected close to the Eiffel Tower and for which the government had chosen to disregard the capital's land-use regulations though, by subsequent court order, the government has been compelled to amend its project.

Matters deteriorated even further at the reappraisal stage of the Master Plan.* The necessity to update this document is clearly apparent but legislation remains rather ambiguous concerning the distribution of powers. In essence it is incumbent upon the government to promulgate the Master Plan after consulting with local authorities. However the Decentralization Acts place territorial planning within the ambit of the regional authority. Three years of consultation/negotiation resulted in stalemate and in January 1993 the Master Plan submitted by the government was rejected by the Departmental Councils and the Regional Council. The passing of this rejection (with a State Council decree) would have meant breaking with the policy of concertation, a position totally unrealistic two months before the general election (March 1993) which was destined to bring a new majority to power. Subsequently the new Master Plan has been promulgated by the government in April 1994.

6.1.3   Political conflicts and planning concepts

The Ile-de-France Social and Economic Council (a consultative body) and local representatives deplored the delay which the rejection entailed for several development projects. Approval of the new document had been keenly anticipated for 78 'ZACs' (Concerted Planning Zones)† which were incompatible with the former Master Plan. However political positions

---

* *The Ile-de-France Master Plan ('schéma directeur')* is a document setting out long-term decisions concerning regional management; local authorities are compelled to comply with its directives.

† The most common town-planning procedure in the Paris conurbation particularly for the redevelopment of built spaces (Webster, 1991).

were fixed and proved too strong to overcome with all the departments and most of the big communes in the Paris region governed by resolute opponents of the socialist government, either communist or right-wing representatives. Furthermore, the Regional Council, elected by proportional representation, has no clear majority. Hence its current right-wing chairman is required to compromise with the ecologists who made significant headway in the 1992 elections and are committed to imposing an environmental friendly approach to town and country planning. Consequently several projects have been shelved or postponed for further examination, as far as comprehensive packages are concerned political consensus is hard to reach and in this context rejection of the Master Plan is easier than its amendment.

This does not imply that events have come to a standstill in the Ile-de-France. As in all the other French regions, a planning agreement (*contrat de plan*) is signed every four years with the government, so as to co-finance joint projects viz industrial parks, railway and road networks and low rent housing programmes. While the central government can refuse to finance some projects and thereby exert some control over regional planning, in most cases selected programmes are priority issues. Concerning the Ile-de-France such contracts place emphasis upon the transportation infrastructure rather than an economic activity. A total of 23 billion francs have been allocated to the *contrat de plan* between 1989 and 1993, 60% of which has been financed by the Regional Council. However when the political context is strained, this co-financing system seriously impedes planning operations, as demonstrated recently with the Seine-et-Marne Departmental Council which cancelled its contribution to the Sénart Super Stadium.

The fundamental issue to arise from this concerns whether divergences are merely political or whether they are a reflection of different approaches to urban planning. Certainly a distinction is apparent, according to the extent of interventionism observed in each case. For example the left is generally more *dirigiste* while right-wing representatives do not always act in a uniform manner; indeed the latter have been just as determined as the socialists or the communists when it comes to controlling communal land.

Various levels of intervention also need to be taken into consideration. The decentralization acts bestow extensive powers upon mayors. Thus planning and development decision-making is dispersed and co-ordination is seriously lacking. Indeed for both ideological and tactical motives, the departments and the region have often backed up local interests to thwart the Government which found itself saddled with thankless arbitration, co-ordination and reallotment responsibilities at a time of budgetary cutbacks and difficulties in the area of transport, housing and employment. In this respect the conservative administration, which took over in March 1993, has inherited a difficult agenda and may be tempted to pass certain matters to the local authorities for resolution. Under such a scenario it remains to be seen whether the Regional Council is powerful enough to prevent spatial discrepancies from widening within Ile-de France, considering that, under the French system, there is no administrative supervision of one local authority over the others. Hence the region cannot impose its decisions on the departments and the communes.

6.2   SPATIAL PLANNING AND LAND MANAGEMENT

6.2.1   The role of towns

In the French system, land management is essentially incumbent upon the communes (Punter, 1989; Vilmin, 1992). Furthermore through decentralization, communes have also been empowered to grant planning permission or rather give administrative clearance prior to a development or ground transformation project. Also mayors have a certain leeway in terms of the interpretation of laws and regulations. This process provides a means of controlling how land is used rather than through the price mechanism yet, recommendations in the *Plan d'occupation des sols* (land-use regulations) are instrumental in the way prices are fixed. Thus, a plot will be much cheaper in an estate with a low floor area ratio (i.e. a 0.4 COS)* than in an area where high-rise buildings can be erected (i.e. a 2.0 COS).

Instead of being a standing document, the *Plan d'occupation des sols* (POS) is increasingly being used as a tool for municipal policy and as such is subject to frequent amendments. Also standby COSs have been created, which are normally too low to make profitable a private development project but may be advanced by a municipality if developers' plans match the municipalities' objectives. It can be argued that POSs free towns from the necessity of accumulating expensive land reserves as private land can be frozen until negotiations enable municipal authorities to put it up for sale.

In addition a statutory density ceiling (PLD), set up in 1975 and amended in 1983, makes a distinction between ownership rights and building permission. Any landowner wishing to develop a plot more densely than provided for by the law must purchase this privilege from local authorities (commune and department). Indeed what used to be a mere dispensation procedure is now a rule. Arguably both parties benefit as over-reaching the PLD is widely used to balance the accounts of concerted planning zones. The consequences of which are an intensification of development where land is expensive, namely in the heart of the Paris conurbation.

---

* *Coefficient d'occupation des sols* is the ratio between the area of a plot and the area of the building on that plot.

The impact of amendments on land price regulations in Paris between 1979 and 1988 has been underlined by Tutin (1990) viz prices initially fell following the enactment of the PLD (1979), rose again when it was upgraded (1983), rose even higher when it was abolished (1987) and rose yet again when land-use indices were raised following the 1988 amendment on land-use regulations. Periodically the municipal authorities reconsider land-use regulations and may increase the COS ratio thereby increasing the permitted intensity of development and thus raising land values. Furthermore, in Paris and its suburbs, large-scale development projects are being carried out within the framework of ZACs, where an 'area development plan' can be set up notwithstanding land-use stipulations. In this respect, municipal authorities have considerable scope for manoeuvre.

Communes can also exert a 'pre-emption right' on all developed or developable areas in their territory. Transactions are required to be notified to the commune authorities which are empowered to override any land transfer. Also when a project is given 'public interest' status by a prefect (the government's official representative), communal authorities can issue a compulsory purchase order, notably inside a ZAC.

Pricing remains the weakness of this system. Pre-emption rights and compulsory purchase orders are theoretically pegged to market prices and any dispute arising from either must be settled in court. In fact, as shown by communist communes in the inner suburbs, pre-emption may contribute not only to curtailing increases in land and property prices but also to avoiding disruption to the social fabric of a town. Furthermore, extensive opportunities are often curtailed by high purchase costs. As communes in the Paris conurbation generally own but a small part of their territory and have accumulated few land reserves, the building of facilities and/or low-rent housing is often hampered by high land prices. In an effort to overcome this problem an Ile-de-France Development Fund was set up in December 1992 by ministerial order. The fund provided subsidies and low-interest loans to encourage land purchase for the erection of low-rent housing, on the condition that construction be completed within five years. This time limit is pitched to enable investors to avail of new land opportunities without having to start building immediately.

Large discrepancies however arise, concerning control over the land and property market. These are partly due to factors beyond the control of local authorities. For example certain communes, where demand is high because of an attractive social and environmental status, have few vacant or reusable plots. However the application of municipal policy may also be instrumental. In this context the split between *laissez-faire* and *dirigisme* is not only to be observed between left-wing and right-wing communes. Certain conservative communes are dogmatic in their development policy favouring the private sector but also including in their ZACs public facilities and low-rent housing. Indeed without subsidy or an equalization of land prices, the ceiling price for low-rent housing would be exceeded in Paris and in the 'smart' inner suburbs. Thousands of low-rent flats can only be built every year by passing part of the land cost burden to office, retail and 'private' housing developers, in accordance with an equalization system provided for concerted development zones.

Until recently, right-wing municipalities have not been unduly worried by increased price levels for land and property, however by the end of the 1980s soaring values were eventually perceived as counterproductive as they made municipal action considerably more expensive, particularly with respect to amenities. In certain cases, some towns had to sell off part of their own property to obtain liquidity to enable the implementation of land policy. A further weakness lies in the lack of collaboration, although co-operation is common in the provinces, it is curiously undeveloped in the Paris conurbation. While 'intercommunal associations' exist in the Paris area, attention is given to managing certain public utility services (viz water supply, waste disposal) rather than undertaking any form of space planning.

Hence suburban towns feel more like competitors and, despite the fact that urbanization is not contingent upon administrative boundaries, have never really embarked upon supra-communal plans. However some initiatives, made easier by political affinities, are noteworthy, particularly in the Plaine-Saint-Denis communist communes (north of Paris) and the Val-de-Seine conservative communes (south-west of Paris). In the former, three communes (Aubervilliers, Saint Denis and Saint-Ouen) and the *conseil général* of Seine-Saint-Denis established in 1985 a research body, La Plaine Renaissance, which played an influential role in the preparation of a zoning plan and more recently (in 1991) has created a public–private partnership, Plaine Développement, to realize urban projects in conjunction with the State. While in the case of Val-de-Seine a syndicate (the Association pour l'aménagement du site de Renault-Billancourt), incorporating local communes, the State and Renault, was formed in 1991 to consider the future utilization of the Renault site.

6.2.2   State intervention

The government can intervene in the affairs of the region through national laws and regulations. The most important measures taken over the last decade include the Decentralisation Acts (effective as of 1982) whereby mayors can now grant planning permission, divide land into plots and set up concerted planning zones. Pre-emption rights were extended in 1985 while the more recent *Loi d'orientation pour la ville* (13 July 1991) has had few effects yet. However it is worth noting that this Act has endowed towns with the possibility of setting up 'public land offices' empowered to buy plots prior to a development project.

The government can also grant loans and subsidies whereby it can influence space planning, more particularly the distribution of offices and low-rent housing. However, at the same time as decentralization was being enforced, the government disengaged from supply-side incentives, as illustrated by the dismantlement of the Urban Development Fund. Rather government is encouraging a policy of contractual partnership with local authorities since many development projects are carried out with the help of the region and/or department.

The government remains the initiator of major development decisions involving supra-regional facilities and transport infrastructures often entailing several compulsory purchase orders. Such large-scale projects may concur to drive up land prices by rehabilitating districts which were previously in little demand (viz la Villette or la Bastille). However in the outer suburbs, land speculation can be frozen through a ZAD (Deferred Development Area) procedure. Originally set up in 1962, this initially included 135 000 hectares in the Ile-de-France at the beginning of the 1970s although decentralization restricted its application to undeveloped plots in towns with no land-use regulations. The procedure was revived in 1989–90 but has come up against strong opposition from communes, though this can be overridden by a State Council decree.

The government can also give a project 'general interest' or 'national interest' status, which imposes special constraints on communes whose territories are subject to such procedures. However being prejudicial to the spirit of decentralization, these measures are seldom taken today, though specific measures have been applied to 'readjust' the Ile-de-France socially and economically. Most noteworthy has been the two square metres of housing for one square metre of office decreed for the west of the conurbation to avoid lengthening home-to-workplace distances.

Concerning land policy the government should not be considered as a monolithic entity; indeed conflicts, between ministries, are actually quite frequent as illustrated by the Renault works controversy. While the Ministry of Industry was backing the carmaker's plan to ask a high price for its plots, the Ministry of Public Works wanted to promote the 'social' dimension of the project whereas the Ministry of the Environment advocated the necessity to protect the site. Such conflicts in the Ile-de-France are generally settled by arbitration involving the President of the Republic or the Prime Minister.

Over the last decade, private business and industrial groups have become major protagonists in the development process in the Paris region and ironically such a large-scale project as la Défense, (which was fully led by the government) would be unthinkable today. Indeed increasingly local authorities are acting in partnership with banks, real estate developers and construction companies. An extreme case is that of Disneyland, where the government granted a private company the right to develop several thousand hectares while extending to it the benefits of farmland compulsory purchase orders. The project as originally envisaged was not only to be a theme park complete with accommodation facilities, but also a complex of industrial and housing estates to be built on the easternmost area of the new town of Marne-la-Vallée.

6.3   THE LAND AND PROPERTY MARKET SPATIAL PERSPECTIVES

6.3.1   Paris and the inner suburbs: an expensive land market

Apart from the former *non aedificandi* military zone whose development was only completed after the Second World War (with the opening of the ring road), Paris had virtually exhausted its developable land by the inter-war period. Hence over the last three decades in particular there has been very little large-scale urbanization although some new building plots have been acquired due to the demolition and rebuilding of office and/or apartment blocks (i.e. the Italie quarter, in the XIIIth *arrondissement*) or the relocation of industrial works (Citroën, in the XVth *arrondissement*) or offices. In addition some of the 'reserves' in the old quarters are not quite used up as illustrated by projects planned for, or ongoing in, the Gare de Lyon (Chalon block) and projects for the Goutte d'Or (XVIIIth *arrondissement*).

Given these contrasts reconstruction, often combined with densification, is frequently carried out on a small scale by private investors. The process normally involves a developer buying one or two wholly or partly built parcels, demolishing what are often still habitable or rehabilitable blocks and erecting a building, which exploits to a maximum the potential allowed by land-use regulations. Demolition costs added to very high land prices inevitably drives up the price of new construction coming on the market. Hence according to Tutin (1990) given the structure of land prices only the construction of luxury flats can achieve levels of profitability acceptable to the private sector. Furthermore, it is argued that by restricting demand to a very narrow market, the rise in prices curtails supply which in turn keeps prices up.

Industrial development follows a similar process except for large complexes requiring state intervention. In these cases the enforcement of the ZAC procedure permits better control over land use to be exerted. However the industrial sector has deserted Paris similar to trends pertaining in the wholesale sector, with the relocation of the Paris food market (Les Halles) to Rungis and the gradual disappearance of the wine warehouses of Bercy.

Opportunities for new land supply arise from the dispersal of railway land assets and public or private buildings which are unoccupied due to the transfer of their end users to the suburbs or to another region. For example two major development projects have materialized from the transfer of the

Ministry of Public Works from Passy (XVIth *arrondissement*) to la Défense and from the relinquishment by the army of the Dupleix barracks (XVth *arrondissement*). Railway land assets represent a major proportion of reusable space, viz the transfer of Montparnasse station gave rise to the Maine-Montparnasse development project while the renovation of Austerlitz station enabled the government to secure a spot for the construction of the Bibliothèque de France. Arising from the pressure upon land supply, wherever possible, disused railway lines, workshops and warehouses are converted and utilized for new development. This process is further highlighted by the fact that at the end of 1992, the government signed a 'corporate real estate plan' (*plan immobilier d'entreprise*) for Paris and its inner suburbs with the SNCF (French Railways). Merlin (1990) estimated that in the mid-1980s land reserves (railway or industrial land assets) amounted to about 600 ha, however this building reserve has already been greatly depleted by several large-scale projects.

The situation regarding building space is similar in Paris's neighbouring communes, viz 'upper-class' Neuilly, 'working-class' Saint-Ouen or the mixed neighbourhood of Montrouge; the renovation of old towns and de-industrialization being the principal means of obtaining building land. Indeed industrial restructuring has made available considerable space through the closure or relocation of plants from the 1960s onwards (Merlin, 1990). This supply source still exists and in 1992, the shut-down of the Boulogne-Billancourt Renault works made available about 50 ha of land (Renard, 1991). The development-led thrust of the 1990s contrasts with the 1970s when such disused plots were often left fallow whereas now the authorities are trying to anticipate plant shut-downs and reloc-ations, so as to pave the way for their transformation. Old industrial suburbs still have potential land reserves which gives municipalities some leeway, though in up-market communes, where land prices are very high, few building opportunities arise.

Many of the former industrial plant sites belonging to the government, to the Paris municipality or to state-run firms are faced with the dilemma of whether to sell plots below their market value so as to encourage the building of low-rent housing and amenities (including green areas) or to price such assets at the current market rate to provide revenue. Currently the latter strategy prevails and Merlin (1990) considers that the decision to reallocate most (75% to 100%) of the proceeds of land sales to administrative bodies can only make such plots more expensive.

6.2.2   The outer suburbs: a traditional market

Ten to fifteen kilometres from Paris a classic property market gradually reappears. Traditionally supply has been met by incorporating even greater amounts of agricultural land, however protection of rural areas has been considerably reinforced over the last twenty years. The idea being to preserve a green belt in the Paris region, though this policy is less consistently applied than that for the Greater London area. Furthermore land supply is often channelled into large units further prolonging already developed areas.

In addition urban development is gradually spreading along the outermost fringes of the Ile-de-France, sometimes into neighbouring northern and western regions. However the present trend is a return to 'central areas' (Paris and the inner suburbs). Paralleling this movement in 1991–2 private house building in the Ile-de-France showed a sharp decrease linked to the growing difficulties associated with home ownership in the current economic climate.

Corporate property is also found in the outer suburbs but rarely in the form of office space with the exception of a few specialized areas viz Roissy-Charles de Gaulle airport and the new towns. As a rule, developers are reluctant to invest beyond the A86 motorway belt which, although less than 10 kilometres from Paris, can be seen as the 'psychological outer limit' of the Paris region's centre. Furthermore, the slump of the early 1990s has curtailed risky projects and the promotion of new areas. As in the case of housing, investments in business and commercial premises are tending to focus upon the centre of the region. In this context it remains to be seen whether in so unfavourable a context Eurodisney will live up to its promises of housing and jobs beyond those provided by a theme park and contribute to an eastward readjustment of the Ile-de-France area.

6.4 PROPERTY PERFORMANCE

6.4.1 Temporal and spatial fluctuations of land and property markets

A survey by the Ile-de-France Regional Land Observatory (1989) showed that price differentials were a function of relative distance from the centre

Table 6.1 Land prices in Paris and in its inner suburbs

	Price per sq m		Rise (in current francs)
	1986	1989	
Paris	FF 6786	FF 22 587	up 228%
Hauts-de-Seine	FF 1741	FF 4457	up 156%
Val-de-Marne	FF 770	FF 1 289	up 67%
Seine-Saint-Denis	FF 609	FF 781	up 28%

Source: Comby, 1990.

of Paris and, to a lesser degree, could also be attributed to the social physiognomy of a commune and the amount of land available for development purposes. Within Paris, a square metre sold for more than FF 13 000 in the western *arrondissements*, and more than FF 5000 in the northern and eastern *arrondissements*. In the western inner suburbs, Neuilly and Boulogne-Billancourt values have reached over FF 10 000 per square metre. Elsewhere prices fall off rapidly viz land values in affluent residential communes averaged between FF 1400 and 4000 per square metre while in industrial communes like Montreuil sales achieved less than FF 900. Land prices reached a record high in the period 1986–9 though the rate of percentage increase showed an uneven spatial pattern across the departments of the inner ring (Table 6.1).

Differences in land prices directly affect real estate since in Paris and the densely populated suburbs land prices often account for 50% or more of the total cost of a building. Among the other factors determining a selling price, construction quality is of less importance relative to the actual occupier of the building. If a location is perceived to be attractive, office users will pay much more than multipurpose occupants or indeed purchasers of luxury housing. Demand for offices drives up land prices and since the mid-1980s, when the government partly abandoned the clearance procedures that were formerly in place, office blocks have been developed throughout the Paris region. However, conservation regulations, which prohibit replacing housing with offices, means that Paris has partly escaped this trend and its office blocks have thus been incorporated into major development projects, as in the Lyon-Bercy district. Availing itself of the La Défense business district, a pleasant environment and a skilled labour force, the Hauts-de-Seine department incorporates several ZACs mostly made up of offices (Levallois-Perret, Suresnes, Sevres, Issy-Les-Moulineaux).

While Paris in terms of property prices has lagged behind other major cities (viz London), from 1985 to 1990 there was an unprecedented rise both in office and housing prices. In some cases, for example highly fashionable locations in the VIIIth *arrondissement*, foreign investors (essentially Japanese) agreed to pay more than FF 100 000 per square metre. Such price growth spread out from 'smart districts' to both eastern Paris and the western suburbs. In 1992, the average market price of old housing was FF 32 000 per square metre in the VIIth *arrondissement* (in the west of Paris) and FF 14 000 in the Xth *arrondissement* (in the east of Paris). Excluding Neuilly (FF 30 000 per square metre), most Hauts-de-Seine towns averaged between FF 11 000 and 18 000 while old industrial and lower-income population departments stayed well below such prices despite significant rises: FF 10 000 to 15 000 per square metre in Val-de-Marne (with occasional higher prices near the Bois de Vincennes), FF 9000 to 12 000 in Seine-Saint-Denis. Again, offices have been to the forefront in fuelling this rise in price levels with even wider variations according to location viz

FF 70 000 per square metre in the central-western *arrondissements* of Paris and below FF 15 000 in the eastern *arrondissements*. In the centre of Paris, offices sold for three times as much as housing in 1989, as compared with a multiplier of 1.5 in 1981.

Performance levels peaked by the end of 1991. In 1992, housing prices decreased by 11% on average in Paris, steadying in 1993 to a rate close to that of the first half of 1989. The slump in real estate turnover including new buildings generally led developers to reduce price levels.

Arguably this has had greatest impact in the commercial and business sectors, particularly office developments due to the considerable size of building projects (2.83 million square metres in 1989) and the amount of capital tied up. At the end of 1992, the amount of available space in the Paris area was estimated at 7% of the total stock (namely 2.5 trading years at the present rate of take-up) with the situation expected to deepen in 1993. While still high, real estate turnover, primarily rental transactions, in 1992 (1 200 000 square metres for the whole region) was below that of 1987. Furthermore price differences narrowed between Paris and its western inner suburbs, where certain sites are still in great demand.

Even though the economic context is less gloomy than in London's Docklands, banks and insurance companies with enormous investments in the real estate business have been badly affected. Considering France as a whole (Paris has naturally the greatest share) the amount of capital which banks, such as Crédit Lyonnais, Groupe Suez or Paribas, had tied up in real estate was estimated at FF 400–500 billion in 1991. Debt levels accrued due to borrowing policies whereby developers and land agents were granted very liberal loans, encouraging new projects and enabling redemption of previous loans. However with the market downturn banks were left with bad debts and generally opted for either the granting of new easy terms and/or the restructuring of development companies to avert bankruptcies which might have impaired the whole system. In the certain situations investors who had bought very expensive blocks in fashionable Parisian districts were forced to make a quick sale at a loss (30% discounts on the initial offering price have not been uncommon and 50% losses have even been reported), instead of making a profit out of their development works. Foreign companies, mostly British and Japanese, which had significantly broken into the market wasted no time in bowing out, further accentuating the imbalance between supply and demand.

6.4.2   The profitability of real estate investments

New rental housing generally does not produce a high-yield investment. In France this became even more apparent during the 1980s, further to the enactment by the socialist government of legislation favouring tenants and the establishment of rent controls. As most new buildings are bought for owner occupation rather than for rental the government has had to grant high tax incentives in the hope of channelling investments back into what had become a much narrower private rental market. This policy has not proved to be successful as housing prices kept on increasing faster than rents, though the 1991–2 downturn will no doubt provide a more favourable yield for would-be investors (rent further increased in 1992). However it is not likely to go over 6% and in the mean time money locked up in property may depreciate further. Considering that there exists gilt-edged short-term investments with a 9 to 10% yearly yield liable to a low tax rate, it is not surprising that investors are shying away from the rented housing market.

The situation is not quite the same for office space, with high rental values, an 8 to 10% yield can easily be secured in attractive locations. Moreover, the office rental market showed a sharp increase in the 1980s, though latterly the highly risky office market with no prior buyers, and essentially targeted for speculative letting has sharply declined. Depending upon how far construction has proceeded, developers and investors alike have suffered. Consequently in the short term new building projects can be expected to become fewer as investors have been seriously weakened by the number of unlet offices in the Paris area. Furthermore, the office market is more open to speculation than that of housing and thus more vulnerable to the economic cycle and market swings. Declining rents are likely to make these investments less attractive, at least in the short term.

6.5   CONCLUSION

The means of land control at the disposal of government and towns are theoretically adequate for the town and country planning system in the Paris region. However monitoring powers are confronted with three main constraints of a legal, political and financial nature.

Concerning legal constraints extensive use has been made of the concepts of 'general interest' and 'state-approval' although the law courts have recently curtailed such excesses (i.e. through rulings against the establishment of certain ZACs), the idea being that pre-emption rights and compulsory purchase orders should not border on the arbitrary. In the political context there is less willingness by individuals to readily accept disruptions to the environment. Hence urban renewal projects and new transport networks face considerable opposition with technical feasibility coming into conflict with political considerations.

In the financial spectrum measures against land and property speculation (pre-emption rights, ZADs etc) are only peripheral to the price structure and land acquisition is placing serious strain on development budgets. In an adverse economic climate, where difficult choices have to be made, ambitions are revised downward. The alternative is to place the private sector increasingly to the forefront and accept a potential downgrading of social objectives. In this context the larger building companies and investors play a prominent role in many programmes as communes seek to minimize their financial risk and balance the budget of development programmes by increasing remunerative elements.

Arguably Paris demonstrates the difficulty of reconciling economic liberalism and voluntarism in planning policies. The apparent contradiction being that over the past 35 years initially the State and subsequent to decentralization the local authorities have displayed a wish to interfere in planning matters but lack the mechanisms for an effective control of the property market, particularly in relation to the evolution of prices.

REFERENCES

Baleste, M., Boyer, J.C., Gras, J., Montagné-Villettes and Vareille, C. (1993) *La France: 22 régions de programme*, Masson, Paris.
Comby, J. (1990) Paris plafonne, *Etudes foncières*, **48** (September), Paris, 15.
Ile-de-France Regional Land Observatory (1989) *Dossier*, **2**.
Merlin, P. (1990) Une politique foncière pour l'Ile-de-France, *Etudes foncières*, **48** (September), Paris, 4–11.
Punter, J. (1989) Decentralisation of the planning system in France, *The Planner*, **75**(4), 12–15.
Renard, V. (1991) L'Ile Seguin, une boucle d'intérêt national, *Etudes foncières*, **50** (March), Paris, 6–8.
Tutin, C. (1990) Pourquoi la hausse? Quatre hypothèses sur une déconnexion. *Etudes foncières*, **47** (June), Paris, 16–23.
Vilmin, T. (1992) Quels opérateurs fonciers pour les communes? *Etudes foncières*, **55** (June), Paris, 19–23.
Webster, P. (1991) An outline of the French Town and Country Planning System, *Journal of Property Finance*, **1**(4), 584–7.

PART TWO ———

NORTHERN EUROPE

———————————

7

Helsinki

_____ *Seppo Laakso and Olli Keinänen*

Helsinki has the appearance of a planned city with only minor problems created by uncontrolled urbanization. Throughout Finland, including Helsinki, landowner's rights are well protected and, at the same time, special emphasis is given to public interests. These two factors, together with the Scandinavian tradition in urban planning and the strong position of private property ownership, are the main characteristics of Finnish urban development. Furthermore Finnish cities are of recent origin due to rather late industrialization, and are mainly post Second World War. For this reason and because of peripherality Finland has been little affected by external influences in spite of being an open, export oriented economy.

Currently (1993) Finland has negotiated membership of the EU thereby counteracting its relative isolation and raising implications for urban development, urban management and urban planning. Relations between property markets and systems of urban planning will be forced to change in the future. Indeed with the Finnish domestic economy opening to international competition, legislation regulating foreign investment and the right to own real estate was changed at the beginning of 1993 to meet the requirements of EEA. Furthermore the Finnish government has started to harmonize other regulations in line with EU legislation. However the influence of foreign companies are not yet significant factors in Helsinki.

This chapter describes characteristics of property markets and functions of planning in the urban development of Helsinki and its metropolitan area. Emphasis is placed upon the development of property markets in the 1980s as well as likely perspectives for the mid to late 1990s.

European Cities, Planning Systems and Property Markets Edited by James Berry and Stanley McGreal. Published in 1995 by E & FN Spon. ISBN 0419 18940 8.

7.1 HELSINKI: AN OVERVIEW

Helsinki as the capital of Finland is the administrative, trade and service centre of the country. In a small and culturally homogenous nation it is natural that the capital occupies a strong position. In population terms Helsinki contains 20% of Finland's five million inhabitants, but in administration, science and education, culture and trade the city assumes considerably greater importance. Indeed the degree of Helsinki-centredness is significantly higher than a decade ago, though during the same time Helsinki's role as a manufacturing city has weakened both relatively and absolutely (Susiluoto, 1992).

Concerning the Helsinki region (total population 1.1 million) the inner metropolitan area is administered by four municipalities, viz the city of Helsinki (population 502 000) as well as three neighbouring cities Vantaa, Espoo and Kauniainen (total population 350 000). The rest of the population of the region, 201 000 inhabitants, is dispersed in an area forming an outer ring, 20–40 km from the city centre (Figure 7.1). This outer ring of suburbs, towns and villages is divided into eight municipalities (*Statistical Yearbook of Finland*, 1992b).

Population growth in the Helsinki region has been 1.1% per annum since 1970. This is an exceptionally high level compared to other European capital cities. Indeed employment growth showed even higher figures until 1990 at which stage severe recession turned the shortage of labour into an unemployment rate over 15%. Hence Helsinki is currently coming to terms with a new set of problems. Formerly the city, the planning system and the market were used to steady growth and planning problems were related to growth management, now questions concern the initiation of new growth.

Geographically Helsinki is situated on a peninsula with the city centre surrounded by the sea from three sides, the ensuing form of urban development following a traditional radial-concentric pattern. This morphology has been an effective hindrance to further enlargement of the downtown area. Prior to the 1960s, and before the construction of main radial freeways, urban development outside the old downtown area was insignificant, but since then urban sprawl has been rapid (Sundman, 1982).

The city of Helsinki has in many respects a similar pattern of development to other core cities within metropolitan areas in Scandinavia or western Europe. The trends in urban development have been characterized by decentralization and regionalization though this development started several decades later than elsewhere. After a period of population decline in the 1970s there has been modest growth over the last ten years, though municipalities in the outer ring still have the highest growth rates. However unlike many central European cities, none of the downtown housing areas of Helsinki has become socially deprived. Indeed the central

HELSINKI REGION

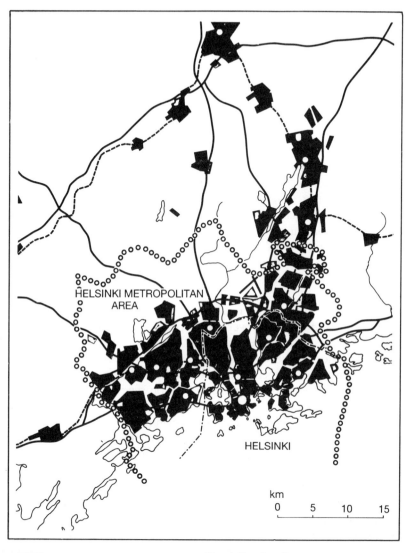

		Population densities:	
▮	Housing areas		
▭	Employment areas	Inner city	4462 inh/km2
——	Roads	Suburbs of Helsinki	2239
-----	Railways	The Metropolitan Area	621
O	Main centre	(excl. Helsinki)	
o	Local centre	The Helsinki region	101
		(excl. Metropolitan Area)	
		Finland	16

Figure 7.1 Helsinki region

parts and inner suburbs have succeeded in preserving and even strengthening their position, and consequently are areas of high-priced housing. The latter has been an important influence behind the wide and seemingly permanent political support which the City Planning Committee has had in carrying out a very strict anti-office zoning policy of downtown areas (Schulman, 1990).

7.2 THE SYSTEM OF LAND-USE PLANNING IN HELSINKI

7.2.1 Basic features of land-use control

A Finnish peculiarity is the landowner's basic right to build. However this general principle can be restricted by zoning plans and by site specific development plans. Consequences of the heritage of freedom to build means that often the landowner gets compensation when the right to build is restricted by planning.

A second feature with far reaching implications is the privilege of planning given to the municipality under which the latter has the right to plan and to make zoning decisions affecting all land, including that in private ownership.

Concerning town plans, up until 1992 these had to be approved by the relevant state authority. However municipalities now have more independence and central government has less direct influence on the land-use policies of cities. Rather the guidance of urban development by state authorities through indirect measures is more important. These are based mainly on regulation of housing finance and on state control of most of the urban infrastructural development, for example, the construction of main roads and railways. Recent changes in planning legislation, in housing policies and in laws regulating the financial relations of central and local government, have given local administrations an even more independent position.

The city of Helsinki also occupies a different situation relative to the other municipalities in that the city is a major landowner not only within its borders but in the whole Helsinki region. The city has used this strength to actively promote the development of new residential areas, hence only a small portion of land zoned for housing has been privately owned. However the situation in the other municipalities in the region is quite the opposite. The outcome being that social housing development is largely concentrated in Helsinki while owner-occupied houses, especially detached properties exist, mainly in the other municipalities.

Regarding industrial and office development the position of the city is different. In the CBD, as well as in other centres in the region, private owners dominate the development process. Important exceptions are certain defined project areas for office development in the downtown area and in most of the new planned subcentres, where development is initiated and actively supported by the city. In this context the city of Helsinki being an important landowner is in a much more influential position than the other municipalities. Furthermore the policy to create independent subcentres and to support office development outside the CBD in order to protect the city image and environment has seen to be fairly successful.

Planning policy, adopted in the 1970s form the principles that still guide urban development. This policy, based upon controlled decentralization, envisaged a polycentric regional structure. Thus the thrust of regional planning policy has been to channel and support growth at defined regional subcentres. Arguably with the Helsinki region consisting of nine municipalities, each with their independent land-use policies, the adoption of a polycentric pattern was a natural planning objective.

7.2.2 Regional planning

There are three levels of urban plans and respective planning authorities viz the regional, the metropolitan and the city level.

Regional planning is compulsory and is organized within the Regional Planning Association formed by the municipalities of the Helsinki region. However the legal status of regional planning documents is rather weak. While decisions on land use by the municipalities should not conflict with the regional plan, in practice it is the regional plan that is changed, not that of the municipality. Therefore the role of regional planning tends to be more active in matters such as recreational issues and in environmental protection.

At the metropolitan level the four central cities of the region have formed a voluntary planning authority to co-ordinate metropolitan public transport and solid waste management. Concerning planning the role of the metropolitan authority is mainly that of research, and planning co-operation which is not binding. Indeed competition between cities and municipalities in the metropolitan region is the most visible feature of the land-use policies adopted by each municipality.

7.2.3 City planning

The process of land-use control has three main stages. First, every munici-pality has to prepare a Master Plan of the city, in essence this is a zoning plan though it also has strategic functions akin to a development plan. Indeed the latter function is becoming more dominant (Master Planning Office, 1993). Formerly master planning was organized as part of the pro-fessional planning administration, which also had responsibility for detailed planning. However by the early 1990s the municipalities had taken over the power to work out and decide the master plans. The situation is nevertheless highly unstable. For instance in the city of Helsinki master planning was reorganized in 1991 and again in 1993. Currently all forms of land-use planning are concentrated in the City Planning Office.

The second stage is the so-called Project Area Master Plan or a component master plan utilized for either large-scale development projects or for especially complicated planning projects over a large area. Normally these plans are an integrated part of the planning process and the first phase in a development project. In a Project Area Master Plan the objectives for urban development, the use of land, the physical structure and building volume are decided by the political decision-makers, initially at the City Planning Committee and finally at the City Council.

From the developer's perspective the principal stage of public control is a town plan. Ratified town plans are legally binding and confirm the right to build but do not directly require it. By combining lease agreements of building sites with the town plan, the planning authority has achieved more influence on developer's decisions, in this way, for example, the timing of construction of housing and services is regulated.

A detailed town plan includes decisions on functions and intensities of land use regarding floor area, number of storeys, parking regulations, precise building sites and external appearance of buildings. These plans are normally very precise and can be considered as site-specific development plans. Normally a detailed town plan covers a building site, a block or a group of blocks.

The last stage in the process of building regulation is the decision on a building permit and building inspection. This activity is organized within a separate authority. The main emphasis is in technical aspects as well as issues of city image. However before a town plan is ratified neighbouring users and other groups with possibly conflicting interests have the opportunity to oppose the plan. Such official hearings can take a considerable length of time.

All stages collectively form a hierarchical planning system, where each previous planning decision is needed before the next step. In Helsinki the

Table 7.1 Land ownership structure in the city of Helsinki 1992

Landowner	Area (sq km)	Percentage
City of Helsinki	119	64
The state	25	14
Private	41	22
Total	185	100

Source: The Urban Data Base of Helsinki.

majority of town plans are initiated by a landowner or a developer. The average time from application to ratification of a town plan is nearly two years. Such a long period can adversely affect investment; indeed it was realized during the boom years of the late 1980s that cities had to speed up their planning process in order to compete successfully with each other.

7.3 ACTORS IN THE PROPERTY MARKET

7.3.1 Land ownership

A special feature of the property market in Helsinki is the fact that the city owns most of the land within its borders, circa two-thirds of the total land area (Table 7.1). However in the other municipalities of the Helsinki region the situation is totally different, with the municipalities owning less than a quarter of the land. Instead development and construction companies are the significant landowners in these municipalities.

Historical and political reasons account for the land ownership structure of Helsinki and the rest of the region. Like most cities, Helsinki has grown from the old city centre outwards and until 1925 only the land within the borders and in the possession of the city could, by law, be exploited for new construction. In 1925 Finnish cities acquired the legal right to incorporate suburbs, and the Town Plan Code of 1931 gave municipalities the privilege of planning the use of privately owned land (Bengs and Loikkanen, 1991). However Helsinki continued to use its traditional means of buying land to be zoned for development and still continues its active role in the land market. The policy is to acquire, for the city, land in new large development areas.

7.3.2 Developers

The development, construction, financing, ownership and use of property has to a large extent become separated from each other in Finland, as in most other industrialized countries. The development of office or retail property is a rather new phenomena in Helsinki and indeed elsewhere in Finland. Until the beginning of the 1980s most major office construction projects were initiated by the owner of the real estate and large companies typically developed headquarters, factories and other buildings for their own use. However in the 1980s there was a significant change in the market: some of the large residential property developers and construction companies, and a number of new firms, many of them backed by large banks, became involved in property investment and development with many new office blocks and shopping centres developed for letting on the open market. Nevertheless the real estate market in Helsinki is still underdeveloped compared with many other European cities. According to the City of Helsinki (1993), the Helsinki real estate market is considered unsophisticated, closed and immature creating sub-optimal conditions for real estate players and inward investing firms from abroad.

The large commercial banks and insurance companies have a powerful role as owners of real estate and development companies. As well as directly owning a large number of office buildings, especially in the CBD of Helsinki, they also control many of the largest construction companies particularly those which were active in office and shopping centre development in 1980s. Generally projects have been financed by purely domestic investors with foreign companies yet to make significant investments in Helsinki.

7.3.3   Construction industry

In 1990 there were almost 12000 firms in Finland active in the building construction industry (Statistics Finland, 1992a), though most are very small. Traditionally the construction sector is an industry with low entry barriers, with new small firms emerging and disappearing from the business. However in spite of the large number of firms the construction industry is extremely concentrated in Finland with three large companies dominating the market. Again foreign companies play no significant role in the industry.

The recession in Finland as in other European countries has had a major impact on the construction sector and a large number of companies have either gone into bankruptcy or merged with others. Consequently since 1991 the construction industry has become even more concentrated and as a result of large ownership changes commercial banks now have controlling interest in many of the largest construction companies.

7.3.4   Financial markets

Finnish financial markets are dominated by a small number of banks; and private institutions specializing in housing or other sectors are lacking. The banking system until the late 1980s was highly regulated with tightly structured and rigid lending policies. Interest rates were administratively controlled and their level was kept low relative to the rate of inflation. These factors together with foreign capital controls resulted in credit rationing. However from 1986 onwards the Bank of Finland gradually deregulated the domestic banking system. Liberalization increased the demand for credit and as a consequence interest rates rose to the highest in Europe, whereas during the 1970s and the beginning of the 1980s real interest rates were negative for most of the time.

Deregulation significantly changed the financing of housing, with loans tied to market interest rates. The requirement for saving in advance of house purchase was loosened and amortizing periods became longer. These changes together with optimistic expectations about the overall economy induced a huge growth of credit leading in turn to a housing market boom during 1987–90 (Koskela, Loikkanen and Virén, 1992). Furthermore deregulation, and especially the abolition of foreign capital exchange controls, also affected the commercial property market with investment in office buildings, shopping centres and hotels increasing rapidly during the late 1980s.

The market responded with a period of exceptionally rapid property price increase during 1987–9. However this was short-lived and prices collapsed during 1989–92 as the Finnish economy slowed down. As a consequence of the boom and bust cycle the banking system ended up with enormous difficulties arising from bankruptcies and declining property values.

7.3.5   The real estate policy of the public sector

In the commercial property market demand and supply are not affected by the public sector as directly as in the housing market. State loans, subsidies or rent/price control have not been used in Finland. Instead, the state has tried to limit the construction of non-residential buildings by a special property investment tax designed to slow down the overheating of investment activity. This form of tax was applied in the Helsinki region several times during the 1970s and the 1980s.

Municipalities may initially affect supply by land-use restrictions. On the other hand, municipalities also compete with each other for firms which offer jobs for inhabitants and pay local taxes. Thus subsidized rents of premises or land, and freedom from restrictions of land-use plans have been used by development oriented municipalities to attract firms. However, the city of Helsinki has traditionally been rather passive in attracting new firms while neighbouring municipalities have been active in attracting firms to move away from Helsinki.

7.4   TRENDS IN THE PROPERTY MARKET

7.4.1   The regional economy of Helsinki

The Finnish economy has grown relatively quickly during recent decades compared with most other industrialized countries; the average annual growth rate of real GDP was 3.4% during 1971–90. Structural and cyclical problems in the economy only emerged at the end of the 1980s, causing an exceptionally deep recession. Real GDP declined by more than 10% during the two years 1991–2 and the unemployment rate soared from 3.9% in September 1990 to 18.5% in April 1993. According to forecasts the growth

Table 7.2 Employment structure (%) the city of Helsinki 1970 and 1989; the Helsinki region and Finland 1989

Industry	City of Helsinki 1970	City of Helsinki 1989	Helsinki region 1989	Finland 1989
Agriculture	0.2	0.3	0.8	8.5
Manufacturing	24.3	11.9	15.6	22.2
Construction	7.6	7.8	7.7	7.4
Trade	23.6	20.2	20.9	15.6
Transport	7.6	8.8	7.8	6.8
Financial and business services	9.9	20.0	17.2	10.4
Public administration and social services	26.7	28.4	27.0	25.9
Total (%)	100.0	100.0	100.0	100.0
(1000 jobs)	327.0	368.4	611.2	2373.7

Source: Statistical Yearbooks of the City of Helsinki.

rate for the economy is expected to be lower in the short term than it was during the 1980s, and the unemployment rate is expected to remain high.

Within Finland the Helsinki region has been the fastest growing area. The annual average growth rate of GDP was 0.1% points higher in the region than for the whole country during the 1970s, and 1.4% points higher during the 1980s. The region's share of total output grew from 24% in 1970 to 28.5% in 1988. Furthermore the population of the region grew by 1.1% annually during the period 1970–89, equivalent to three-quarters of the total population growth of Finland over that period. Employment growth has also been fast: the average annual growth rate was 1.7% in the Helsinki region compared with only 0.5% in the whole of Finland during 1970–89. However the recession has caused problems to the regional economy of Helsinki. Output and employment in the region have declined since 1990, and the unemployment rate has increased to 15.4% (April 1993).

A significant change in employment structure has taken place in the Helsinki region during the last two decades (Table 7.2). The proportion of manufacturing has declined while financial and business services have increased. Thus by the end of the 1980s the employment structure both in the city and in the region of Helsinki resemble that of a typical capital city: public administration, financial and business services are well represented while manufacturing has only a minor role.

7.4.2 Demand for office and retail floor space

A close association exists between the demand for office and retail floor space and the performance of the real economy of the region. Office

Table 7.3 Employment in main service sectors in the city of Helsinki in 1970, 1980 and 1989, and in the Helsinki region in 1989 (1000 jobs)

| | City of Helsinki | | | Helsinki region |
	1970	1980	1989	1989
Finance and insurance	16.4	20.1	29.8	36.2
Business services	18.4	26.4	44.0	64.9
Public administration	21.2	26.4	26.6	37.3
Public services	41.1	54.1	53.3	88.5
Other services	22.5	16.7	24.6	31.0
Total main services	119.6	143.7	178.3	257.9
Total all industrials	327.0	315.2	368.4	611.2

Source: Statistical Yearbooks of the City of Helsinki.

premises are basically used by the service sector, hence the development of banking, insurance, business services and public administration are of crucial importance in terms of generating demand. While in the retail property market the development of private consumption is a crucial demand-side factor.

Employment within the service sector increased by 50% in the city of Helsinki from 1970 to 1989 (Table 7.3). Indeed the total number of jobs in the sector were 180 000 in the city and 258 000 for the whole region at the end of the 1980s, representing 45% of total employment in the latter. However current forecasts (1993) concerning future development of the service sector are pessimistic with employment in the public sector as well as in banking expected to decrease, while employment in other services is uncertain because of poor prospects for private consumption.

A factor influencing the demand for office space is the floor space to person ratio. This was approximately 29 m^2 per person in office buildings in 1985, the ratio having almost doubled over the previous 15-year period (Laine, 1988). According to the City of Helsinki (1993) office floor space per person ratio is 40–70% higher in Helsinki than in typical European metropolitan cities, but at a similar level to other Scandinavian centres. It is expected that the ratio will decrease in Helsinki in the future, towards the level of other west European cities.

7.4.3 Construction of office and retail space

Construction of new residential and commercial buildings has been extensive in the Helsinki region due to the rapid increase of employment and population. Annually completed floor space was on average as much as 3.0% of the existing stock during 1982–91, 59% being residential

Table 7.4 Construction in the Helsinki region (annual averages) by the use of the building, in 1982–91

	1000 m²	% of stock
Residential	1069	2.8
Office	171	3.4
Retail and hotels	68	2.2
Factories	154	2.6
Other	352	3.9
Total	1814	3.0

Source: The Statistical District Data Base of Helsinki.

construction and 41% in other sectors. Concerning the construction of new office buildings the annual rate of completions amounted to 3.4% of the stock, for retail and hotel buildings the ratio was 2.2%, and for industrial buildings 2.6% (Table 7.4).

However construction activity has not been distributed evenly through the region. Since the 1950s decentralization of both housing and employment has characterized Helsinki like most other metropolitan areas with the principal difference being that in Helsinki the process started later. For example in 1960, 42% of the population and 65% of the jobs of the region were still located in the inner city of Helsinki, by 1989 the respective figures were 15% and 36%.

Reasons for decentralization are basically the same in Helsinki as in any metropolitan area. The inner city became fully developed during the 1960s and 1970s and as the city core has been protected by the planning authorities, for architectural and other reasons no large sites have been released for redevelopment within this area. The lack of development opportunities together with traffic problems in the inner city have targeted the demand for and supply of new office and retail space towards the suburbs and the rest of the region. Indeed the biggest neighbouring municipalities, Espoo and Vantaa, have had a systematic strategy for growth, and have been active in supplying possibilities for both residential and commercial development.

Consequently one-third of construction activity took place within the city, and only one-tenth within the inner city, during 1982–91 (Table 7.5). More specifically regarding office construction the proportion within the inner city was 30%, and in retail and hotel construction only 9%. In contrast the most intensive areas of commercial construction have been outside the city borders, along highways, ring roads, and railways, near the airport, and in new subcentres.

Approximately half of the new office buildings in the city of Helsinki have been developed by commercial real-estate companies during the

Table 7.5 Construction in the Helsinki region by location, in 1982–91

	Buildings completed (annual average)		City of Helsinki		Rest of the region
	1000 m²	%	Inner city %	Suburbs %	%
Residential	1069	100	6	27	67
Office	171	100	30	17	54
Retail and hotels	68	100	9	24	68
Factories	154	100	19	21	61
Other	352	100	10	21	69
Total	1814	100	10	25	65

Source: The Statistical District Data Base of Helsinki.

Table 7.6 Construction in the city of Helsinki by owner group, in 1980–91 (%)

Developer	Office building %	Retail and hotel building %
Real-estate company	48	81
Public sector	14	—
Banks and insurance companies	8	—
Other private companies	30	19
Total	100	100

Source: The Urban Data Base of Helsinki.

1980s for letting on the open market, one-third by banks, insurance companies, and private firms mainly for their own use; and the rest by the public sector, especially by (and for) the state. Concerning retail construction 81% of this was realized by real estate companies, the rest by other private interests (Table 7.6). However the outlook for the construction of new office and retail space is likely to be modest during the 1990s. The market is currently over-supplied due to intensive construction during the 1980s, while the demand for office space is set to decline due to decreasing employment in the service sector. Furthermore there are no reasonable prospects for new large shopping centre development, because of declining private consumption.

7.4.4 Stock analysis

The total office stock in the Helsinki region was approximately 6.4 million m², in 1992, making Helsinki one of the 12 largest office centres in Europe

Table 7.7 Age and location of the office and retail and hotel stock in the Helsinki region in 1992

Office stock	Total stock Millions m²	%	−1959 %	Year of construction 1960–69 %	1970–79 %	1980–92 %
CBD	1.7	100	74	15	8	4
Other inner city	2.2	100	43	14	18	25
Helsinki suburbs	1.0	100	6	21	27	45
Rest of region (*)	1.5	100	—	6	27	67
Total region (*)	6.4	100	35	13	19	33
Retail and hotel stock						
CBD	0.4	100	67	4	3	26
Other inner city	0.2	100	44	3	37	16
Helsinki suburbs	0.5	100	11	26	22	41
Rest of region (*)	1.4	100	—	15	21	64
Total region (*)	2.5	100	16	14	20	50

*Approximations by writers.
Source: The Urban Data Base of Helsinki.

(City of Helsinki, 1993) with office supply approximately the same size as for example Vienna, Brussels or Madrid. Indeed since 1980 the office stock in the Helsinki region has increased by more than 50%. Regarding retail and hotel buildings the total stock is 2.5 million m², an increase of 30% since 1980. Furthermore most of the building stock is relatively new because of intensive construction activity during the 1970s and the 1980s (Table 7.7).

In spite of decentralization of employment the inner city still retains the main concentration of office stock with two-thirds of the office space still located in this area. In contrast retail and hotel building stock is more evenly distributed with the proportion located in the inner city only 15%.

About half of the office stock of the city of Helsinki is let on the market. Banks and insurance companies are the most significant investors, the rest of the stock is owner-occupied by city, state and private companies. Although the rate of owner-occupation has declined during recent decades and the proportion of rental stock has increased, the office market and investment in office property in Helsinki is much less developed than in many other European cities.

7.4.5 Vacancy rates

Office vacancy rates in the Helsinki region were low during the 1980s, in spite of the increase in supply. The average vacancy rate was 2% during

1981–90 but by 1992 this had risen to 11% of stock. Internationally this level is not exceptionally high, according to the City of Helsinki (1993) higher levels of vacancy were recorded in for example Oslo, London and Amsterdam at the end of 1992. However a further increase in vacancy levels is expected in Helsinki, and by 1995 rates will probably be among the highest in Europe. It is anticipated that vacancy will be within the range 16 to 22% by the end of this decade.

Also there are large regional differences in vacancy rates within the Helsinki region. These are highest in peripheral locations where considerable new space was completed during the last five years. It is estimated that vacancy is less than 8% in the CBD, but over 15% in municipalities of Espoo and Vantaa.

7.4.6 Performance analysis

While the demand for office space was high in Helsinki in the 1980s the supply-demand ratio seemed to be in balance, thus rents increased, but not at an exceptionally high rate. According to Olkkonen and Miettinen (1993) the annual nominal rent increase of new contracts in the inner city of Helsinki was 11–12% during 1981–90 while the average annual inflation rate was 7%, on average. Rents started to decline in 1991, and by the spring of 1993 the nominal level of new rentals had declined by 15% from the market peak reached in 1990. At this stage the average office rent in central Helsinki was 75 FIM/m²/month, and prime rents (top rent for the best quality space) was 95 FIM/m²/month (100 FIM = appr. 18 US$). Following the decline from the top levels reached in 1990, office rents in Helsinki are clearly below the level of Paris, London, Brussels and Frankfurt, and also cheaper than in the Scandinavian capitals of Stockholm and Oslo (City of Helsinki, 1993; Leiwo, Miettilä and Olkkonen, 1993).

There are also large variations in rent level according to location within the region as well as by the age and quality of the building. Prime office rents in the suburban centres of the city of Helsinki (5–10 km from the city centre) are 60–70%, and in the sub centres of neighbouring municipalities (10–20 km from the city centre) 50–65% of the rent level of the CBD (City of Helsinki, 1993; Leiwo, Miettilä and Olkkonen, 1993). However, the office rent gradient is not as steep in Helsinki as in most other European cities, though office rent levels are expected to decline further in Helsinki, and the rent deviation between top quality space in best locations and poor quality space in peripheral locations is expected to increase.

The capital value of real estate increased rapidly during the 1980s and the possibility of capital gains attracted investors. Yields for prime CBD offices were estimated to be 5% in 1990. However, as in the case of rental values, capital values have fallen from the high levels of 1990, in some circumstances by as much as 40–60%. Present estimates of yields for CBD offices vary between 6.5 and 9% and outside the CBD between 8 and 11%, reflecting the greater uncertainty of the property market.

7.5   CONCLUSION

Until the early 1990s the relationship between planning and property markets was considered to be an ideological issue; either planned development or market forces should dominate. Thus for example during the boom years of 1985–9 the planning system attracted criticism and was seen to be too rigid and too slow in producing new development opportunities. However, very little happened to make the system more effective, though it should be appreciated that considerable development was realized during this period. Furthermore relatively independent municipalities within the region compete with each other by offering the market building sites and projects, which the planning system as a whole could neither effectively oppose nor satisfy. As a result the urban sprawl has the potential to accelerate further and fluctuations in the construction industry are likely to be steep. Furthermore there is no sign of any growing willingness to improve regional co-operation.

Currently (1993) Helsinki, in common with many other metropolitan regions, suffers problems of economic decline and high rates of unemployment. The need for structural change in the local economy as well as in the public sector is evident. The fiscal crisis at both the central and the local level of the public sector makes it difficult to finance necessary infrastructure investments. New ideas are needed to channel private resources to projects previously considered purely as public. In this context planning systems should be more flexible and change their goal of restricting development to support growth by adopting an active strategy, from regulatory plan-led development to more discretionary policy-led development. It seems that separately each city and municipality within the Helsinki region will have to alter their approaches to urban planning and management practice. However planning systems may prove too rigid to be changed.

REFERENCES

Bengs, C. and Loikkanen, H.A. (1991) The Finnish housing market: structure, institutions, and policy issues, in B. Hårsman and J.M. Quigley (eds), *Housing Markets and Housing Institutions: an International Comparison*, Kluwer Academic Publishers, Norwell Mass, 63–112.
City of Helsinki (1993) Helsinki Market Report. Unpublished information and evaluation provided without warranty by Jones Lang Wootton Consulting and Research.

City of Helsinki, Master Planning Office (1993) *Master Planning in Helsinki: From Strategic Planning Advice to Implementation Schedule*, Ministry of the Environment, Planning and Building Department.

City of Helsinki Information Management Centre (1975) *Statistical Yearbook of the City of Helsinki 1975*, Helsinki.

City of Helsinki Information Management Centre (1992) *Statistical Yearbook of the City of Helsinki 1992*, Helsinki.

City of Helsinki Information Management Centre: The Urban Data Base of Helsinki.

City of Helsinki Information Management Centre: The Statistical District Data Base of Helsinki.

Koskela, E., Loikkanen, H.A. and Virén M. (1992) House prices, household saving and financial market liberalization in Finland, *European Economic Review*, **36**, 549–58.

Laine, M (1988) *Työpaikkaväljyyden muutokset Helsingissä 1970–1985* (The change in floor space per worker ratio in Helsinki 1970–1985), Publications of the City Planning Department of Helsinki YB 7/88, Helsinki.

Leiwo, K., Miettilä, A. and Olkkonen, O. (1993) *Toimitilojen vuokrat Helsingissä 1992* (Rents of commercial premises in Helsinki), Research reports from the City of Helsinki Information Management Centre 1993, **2**, Helsinki.

Olkkonen, O. and Miettinen, A. (1993) *Liike- ja toimistotilojen vuokrat ja niiden kehitys* (Rents of retail and office premises and their development), Turku School of Economics, Turku.

Schulman, H. (1990) *Alueelliset todellisuudet ja visiot. Helsingin kehitys ja kehittäminen 1900-luvulla* (Spatial realities and visions. Urban development and planning in Helsinki in the 20th century), Diss., Helsinki University of Technology. Centre for urban and regional studies publications A 18, Espoo.

Statistics Finland (1992a) *Corporate Enterprises and Personal Businesses in Finland 1990*, Helsinki.

Statistics Finland (1992b) *Statistical yearbook of Finland 1992*, Helsinki.

Sundman, M. (1982) *Stages in the Growth of a Town: A Study of the Development of the Urban and Population Structure of Helsinki*, Helsinki City Planning Department Publication YB 1/82, Helsinki.

Susiluoto, I. (1992) *Helsingin seudun elinkeinorakenne ja taloudellinen kasvu* (The economic structure and growth in the region of Helsinki), Research reports from the City of Helsinki Information Management Centre 1992, **3**, Helsinki.

8

Stockholm

*Håkan Bejrum, Göran Cars
and Thomas Kalbro*

During recent decades the property market of Stockholm has, to say the least, been turbulent, characterized by large swings in demand, supply and prices. At the same time new conditions for decision-making on land use and construction have emerged. Structural changes in society have altered the framework for urban planning and development. In this chapter the characteristics of these changes and the new decision-making framework with regard to the planning and property market are identified. Initially a short description of the Stockholm region and the Swedish planning system is presented; this is followed by a discussion of the recent changes in the framework surrounding planning activities. The opportunities and constraints presented are related to questions concerning transportation, infrastructure environment and conservation. Special interest is focused on the question of public–private partnerships as a method for urban development. The analysis is set against the background of the Swedish economy during the 1980s and early 1990s and the performance of property over this period.

8.1 THE STOCKHOLM REGION

8.1.1 Administrative structure and population

Sweden has three levels of government. At the national level is the central government and parliament (Riksdag), while the regional level is composed of 24 counties with popularly elected county councils. The main responsibilities of the latter are medical care and public transport. Central government is represented at the regional level through the county administrative boards, whose responsibilities include reviewing local planning decisions

European Cities, Planning Systems and Property Markets Edited by James Berry and Stanley McGreal. Published in 1995 by E & FN Spon. ISBN 0419 18940 8.

Figure 8.1 Local government boundaries in Stockholm County
Source: reproduced with permission from Stockholm County Council, Office of Regional Planning and Urban Transportation.

to ensure agreement with 'national interests'. Each county is divided into municipalities (286 in total) which play a key role in Swedish society with responsibilities for housing provision, education, child care, care of the elderly, social services and protection of health and the environment. In addition, the municipality is directly involved in land-use changes through its responsibility for planning, development control and provision of urban infrastructure (streets, water and sewerage systems, parks, playgrounds, etc.). The municipality often owns land for development and recreation, and sometimes acts as developer. There are three major sources of financing for municipal activities: taxes, fees and government grants. On average taxes account for almost 50% of revenues, fees for slightly less than 20% and government grants for about 25%. This, for instance represents the financial profile for the City of Stockholm.

The region, Stockholm County, is divided into 25 municipalities (Figure 8.1) and of Sweden's 8.7 million inhabitants, almost 1.7 million live in Stockholm County, approximately 20% of the national population. However, the municipalities vary greatly in terms of populations. The City of Stockholm is the dominant entity with almost 700 000 inhabitants, the next largest municipality, Huddinge, has a population of about 75 000, and the smallest, Vaxholm, has only about 7000 residents.

8.1.2   Regulations related to land use

In principle, all land in Sweden is divided into real estate units (which are registered with a unique designation). In Stockholm County there are 340 000 real-estate units of which 85% are single-family lots, 5% are blocks of flats, 5% industrial properties and finally 5% are farming or forest properties. Focusing on the City of Stockholm there are 60 000 real-estate units, circa one-third of the County's real-estate units when holiday cottages are excluded. Urban land is often held by leasehold (*tomträtt*), with the common forms of tenure being fee simple ownership, tenancy and co-operative tenancy.

Leasehold means that the municipality (or the state) grants exclusive possession of the land to the lessee for an unspecified term in consideration of an annual rent. The rent is constant for a fixed term of no less than ten years. In other respects leasehold is quite similar to freehold. For example, the lessee has the right to transfer the leasehold property to a third party. The lessee may also use his lease as collateral for a loan. In the Stockholm region, especially within the City of Stockholm, leasehold plays an important role. In the County as a whole, there are 40 000 leasehold properties of which 30 000 are found within the City of Stockholm where most lots are held by leasehold. In 1991 leasehold rents in the City amounted to over one billion SEK, accounting for 5% of the City's total revenues.

Renting (hyra) is a very usual form of tenure in Sweden. A building or a part of a building can be leased for use as a residence or for other purposes; indeed 60% of the housing stock in the City of Stockholm (390 000 dwellings) are rental units. Concerning commercial property about eight million sq m of space is rented.

Co-operative tenancy (*bostadsrätt*) is a form of tenure offered only by co-operative housing societies (*bostadsrättsföreningar*). The co-operative tenants are the members of the society. In the legal sense, the society owns all the dwellings, but the member has certain ownership rights in the property. For instance, the co-operative tenant may sell the lease. Co-operative ownership is quite widespread, accounting for about 15% of the total housing stock in the City of Stockholm.

Floor area ratios (gross floor area over the site area) for different parts of the city varies from close to 0/1 in undeveloped districts to 2.6/1 in Norrmalm, the district containing Stockholm's commercial centre.

The percentage mix of housing and commercial facilities also varies among the districts. Analysis based upon the ratio of commercial premises to total gross floor space indicates the occurrence of a number of typical employment zones (more than 75% commercial premises) including Norrmalm and the harbour areas.

8.1.3   Land ownership

The municipalities have substantial land holdings. For example the City of Stockholm owns almost 70% of its total land area of 188 sq km, the remainder, which consists primarily of open space and parks, is mainly owned by the State. In addition the city owns land in other municipalities in the region. The holdings in these municipalities amount to 431 sq km, i.e. Stockholm's holdings in other municipalities are twice as big as the city itself (and more than three times as large as the city's holdings within its own territory).

The city – or its corporations – can also act as developers, i.e. implement residential, commercial or industrial development. For example, a large percentage of Swedish housing is in blocks owned by municipal housing corporations (*allmännyttiga bostadsföretag*). In the City of Stockholm these companies manage almost 50% of the total stock of rental flats, corresponding to 30% of all dwellings in the City. Furthermore single-family housing plays a relatively subordinate role, with 42 000 private dwellings, corresponding to 10% of the total housing stock.

8.2 THE SWEDISH PLANNING SYSTEM

In 1947 building legislation was adopted, which gave the public authorities a strong position in decisions on land use. This gave the authorities the ability to decide not only where, and when construction could take place. Most of the planning powers were allocated to the municipalities but the state was given an overriding responsibility, including examination and ratification of municipal development plans. However new legislation was adopted in 1987, including the Planning and Building Act and a parallel special Act on Conservation and Management of Natural Resources. These have changed the conditions for planning by offering the municipalities greater independence. State ratification of development plans has ceased with the state only likely to take action against plans for extraordinary reasons, such as a conflict with specified national interests.

In the municipalities the Executive Committee has overriding responsibility for planning activities though normally planning and building issues are handled by the Department of Planning and Development Control. However, when the development is comprehensive or complex, the decision to produce a plan, and guidelines for the preparation are given by the Executive Committee. In these cases, a programme for the plan is often formulated.

The planning system contains three types of plans. The **regional plan** (*regionplan*) may be set up whenever two or more municipalities find the need for a joint plan covering such common matters as highway systems, airfields, recreation areas, and common water-supply and sewage systems. The regional plan can be seen as a guideline for the municipalities involved. However, a compulsory **comprehensive plan** (*översiktsplan*) should be set up in all municipalities. This plan covers the entire municipality and gives a broad indication of how land is to be used for different purposes, such as housing, traffic arteries and public areas. The comprehensive plan is based on a population forecast, analyses of economic conditions and special surveys thus constituting a guideline for the detailed planning.

Detailed development plans (*detaljplan*) regulate in detail the boundaries for buildings, blocks, streets and public places. The plan often specifies the number of buildings that may be put in a lot, the height of the buildings, the maximum floor space area and other details as may be considered necessary. An adopted plan is legally binding and entitles the municipality to acquire land to be employed for public purposes. A detailed development plan is required before urban development can take place. The plan creates a building right for a specific purpose and extent and usually encompasses between two to ten blocks. The two main purposes of the plan are to demarcate common areas (streets and parks) from building sites, and to regulate the development of the building site with regard to use, building area, building height, number of storeys, etc. The property owner is permitted to use the land in accordance with its provisions although these development rights are limited in time to an 'implementation period', which can vary between 5 and 15 years. Within the area covered by a detailed development plan, a **property regulation plan** (*fastighetsplan*) can be prepared if deemed necessary. The plan lacks stipulations concerning building volume or architectural design, its purpose being rather to regulate subdivision, easements for mains and so forth.

Finally, a **building permit** (*bygglov*) is required to erect new buildings, make additions, use the premises for substantially different purposes, and undertake important changes in the layout or structure, etc. In areas covered by a detailed development plan, a building permit is also necessary for changing the colour of a façade and for other measures which substantially affect the exterior appearance of a building. A permit is also required to demolish a building within an area covered by a detailed development plan (*rivningslov*). Furthermore, a permit may be required for grading, filling, tree-cutting etc. (*marklov*). In principle, a building permit may not be granted for measures which conflict with the detailed development plan (or the property regulation plan). Minor deviations are allowed, if they are in accordance with the purposes of the plan.

In preparing a detailed development plan and property regulation plan, the municipality shall confer with property owners, co-operative tenants and tenants in rental units as well as with organizations and individuals who have a vital interest in the planning proposal. Concerning building permits, the municipality must inform such parties that an application has been made for a building permit. The parties concerned then have the right to appeal against the municipality's decision regarding the plan and the building permit.

8.2.1 Provision of local infrastructure

Within an area covered by a detailed development plan, the municipality normally is responsible for water, sewerage, streets and parks. In order to cover its costs, the municipality has the right to collect fees from property owners. For water and sewerage facilities, the fee may be collected partly in the form of a one-time charge to cover construction costs and partly as an annual fee for operating and maintenance costs. The degree of cost defrayment for a municipal water and sewerage system is normally 100%. In areas covered by detailed development plans, the municipality has the right to charge a fee covering construction costs for local streets and parks. Operating costs, however, must be financed by local taxes. The inclination of the municipalities to actually collect street fees varies within Sweden as a whole, but in the Stockholm region, the goal is normally to defray 100% of the costs.

It should be emphasized that the system described above does not apply when the municipality leases the land. In this case fees are not charged for construction costs (however, the lessee must pay special use charges for water and sewer services).

8.3   DIFFERENT WAYS TO IMPLEMENT A DEVELOPMENT PROJECT

Generally the implementation of a development project in Sweden can be classified according to two key factors (Kalbro, 1992). First, land ownership within the development area and whether the land is in private or municipal ownership when the development is initiated. Second, the developer's role in the process and specially whether the municipality prepares the detailed development plan on its own, or involves the developer in plan preparation. Based on these two factors, four models for implementing a development project can be discerned (Figure 8.2).

The Swedish planning and approval system is constructed largely on the basis of model 1, i.e. it is based on private land ownership where the property owner is not expected to take an active part in shaping the detailed development plan. In reality, however, a large proportion of the projects which are implemented are more closely related to one of the other three models. Indeed the majority of development projects in the City of Stockholm are implemented according to model 4. In this case the land is owned initially by the City which chooses a developer at an early stage of the process. After this the City prepares the detailed development plan in co-operation with the developer. In other words, the developer is chosen before work on the development plan is started.

The City can then either freely choose the developer it deems suitable, or organize a competition. Usually, sites are allocated according to a system with different quotas for each category of developer according to a specific order of priority or on other politically determined grounds. Site-allocation competitions are sometimes arranged whereby a municipality invites developers to submit proposals for a certain site, and the developer who submits the best proposal with regard to quality and cost is allowed

	The developer does not participate actively in plan preparation	The developer and the municipality prepare the development plan jointly
The developer owns the land	Model 1	Model 2
The municipality owns the land	Model 3	Model 4

Figure 8.2   Models for implementing a development project

to purchase the land. Once the developer is chosen, a preliminary development agreement is drafted by the municipality and the developer to regulate matters such as responsibility for further planning and design, and distribution of costs between the municipality and the developer. When the detailed development plan has been completed, a final development agreement is drawn up, which regulates transfer of land, economic matters, and responsibility for various measures (Kalbro *et al.*, 1989).

8.3.1   Development activities in the City of Stockholm

In the City of Stockholm between 2000 and 3000 dwellings were constructed annually during the latter part of the 1980s and the early 1990s with single-family houses making up a small fraction of the total. Regarding commercial property new space was created in the City of Stockholm at the rate of between 200 000 and 600 000 sq m annually, peaking in 1989 (Figure 8.3). However this rate of input declined rapidly in the early 1990s to a situation where virtually no new commercial premises were being built.

8.4   PUBLIC–PRIVATE PARTNERSHIPS: OPPORTUNITIES AND CONSTRAINTS IN URBAN PLANNING

8.4.1   The framework for planning, construction and the property market

During the last decade the structure for decision-making has changed in Sweden. This change can be observed in the private market as well as in

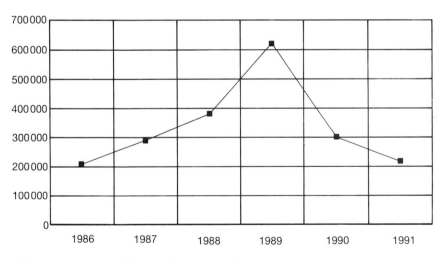

Figure 8.3 Net addition of commercial space, 1986–91 (sq m), the city of Stockholm

the public sector. In the private sector, traditionally, decisions have been made in accordance with the economic principles of the market while to a large extent decisions in the public domain have occurred within the framework set by laws and regulations. One feature of this change is an increased collaboration between public and private interests, which has significantly impacted upon the field of urban planning (Statens Offentliga Utredningar, 1990). In addition the methods for planning have essentially changed and within this formal structure for decision-making sit other administrative frameworks.

In these circumstances where laws and regulations are not providing the basis for planning activities a number of informal channels are often operating between the actors. For example, relationships of different origin can be observed between the political system and the private corporations. In some cases the initiative is taken by the private actor with the aim of influencing the focus, comprehensiveness or design in a development project. When the initiative is taken by the public authority, the usual aim is to obtain external economic support for investments in infrastructure. In addition, a network of informal relationship has also emerged between the citizens on the one hand, and municipal boards and bureaucracy on the other. For example, citizens may make demands and suggestions concerning urban development and service provision with the role of the traditional planning system reduced to merely uttering a juridical expression of prior decisions that have been made within the informal decision-making system (Cars, 1992).

8.4.2   Public–private partnerships

As a result of structural changes in society, incentives have developed for both private and public actors to change their traditional behaviour and roles in the urban planning process. The need for direct collaboration has subsequently increased. Regarding these actors in the private market, the explanation for the changed behaviour can be sought from two sources. First, interest among private corporations to participate actively in the development of creative and profitable niches in the urban environment has increased. This interest concerns space for commercial use and employment as well as infrastructure investments in, for example, roads and other transport facilities. The second reason for private actors to engage actively in the urban planning process is a desire to promote urban developments that could be regarded as profitable long-term investments (Cars *et al.*, 1991).

In parallel to this change are motives by the public authorities to include private actors in the planning and decision-making process. Due to constraints on the public economy the resources available for maintaining existing infrastructure and investing in new structures has declined. For this reason collaboration with private actors is sought, with the aim of financing necessary infrastructure investments. This is not, however, unique to Sweden. The same pattern can be observed in most industrialized countries (Kaiser and Burby, 1988).

8.4.3   Negotiated agreements versus public planning

The described changes in the process have caused different reactions among the affected actors. Analysis show that the actors are pleased with the use of negotiation as a method for decision-making in urban planning as well as the outcome of the negotiations. In most cases both muni-cipal decision-makers and corporate representatives have judged the actual outcome better than if alternative methods for decision-making had been used. However, collaboration between private–public and negotiated agreements has also faced extensive criticism in the arena of public debate. The critique addresses two problems: democracy and efficiency in the chosen methods for decision-making.

8.4.4   Democratic aspects

Critics claim that political guidance in the planning process as well as public information and participation have suffered when negotiations are chosen as a method of decision-making in planning. It is claimed that negotiations have put legitimate political interests aside. In negotiated agreements on urban development, the contracts between municipalities and private investors are often signed early in the process, either before or in connection with that part of the planning phase where programme activity is carried out. Despite the fact that such agreements are normally con-ditioned by the municipal council's adoption of a development plan, they exercise substantial influence on planning activities that follow in the latter parts of the planning process. The municipality is obliged to give support to the agreement in order to keep up its credibility. If for example the municipal council were to make deviations, it would harm the relationships with the private actor and make further collaboration difficult.

From a public perspective criticism may be raised from a similar starting-point. During the 1960s and 1970s Sweden experienced an inten-sive debate about public participation in the planning process and issues concerning urban development. In this debate the authorities were criti-cized for being insensitive to demands from the public. It was also claimed that public opinion was sought only in the latter stages of the process, too late to be considered seriously. With the adoption of a new Planning and Building Act in 1987 many people perceived that this legislation was in response to the demands for improved public information and influence.

Thus the controversial nature of negotiated agreements is not too surprising as such negotiated agreements between municipalities and private investors were in opposition to the legal system which formerly prevailed.

8.4.5 Rationality of the chosen methods for decision-making

Criticism has also been raised concerning the efficiency of negotiated agreements. From a general point of view, the question of efficiency is relevant as many negotiated development projects have actually become impossible to implement. Groups and individuals adversely affected by a project often express their disapproval with public planners and politicians through widespread media coverage. The pressure has led to alterations of plans as well as postponements and delays in implementation representing a waste of intellectual resources and a loss of money. As the Planning and Building Act require that detailed plans should be subject to consultations with affected parties and put on public display before adoption this offers opponents a strong position for challenging the negotiated agreement which as a result is placed in jeopardy.

8.4.6 Public–private collaboration in urban development

The effectiveness of negotiations in urban planning can be measured in relation to the expediency of the agreements which are reached. Evaluation shows that in certain cases the municipality has gained advantages by implementing the best alternative to a negotiated settlement instead of the current agreement. In other cases the municipality would have obtained a better outcome if the negotiating situation had been formulated in an alternative way. This scepticism and criticism is primarily related to concerns about the availability of information and knowledge as well as the preparations which are made before the negotiations commence (Cars, 1992).

From a democratic viewpoint there is a demand for a model for decision-making which facilitates public participation as well as political discussion and the formation of attitudes before strategic decisions are made. Criticism is often based on the fact that public participation and grass-root expressions came much too late in the planning process in order to be considered seriously. A planning process with a different structure would be able to satisfy some of these requirements. It is not the negotiations in themselves which are the problem, but rather the way in which they are handled by the parties involved. In essence, negotiated agreements on urban development provides advantages. At the same time implementation is often criticized. Thus in order to maintain advantages and at the same time eliminate or reduce problems, changes in the established planning practice is required.

The role of comprehensive planning must alter in order to facilitate changes that are needed to make the urban area more attractive and compatible. Two perspectives should be established. First, from the municipality's point of view, it is vital to develop a physical structure which is desirable in the long-term and which should facilitate discussions and detailed planning in the future. This outline phase should also be formulated in a manner that clearly illustrates any conflicts in the form of land use contemplated, as well as describing all of the possible alternatives to the development which is recommended by the municipal administration.

Second, this should occur within a framework that recognizes that non-municipal actors may also wish to express opinions about development and to take measures to push it in a certain direction or to favour a particular geographic location. For this reason, it is very important during the work on the comprehensive plan to make a careful study of those areas which are likely to be in demand for new developments by parties outside of the municipal apparatus. These demands may involve centrally located areas of land which have lost most of their earlier economic attractiveness, such as harbours, industrial estates, and other sites. This also applies to zones, corridors and municipal districts with a strong growth potential, areas which require more detailed studies to be carried out in conjunction with the comprehensive plan. These studies should attempt to survey the nature of the claims that are likely to arise in relation to the development of the area in question, as well as the source of such claims. Through such preparations, the municipality will be better equipped for future negotiations as potential development alternatives are evaluated.

Based on comprehensive planning activity a programme for development is worked out, including a detailed description of the actual conditions in the area. The latter should reflect the ownership of land, the character of the built environment, traffic and environmental conditions. Under these circumstances where competing development interests exist, the programme should propose alternative paths for development. The consequences of the development alternatives should also be considered, with respect to the way in which the development may influence the plan area, as well as its surrounding locality. Once the political stance is clarified, preliminary agreements can be reached. This may involve agreements about land appropriation as well as arrangements which regulate the relationships between parties.

When the programme conforms to such guidelines the main grounds for the criticism which is mounted against negotiative planning from a democratic viewpoint can be set aside. Thus this process simultaneously facilitates political discussion and steering, while giving the general public the opportunity to observe and participate in the process, and the media opportunity to scrutinize it. Also from the perspective of efficiency, the suggested alterations of the traditional planning process makes improvements possible. Furthermore the openness of the procedure reduces the risk that a project will be stopped or postponed in its later stages. At the same time the structure of the process encourages both private and public actors to develop creative solutions with achievement of mutual gains providing a guiding incentive. In this way the plan can be formulated with a potential for better results than if other methods of decision-making had been chosen.

8.5 BASIC CHARACTERISTICS OF THE SWEDISH ECONOMY AND PROPERTY MARKET DURING THE 1980s AND EARLY 1990s

The Swedish economy around 1980 was characterized by high inflation and slow growth; the budget deficit was largely due to high public-sector expenditure and private savings were very low or negative. The government and the municipal public sector mainly financed their growth by increased taxes and new loans. In 1980, the minority Liberal government in conjunction with the Social Democrats limited tax deductibility of interest payments to 50%. This reform caused the after-tax interest rate to rise dramatically, directly causing property prices to remain nominally unchanged or sink, whereas the high inflation rate (10–12%) at that time should have promoted nominal growth in property prices.

In 1982 the new Social Democratic government twice devalued the Swedish currency, the total effect being a devaluation of some 20% relative to the main currencies of competitors on the international markets. As a consequence the Swedish economy accelerated dramatically. The international upswing in business cycles, that started at about the same time, helped to create boom conditions in Sweden. Since the Stockholm area for decades has been the driving force in the Swedish economy, it was obvious that the greatest interest for investment was focused on Stockholm. The demand for commercial space, as well as housing, rose and rents and property prices started to increase in real terms in the middle of the 1980s. Investments in property grew rapidly, led by insurance companies, real estate and construction firms. The investment activity of insurance companies was augmented by the abolition of limits for direct investment in real estate. In the case of construction and real estate firms tax-free funds built up under the earlier tax system were used for new investment without any tax consequences. The Stockholm Stock Exchange had a boom, which created large amounts of capital looking for investment opportunities.

Furthermore in 1986 the regulations of the capital market were abolished, followed one year later by removal of limits in exchange controls.

Table 8.1 Indicators of the Swedish economy 1980–92

Year	1980–90	1991	1992
GNP	+2,0	+1,8	−1,2
Inflation	+7,6	+9,7	+2,3
Real interest rate	+4,4	+5,1	+5,8

The deregulation of the capital market led banks and financial firms to switch to long-term financing of real estate investments, previously only long-term mortgage firms had the right to issue long-term bonds. New actors tried to expand their market share and explicit risk analysis was often considered not to be necessary. The real estate market suddenly had 'free' access to low-cost borrowed money and increasingly real estate investments were financed by less equity investment.

At the beginning of the 1990s economic indicators suddenly became negative compared to both the economy of the late 1980s and major competitor countries. Sweden was forced to accept a floating currency in the autumn of 1992, amounting to a *de facto* devaluation of some 20%. A large budget deficit, the worst economic recession since the 1930s and some political instability in the parliament has led to a Swedish interest rate that is higher than most of the OECD-countries (Table 8.1).

The outcome has been decreased demand for business and commercial space as banks and mortgage firms have raised their interest margins to cover losses, caused by the property boom. This inevitably increases the cost of capital for construction and real estate firms. In combination with a higher frequency of mortgage foreclosure, the effective squeeze of borrowed money has forced many well-run real estate firms into bankruptcy. The mortgagees, mainly banks, have been forced to accept a *de facto* ownership of property, formerly owned by real estate firms. The government has had to step in to guarantee and reconstruct the banking system, with strict guidelines being set for valuation, risk analysis and property management.

8.5.1 Rents, prices and yields

The prices of single-family homes were unchanged in nominal terms during the early 1980s. In 1985 prices started to rise, a trend which accelerated during 1987–90, the period of real boom in the Swedish economy. Prices peaked in early 1991 and during 1992 prices of single-family homes declined by some 25% in nominal terms (Figure 8.4).

The real prices show a cyclical pattern, with falling prices for approximately 5 years followed by a price appreciation for 4 to 5 years during the

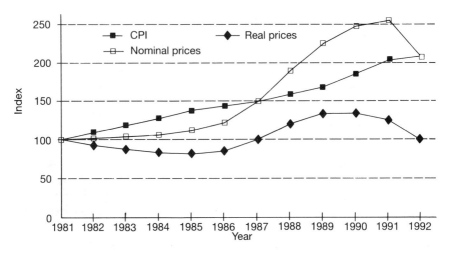

Figure 8.4 Nominal and real price indices for single-family homes in Greater Stockholm and consumer price index

late 1980s after which the trend swings back. Turnover on the market is normally 4–5% of the stock and net additions circa 3% of the stock were highest in the early 1980s. However at the end of the 1980s new construction decreased to about half this volume; indeed building of new single-family homes in the City of Stockholm is about 0.5% of the stock per year and forecasts for 1993 indicate an even lower volume. The decline in construction activity is largely due to the recession of the economy, high real interest rates, falling household incomes and reduced subsidies to housing from 1993. These changes have affected site prices negatively. For example in the City of Stockholm site prices in good locations were more than a million SEK in 1990, but by 1993 the price level of sites for single-family homes was less than half the 1990 level.

In Sweden all housing rents are subject to control, with rents determined by the average cost of capital, operating and maintenance expenses of the public housing companies. The rents of dwellings owned by private companies are compared with rents in the public housing sector, and are accepted if they do not deviate more than 5% from public housing rents. Since the mid 1980s these rules have been questioned and expectations of more market determined rents raised. Rents in real terms were approximately unchanged during the early 1980s although increases in construction costs, tax reform and introduction of VAT on operating costs has led to a sharp rise in costs of public housing companies. These cost increases were directly transformed to rent increases and between 1989 and 1992 the nominal housing rents were doubled throughout Sweden, corresponding to a real increase of about 50%. These cost increases have led to rents near the market level almost everywhere in the Greater Stockholm area, except for the central parts of the City of Stockholm and in special locations, like waterfronts. In peripheral locations vacancy rates have increased from almost none to about 3–4%, which is considered high in a market used to excess demand caused by the rent control. The turnover has also increased and is about 8% a year on average, though lower in older houses in central locations and higher than average in new houses in the periphery.

The market for cooperative dwellings shows the same pattern as the single-family home prices (Figure 8.4). Price differences due to location are large. In prime locations a cooperative apartment was priced at about 15.000 SEK per sq m when prices peaked in 1990; since then urban prices have fallen 40 to 50%. In more peripheral locations cooperative apartments can be bought for about 1000 SEK per sq m (1993 prices).

Rents for commercial space, mainly offices and shops, are determined by the market. The 1980s and especially the latter half of the decade was characterized by a rapid growth of commercial rents. This was most pronounced in the central business district of Stockholm, but rents in more peripheral locations also increased. The duration of most rental agreements is 3 to 5 years and rents are normally indexed annually. Due to the increasing inflation in the end of the 1980s market rents for new agreements peaked in 1989–90. Retail rents in prime locations are normally higher than for offices (Figure 8.5) and average rents in central parts of the City of Stockholm are 30 to 40% lower than top rents.

Since 1990 rents for both offices and shops have fallen dramatically,

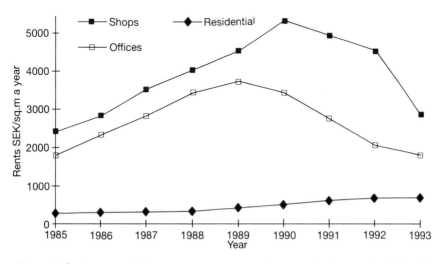

Figure 8.5   Rents in SEK/sq m per annum, prime location Stockholm city, 1985–93

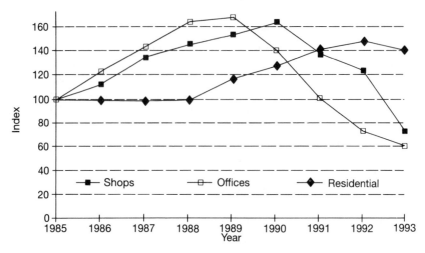

Figure 8.6 Real rent indices (1985 = 100), prime location Stockholm

indeed in 1993 real rents were lower than those in the middle of the 1980s. (Figure 8.6). The main explanation being due to the massive overproduction of new commercial space during 1980s. Excess supply has been 100.000 to 200.000 sq m or more per year or about 1.5 to 3% of the stock. Even in 1990–1, after the market turned downward the excess supply was 2% of the stock. The net additions to the stock remained high in 1992 and the absorption rate is likely to remain low for several subsequent years. Furthermore the vacancy rate which was 2 to 3% during the 1980s but increased to 10–15% in 1993, the highest level in recent times. Even if demand levels reached those of the 1980s it would take 4–5 years before vacancy rates reduced to 2–3% again. Hence construction activity has been reduced to completing existing projects, with new projects either cancelled or postponed.

Regarding income property in prime locations, residential rents had increased by 16% in real terms over the period 1985–9. At the same time yields fell from approximately 8% in the beginning of the 1980s to approximately 2.5% in 1989, since then yields for residential income property have increased to 8–10% by 1993. However the market has a low turnover – 2 to 3% and market information is thin and uncertain. The extraordinary price trends for residential income property in central parts of Stockholm are more apparent in the long-term perspective. With specific reference to buildings erected in the 1930s and 1940s and subject to only normal maintenance (Figure 8.7).

Nominal prices were more or less unchanged up to 1970, when a slow appreciation started, mainly due to the increasing inflation rate and introduction of government subsidies for renewal of older buildings. Also

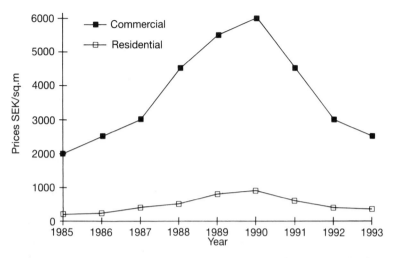

Figure 8.7   Prices per sq m of income property, prime location Stockholm city, 1985–93

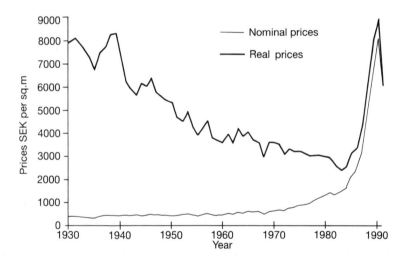

Figure 8.8   Market prices 1930–91 in Stockholm inner city for residential income property, nominal and real (1991 prices) price per sq m
Source: Bejrum *et al.*, 1992.

favourable tax rules encouraged investment in real property. However these prices escalated from 1985 (Figure 8.8). In real terms the extraordinary price trend is even more obvious, due to obsolescence and wear and tear, market prices declined about 2% a year up to 1985, but from

1985 to the peak in 1989–90 prices of 50-year-old buildings increased to
the same level as when buildings were new, that is, around 8000 SEK per
sq m. The price fall in real terms is very dramatic when the market adjusts
to the 'normal' level.

Likewise the price of commercial real property increased throughout
the 1980s, in prime locations prices increased by 200% between 1985 and
1989/90 with yields falling from 7 to 8% to less than 4% in 1989–90.
However since then an oversupplied rental market has seen property
prices in good locations fall back to the nominal level of 1985, which in real
terms means a depreciation of at least 30%. If the drop in prices is
measured from the peak level of 1990, the loss in value is more than two-
thirds. In less attractive locations the supply and demand situation is even
more unbalanced and market rents achieved during 1993 barely cover the
operating expenses. The yields of commercial property in prime locations
is between 8 and 10% in 1993, and for new construction in less attractive
locations in the Greater Stockholm area the market yields are up to 12%.
Investments in commercial property is increasingly being achieved by share
dealings in real-estate firms (indirect real estate). As such transactions are
not registered in the official real-estate sales database, market information
is hence very thin and difficult to interpret. However uncertainty is large
and gives rise to speculation among the parties of the real-estate market
concerning the 'right' price level.

8.6   FUTURE OF INTERACTION BETWEEN THE PLANNING
SYSTEM AND PROPERTY MARKETS

In this chapter recent developments in the Stockholm region with respect
to the planning system and property market have been discussed. In
conclusion it is appropriate to consider those lessons that can be learned,
and also to point out some directions for the future.

During the last decade the property market has been characterized by
large variations in demand and supply. Furthermore in the latter part of
the 1980s supply could not meet the demand and despite dramatically
increased construction activity there remained an unfilled demand with
prices escalating. From an analytical point of view it was obvious that this
situation could not last, and that inevitably a situation would occur in
which the supply would be far larger than demand. Despite this awareness
the main actors did not respond to these signals. Early in the 1990s this
scenario turned to reality and in a very short period of time the shortage
on the market turned into a surplus. In retrospect it seems obvious that
the organization of and the roles played by different actors in the property
market was not efficient. The situation was characterized by the fact that
new roles and relations had emerged within and between the public and
private sectors. In particular the planning system did not meet the needs

and demands of the key actors and as a consequence other methods for planning and collaboration evolved.

Ever since the planning and development process was regulated by law there has been a degree of interdependence between planning authorities and building entrepreneurs in Sweden. During the growth years of the 1960s, politicians had substantial power over the development of urban settlements by virtue of a strong planning system and a stable economy in which plentiful resources were available to individuals as well as to municipalities and county councils. High-standard provision of infrastructure and services were integral parts of the large scale urban building projects which were carried out. The financing could be guaranteed via economic growth and increased tax revenues. However the situation was significantly different in the 1980s. The economy of the municipalities were characterized by constraint and collaboration was sought with private actors, with the aim of financing infrastructure and other public investments. Paralleling this, changes also could be observed in the private sector which became increasingly characterized by specialization, dominated by the production of services for high technology, trade, transport and marketing firms. In expanding regions there was a substantial increase in the demand for office space and the real estate stock in metropolitan areas was considered to be a more secure investment for capital growth than other alternatives. As a consequence strong growth occurred in the real estate market and private actors sought an active role in the planning process. Negotiations became an important method for fulfilling this ambition.

Hence there emerged the need for new methods and a new framework for collaboration between public and private actors. Also, the necessity for a reformulation of the respective roles played by the public and private sectors became obvious. This in turn promoted a political debate and demands for a reorganization of the planning system. However there are a number of questions of principle concerning the *raison d'être* and practice of negotiative planning. As a method, negotiative planning is not a replacement for the established planning processes, rather it implies that planning is an activity which cannot be carried out efficiently if it is restricted to being a completely public activity undertaken within the framework of a formal set of rules. The public sector certainly has a planning monopoly, but it cannot monopolize the pursuit of planning activities. It is not by drawing up the plan blueprint itself that the public sector gains its power over the built environment, but rather by having the right to make decisions about other actors' initiatives. Planning involves a series of decisions which are reached as a result of informal contacts and procedures. This insight constitutes the base for the present discussion on how the professional roles among actors and the system for urban planning can be developed.

8.6.1   The future development of the planning system

In addition to bringing about a suitable pattern of land uses, a planning and approval system must also serve two functions. In the first place the system must be 'simple'; it must be possible to process the developer's/owner's project quickly and smoothly so as to save time and money. Second, the system must be 'democratic', in that other property owners, tenants and municipal residents must be allowed to influence changes in land use. It is often difficult to combine these two functions since 'simplicity' and 'democracy' normally are conflicting requirements for constructing a planning and approval system (Figure 8.9).

Thus, an 'effective' planning and approval system is characterized by the fact that it cannot be changed except at the expense of either 'simplicity' or 'democracy'. In an 'ineffective' system, however, simplicity as well as democracy can be improved. Without a doubt, the Swedish planning system belongs to the latter category, i.e. it is possible to make changes which are positive both from the point of view of simplicity and democracy.

The role of the detailed development plan in the building process should be analysed from the perspective of simplicity. An explicit purpose of the development plan is to legally regulate the relationship between the municipality and the developer, but this form of regulation is unnecessary in many development situations. A building permit in combination with a development agreement is often sufficient. From this point of view, the requirement to prepare a development plan should be relaxed substantially. However, the problem is that this would create a conflict with another important purpose of the development plan, i.e. to allow other actors to influence changes in land use. Many of the formal rules regulating the contents, preparation and approval of the detailed development plan were formulated to satisfy this democratic requirement.

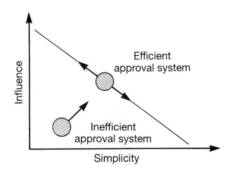

Figure 8.9 'Efficient' and 'inefficient' systems for planning and development control

In terms of resolving this political conflict it is possible to deal with democratic issues in other forms. An obvious solution would appear to be to move opportunities for influence from the detailed development plan – where influence is often more formal than actual – to a less detailed level, where decisions on the broad outlines of land use are made. This means that democratic issues should be linked to a level of decision making somewhere between the current comprehensive plan and the detailed development plan. It could be mentioned that within the framework of the present legislation, the City of Stockholm is trying to resolve the problem by linking democracy and influence to the process of preparing a detailed development plan. In summary this means that municipal planning activities should focus less on the detailed regulation implied by the development plan to a more comprehensive, strategic level. This should enable the building process to function more effectively at the same time as democratic aspects are actually given greater emphasis.

8.6.2   The future development of property markets

The construction, rental and property markets will always move around some indefinite equilibrium point. The slow adjustment of supply to demand give rise to more or less inevitable unbalances. These lags mostly depend on the slow and cumbersome process of programming and production of space for rent or sale and of course upon the special characteristics of the property market, viz locational monopoly, heterogeneity and durability of assets.

On the rental market, changes in demand are registered in one to three months. Vacant space is absorbed subsequently, if there is an initial excess supply. When vacancy rates fall, the decline in rents level out and subsequently cause rents to increase. The property market often has a time lag of half a year or more and real prices of property start to rise because of increased demand for existing property. The construction firms register the increased demand and update old projects or start new ones. However, because of the long programming and production time the new projects will enter the market in, say three years. With ordinary business cycles of 4–8 years, the new construction often has a time lag of 2–3 years. This is apparent in all developed countries. To achieve a more efficient synchronization of demand and supply there is a need for more demand-oriented programming, production and management processes. The forecasted probable net income, largely market rent, has become the benchmark for the possible construction cost, while the reversed reasoning was frequently applied in the period from 1970 to 1990.

In stimulating a more demand-oriented process, there is the need to develop techniques for shortening the time of the programme and production. More market analysis and real estate firms that are financially

160   STOCKHOLM

strong are essential features of a market-oriented approach. In such a market investors and construction firms receive returns on capital related to the risk they conceive. If the real returns of property investment, regardless of new construction or older property, exceed the real interest rate for borrowed money, a functioning capital and real-estate market will be critical in the long run.

Arguably a 'cultural change' in the construction and real estate firms is required. The same argument also holds for the municipal authorities. A new rental law with more market orientation, a working system of managing credit risks in real estate, and more simple and firm taxation of real estate are also needed. This will, hopefully, give a robust framework for the construction and real-estate sector of the economy. On the way, from regulation to market orientation, a lot of effort must concern educational activities aimed at construction and real-estate companies and other actors in the market, for instance tenants and their organization. An efficient market is a market where 'consumer is king', competition among producers is high and transaction costs are low. In Sweden considerable progress is already been taken in that direction.

REFERENCES

Bejrum, H., Lundström, S. and Szynkier, S. (1992) *Marknadsvärden och direktavkastning för bostadshyreshus i Stockholm 1930–1991* (Market values and yields for residential income property in Stockholm 1930–1991), Department of Real Estate Economics, Report No. 19, Royal Institute of Technology, Stockholm (in Swedish).

Cars, G., Lanesjö, B., Westin, P.-H. and Åkerlund, P.-O. (1991) *Public/ Private Co-operation in Urban Planning in Sweden – a Review*, Swedish State Railways and Department of Regional Planning, Royal Institute of Technology, Stockholm.

Cars, G. (1992) *Förhandlingar mellan privata och offentliga aktörer i stadsbyggandet* (Negotiated agreements in urban planning), Department of Regional Planning, Royal Institute of Technology, Stockholm (in Swedish).

Kaiser E.J. and Burby, R.J. (1988) Exactions in managing growth: the land-use planning perspective, in R. Alterman (ed.), *Private Supply of Public Services*, New York University Press, New York and London.

Kalbro, T. (1992) *Markexploatering* (Land development), Lantmäteriverket (The National Land Survey of Sweden), Report 1992:4, Lantmäteriverket, Gävle (in Swedish).

Kalbro, T., Mattsson, H. and Miller, T. (1989) Development Agreements for Residential Development in Sweden, in D.R. Porter and L.L. Marsh (eds), *Development Agreements: Practice, Policy and Prospects*, The Urban Land Institute, Washington, DC.

Statens Offentliga Utredningar (1990) *Demokrati och Makt i Sverige – Maktutredningens huvudrapport* (Democracy and Power in Sweden – Report from the government investigation on powers in the Swedish society), Allmänna förlaget, SOU 1990:40, Stockholm (in Swedish).

9

Copenhagen

_____ *Kai Lemberg*

In this chapter characteristics of the Danish planning system are considered with particular reference to the metropolitan land and property market in Copenhagen. Generally private ownership prevails but there are a number of partly independent property markets and a large semi-public sector of non-profit building societies concerned with high-quality social housing. Key influences on the property market include the macro-economic cycle, and the phasing of regional and urban development.

Danish planning legislation (Ministry of the Environment, 1991) dates from 1938 with the Communal (Municipal) Planning Act, followed by the Regional Planning Act of 1949. Reform was carried out during the 1970s, with four main planning acts, establishing three levels of planning: national, regional and municipal, with emphasis placed at the municipal level. In 1991 all planning laws were embodied in one general Planning Act. Against this background, visions of metropolitan planning in the Greater Copenhagen Region and of municipal planning in the City of Copenhagen are presented. This is related to the operation, structure and performance of the property market. However, statistical limitations imposed by data means that these relationships cannot be assessed quantitatively, but only in qualitative terms. A case study of major interest, the development of the central harbour area in Copenhagen, is discussed in relation to planning policies and the scope for public private partnership arrangements.

9.1 THE PLANNING SYSTEM

9.1.1 Danish planning legislation

The first meaningful planning legislation in Denmark was the Town Planning Act of 1938, the effect of which was delayed by the Second World War. This legislation introduced rational, comprehensive town planning at

European Cities, Planning Systems and Property Markets Edited by James Berry and Stanley McGreal. Published in 1995 by E & FN Spon. ISBN 0419 18940 8.

the municipal level focusing on a detailed land use plan. Later the act was supplemented by regional zoning legislation, starting in Copenhagen and the largest provincial towns in 1949. Following general municipal and county reform in 1970 planning changes were introduced. These comprised urban/rural zoning whereby all land in Denmark was classified as either urban land where development might proceed within the framework set by municipal town plans, or rural land where urban development was prohibited and land had to remain in agricultural, woodland or recreational use. Furthermore two Regional Planning Acts in 1973 (one for the Metropolitan Copenhagen Region, one for the rest of Denmark and for national planning) introduced obligatory regional planning for all Danish counties and the combined metropolitan region consisting of the two central cities of Copenhagen and Frederiksberg and three surrounding counties. The Town Planning Act of 1975 further decentralized planning to the municipalities with only a minor degree of state control, and introduced public participation at a much broader scale. A final measure, the Urban Renewal and Residential Rehabilitation Act of 1982 superseded former slum clearance laws.

Municipal town planning comprises a general communal plan and, within this structure a large number of successive small, detailed plans (local plans) for a single block or more usually for a few blocks. However it is only the local plans that are directly binding on land and property owners, developers and construction companies. The 1991 Planning Act simplified matters and at the same time provided more decentralized planning powers to counties and communes. However in the City of Copenhagen, where a more complicated administrative structure prevails (including six mayors and one lord mayor) relative to other communes, town planning originally was under the direction of the mayor for technical affairs, architecture and planning. Later responsibility for planning was transferred to the lord mayor in order to increase his power as the responsible politician for economic planning as well as physical planning.

9.1.2   Planning in the metropolitan Copenhagen region

Immediately after the Second World War there was general political concern regarding public control of the expected urban growth of Greater Copenhagen. An unofficial plan, but nevertheless backed by public-sector finances, the so-called Finger Plan of 1947 encompassed Copenhagen, Frederiksberg and the surrounding suburbs up to a distance of 15 km. The proposal was to concentrate further urban development in this metropolitan region along existing and planned suburban radial railway lines ('S-lines') and to keep the wedges between them free of urban development, as agricultural areas, woodlands or for recreational use. Following negotiations with the communes, all land in the metropolitan region was subsequently classified in urban and rural zones. In the latter urban development was forbidden.

The Finger Plan report was accepted by all political parties of the Folketing (Parliament) and enshrined in the 1949 Urban Regulation Act. As rural classification of land did not deprive the owners of any existing market value, but only of a possible property profit in the case of unplanned urban growth, this was not considered an expropriation, but a general planning regulation. Thus, no compensation was paid, except in a few cases, where expenses actually had been incurred by the owners to prepare a parcelling out plan. The Finger Plan through the clear distinction between urban and rural land established two levels of land prices with a marked difference in value. The plan functioned reasonably well during the suburbanization process until the 1960s, when it proved necessary to regulate the land market outside the borders of the Finger Plan. Consequently the concept of the metropolitan region was widened to include the whole of North Zealand, from Elsinore in the north to Roskilde in the west and Koge in the south.

A new regional plan, strongly influenced by the growth of population and traffic during the 1960s, was published by the Regional Council, a cooperation between all counties and communes in North Zealand, in 1973 (Metropolitan Council, 1978). This supplemented the existing one-centre metropolitan structure (the old city in Copenhagen) with a diagonal 'A-zone' of superior regional activities comprising four regional nodes of concentrated shopping, service trades and public service centres. West of this activity corridor new reserves of land for urban development including dwellings, work places, shops and local public services were located, producing space for up to 2.5 million inhabitants. Thereby, the prospective urban land market was considerably widened.

The regional plan was based on growth assumptions, but in reality 1973 was to become the last year of total regional growth with the population of 1.8 million reducing in subsequent years to 1.7 million. The Copenhagen metropolitan agglomeration had entered the desuburbanization phase, in which population growth mostly occurred in small towns with less than 5000 habitants.

9.1.3 Planning in the City of Copenhagen

In 1954 a blueprint Master Plan for the City of Copenhagen was published (Copenhagen Chief City Engineer, 1954). This proposed three strategies, namely in the historic city and Christianshavn, areas classified for preservation, a stop to high-rise urban building; second, promotion of large-scale residential urban renewal in the nineteenth-century working-class quarters surrounding the old centre; and finally for the outer parts of the commune, mostly built during the twentieth century after incorporation into Copen-

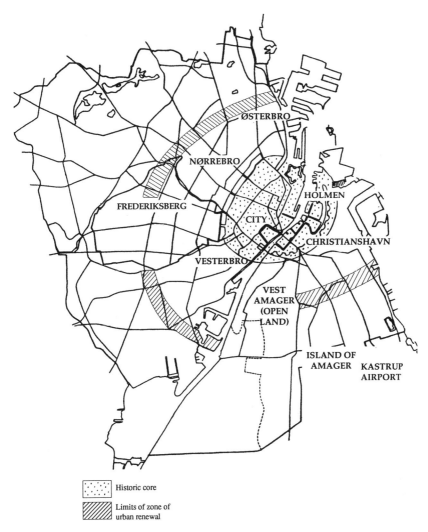

Figure 9.1   Zones relating to the strategies proposed in the 1954 Master Plan

hagen in 1901–2, the status quo was to be observed in principle in which local centres performed an important role (Figure 9.1). The plan also proposed a primary road network for through traffic and improvements of public transport including underground metro lines through central Copenhagen. While serving as a basic framework for detailed town plans through the following twenty years, it was never followed up by a 'final' master plan. Indeed subsequent town planning policy adhered to the functionalistic planning theory of le Corbusier, aiming at functional separation into residential, industrial and commercial quarters, and keeping the central city as a multifunctional superior centre.

The Master Plan (and the Finger Plan) largely underestimated the development of private car traffic, and correspondingly over-evaluated the competitiveness of public transport. Rapid growth in road transportation from the mid 1950s and during the 1960s raised questions of road capacity, congestion, deteriorating public transport passenger figures, and environmental hazards of noise and air pollution. This period of rapid economic growth resulted in ambitious transport infrastructure plans focusing primarily upon urban motorways, but also including plans for a large underground metro network, a new port at the eastern part of Kastrup airport, which was planned to be removed to Saltholm island in the middle of the Sound, and a proposed bridge for road and rail transport between Denmark and Sweden. A commercial city centre extension ('City West') was planned west of the central station (Inner Vesterbro), and a belt of new towns with a total of more than 100 000 inhabitants was planned on the vacant publicly owned West (Vest) Amager which had been freed from its former military use. At the same time very successful pedestrianization took place of city centre shopping streets and small squares.

The growth philosophy broke down in the early 1970s, with the first oil crisis, economic recession and financial austerity. The state withdrew promises of 100% payment of urban motorways and the private sector became increasingly reluctant to invest in sites and property. Furthermore the population began to react against major road plans. Against this background and to comply with the Planning Reform the City of Copenhagen had, like all other communes, to prepare an overall communal plan for physical development. This gave rise to political conflicts within the City Council, between the city and the state, and between municipal politicians and citizens. The worst of these conflicts, relevant to the land and property market, concerned urban renewal methods in the old working-class residential quarter of Inner Norrebro containing many slum dwellings from the second half of the nineteenth century. The city council undertook, without much public consultation, a large-scale renewal with clearance of whole blocks, followed by the building of new modern social tenement blocks of high material standards (Svensson, 1981; Lemberg, 1981) resulting in large-scale displacement of low-income residents.

The Copenhagen Communal Plan of 1985 (Casabella, 1987) experienced many years of delay and only was adopted and accepted by the State in 1989. Infrastructure plans for motorways, metro lines, a new Saltholm Airport, the City West plan and the West Amager plan were abandoned. What emerged was a more pragmatic Communal Plan without specific vision, apart from the desire to change Copenhagen from an industrial to a service city. The plan also envisaged the continuation of more modest urban residential renewal, a concentration of commercial harbour activities to the north and east harbours and the conversion of the inner and south harbour sections to other urban functions, primarily service trades. Instead of a comprehensive general planning framework the initiative for change was left to private developers and landlords. In essence the Communal Plan was structured as a strategic plan to enable detailed decision-making, one outcome being a rapid increase in land values in areas with investment plans.

A revision of the plan in 1991 (City of Copenhagen, 1991a, 1991b, 1993) added a more European perspective, taking account of the Single Market, presumed Danish and Swedish membership of the EC, and increased competition between European metropolitan cities. Revitalization of the economic growth philosophy of the 1960s was introduced based partly on the new wave of prosperity in the 1980s, and in the belief of a large growth potential stemming from the decision to build a combined road and rail bridge and tunnel between Copenhagen and Malmoe. This, it was assumed, would offer the possibility to create a brand new international service trades city on West Amager, called Orestaden ('The Sound City') with 50 000 service trade work places, including international organizations and firms. The resulting extra traffic was to be managed by building an extra north–south motorway, a central metro line and two light railway lines on the island of Amager, financed by sales of building sites on the publicly owned West Amager (Figure 9.2).

The 1991 revised Communal Plan contained other elements of interest including an emphasis on four specific themes: areas near S-line stations; the waterfront; the Green City; and the historical dimension including building heights. However, the Sound Bridge and the Sound City Plan

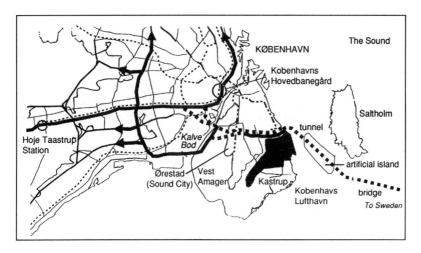

Figure 9.2 Proposed transportation links and associated Sound City development

raised new conflict between economic growth supporters, and ecologists and environmentalists who wished to see higher priorities attached to maritime and urban environmental qualities and to ecological balance than to quantitative growth in population, production and incomes.

9.2   PROPERTY MARKET

9.2.1   Planning policies and the property market

In general, planning policies for Copenhagen can be characterized as primarily trying, usually without success, to pursue goals of economic growth, employment and attraction of enterprises and tourists. Second, goals of improved housing, living conditions and, since the late 1970s, environmental issues are also pursued. Therefore, politicians are sensitive to the presumed benefits of large private projects and infrastructure investments, and try to attract investors through the provision of infrastructural elements. Changing economic conditions, however, affect the financial possibilities of carrying out private as well as public investment plans. Furthermore private investors are for good reason sceptical towards the realism of large public investment plans, such as the City West and the Sound City and are reluctant to start large building projects which depend on the realization of public infrastructure provision.

Private landowners and landlords also must take into consideration the political risk that a governing party or coalition may lose power and be followed by another party with other priorities. Also, most of the grandiose transport and town plans for Copenhagen have collapsed as a combined result of economic recession, lack of financial means and a growing awareness among citizens of the conflict between growth, and ecological and environmental goals. Thus, the general picture has been an unstable public policy towards the property market, sometimes offering extremely promising developments at certain locations, sometimes giving only marginal stimulation to investors and occasionally heavily disappointing them.

Planning policies, regional and local, may be described in three time phases each with a distinctive emphasis. During the 1960s and early 1970s large-scale planning for population growth, work places and transport investment, especially into roads dominated. The late 1970s and the initial years of the 1980s placed emphasis upon planning for residential urban renewal, transition from industrial to service trades, and adoption of public investment to overcome stringent economic conditions. The third phase commencing in the mid 1980s was based upon an internationally oriented growth philosophy and the expected dynamics of the EC, and focused on the road/rail Sound Bridge and a new Sound City on West Amager (Lemberg, 1992).

However to private sector owners, investors and developers many factors other than physical planning are important viz the rate of interest; the rate of inflation; rental levels and legislation; demographic decline in Copenhagen and the inner suburbs; rules of property taxation; the changing phases of the business cycle and structural changes in trade and industry. Most of these affect the general level of land prices, but some are specific to certain areas or districts.

9.2.2   Structure and operation of the property market

According to Danish legislation and planning traditions private ownership of land and premises is not connected to any automatic building right. The latter, if any, depends on land-use decisions according to urban/rural zoning and to town-planning decisions made by the municipalities. All construction requires a building permit from the municipal council, to which different conditions are stipulated, including accordance with a local (town) plan for the area. Thus, beyond locational qualities of the site and usual supply/demand factors such as scarcity of land and floor space, the site price depends upon its urban/rural zoning status, allowed land uses, plot ratios and accessibility.

Furthermore the operation of the land market represents the interaction of a myriad of factors and interest groups incorporating public and private interventions; national, regional and local interests; legislative controls; use sectors; financial and fiscal inputs; and the economic cycle (Figure 9.3). Key actors in the market include on the supply side: landowners, builders and construction companies, building societies, urban renewal societies, the building industry and financial institutions (banks, mortgage societies). On the demand side current and future users, split by sector into residents, trades and industries, and public institutions. Also there is an 'intervening side' with politicians representing the general public or specific group interests as well as claims and pressures directly from citizens.

The different actors influencing planning and urban development possess varying degrees of economic and political power. Generally the hierarchy of power can be considered as a succession of layers, ranked according to decreasing levels of influence (Lemberg, 1989). The various layers are, however, linked together. Arguably, the most powerful position is ownership of land and premises, together with the market mechanism and the private initiative in production. Landowners and property owning institutions make the final decision, acting within the context set by laws and town plans. Next to ownership the second- and third-power layers are politicians and public officials, followed by interested organizations and the mass media. Less powerful layers include public participation instituted by law and spontaneous citizen participation, while at the base of the hierarchy, without noticeable influence, are 'the silent majority' of passive citizens.

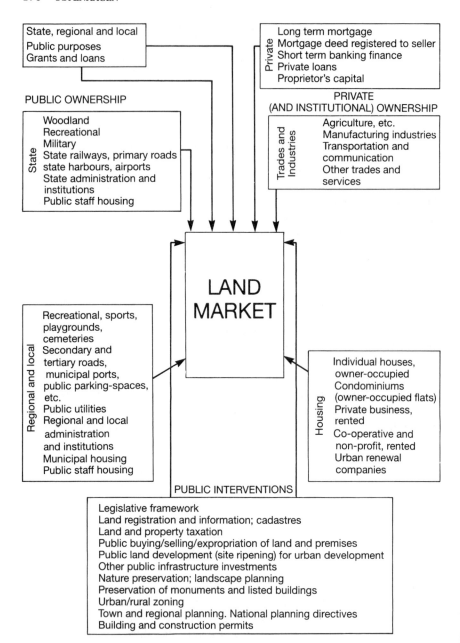

Figure 9.3 Urban land markets and interactions between public and private ownership in land acquisition and development

Such a power structure implies that the relationship between planning and property is not solely restricted to planning influences on the market. Rather owners of land and premises and their organizations try to influence communes, counties and the state through lobby activities to protect their interests with regard to legislation, plans and building permits.

The long run trend, up until about 1980, was for property prices to increase due to inflationary conditions and property from the investors perspective appeared to be a source of high and secure return. In Denmark property taxes are not high as both the state as well as the communes obtain their main revenue from income tax (also in the case of the state from VAT and other consumption taxes). Until the 1980s property taxes were deductible in the tax return (contrary to all other taxes), and the very high marginal income tax (68%) meant that deduction of interest on mortgage loans was an important relief for house owners.

However several factors have contributed to dismantling the advantageous position of property owners namely the reduction in inflation levels to circa 1–3% per annum; the relatively high real rate of interest; and the reduced value of deductions for interest payments in taxable personal incomes. Furthermore recessionary conditions starting in 1990 resulted in high levels of vacancy in commercial property with large new and expensive office buildings very difficult either to sell or lease out. This weakness in the property market is only slowly beginning to recover (mid 1993). However the shake-out has been severe with many contracting firms, including most of those planning to build on former harbour areas, having gone into liquidation. Austerity in public finances has resulted in reduced public building and reduced quotas for construction of dwellings with public support. Also the financial institutions, banks and mortgage companies have lost considerable sums of money invested in both new and old premises.

9.3 CASE STUDY OF COPENHAGEN PORT AREAS

Technological change in maritime transport, the concentration of intercontinental transport to a few European ports, of which there is none in Denmark, and competition from road and partly rail and air transport have, together with the transition from an industrial society to a service and information society, reduced the turnover of goods and passengers in the Port of Copenhagen. Also, savings of energy consumption (oil) and the geographical decentralization of oil and coal imports deprived the Port of Copenhagen of large quantities of goods. With most of the quay area now disused the Port of Copenhagen Authority (PCA), a public body independent of the City of Copenhagen and of the state, has been interested in revitalizing the area by either selling PCA-owned sites or leasing them on a long-term basis for office construction and other tradable services.

At the same time the City of Copenhagen hesitated in preparing a comprehensive town plan for the transition of large harbour areas into other types of urban functions, although proposals had been presented as a result of a Scandinavian competition in 1984–5 on the future of the Port of Copenhagen. Rather the City of Copenhagen preferred an incremental approach by treating projects from private construction companies and businesses individually, and evaluating each project separately. In practice, very little happened and in 1988 the Danish State lost patience and appointed a Copenhagen Harbour Commission to discuss and evaluate the future of the Port of Copenhagen. In its report (Port of Copenhagen Commission, 1989) the Commission proposed to close the South Harbour and the Inner Harbour to commercial maritime transport (over a number of years), convert these areas to other urban uses, especially dwellings and public parks and spaces, and concentrate commercial harbour activities in the North Harbour (including the Free Port) and the East Harbour (Figure 9.4).

Furthermore the Commission presented alternative administrative struc-

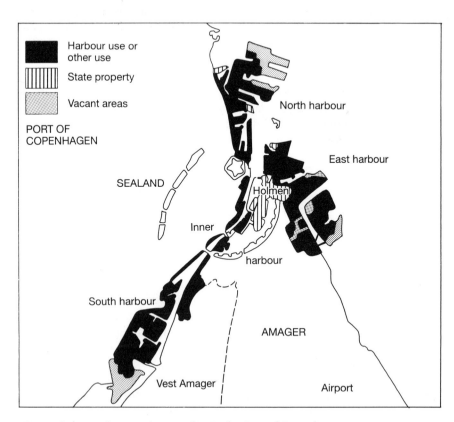

Figure 9.4 Land use and ownership in the Port of Copenhagen

tures with a proposal to split up the Port of Copenhagen Authority in two independent bodies. There was to be a continuous role for the PCA in terms of the maritime port activities, but a new planning and management board (Development Board) was proposed to own, plan and manage the areas to be withdrawn from maritime harbour activities and converted to other land uses. These areas were to be transferred from the present PCA to the new board without payment – the transferral of property from one public body to another unlike private property is not protected by the Danish Constitution (Grundlov) and is therefore not an act of expropriation. The Development Board could then sell areas to developers for residential and commercial land uses at market values, and use part of the revenue generated for cultural buildings, the creation of public open space and purification of the contaminated Inner Harbour. However both the PCA and the Ministry of Transport protested, claiming that the PCA should be paid full value for all property taken over. This, however, would eliminate the financial basis for the public buildings and open spaces to be created by the Development Board. Privately owned areas along the waterfront, including those recently sold by the PCA, were of course not affected by the free transition to Development Board ownership, except in the case of an ordinary expropriation against which full compensation may be sought.

A prolonged juridical-political battle over the non-payment takeover resulted finally in 1992 in legislation concerning the Port of Copenhagen. This constituted a victory for the PCA and the City of Copenhagen over the comprehensive planning and management visions of the Harbour Commission. Thus the PCA remains the sole authority over all parts of the Port of Copenhagen and also becomes the body responsible for the areas to be removed from harbour activities. However with the emergence of the concept of the Sound City it is unclear whether the City of Copenhagen will concentrate growth efforts in that part of West Amager or in renewal of the waterfront in the former harbour area.

Furthermore the now disused military area of Holmen, just north of the Inner Harbour at the Amager side of the harbour fairway opens up a hitherto closed area with many historical monuments of high architectural value to urban use. Proposals have been made from private organizations and architects for the use of this area primarily for cultural purposes particularly as Copenhagen has been selected as the EU Cultural City of Europe in 1996. Again in this locality public ownership, although accounting for a small share of the total property market in Copenhagen, dominates in the most strategic area for new urban development.

9.4   CONCLUSION

In Denmark emphasis is upon the private ownership of property but the market operates within a well-established regulatory framework with planning legislation dating back to 1938. Since this period responsibility for town planning has been increasingly devolved through various legislative measures to the municipalities, and counties with the state now having little overall control. Also through public participation some degree of control has been further devolved though practice has not fully lived up to intentions.

Regional zoning legislation was enacted for Copenhagen in 1949 with the Finger Plan making a clear distinction between urban and rural land. This introduced a differential land market with implications in value terms. Both the Master Plan for the City of Copenhagen (1954) and the regional Finger Plan (1947) underestimated the degree of expansion, especially of private transportation. As a consequence of economic and population growth in the 1960s there was a widening of the metropolitan region and a new plan based upon growth assumptions was prepared. Such conditions were however never fulfilled and it was only in the late 1980s that an economic growth philosophy once again came to the fore, boosted by wider European influences. Indeed the 1989 Copenhagen Communal Plan was revised in 1991 to take specific account of the Single European Market.

Although the Communal Plan placed emphasis upon the private sector as the main vehicle initiating change, investors have remained sceptical of some of the large-scale plans, particularly those dependent upon public infrastructure provision. The level of sceptism has been heightened by a history of relatively unstable public policy towards the property market. Furthermore low levels of inflation coupled to relatively high real interest rates and economic recession has in recent years been a further disincentive to property investment. However with the public sector being the major land-owner in a number of key development sites including the harbour, West Amager and Holmen the evolution of public–private partnership arrangements will be critical if new investment potential is to be achieved in the mid-late 1990s.

REFERENCES

Casabella (1987) *Kai Lemberg: Un piano generale per la citta* di Copenaghen (in Italian and in English), 5.
City of Copenhagen Overborgmesterems Afdeling (1991a) *Kobenhavns Kommuneplan Forslag til revision* (in Danish), 272.
City of Copenhagen, Department of Lord Mayor (1991b) *Strategies and Planning*, 32.
City of Copenhagen, Department of Lord Mayor (1993) *Copenhagen: Views and Visions*, 32.
Copenhagen Chief City Engineer (1954) *Kobenhavn. Skitse til en generalplan*, Copenhagen, 32.
Lemberg, K. (1981) *Danish Cultural Institute: Nordic Democracy* (an-

thology), 780.

Lemberg, K. (1989) The need for autonomy improving local democracy, in R.V. Knight and G. Gappert (eds), *Cities in a Global Society*, London, 339.

Lemberg, K. (1992) *Cultural Institute: Discover Denmark* (anthology), 240.

Metropolitan Council (1978) *Regional planning in the Greater Copenhagen Region 1945–75: From the Fingerplan to Regionplan 1975*.

Port of Copenhagen Commission (1989) *Kobenhavns Havn*, Copenhagen.

Svensson, O. (1981) *Danish Town Planning Guide*, Dansk Byplanlaboratorium (Danish Town Planning Institute).

10

Edinburgh

Greg Lloyd and Stuart Black

Scotland remains a peripheral regional economy within the UK context. It has a unique political and cultural experience (McCrone, 1992), and its present economic structure and economic problems reflect its industrial and urban history (Randall, 1987). The principal characteristics of the economy have included a continuing dependence on heavy manufacturing industries (with weak growth prospects) and relatively low internally generated economic growth (Danson, Lloyd and Newlands, 1992). Furthermore, Scotland's location creates cost disadvantages in terms of its industrial competitiveness and ability to attract inward investment. There are, in addition, relatively marked differences within the Scottish economy. The declining industrial-urban areas of the central belt and the remoter rural economies of the Highlands and Islands represent problem areas, while the oil-dependent economy of the north-east of Scotland and the concentration of high technology activity in the eastern central belt represent areas of economic potential (Ashcroft, 1983). Within this broad context, Edinburgh has played a key role. The city was established as a Royal Burgh in the twelfth century, enabling it to operate as a centre for commerce and trade. Between the fourteenth and eighteenth centuries, the city became the leading and largest administrative and commercial urban centre in Scotland. Its growth and development was supported by its hinterland which was rich in resources including agricultural land, coal and oil shale (Adams, 1978). Edinburgh assumed primacy in the economic life and administration of Scotland becoming a national capital and a regional city (Gordon, 1986).

This chapter examines the nature and effects of the land-use planning system and property markets in Edinburgh, the capital city of Scotland but lacking the full functions of the capital of a nation. After a brief introduction to the Scottish arrangements for land-use planning and economic deve-

European Cities, Planning Systems and Property Markets Edited by James Berry and Stanley McGreal. Published in 1995 by E & FN Spon. ISBN 0419 18940 8.

lopment, the chapter specifically examines Edinburgh which after London is the second foremost financial centre in the United Kingdom.

10.1 PLANNING AND GOVERNMENT IN SCOTLAND

The various administrative and management structures for land-use planning and economic development in Scotland are considered in this section. This includes an appraisal of the role of central government, local authorities and the structure of agencies operating within the country.

10.1.1 Scottish Office

Scotland has had a separate political administration since the late nineteenth century. The Scottish Office has subsequently developed important and integrated functions of public administration. A distinctive feature has been its strategic approach to land-use planning policy formulation and implementation (Begg and Pollock, 1991). Strategic planning policy guidance has been achieved by the (then) Scottish Development Department by means of a number of individual but complementary policy instruments. These have included Circulars, National Planning Guidelines and Planning Advice Notes. Circulars have provided statements of ministerial policy on a range of land-use planning issues, information about legislative changes implementing government policy and advice on procedural matters. The Planning Advice Notes set out advice to planning authorities on specific issues, such as the siting and design of new housing in the countryside. Collectively these principal instruments have contributed to the operation of a positive land-use planning system (Nuffield Foundation, 1986).

The National Planning Guidelines identified land resources having national significance which should be safeguarded from or for development, namely prime agricultural land resources, single-user high-amenity sites for technology development and land for skiing developments. Such guidelines were uniquely Scottish and the policy instrument represented a pragmatic yet radical and innovative departure from conventional traditions of British land-use planning. This is primarily regulatory or negative in effect (Pearce, 1992). National Planning Guidelines, however, were such an attempt to set out a positive framework of indicative planning for local decision-making over land and property development by individual planning authorities.

In 1991, the Scottish Office Environment Department (SOEnD), the renamed Scottish Development Department (Parry, 1992), put into effect a rationalization of its strategic planning policy framework. A significant change was the replacement of the National Planning Guidelines by National Planning Policy Guidelines. Notwithstanding the similarity of the nomenclature the two sets of policy instruments differ both in substance and detail (Lloyd and Rowan-Robinson, 1992). The new instrument was introduced in an attempt to sharpen the clarity of the strategic land-use planning guidance of the SOEnD. Furthermore, Circulars are no longer used to convey ministerial policy on land-use planning issues but will be confined to providing advice on legislative change and on procedural matters. In contrast, the National Planning Policy Guidelines will assume more significance in conveying strategic guidance in terms of locational and policy advice to local planning authorities and potential developers. These instruments provide the present context to the Edinburgh case study.

10.1.2 Local government

The present structure of local government in Scotland is a consequence of the Local Government (Scotland) Act 1973. This followed the broad recommendations of the Wheatley Commission that a two-tier structure of local government was appropriate to the Scottish circumstances. The legislation established a system which was based on a two-tier system of 12 regions and 53 districts which varied in population and geographical size. Of these the 3 island councils (Shetland, Orkney and Western Isles) were established as unitary authorities responsible for all local authority matters and 3 mainland councils (Highland, Borders, Dumfries and Galloway) were established as 'general planning authorities' responsible for both structure planning and local planning. In the remaining mainland regional councils (Grampian, Strathclyde, Lothian, Tayside, Fife, Central) a two-tier system operated with an appropriate division of responsibilities between strategic and tactical functions over their respective geographical areas. The distinctive mix of unitary and two-tier arrangements and the division of planning responsibilities was a deliberate measure to reflect and accommodate the balance of geographical area and population distribution in Scotland. Indeed Cullingworth (1988) suggested that the division between strategic and local responsibilities and functions in Scotland was also much more clearly defined than was the case in England and Wales.

The Scottish Office's case for reform of the two-tier local authority structure in Scotland was outlined in 1991 and 1992 (Scottish Office, 1991, 1992). It was argued that the two-tier structure was no longer valid or appropriate as changing circumstances had weakened the case for a two-tier model of local government. These included an approach to local economic development which emphasized a partnership between the public and private sectors, the existence of other executive agencies and changed expectations on the part of the public particularly with respect to the costs of local government in delivering local services. Further, the Consultation Paper was critical of the effectiveness and efficiency of the existing structure and operating arrangements of Scottish local government. It argued that there was duplication, overlap, waste and confusion over the division of responsibilities and functions. A subsequent White Paper set out its proposals for 'a structure of single tier, all-purpose councils' (Scottish Office, 1993). A framework of 28 local authorities for Scotland – to be called Councils was set out. However, the new structure of local government in Scotland will not be of uniform population size nor uniform geographical area. There will be four city authorities – Edinburgh, Glasgow, Aberdeen, Dundee – which will 'restore full responsibility for local affairs to these traditional centres of Scottish life'. The new Councils are intended to satisfy the Government's requirements concerning the increased efficiency and effectiveness of service delivery, enhanced accountability, and strengthening local loyalties and allegiances. The new City of Edinburgh Council will therefore assume all responsibilities for strategic planning, local planning and development control for the area over which it has jurisdiction.

10.1.3   Scottish Enterprise

A consequence of Scotland's relatively disadvantaged economic position within the national economy is the extent to which successive governments have intervened in the form of policy initiatives and assistance (Randall, 1987). Thus, throughout the greater part of the post-war period, Scotland was eligible for a considerable range of incentives under the conventional regional policy framework in an attempt to address its structural and locational disadvantages. The regional policy framework reflected the geographical concentration of industrial problems in Scotland's main metropolitan centres, particularly in the Glasgow–Edinburgh axis. Regional policy in Scotland was supplemented by the creation of development agencies. These

> are the creatures of central government, reflecting its reluctance to put resources directly in the hands of local authorities ... This mode of intervention has been deployed and sustained in Scotland and Wales essentially because of its advantages, from central government's viewpoint, as a way of responding to well articulated regional interests there, rather than because it is intrinsically superior to alternative arrangements. (Damesick and Wood, 1987)

In 1991 new institutional arrangements were introduced in Scotland concerning the organizational arrangements for the provision of training, business development measures and environmental improvement (Lloyd and Black, 1992). The new institutional arrangements complement conventional regional industrial policy aimed at the regeneration of the Scottish economy by securing conditions appropriate to local business and economic development. Two bodies – Scottish Enterprise and the Highlands and Islands Enterprise – replaced respectively the Scottish Development Agency and Highlands and Islands Development Board. The distinguishing feature of the new institutional arrangements is the delivery mechanism whereby the services for training, business growth and environmental improvement have been decentralized to a network of constituent Local Enterprise Companies (LECs).

In formal terms, Scottish Enterprise and Highlands and Islands Enterprise are charged with the responsibility of stimulating self-sustaining economic development and the growth of enterprise, securing the improvement of the environment, encouraging the creation of viable jobs, reducing unemployment and improving the skills of the Scottish workforce. Scottish Enterprise and Highlands and Islands Enterprise both comprise a central strategic administration and policy-making role in addition to monitoring and enforcement. The LECs are responsible for a range of functions, namely assessing the circumstances and requirements of local labour markets in Scotland; arranging for the delivery of national training programmes; developing training initiatives for specific local needs, designing business development services; and raising private sector money – a process referred to as leverage – to supplement the public-sector resources being made available to them. Essentially, however, the LECs involve increased private sector control of public sector resources. Indeed the local bodies are bound by a contractual arrangement to Scottish Enterprise and Highlands and Islands Enterprise to deliver the national training programmes and business development measures. Individual projects over a certain financial threshold are referred back to the parent bodies for approval.

In the context of Edinburgh, the appropriate LEC is the Lothian and Edinburgh Enterprise Limited (LEEL) which has defined responsibilities for the city and its economic hinterland. LEEL's remit is essentially to promote the economic, environmental and human resource development of the area under its jurisdiction. LEEL attempts to secure this through a property led development strategy, a training strategy and a business growth strategy. LEEL now has, in common with other LECs, a new land development based measure available for its work – Resources and Action for Private Industrial Development (RAPID). This is the most recent local economic development incentive to be introduced in Scotland and is to be administered through the Scottish Enterprise network. The measure applies to all sectors of commercial and industrial property but excludes the residential sector. The availability of RAPID will be determined by individual LECs depending on the localized property market circumstances and their individual development strategy laid down in their agreed business plan. In 1991–2, LEEL invested £16 million in 250 projects concerned with the acquisition, development and regeneration or refurbishment of land and property in the Edinburgh sub-regional economy. In particular, LEEL purchased land in anticipation of redevelopment and in order to provide for the needs of inward investment. It also developed property for specific needs, reclaimed derelict land and undertook measures to improve the quality of the urban environment.

10.2   STRATEGIC VISION IN LOTHIAN

This section discusses the strategic framework to land-use planning and property development in Edinburgh. In this context Hague (1993) notes that the dominant political ideology of the city region was essentially conservative – 'caution verging on complaisance, an attitude of mind which had been cemented into the city's local government bureaucracy'. Concerning the development of a strategic vision for Edinburgh and its metropolitan region, Hague (1984) described this as 'convoluted' with a discernible cyclical pattern of intervention. Thus

> planning is low key, pragmatic and non-interventionist for long periods until some development crisis which by common consent needs major strategic planning action. In such stirring times grand plans are produced, but these are then rejected by the civic leadership as the crisis wanes and a new era of normality dawns. (Hague, 1993)

Traditionally, local land-use planning has tended to be relatively low key and indeed the creation of Lothian Regional Council in 1975 continued in this tradition with substantial continuities with the past. However, over the period 1978–82, Lothian Regional Council was controlled by a Labour administration committed to reversing the long period of under-investment in public services in the city. This brought the authority into conflict with central government over its spending plans although, throughout this period, planning of land and development remained highly conservative with an over-riding emphasis on development control and conservation issues.

By the early 1980s, Hague (1993) observed that Edinburgh had an abundance of long-term gap sites, the legacy of frustrated ambitions, abandoned road plans, and was suffering from the post oil crisis collapse of the property market in the 1970s. Indeed the dominant urban image of the city was of the historic and cultural tourist core. However, in the 1980s, the strategic vision of Edinburgh changed. This was a consequence of three factors.

First, there was a change in political administration. Lothian Regional Council became controlled by a Conservative and Alliance grouping and Edinburgh District Council became Labour controlled. Second, the SDA initiated the Leith Project, to the north of the city. This was an integrated area project aimed at securing urban and property regeneration through an injection of private-sector investment. In an effort to lever the latter the

SDA undertook considerable environmental improvement and landscaping of derelict sites. Third, in 1985 the Edinburgh Chamber of Commerce established a business agenda for the future. This strategic vision for business interests set out a new agenda for development in and around the city. Arguably these factors served to change attitudes to planning practice in Edinburgh. Thus, Lothian Regional Council in 1992 declared that planning in Lothian is about improving and sustaining the quality of the environment in the long-term interests of the community while, at the same time, ensuring a buoyant economy with lively cultural activities.

At the present time the strategic vision for the region and city has been set out as follows by Lothian Regional Council:

> The objective of planning at the regional level is to enable development in the interests of the community at large and to provide guidance for Local Plans. The Structure Plan allows market forces to be harnessed in ways which enhance the environment, spreads benefits to be gained from the Region's economic strengths and uses resources efficiently.

It is clear from this that the strategic vision is more assertive while remaining pragmatic in terms of the relationship between planning and the market.

10.3   PLANNING IN EDINBURGH

In examining planning policies for Edinburgh this section seeks to identify the extent to which the planning process is contributing to the stimulation of commercial property markets and the attraction of property investment activities into the city.

Lothian Regional Council published its first Structure Plan in 1979 which was subsequently reviewed in 1986. The strategic themes of the Structure Plan framework included the provision of inner-city housing in Edinburgh, securing the phased supply of housing land with adequate infrastructure provision, facilitating economic development (through the identification of sites for high technology industry and encouraging the development) of the financial and service sectors.

At the present time, Lothian Regional Council is in the process of preparing a new Structure Plan. The draft Structure Plan (1993) sets out an overall strategy which seeks to improve the natural and built environment of the region, spread the benefits of economic opportunities, protect urban areas from overdevelopment, regenerate disadvantaged areas, promote improved public transport and traffic management, and make the best use of infrastructure. A principal issue in this strategic planning framework concerns the green belt. In order to avoid over-development of Edinburgh's core, the Structure Plan proposes to develop greenfield land for residential and industrial purposes. The greater part of this land will be found outwith the defined green belt in areas which are accessible to jobs and public transport and in locations where the best landscapes will be protected. It is evident that the green belt is a pivotal element in the strategic planning framework for Edinburgh.

10.3.1   Lothian Region green belt

The Edinburgh green belt, designated in 1957, was the first to be officially declared in Scotland. It encircles the city from Dalmeny in the west to the coast and Prestonpans in the east. While the average width of the green belt is only three kilometres, there are nine settlements within the area, designated as 'urban envelopes'. There are also 'green wedges' which are entirely separate from the main green belt; these have an important amenity and recreational role. In the rest of the green belt, recreational use is limited, due to the intensive arable cropping. Some 90% of the green belt is privately owned. The objectives of the green belt were to: 'prevent expansion of the city..., to prevent coalescence..., to prevent use of agricultural land for development..., and to preserve and enhance the landscape setting of Edinburgh' (Lothian Regional Council, 1990). In total, some 14 000 ha were designated. Over the following period to 1965, significant incursions into the green belt were made through planned releases of land for residential and industrial purposes. The outer boundary, however, was extended to include the 'green wedges' to preserve green landscape corridors into the city. As a consequence, the size of the green belt increased to 15 000 ha (Edinburgh Green Belt Initiative, 1990).

However, the areas designated as green belt have recently become extremely difficult to uphold as all the major greenfield sites reserved since the 1960s for housing within the city itself have been used up. Furthermore there is a demand for low-density housing, with additional community facilities, together with some industrial sites. Indeed there is evidence of development 'leap-frogging' across the green belt as settlements outwith the designated area have shown a trend of increased growth. Nonetheless due to the prime quality of agricultural land around Edinburgh, protection remains a primary objective. This is linked with the maintenance of the overall landscape quality, since Edinburgh's dramatic setting is very much due to the surrounding agricultural resource base.

Following the publication of the Structure Plan in 1979, Lothian Regional Council undertook a major survey and review of the green belt. This led to the implementation of a Green Belt Agreement and Code of Practice which was signed by the Region and the Districts in November 1983. The agreement was to be binding on all these authorities, with planning applications being 'called-in' to the Regional Planning Authority, and consultation with all relevant bodies, before decision. This is, in effect, treating major applications like a Structure Plan alteration, in requiring a level of public debate and consensus of all parties, even those not directly affected, in order to ensure a consistency of policy is seen to be applied. In addition, the Green Belt Agreement included a commitment on the part of the authorities to adopt a programme of remedial landscape measures in those areas of poor environmental quality, as identified by the survey. There was also the opportunity to improve recreational and amenity potential. The environmental improvements began in 1984 with support from the Countryside Commission for Scotland, the Scottish Development Agency and the constituent local authorities. In 1987 the Edinburgh Green Belt Initiative evolved as the appropriate institutional vehicle for management of the green belt. Furthermore, in 1991, the Edinburgh Green Belt Trust was established as a new, independent organization entirely responsible for the green belt. The Trust can hold land, in order to achieve landscape enhancement, rather than stop land being bought for development and while it has major public funding it is 'private' sector led. The desire is to get the private sector interested in maintaining an enhanced green belt and therefore a pleasant Edinburgh environment for all.

The 1985 Lothian Structure Plan (Lothian Regional Council, 1985) identified the need for the allocation of up to 5500 houses by 1991–6 within the Edinburgh area though the Region left the actual allocation of sites to the discretion of the district authorities. A review of green belt boundaries was undertaken and housing sites found but these meant an extension to and revision of the green belt designated zone. Furthermore, pressure from both the Region and developers increased, when it became obvious that these sites would not be available until 1992. In addition, the 1990 Structure Plan Review (Lothian Regional Council, 1990) stressed the need for housing up to the year 2005, however, there were no sites available within the inner city, either infill or brownfield, as all available land had been allocated or developed upon. Hence, pressure on the green belt has now increased, though this relates to development demand and not necessarily need. A generating growth of pressure is apparent at certain sites. Indeed throughout the 1980s, the same sites kept recurring as having development potential with regularly submitted planning applications often relating to sites of long established developer ownership.

The west of the city is the most pressurized location, it is already a major transport and infrastructure corridor, and as such strategically significant. Essentially it is the 'key area' in the 'market'. Furthermore, many offices are situated on the western periphery of the city and currently the market is particularly buoyant with high rents. There have been several proposals in this area of green belt for major developments including a District Council Business Park, Hi-Tech Industry, a Football Stadium, and a Motor Racing Research and Development Centre. Also there is a strategic need, due to ageing facilities within the city, for a 20 ha new hospital site, which has Secretary of State approval to be located in the green belt. Thus land releases have been *ad hoc* responses to individual proposals rather than controlled phasing as part of an overall settlement strategy through Structure Plan Review.

The result of the Structure Plan Review leaves two options, development of greenfield sites within the green belt or 'leap-frogging' across, to bordering settlements. If the green belt stays fairly rigid the pressure will be on the countryside and settlements around the city. However, investors favour what is perceived as the 'hub' of activity and will thus have to accommodate and adjust to green belt and development pressures as best it can. It is unlikely that pressure from the 'market' will question the survival of Edinburgh's Green Belt as a major element of the planning process, since the city and its green belt have strategic, economic, and political significance. Liaison with the private sector through the Green Belt Trust may ease conflicts that arise, if developers can appreciate that the very attractiveness of Edinburgh relates to its 'green' image. Indeed the economic prosperity of the city and the green belt concept are closely linked though there will have to be certain flexibility of the green belt to development pressure, with likely future changes in its green belt boundaries to accommodate this. Arguably more positive moves from Central Government are also required to encourage development to the other local areas, if the green belt boundaries are to remain broadly similar to those currently operative.

10.4   EDINBURGH OFFICE MARKET

Edinburgh is the administrative and financial capital of Scotland. It is the location of the head offices of five of Scotland's eight life offices, three of Scotland's four major clearing banks, seven independent investment fund managers, seven Merchant Banks, and three Securities Brokers (Ryden, 1990). The Scottish financial services sector employs over 208 000 people, or 11% of the Scottish workforce and accounts for 15% of GDP, which is twice the EC average (Scottish Financial Enterprise, 1993). Indeed Edinburgh is the second most important centre for fund management in the UK, after London. In the Life Assurance sector, the Scottish Life Offices, including Standard Life, Europe's largest mutual assurance society, manage assets of almost £72bn. Scottish based independent fund managers control total assets of £35.7bn (Scottish Financial Enterprise, 1993).

During the services boom of the late 1980s, employment in financial services grew by 60% in Edinburgh. This growth, however, has recently been checked and in some cases major restructuring is leading to employment loss. The Royal Bank of Scotland, for example recently announced plans to shed 3500 jobs over the next five years (*Estates Gazette*, 1993), though the financial service sector in Scotland has weathered the recession much better than has been the case in London and the South-East of England. Latest figures suggest that during 1992 employment in Scottish financial and business services fell by only 1000 to 208 000, while in the South-East the fall was by 29 000 to 1 213 000, with over 80% of these losses in Greater London.

In 1989 it was estimated that Edinburgh's office stock was 1.51 m sq m, 27% of this was located in the so-called 'Golden Rectangle' in the city centre, and 62% in the central area office policy zone operated by Lothian Regional Council. Concerning the composition of the stock, 36% was occupied by public sector bodies (including the Scottish Office) and 19% by the financial services sector. Major corporate head offices tend to be owner-occupied (Lothian Regional Council, 1989).

During the late 1970s the possibility of devolution from Westminster and a Scottish Assembly led to the build-up of office development activity. The Assembly failed to become a reality and as the UK economy moved into recession in the early 1980s Edinburgh was affected by an oversupply of office space and poor rental growth. Indeed until 1987 very little speculative office development took place with the exception of Capital House, a 5500 sq m development outwith the traditional office core on Lothian Road, which was completed in 1985 (Lothian Regional Council, 1989).

The City of Edinburgh District Council Planning Department provides

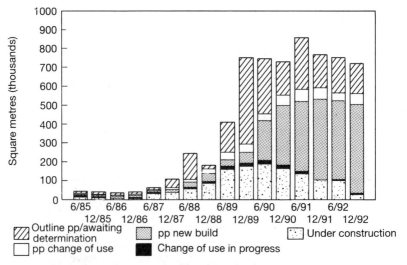

*From 6/90 outline pp becomes awaiting determination

Figure 10.1   Edinburgh office development pipeline
Source: City of Edinburgh District Council.

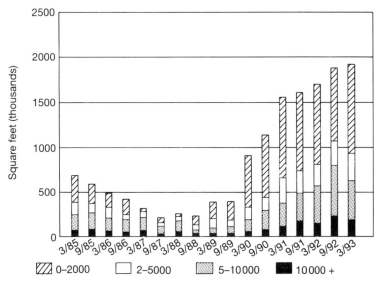

Figure 10.2   Edinburgh office supply (by unit sizes)
Source: Ryden Property Consultants.

schedules of all current office developments in the city over 200 sq m on a twice yearly basis. These statistics show very little space in the pipeline during the mid 1980s reflecting the recession and the extent of oversupply in the market (Figure 10.1). On average over the period 1985 to 1992 there was 82 027 sq m of new office floorspace under construction in each six-month period for which data are available. This was at its lowest ebb in mid 1986 with only 2242 sq m under construction. In contrast, building activity peaked in June 1990 when there was 189 596 sq m under construction. Office development has subsequently fallen back to around 28 062 sq m at the end of 1992. In addition, there is also a great deal of new office space with planning permission, at the end of 1992 this represented some 470 861 sq m (ignoring conversions). However, completion data are only available from December 1989. These statistics indicate that completions peaked in the final half of 1990 at 71 119 sq m whereas the latest figures (at December 1992) show that the total amount of office floorspace in the pipeline is 567 367 sq m. Comparing this to a rate of take-up of 49 445 sq m in 1992 the current office pipeline is equivalent to over 11 years of take-up at current rates, although this includes speculative space which is unlikely to be developed.

Regarding the supply of office space on the market by unit size, statistics illustrate the increased availability of space over the period March 1985 to March 1993 (Figure 10.2). This can be correlated to the declining rate of construction activity. Indeed at December 1992, there was very little

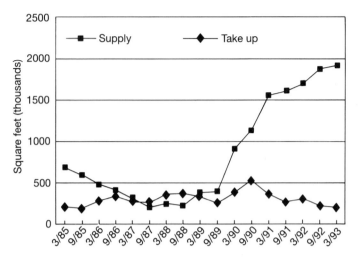

Figure 10.3 Edinburgh office demand and supply
Source: Ryden Property Consultants.

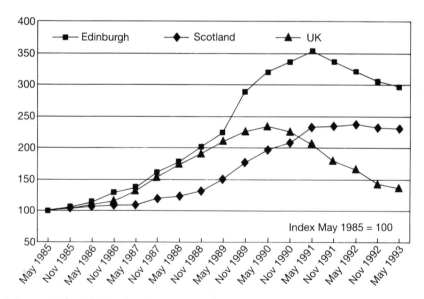

Figure 10.4 Edinburgh office rent trends
Source: Hillier Parker.

speculative space under construction with building only starting on the basis of pre-lets or for owner-occupation (City of Edinburgh District Council, 1993). Of particular significance is the growth in larger floor plate offices reflecting an increasing trend towards out-of-town business park developments.

The increasing mismatch between supply and demand (Figure 10.3) can be compared with rental trends (Figure 10.4) and development trends (Figure 10.1). As availability fell in the mid to late 1980s speculative development led to an oversupply situation which in turn dampened rental growth and precipitated a decline in rents. Vacancy rates over the same period have fluctuated between 5 and 12% of total office stock. Furthermore, it is interesting to note that while rentals peaked in mid 1991 take-up rates fell from late 1990; also the amount of new floorspace under construction peaked in mid 1990, just before the decline in take-up rates back to more historically normal levels. Latest figures show take up for the six months to March 1993 (20 105 sq m) the lowest level since the six months to September 1985, and almost one-third below the average take-up level for the period (Ryden, 1993).

Concerning the performance of prime office rentals (Figure 10.4) Edinburgh shows better than average rental growth, notably over the period May 1989 to the rental peak of May 1991. At this time prime rentals achieved £260 sq m (Ryden, 1991). However, the Edinburgh office market has fallen, with latest figures (1993) suggesting rental levels of around £230 per sq m for prime office space. The rental falls have been less dramatic than in the City office market in London where rents have declined by 50% from their peak levels in the late 1980s. Indeed office rents in Scotland as a whole have been less dramatically affected than the rest of the UK and indeed Edinburgh. Furthermore, Scotland has also been less affected than the rest of the UK by falls in capital values in the office sector, for example Hillier Parker figures for the period May 1992 to May 1993 show that capital values in Scotland fell by 5.2% compared to 16.9% for the UK as a whole (Hillier Parker, 1993). Prime office yields in Edinburgh have ranged between a low point in 1987 of 6% and for April 1993, 8.25% (Ryden, 1993).

10.4.1   Case study: Saltire Court

Saltire Court is one of the largest speculative office developments in Edinburgh; it was built by Scottish Metropolitan and completed in late 1991. The 20 000 sq m office complex lies in the shadow of Edinburgh Castle, immediately behind the Usher Hall on Lothian Road. It therefore reflects the shift in the office core from the 'Golden Rectangle' area concentrated around Charlotte Square to the more modern developments in the vicinity of Lothian Road.

Saltire Court was built on a site which infamously became known as Edinburgh's 'hole in the ground'. In 1962 redevelopment of the site which was then a cinema, was discussed by the City Corporation. The plans included a national theatre for 1700 people but financial constraints prevented this development, which was costed at £1 m from going ahead. In 1966, the existing buildings on the site were demolished, and there followed a period of vacancy from 1966 to 1988 as plans for an opera house and hotel were shelved. In May 1987 Edinburgh District Council issued a development brief for the site. This document invited submissions for proposals for the site. As it stated

> any development will be expected to make a civic contribution both in visual terms, by high quality of design, materials and finishes; and in function by encouraging public access. If a commercial centre is proposed this should be in the form of a trade 'centre' rather than an inaccessible purely office scheme. (City of Edinburgh District Council, 1987)

In total, 22 proposals were forthcoming from different developers reflecting the importance of the site, eight of which were put on public display. The public were asked to vote on the proposals and the development by Scottish Metropolitan gained the largest share of the votes (49%) with the next closest rival only gaining 6%. This is not standard planning practice in the UK but it does reflect the importance attached to the site by the Council. Hence the so-called 'Scottish Financial Centre' later named 'Saltire Court' was born. The completed development includes office floorspace, a theatre complex with associated bars and foyer which is leased to the City Council and sublet to the Traverse theatre. At the current time (September 1993) the offices are 98% let, and Saltire Court is on the market for £45.8 million (*Glasgow Herald*, 14.9.93).

10.5   CONCLUSION

Edinburgh has played a key role in Scotland's economic and political history. It has assumed the role of national capital but remains essentially devoid of the powers and responsibilities of such a status. Edinburgh has retained a powerful economic role, particularly in terms of the financial sector and services. This is reflected in the buoyant office development sector in the city and demonstrates the rationale for a strong policy of restraint through the green belt. Edinburgh's principal strategic problem is accommodating the growth in indigenous development and inward investment while retaining the essential urban characteristics of the city. The conflict of interest here is likely to become more acute and will demand more innovative land management policies from the city.

REFERENCES

Adams, I.H. (1978) *The Making of Urban Scotland*, Croom Helm, London.

Ashcroft, B. (1983) The Scottish region and the regions of Scotland, in K. Ingham and J. Love (eds), *Understanding the Scottish Economy*, Martin Robertson, Oxford, 173–87.

Begg, H.M. and Pollock, S.H.A. (1991) Development plans in Scotland since 1975, *Scottish Geographical Magazine*, **107**(1), 4–11.

City of Edinburgh District Council (1993) *Office Development Schedules*, Department of Planning, City of Edinburgh District Council, Edinburgh.

City of Edinburgh District Council (1987) *Castle Terrace Edinburgh: a Site for Prestigious Development*, Department of Planning, City of Edinburgh District Council, Edinburgh.

Cullingworth, J.B. (1988) *Town and Country Planning in Britain*, Allen & Unwin, London.

Damesick, P. and Wood, P. (1987) Public policy for regional development: restoration or regeneration?, in P. Damesick and P. Wood (eds), *Regional Problems, Problem Regions, and Public Policy in the United Kingdom*, Clarendon Press, Oxford, 260–6.

Danson, M., Lloyd, M.G. and Newlands, D. (1992) Scotland, in P. Townroe and R. Martin (eds), *Regional Development in the 1990s: The British Isles in Transition*, Jessica Kingsley Publishers, London, 108–16.

Edinburgh Green Belt Initiative (1990) *Edinburgh Green Belt Initiative*, Second Report, Edinburgh.

Estates Gazette (1993) Region attempts a balancing act, *Estates Gazette*, 1 May, 38–44.

Gordon, G. (1986) Edinburgh: capital and regional city, in G. Gordon (ed.), *Regional Cities in the UK 1890–1980*, London, Harper & Row, 149–70.

Hague, C. (1984) *The Development of Planning Thought*, London, Hutchinson.

Hague, C. (1993) *Imagery and Property Devleopment: Taking Planning into the Market*, Heriot Watt University, School of Planning and Housing, mimeo.

Hillier Parker (1993) *Property Market Values*, Hillier Parker, London.

Investors Chronicle/Hillier Parker (1990) *Property Market Indicators: Scotland*, Hillier Parker, London.

Lloyd, M.G. and Black, J.S. (1992) Scottish Enterprise: casting a shadow over continuity and accountability?, *Town and Country Planning*, **61**(4), 109–11.

Lloyd, M.G. and Rowan-Robinson, J. (1992) Review of strategic planning guidance in Scotland, *Journal of Environmental Planning and Management*, **35**(1), 93–9.

Lothian Regional Council (1985) *Lothian Structure Plan*. Edinburgh.

Lothian Regional Council (1989) *Offices in Edinburgh: Trends and Prospects*, Department of Planning, Lothian Regional Council, Edinburgh.

Lothian Regional Council (1990) *New Structure Plan Review*, Edinburgh.

Lothian Regional Council (1993) *Draft Structure Plan Review*, Edinburgh.

McCrone, D. (1992) *Understanding Scotland: The Sociology of a Stateless Nation*, London, Routledge.

Nuffield Foundation (1986) *Town and Country Planning*, The Report of a Committee of Inquiry Appointed by the Nuffield Foundation, London.

Parry, R. (1992) The structure of the Scottish Office (1991), in L. Paterson and D. McCrone (eds), *The Scottish Government Yearbook 1992*, Edinburgh, Edinburgh University Press, 247–55.

Pearce, B.J. (1992) The effectiveness of the British land use planning system, *Town Planning Review*, **63**(1), 13–28.

Randall, J. (1987) Scotland, in P. Damesick and P. Wood (eds), *Regional Problems, Problem Regions and Public Policy in the United Kingdom*, Clarendon Press, Oxford, 218–37.

Ryden (1990) *The Edinburgh Office Market: A General Overview*, Ryden Property Consultants, Edinburgh.

Ryden (1991) *Scottish Industrial and Commercial Property Review*, Ryden Property Consultants, Edinburgh.

Ryden (1993) *Scottish Industrial and Commercial Property Review*, Ryden Property Consultants, Edinburgh.

Scottish Financial Enterprise (1993) *Scottish Financial Enterprise Facts*, SFE, Edinburgh.

Scottish Office (1991) *The Structure of Local Government in Scotland: The Case for Change: A Consultation Paper*, Edinburgh, HMSO.

Scottish Office (1992) *Local Government in Scotland: The Shape of the New Councils: A Consultation Paper*, Edinburgh, HMSO.

Scottish Office (1993) *The Structure of Local Government: Shaping the Future – The New Councils*, Cm 2267, Edinburgh, HMSO.

11

Dublin

Joseph Davis and
Terry Prendergast

Dublin, situated on the east coast, is the capital city of the Republic of Ireland. The Republic together with Northern Ireland, which forms part of the United Kingdom, constitute the territory of the island of Ireland. Total population is approximately 5 million of whom 3.5 million reside in the Republic. The city of Dublin and the evolution of its built environment mirror in many respects the political and economic history of the island. In a time dimension which extends from pre-Celtic origins to the still evident Viking, Norman and late medieval influences; the distinctive scale of eighteenth-century Georgian architecture through post-1960s development to the modern European capital city of the 1990s.

The two distinctive development phases which define the city, as it exists today, are separated by two hundred years. The development of Georgian Dublin reflected the economic prosperity of the nation at that period (1780–1800) and promoted its status as the second city, after London, within the British Empire. However nineteenth-century Ireland was characterized by falling population and a static economy, and indeed a similar scenario persisted for almost forty years following the establishment of an independent Irish State in 1921. In Dublin substantial Victorian and Edwardian suburban housing, developed for the professional and merchant classes, co-existed with what were regarded as some of the worst slums in Europe. Apart from the rebuilding of the city centre following the destruction caused by the 1916 Rising, the property development efforts of the new Irish State were predominantly directed to the elimination of these slum conditions. Thus by 1960, the beginning of the modern development phase in Dublin, the turn of the century city, as chronicled in detail in James Joyce's *Ulysses*, was largely intact.

European Cities, Planning Systems and Property Markets Edited by James Berry and Stanley McGreal. Published in 1995 by E & FN Spon. ISBN 0419 18940 8.

The objective of this chapter is to review how the planning system and property investment in Dublin have shaped the expansion and transformation of the city from 1960 onwards. Arguably this date marks the beginning of the first sustained period of economic prosperity and development since 1800.

11.1 SOCIO-ECONOMIC CONTEXT

In 1991, the Greater Dublin area contained a population in excess of 1.1 million persons, representing one-third of the population of the Irish State. Within this functional urban area there is a number of demographic bands associated with distinctive development phases in the evolution of the city.

The inner city is defined as that area bounded by the two canals and containing the historic core of the medieval and Georgian city as well as the Central Business District. The resident population of the inner city has continuously declined over the past 60 years, halving to a mere 76 000 persons over the 25-year period to 1991 (*Census of Population*, 1966, 1991).

The predominantly late-nineteenth-century and earlier twentieth-century inner suburbs, located outside of the canal rings, which together with the inner city constitute the County Borough or Dublin City area, contain a resident population of some 404 000. The 'hard' suburban ring which, in the main, consists of post-1950 development, contains a population of 544 000. Finally, the 'soft' suburban commuting ring beyond the periphery in the adjoining counties of Wicklow, Kildare and Meath, which is broadly but not exclusively characterized by 1980 development, houses a population of 115 000 (*Census of Population*, 1991).

While the resident population of both the city and inner city has declined in absolute and relative terms, the Greater Dublin area has in contrast expanded rapidly. The decline of inner-city population, accompanied by the rapid suburban population growth with its associated development and spatial expansion, has created the characteristic 'doughnut' effect widely observed internationally. This process has been the inevitable outcome of market forces facilitated by national and local planning policies pursued over a period of 25 years. However, there is now clear evidence of a process of re-urbanization taking place in Dublin facilitated by public policy measures which reflect changing community and government attitudes, influenced by international experience and having regard to spatial policy.

A further important factor to highlight from the demographic trends is the rapid expansion of the Dublin Metropolitan area between 1966 and 1981 (Table 11.1). Indeed Dublin had the distinction of being the fastest growing urban area in Europe at that time, although the rate

Table 11.1 Population change in the Greater Dublin area

Year	Population of Greater Dublin area (000s)	Annual average % change	Greater Dublin as % of State	Dublin* as % of Greater Dublin	Dublin* as % of State	Dublin City as % of State	Inner city as % of Greater Dublin
1966	840.9	—	29.2	94.5	27.6	19.7	17.7
1971	892.1	1.2	30	95.5	28.6	19.1	
1981	1091.9	4.1	31.7	91.9	29.1	15.3	
1986	1127.1	0.6	31.8	90.6	28.8	14.2	
1991	1139.7	0.2	32.3	89.9	29.1	13.6	6.7

*Dublin City and Dublin County.
Source: *Census of Population*, 1966–91, Central Statistics Office.

of growth has slowed down very considerably since, reflecting overall national population trends.

The growth in and movement of population in the Dublin Metropolitan area have been accompanied by significant changes in urban economic and land-use structures shaped by socio-economic and spatio-economic policy initiatives. The decade of the 1960s represented a turning point in Irish economic and spatial development with the introduction of national economic and physical planning policies. Over the succeeding three decades the State has been gradually transformed from a largely agricul- turally based protectionist economy into a modern internationally trading, industrialized and increasingly urbanized society with national GNP grow- ing at an annual average real rate of 3.2% over the period 1960–90 (NESC, 1992). The effects of these national structural changes are most strikingly manifested in Dublin.

The 'New Towns' strategy for the accommodation of Dublin's growing overspill population recommended in the Myles Wright Report (1967) was incorporated as the key policy objective in the First County Devel- opment Plan (1972). This was to have profound consequences for the subsequent physical development of the overall Dublin Metropolitan area. Furthermore substantial property development and the emergence of a property investment market focusing primarily on Dublin have been es- sential elements of the socio-economic and physical transformation.

11.2   THE PLANNING SYSTEM

At local level, the Dublin Area was, until 1 January 1994, divided into three separate authorities – Dublin Corporation, established in 1899 with re- sponsibility for the city area, Dublin County Council, also established in 1899, with responsibility for the growing suburban and rural areas sur- rounding the city, and Dun Laoghaire Corporation, established in 1930. While the structure of local government has, until recently, been left almost intact since the late nineteenth century, internal reorganization has been considerable. A system of city management was introduced in Dublin in 1930. The basis of this system is that the functions of a local authority are separated into reserved and executive functions, the former performed by the elected representatives and the latter by the City or County Manager. One of the most important reserved functions is the power to adopt a development plan or materially contravene it. The grant or refusal of planning permission to carry out development is an executive function.

On the technical side, the Dublin Planning Officer has had responsibility for planning in Dublin city and county, but has no direct responsibility in Dun Laoghaire Borough. Nevertheless through the city management system and the Dublin Planning Officer some degree of co-ordination and consistency in decision-making has been possible regarding planning and infrastructural provision.

The local government system in the Dublin area has been reorganized into four separate authorities. While the Dublin Corporation has remained, possessing as it does a considerable degree of public acceptance, the Local Government Reorganisation Act (1985) established three new electoral counties. One of these is based on an extended Dun Laoghaire authority – Dun Laoghaire Rathdown, another on the north county area – Dublin Fingal, and a third to the south of the city, west of the extended Dun Laoghaire Authority area – South Dublin (Figure 11.1).

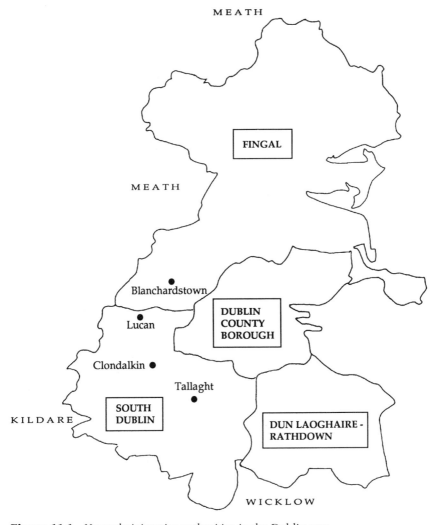

Figure 11.1   New administrative authorities in the Dublin area

At a national level two main organizations have responsibility for planning, namely the Department of the Environment and the Planning Appeals Board (An Bord Pleanala). A third organization, the Environmental Protection Agency, established in 1993, is likely to play a major role with regard to control of large-scale industry and protection of the environment. The responsibilities of the Department of the Environment include planning legislation; general guidance to planning authorities and the Planning Appeals Board; formulation of planning policies and objectives; the issuing of general policy directives; the confirmation of Special Amenity Area Orders and Compulsory Purchase Orders; and the certification of development proposed by a planning authority which requires an environmental impact statement.

As the main overseer of the planning system in Ireland, the Department of the Environment takes an active role in the framing of planning legislation, but takes a less prominent role with regard to policy formulation and guidance. The Minister of the Environment has had the powers since 1982 to issue general policy directives to local planning authorities and the Planning Appeals Board. To date only two such directives have been issued.

The Planning Appeals Board, established in 1977, is an independent corporate body with responsibility for all planning appeals in addition to other forms of appeal. The Board has absolute independence in making decisions on planning appeals. While the Minister may give direction as to policy and may issue general policy directives, no ministerial influence is exercised over individual cases. The Board must however keep itself informed on the policies of public authorities. A decision of the Board is final in planning terms, though a further appeal can be made on a point of law to the High Court.

11.3   THE PLANNING PROCESS

The principal Act relevant to the Irish planning system is the Local Government (Planning and Development) Act (1963). This Act has been substantially amended and extended by subsequent legislation to make up the planning code.

The 1963 Act came into operation in October 1964 and required each planning authority to make a development plan within three years, and thenceforth review it every five years. This time-scale proved difficult to achieve and the first round of plans in the Dublin area were adopted in 1970 in Dun Laoghaire, in 1971 in Dublin City and in 1972 in Dublin County. Only Dun Laoghaire Corporation has succeeded in regularly reviewing its plans in 1976, 1984 and 1991. Delays in the other two authorities have been considerable. The second round of plans were adopted in Dublin City in 1980 and in Dublin County in 1983, resulting in a 9-year and an 11-year gap respectively between plans. The latest Dublin City and County Development Plans were finally adopted in 1991 and 1993, the former only after the elected representatives decided to omit a controversial road proposal for later consideration.

Clearly the preparation and adoption of development plans is not operating satisfactorily in the case of the larger authorities of Dublin City and Dublin County. A development plan simply cannot remain relevant over a period of a decade in an urban area of Dublin's scale. The size of the areas, the scale and complexity of the issues, the staffing levels in the authorities and the procedures involved all contribute to delays. A facility in the 1963 Act to prepare local plans relating to a particular district or aspect of planning has recently been explored by Dublin Corporation and Dun Laoghaire Corporation. In Dublin City two such local plans have been prepared on the Temple Bar and the Grand Canal areas and others are proposed. This option has the potential of introducing much needed flexibility into the development plan system. The reorganization of local government will result in smaller more manageable authorities and the time-scale of the development plan process may improve.

A development plan is generally binding on a planning authority. This fact, combined with the lengthy review period for plans, could give rise to an inflexible and unworkable system were it not for the fact that the Planning Appeals Board is not bound by development plans and that planning authorities can materially contravene their own plans provided certain procedures are observed. In 1991, the latest year for which figures are available, 17 material contraventions were passed by Dublin County and four by Dublin City (Griffin, 1992). The relatively limited use of this procedure not only by the Dublin authorities, but also nationally, reflects the fact that an appeal procedure is available if a planning application is unsuccessful at local level, even if the proposed development contravenes the plan for the area. These provisions, and in particular that relating to the Planning Appeals Board, have allowed the planning system to operate reasonably efficiently despite outdated provisions in development plans. The introduction in the Local Government (Planning and Development) Act (1992) of a time limit of four months on appeal decisions by the Planning Appeals Board should lead to an increase in efficiency.

Permission to carry out development must be sought from the local planning authority. The authority must respond to a planning application within two months, unless the applicant agrees to a time extension. In its response the planning authority can either grant or refuse an application, or seek additional information. If the planning authority fails to make a decision within two months, the applicant is entitled to a grant of per-mission by default. Decisions are an executive function of the planning authority and are made by the city or county manager. The refusal rate in both Dublin County (including Dun Laoghaire Borough) and City for 1991 was circa 14% compared with a national average of 12.5% (Griffin, 1992). An appeal against a decision of a planning authority can be made by the applicant or by any third party within one month of the planning authority's decision. Third party rights are thus a fundamental feature of the Irish development control system. Appeal rates in the Dublin area are considerably above the national average, for example in 1991 the appeal rate in the Dublin area was circa 15.3%, compared with a national rate of 7.9% (Griffin, 1992). Each year 20–25% of planning authority decisions are reversed by the Planning Appeals Board (Griffin, 1992).

11.4 PLANNING POLICY

The single most important influence for the development of Dublin has been the Myles Wright Plan commissioned by government and prepared over the years 1964–7. Wright proposed that the bulk of the anticipated population increase in the region, estimated at 320 000 persons between 1961–85, be accommodated in four new towns located circa 10 km to the west of Dublin city.

The subsequent Dublin County Council Development Plan (1972) adopted the Wright strategy, modified to provide for the development of three towns, Tallaght, Lucan/Clondalkin and Blanchardstown. Thus a coherent settlement strategy was set in place though difficulties arose in the implementation of the policy. Unlike the United Kingdom experience, no single purpose corporations were established to oversee development of the towns. Instead this was dependent on the individual actions of the private sector and public agencies with the local authority both servicing the land and co-ordinating and attempting to stimulate development. The subsequent slow down of population growth in the towns, combined with their perceived lack of attractiveness for the private residential sector had serious repercussions for development, and the target population of 100 000 per town currently appear unlikely to be achieved.

Tallaght, with a population of circa 73 000, only obtained its town centre after 20 years and this was only achieved due to designation of the site for financial incentives by central government. The town centre has since acted as a pump primer for further commercial and recreational development in its vicinity. However, the fate of the other two new towns Blanchardstown and Lucan/Clondalkin, with current populations of circa 43 000 and 55 000 respectively remains uncertain. Perceived as unattractive by private-sector residential developers, who have opted to develop in the south and south-east suburbs and in the northern fringe of the city, these towns have experienced a significant downturn in development activity. This has serious implications for the achievement of target populations and the provision of the range of services typically found in urban areas.

The settlement strategy which has been pursued in the Dublin area for over 20 years has not been the subject of review and reassessment. The ill-fated Eastern Region Settlement Strategy 2011, failed to gain public or political acceptance, and was never adopted. Meanwhile the sphere of influence of the Dublin Urban area has now extended to the adjoining counties of Meath, Kildare and Wicklow, giving rise to considerable development pressures and long-distance commuting. These factors, together with the lack of confidence in the settlement strategy displayed by private developers and elected political representatives, point to the need for a fundamental reassessment of the strategy.

Furthermore the lack of a regional level of government in Ireland has meant that, to date, no forum has existed for strategic planning. This fact, combined with the relative lack of national policy guidelines has left local planning authorities operating in a policy vacuum. A provision of the Local Government Act (1991) allows for the establishment of regional authorities 'with the limited role of promoting co-ordination of public services'. Such regional authorities will be established in 1994. The establishment of an authority for the Dublin region with appropriate powers is critical as 'it is only in this regional context that strategic planning and co-ordination will be meaningful for this area' (Advisory Expert Committee Report on Local Government Reorganisation and Reform, 1991).

The large-scale suburban growth in the County area in the 1960s and 1970s corresponded with a marked decline in population in central Dublin. Apart from the high-quality south-east sector of the city which experienced considerable development pressure, other areas continued to decay. The response of Dublin Corporation was the formulation of policies aimed at the encouragement of public transport, reduction of dependency on the private motor car, curtailment of office development outside the city centre, environmental improvement, conservation of the historic heritage and protection of residential communities. However due to stringent central government control of local authority finance, combined with limited independent financial resources and the lack of a spending budget, the planning department is dependent on the actions of the private sector and on central government to achieve its policies. Lack of national policy guidelines also create difficulties for the planning authority in the formulation of development plan policies. For example the Dublin City Draft Plan (1987) proposed the construction of a rapid transit system with a central transportation centre in the Temple Bar area of the city.

However, a subsequent announcement by government that finances were unavailable and that the Temple Bar area was to be conserved, undermined a central strategy of the draft plan. This specific case highlights the difficulties of planning in a large urban area, particularly in the absence of national guide-lines and the financial means to achieve objectives.

The Dublin planning authorities thus depend largely on development control to achieve policies. This operates effectively when planning policies are in agreement with market forces as, for example, the current increase in the construction of residential development in the inner city and the development of office buildings near to transportation routes. However policies which seek to direct or contain the market have met with less success for example a requirement of the Dublin City Development Plan (1980) that office developments in the south-east sector of the city contain a 60% residential content proved unsuccessful and has been abandoned. Likewise attempts to encourage development in the north inner city by flexible zoning objectives failed to attract much needed investment. It was only after the introduction of financial incentives by central government, in selected areas in the 1980s that development activity took place (Berry and McGreal, 1993).

One important recent initiative has been the commissioning by government of the Dublin Transportation Initiative (DTI), the final report of which is due in 1994. This study forms the first transportation/land use plan carried out for the Dublin area since the publication of the Dublin Transportation Study in 1971. Unlike the latter study, the DTI involved a considerable element of public participation. The proposals put forward in the study favour the encouragement of public transport by the introduction of light rail and quality bus services and the curtailment of road construction and widening within the motorway ring under construction around the city (DTI, 1993). The DTI proposals relating to public transport are consistent with the development plan policies of Dublin Corporation and, if implemented, would lead to improved accessibility to the inner city and a strengthening of its commercial core. Application is being made by government (early 1994) for EC Cohesion Fund support to assist in the funding of the DTI proposals.

11.5   PROPERTY MARKET SECTORS

11.5.1   Industrial

Reflecting international experience, industrial employment in the Dublin area declined both absolutely and relatively over the period 1971–89. Numbers employed fell by 32% and Dublin's share of national industrial employment decreased from 37% to 27%. The major source of employment loss was in traditional manufacturing industry, much of which had been located in the inner-city area. The changing industrial structure in Dublin involving closures, relocations and the establishment of new foreign-owned high-technology industries led to major changes in land use in the inner city as well as in suburban areas. These market-driven closures and locational changes were facilitated by planning policies regarding industrial location (Drudy, 1991).

Since 1961, approximately 2800 industrial units containing more than 2 million sq m of space, of which 20% is classified as post-1981 modern space, have been developed in the Dublin area. These are located predominantly in industrial estates in the south-western suburbs of the city. The provision of this space has been marked by three periods of intensive development activity in 1968–72, 1978–81 and more recently in 1990–2, corresponding in each case to increases in economic growth rates nationally. Since the basis of national economic policy was export-led growth in manufacturing output, generous tax concessions involving 100% relief on cost of construction have acted as a stimulus to occupiers of and investors in industrial space. Over 40% of industrial floor space was held by institutional investors in the early 1980s. However, substantial disinvestment by institutions and the disposal of industrial property by the semi-state agencies, the Industrial Development Authority and Industrial Credit Company, has resulted in the current situation whereby only 25% of industrial floor space is owned by institutional investors, under 3% is held by commercial developers and the vast bulk of the remainder is owner occupied. Irish institutional property portfolios currently hold on average from 8–10% in industrial property (Centre for Urban and Regional Studies, Trinity College, Dublin/Sherry Fitzgerald, 1992).

Industrial rental levels are determined by a combination of unit size, location, age and design. Significant variations in rental levels and yields are evident between third-generation space, incorporating a substantial office component and generally enhanced design/construction standards, and older larger units for which there is little demand. Although there is a current vacancy rate of circa 12%, much of this is in older obsolete space and shortages of well located larger modern units are beginning to emerge.

11.5.2 Offices

Service sector employment grew rapidly in Ireland from 1960 onwards with total employment rising from 39% of the labour market in 1961 to 59% in 1992. A considerable part of this growth in numbers has been concentrated in Dublin. Indeed between 1971 and 1989 service employment in the Dublin Metropolitan region rose by 34% almost exactly counterbalancing the decline in industrial employment, and increasing the share of service employment in the region from 60% to 75%. Within the white-collar services sector, the main area of employment growth has been in the insurance, finance and business services sector which increased its employment base almost fourfold between 1961 and 1990. Non-market services, including public-sector office employment, grew particularly strongly during the period 1970–80, at a rate of 4.2% per annum (Bannon, 1991).

Approximately 1.35 million sq m of dedicated office space was developed in Dublin over the period 1960–92 in response to this growth in demand. Supply was facilitated by the development of the financial sector which both assisted in the funding of development and invested in completed developments. Three distinct development cycles with a lagged relationship to national economic cycles and peaking in 1973, 1982 and 1990, characterized the provision of this space (Malone, 1990; Hamilton Osborne King/Department of Geography, Trinity College Dublin, 1990–3).

Market forces have dictated that office space in Dublin is highly concentrated in the south-east segment of the city particularly in districts Dublin 2 and 4 (Malone, 1990). This has been the case despite strong planning policy provisions to encourage office development in the north inner city – an area in urgent need of renewal.

Office displacement of residential and industrial uses often resulted in conflict between conservation and development interests, particularly in the earlier stages of the development boom (McDonald, 1985). However, planning policy, as expressed in plot ratio, site coverage, residential content and listing provisions, has been largely successful in preserving the Georgian scale and much of the better housing stock in the high-pressure south-eastern segment of the city. In contrast many Georgian residential buildings in the south inner city underwent change of use to office accommodation while those in the north inner city continued in long-term decline, occupied by rent-controlled tenants.

Several features distinguish the office property sector in Dublin. The principal owner of completed space is the financial sector (58%); the bulk of occupied space is leasehold (67%); the dominant occupation of space is by the state sector (51%) and the majority of space developed is traded space (77%). Concerning the latter the greater part was realized by development interests, the remainder by institutional investors. Institutional property portfolios hold approximately 55–60% in office investments (Malone, 1990).

The emerging trend in the Dublin office sector is towards a tiered market consisting of new third-generation space in established prime areas, for example in Dublin 2 and 4, and in the better located urban renewal designated areas. The current vacancy rate (1993), approximately 11% of stock, is dominated by second-hand space, both Georgian and second generation, and by new space in secondary designated areas.

11.5.3 Retail

Since 1960, 54 new planned shopping centres of over 2000 sq m each, containing a total of 360 000 sq m of net retail space have been developed in the Dublin Metropolitan area. Two of these are major city centre developments namely the Ilac Centre, which opened in 1981, contains 22 000 sq m of net retail space and the Stephens Green Centre, opened in 1988, contains 23 600 sq m of net retail space. The Square, Tallaght, the largest shopping centre in Ireland, which opened in 1990, has 38 000 sq m of net retail space, 70%, of which is devoted to comparison goods and services. It functions as a regional shopping centre. The remaining centres, varying in size, are widely distributed throughout the inner and outer suburbs.

Ownership of retail space is shared between retail interests (29%), property development/holding companies (44%) and institutional investors (27%). The latter is principally accounted for by institutional ownership of the Ilac Centre and a significant portion of the Square, Tallaght, which between them account for 17% of all new retail space (Parker and Kyne, 1990). The share of retail investment in Irish institutional portfolios is of the order of 35%. Apart from investment in large new shopping centre developments, institutions exercise caution in respect to suburban retail investment, concentrating instead on prime city centre leasehold and freehold retail interests.

Despite the increased provision of suburban space devoted to comparison goods shopping, up to 1988 the city centre had maintained its dominant share in this sector with 63% of total comparison goods turnover in the Dublin area. However, with the opening of the Square, Tallaght, this share is likely to decline and will come under further pressure with the opening of the 60 000 sq m Blanchardstown Centre. Consequently city centre retailing has become highly concentrated into two prime streets, Henry Street and Grafton Street, where rents have increased on average by 50% during the 1980s. The relative decline in the city's secondary shopping streets is highlighted by a rental growth of only 15% over the same period.

The conflict between the provision of extensive retail facilities in the new towns as provided for in the County Development Plan, and the enhancement of city centre retailing, as provided for in the City Development Plan, in a scenario in which population growth has ceased, disposable income has slowed and unemployment levels have remained persistently high, is an issue of concern to property investment interests. This perception of the city becoming overshopped allied to doubts concerning the future viability of older medium-sized district centres is making institutional investors wary of the retail sector.

11.6 THE PROPERTY INVESTMENT MARKET

The property investment market in Ireland is small, reflecting both the relative size of the country and its population, as well as its comparative

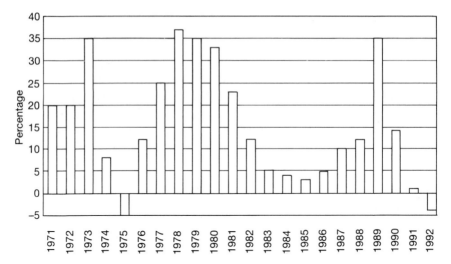

Figure 11.2 Investment property, annual growth
Source: reproduced with permission of Hamilton Osborne King from Property Outlook, June 1993.

stage of development and level of GNP in relation to other EC member states. The market consists almost exclusively of prime Dublin office, retail and industrial properties traded and held mainly by institutional investors, as part of pension and life assurance funds. Institutional property portfolios broadly comprise 60% office, 30% retail and 10% industrial.

The current capital value of property investment holdings in Dublin is estimated at £1.75 billion, of which £1.4 billion represents institutional investment. The equity market is valued at £11 billion and the gilt market at £30 billion. Furthermore as in the United Kingdom and other European countries institutional investment in property has declined sharply over the past decade from a high of 21% of investment portfolios in 1981 to 7% in 1993 (French, 1993).

While the investment market is subject to cyclical variation in demand and output (Figure 11.2), the extent of these and the more cautious approach of lending and investment institutions to property development and investment has meant that the market has not been subject to the level of variation experienced in larger and more highly developed urban economies. In recent years the annual amount of investment in commercial property has varied between £220 million in 1989 to £30 million in 1992, the bulk of it being held by private-sector non-institutional investors.

In relation to alternative investments, over the long run, 1970–92, property comfortably outperformed gilts and cash by two percentage points but underperformed by a similar margin relative to equities. The

Table 11.2 Returns and risk: Irish investments 1970–92

Investment category	Returns % p.a.	Risk % p.a.
Property	14	12.6
Equities	15.9	37.6
Gilts	12.1	12.8
Cash	12.1	3.2

Source: reproduced with permission from Cunneen (1993).

Table 11.3 Comparative performance by sector, property and equities and consumer price index 1973–92

	Compound annual average percentage change
Consumer price index	9.79
Overall property index	12.70
Total returns equity index	16.15
Property capital value index	5.71
Industrial equity price index	9.14
Property net income index	5.92
Total market dividend index	7.91
Property estimated rental value index	8.08
Offices	
Capital value index	8.49
Estimated rental value index	5.43
Retail	
Capital value index	8.36
Estimated rental value index	7.14
Industrial	
Capital value index	7.75
Estimated rental value index	5.69

Source: adapted from Irish Property Index (1993); reproduced with permission of Jones Lang Wootton.

analysis also shows that in terms of risk exposure, property performed substantially better than equities and marginally better than gilts (Table 11.2).

The performance of property and of the different property sectors measured by overall returns, capital values, rental income and estimated rental values *vis-à-vis* comparative returns from equities and the consumer price index shows that in terms of overall returns, equities outperformed property while both yielded real rates of return in excess of inflation of

Table 11.4 Annual average percentage compound growth in rental income and the consumer price index 1970–92 (current market prices)

Time period	No. of years	Industrial	Modern office	Georgian office	Retail	Composite	Consumer price index
1970–80	10	15.63	17	18.47	16.69	16.36	13.85
1970–85	15	10.96	11.43	12.01	12.27	11.24	13.11
1970–90	20	12.11	11.84	10.63	13.27	11.84	10.89
1970–92	22	11.25	9.85	8.4	11.32	10	10.15

Source: adapted from Lisney Property Rental and Unit Linked Indices (1993); reproduced with permission of Lisney.

Table 11.5 Annual average percentage real compound growth in rental income 1970–92

Time period	No. of years	Industrial	Modern office	Georgian office	Retail	Composite
1970–80	10	1.78	3.15	4.62	2.84	2.51
1970–85	15	−2.15	−1.68	−1.1	−0.84	−1.87
1970–90	20	1.22	0.95	−0.26	2.38	0.95
1970–92	22	1.1	−0.3	−1.75	1.17	−0.15

Source: adapted from Lisney Property Rental and Unit Linked Indices (1993); reproduced with permission of Lisney.

6.36% p.a. in the case of equities, and 2.91% in the case of property (Table 11.3). The differences in performance between the sectors are reflected both in income and capital value variations. Property net income, capital value and estimated rental value, both overall and in the different property sectors, underperformed relative to industrial equity prices and total market dividends. The best performing property sector in terms of combined capital growth and estimated rental value is retail followed by offices and industrial.

The rental performance of the different property sectors *vis-à-vis* the consumer price index over four different time periods, namely 10, 15, 20 and 22 years, is presented in Table 11.4 and translated into real terms in Table 11.5.

The analyses show that in terms of rental growth there are variations between the different time periods considered, both within and between the sectors. Retail was the best performing sector over a 15, 20 and 22 year period, while Georgian office rentals failed to match inflation over the same periods. The effect of downturns in economic activity in the early 1980s transformed real rental growth in all property categories between 1970 and 1980 into negative growth over the 15-year cycle between 1970 to 1985. Economic recovery following 1986 resulted in positive growth to

1990. Since then economic difficulties combined with an overhang of vacant space is again reflected in negative composite property growth caused particularly by decline in the office sector.

11.7   STIMULATING THE PROPERTY INVESTMENT MARKET IN INNER-CITY DUBLIN

The extensive redevelopment of inner-city Dublin, over the past three decades, has been concentrated in the south-eastern part of the city leaving large areas of dereliction particularly, but not exclusively, in the north inner city. Renewal of the latter area has been a major focus of attention since 1985. Unlike other countries where regeneration has been facilitated by substantial government investment in infrastructure, Ireland has relied on a system of fiscal incentives supported by the establishment of special purpose public agencies to secure the renewal of two key areas in inner-city Dublin – Custom House Docks and Temple Bar.

Apart from one notable exception, that of the Ilac Shopping Centre, opened in 1981, which was a joint venture between the Irish Life Assurance Company and Dublin Corporation, commercial property in Dublin has been, until recently, exclusively initiated, managed and funded by private-sector interests. Participation of the public sector other than through meeting the requirements of the normal planning process has been absent. However a number of legislative initiatives has now provided for public–private partnerships based on the availability of fiscal incentives for developments, within designated areas, concluded within a stated time period.

The Urban Renewal Act (1986) and Finance Act (1986) with subsequent amendments provide the legislative and fiscal basis for designation. In addition, Section 27 of the Finance Act 1988, reintroduced the former Section 23 of the Finance Act 1981, in respect of taxation relief for the provision of rented residential accommodation (this provision has now lapsed outside of the designated areas).

The 1986 Acts enable investors/developers, owner occupiers and lessees of new and refurbished commercial and residential development undertaken within a specified time period in the designated areas to qualify for a range of fiscal incentives extending over a ten-year period. Excluding the Custom House Docks and Temple Bar areas where the tax savings are greater (100% capital allowances as opposed to 50% for other Dublin designated areas), the effect of the incentives for investors/developers of new/refurbished commercial buildings in designated areas is to reduce development/refurbishment costs by approximately 20%. Additionally, owner occupiers of such buildings qualify for complete rates remission for a ten-year period. In the case of business lessees, as a result of double-taxation allowances and rates remission, the total savings over ten years can amount to approximately ten times the initial annual rent payable (Dublin Corporation, 1991).

A measure of the success of the incentives is that approximately £265 million or 37% of all non-residential investment sales over the period 1987 to 1993 have been tax-based (Hamilton Osborne King, 1993). Owner occupiers of new houses and apartments qualify for savings of approximately 25% of development costs while investors/developers can qualify for tax savings of up to 60% of development costs of residential units for renting under the provisions of Section 27 of the 1988 Act (Dublin Corporation, 1991). The effect of the incentives is that a single person purchasing a new two-bedroom apartment in a designated area in Dublin's inner city can do so at 49% of the monthly outlay required to rent a similar sized apartment in Dublin districts 2 and 4, and at 75% of the monthly outlay required to purchase a new three-bedroomed house in suburban Dublin. The respective monthly outlays on the purchase of an apartment within a designated area by a married couple are 35% and 60% respectively of renting an apartment in Dublin 2 or 4, or of purchasing a suburban house.

The 1986 Urban Renewal Act was originally intended to regenerate the inner areas of the major urban centres of the country, and its perceived success prompted the government substantially to extend the number of urban centres and designated areas in 1988 and 1989. The significant extension of designated areas in Dublin has, however, been criticized by property interests as undermining the original intention and effectiveness of the scheme as an instrument of urban regeneration (Mulcahy, 1991; Williams, 1993). The inner city renewal focus was also extended by designating the suburban Tallaght New Town Centre which provided the catalyst for the development of the Square Shopping Centre and other adjoining commercial developments. Likewise the town centre of Ballymun, a north city suburb, which consists of a large shopping centre developed in 1969 and urgently in need of refurbishment, has also recently (1993) been designated.

11.7.1 The Custom House Docks

The 1986 Urban Renewal Act established the Custom House Docks Development Authority, a single-purpose agency charged with securing, within a period of five years from the date of initial commencement of site development work, the redevelopment of the 11 ha redundant Custom House Docks site adjoining the north central business district of Dublin. Development certified by the authority as being in accordance with its development plan, already approved by the Minister, is classified as being exempt. Such exemption from the normal planning process has undoubtedly expedited the pace of development activity on the site.

In 1988, the Authority entered into a master project agreement with a development consortium, the Custom House Docks Development Company, to undertake a mixed scheme of offices, hotel, museum, retail leisure and residential development totalling 200 000 m^2 and representing an investment of some £300 million. To date five buildings, including the flagship International Financial Services Centre (45 000 m^2) and representing some 40% of planned development, have been completed and are occupied by more than 2000 office staff. This has been achieved despite a turndown in the Dublin property market, although concern has been expressed about delays in commencing the less commercial elements of the development. Overall what has been realized to date and the speed at which it has been achieved are a testament to the success of Ireland's first formal statutorily established public–private sector development vehicle.

11.7.2 Temple Bar

With financial support from the European Community and forming part of the Dublin European City of Culture 1991 project, the Temple Bar Renewal and Development Act (1991) established two associated companies, Temple Bar Properties Limited and Temple Bar Renewal Limited, the objective being to create within a five-year period, a cultural, residential and small business quarter in the historic but run-down Temple Bar area in the heart of Dublin (Temple Bar Properties, 1992).

The function of Temple Bar Renewal Limited is to ensure that development is in accordance with the provisions of the Act with regard to uses, activities and other criteria and to certify such development as qualifying for the specified tax incentives. The function of Temple Bar Properties Limited is to act as development company for the area. Unlike the Custom House Docks Development Authority, the company is obliged to conform fully with the provisions of the planning system. In seeking to achieve renewal, Temple Bar Properties is undertaking, directly and in partnership, development to a value of £100 million, financed from the European Regional Development Fund and by loans from the European Investment Bank and from the Bank of Ireland, guaranteed by the Minister for Finance. The development is being planned on the basis that the commercial elements will cross-subsidize the less commercial activities. Matching funding of a further £100 million is expected to come from the private sector.

The preparation of an architectural framework plan and a development plan are key stages already completed in the developing concept of Temple Bar. Currently (mid 1993) substantial property acquisition and infrastructural work has been undertaken, some development has been completed and more is under construction. In total 24 planning permissions for major developments have been sought. By the end of 1994, it is estimated that there will be five hotels, 200 shops, 40 restaurants and close to a dozen expanded or new cultural centres in Temple Bar with a residential population of 2000.

All of the Temple Bar Property Company's holdings will be transferred to a trust after the company's mandate ceases in 1996. This and the provision that all commercial leases contain covenants that make any future proposed change in use subject to the agreement of the company or its successor, as well as the fact that commercial development will be small-scale in nature, mean that the 'Left Bank' character of the area is likely to be preserved and lower-valued uses not displaced by higher-valued larger-scale high-street uses.

11.7.3   Evaluation of designated areas

The success of the designated area schemes in stimulating development may be measured by the amount of development completed, in progress and planned, virtually all of which is privately funded (Tables 11.6 and 11.7).

The statistics indicate (Table 11.7) the marked shift from office to residential development as schemes have developed. The take-up of office space particularly of smaller units in the more peripheral areas has been slow, despite the incentives, in a situation of low demand and considerable vacant space throughout the city. As a result, almost by default, there has been a remarkable inner-city residential renewal following a period in which for many years there had been a complete absence of private residential development in the inner city. Since 1990, 2589 private apartments have been completed or are under construction in the inner city, while a further 4165 are at planning stage (mid 1993). There has also been a marked shift in ownership from investment in units for renting to

Table 11.6   Urban renewal schemes in Dublin as at 31 December 1992

Project type	No.	Sq metres	Estimated cost £S
Projects completed in designated areas	115	107 130	72 594 082
Projects in progress in designated areas	33	111 738	99 777 636
Projects in planning in designated areas	136	282 659	223 788 272
Urban renewal schemes on Corporation owned sites outside of designated areas	22	58 643	41 336 722
Custom House Docks Development		200 000	300 000 000
Tallaght Town Centre		65 000	85 000 000
Total	306	825 180	822 496 762

Source: reproduced with permission of Dublin Corporation.

Table 11.7 Distribution of development type in designated areas as at 31 December 1992 (percentages)

	Offices	Commercial	Offices/ commercial	Hotel, bostel, pub, leisure etc.	Residential	Residential/ other	Industrial	Total
Completed projects	41	18	11	13	8	9	—	100
Projects in progress	17	0.05	0.05	23	33	26	—	100
Projects in planning	27	7	14	10	25	15	2	100
All projects	27	8	10	14	24	16	1	100

Source: reproduced with permission of Dublin Corporation.

owner occupation by first time buyers reflecting market response to the attractive tax savings available to owner occupiers.

11.8   CONCLUSION

Driven by market forces generated by national and regional economic growth and shaped by planning policy, Dublin has undergone major changes and expansion over the past 35 years. The city has grown sub-stantially both in area and population. In terms of occupational structure, it is now pre-eminently a services city. A significant volume of industrial and commercial property investment has been undertaken yielding re-latively stable and satisfactory long-term real returns.

The rapid expansion of the suburbs has been accompanied by a cor-responding decline in the inner city. Industrial and retail development has followed the decentralization of population to the suburbs, and office development has been concentrated in the prime south-eastern segment of the city. While considerable areas of dereliction still remain, urban renewal fiscal incentives are having an important impact in reversing inner city decline, resulting in a substantial addition of commercial and office space as well as a significant return of private residential land use to the city core.

Since its inception in 1963 the planning system in Dublin has been more successful in controlling than in promoting and facilitating development. The development control element of the system operates relatively ef-ficiently due to a combination of strict time limits and a right of appeal to the Planning Appeals Board, which itself is not bound by local devel-opment plans. Third-party rights are a fundamental feature of the system and account, to a large extent, for its acceptance by the general public. In contrast, in the Dublin area, the development plan system is hampered by excessive delays, resulting in dated policies and objectives. This fact, combined with a severe lack of resources at local authority level, has resulted in the perception of development plans as a controlling, rather than a promoting, mechanism.

Local planning authorities, in turn, have been operating in a policy vacuum, caused by lack of direction and guidance at national level and the lack of a regional level of government. The publication in January 1990 of the first ever Environment Action Programme by an Irish government is a positive indicator of increased involvement by central government in spatial policy-making. The establishment of a regional authority for the Dublin area is also under way, albeit with restricted functions.

The settlement strategy pursued over the past 20 years for the devel-opment of the Dublin area, based on the United Kingdom new towns model, is in urgent need of review and reassessment. Failure to establish single-purpose corporations to oversee development of the towns, combined with a lack of resources, has had serious repercussions for the implementation of the strategy. Furthermore the lack of interest displayed by the private residential sector to development in the new towns and the likelihood that the towns will not achieve their target populations, point to the need for new approaches to their planning and development.

Future prospects for the city and opportunities for profitable property development and investment will be influenced not only by planning policy but also by the continuing situation of stabilization of population, economic slowdown and high rates of long-term unemployment. Meanwhile planned transport improvements will ease traffic congestion and proposed changes in administrative structures should improve urban management.

REFERENCES

Advisory Expert Committee (1991) *Report on Local Government Reorganisation and Reform*, Stationery Office, Dublin.

Bannon, M.J. (1991) Service industries, paper presented to Conference, *Priorities Now: Dublin's Economy in the 1990s*, Dublin Chamber of Commerce.

Berry, J.N. and McGreal, W.S. (1993) Fiscal mechanisms and inner city development in Dublin, *Journal of Property Finance*, **3**(4), 543–52.

Census of Population (1966, 1991) Stationery Office, Dublin.

Centre for Urban and Regional Studies, Trinity College, Dublin in conjunction with Sherry Fitzgerald (1992) *Industrial Property Development in Dublin 1960–1991*, Sherry Fitzgerald, Dublin.

Cunneen, P. (1993) The role of property in investment portfolios in the 1990s, paper presented to Conference, *Prospects for Property Investment*, Society of Chartered Surveyors in the Republic of Ireland, Dublin.

Drudy, P.J. (1991) Demographic and economic change in Dublin in recent decades, in A. McLaren (ed.), *Dublin in Crisis*, Trinity Papers in Geography No. 5, Trinity College, Dublin.

Dublin County Council (1972, 1983) *Dublin County Development Plan*.

Dublin Corporation (1980, 1991) *Dublin City Development Plan*.

Dublin Corporation (1987) *Draft Dublin City Development Plan*.

Dublin Corporation (1992) *Financial Incentives in Dublin*.

Dublin Transportation Initiative (1993) Interim Report, Stationery Office, Dublin.

French, I. (1993) Paper presented to Seminar organized by Irish Association of Pension Funds, Dublin.

Griffin, L. (1992) *Planning Statistics 1991*, Environmental Research Unit.

Hamilton Osborne King/Department of Geography, Trinity College, Dublin (1990–1993) *HOK Offices*, Hamilton Osborne King, Dublin.

Hamilton Osborne King (1993) *Property Outlook*, Hamilton Osborne

King, Dublin.

Jones Lang Wootton (1973–1993) *Irish Property Index*, Jones Lang Wootton, Dublin.

Lisney (1970–1993) *Property Retail Indices*, Lisney, Dublin.

McDonald, F. (1985) *The Destruction of Dublin*, Gill & MacMillan, Dublin.

McDonald, F. (1989) *Saving the City*, Tomar Publishing, Dublin.

Malone, P. (1990) *Office Development in Dublin 1960–1990*, School of Architecture, University of Manchester.

Mulcahy, J. (1991) paper presented to Conference, *The Role of Fiscal Policy in Urban Renewal*, 4 October, Foundation for Fiscal Studies, Trinity College, Dublin.

NESC (1992) *The Association between Economic Growth and Employment Growth in Ireland*, Stationery Office, Dublin.

Parker, A.J. and Kyne, D.M. (1990) *Dublin Shopping Centres: Statistical Digest 11 and Update*, The Centre for Retail Studies, University College, Dublin.

Temple Bar Properties (1992) *Development Programme for Temple Bar*, Temple Bar Properties, Dublin.

Williams, B. (1993) Encouraging demand is key issue in commercial property, *Irish Times*, 2 June, Dublin.

Wright, M. and Partners (1967) *The Dublin Region: Advisory Plan and Final Report*, 2 vols, Stationery Office, Dublin.

PART THREE

SOUTHERN
EUROPE

12

Barcelona

Pere Riera and Geoffrey Keogh

Barcelona, the capital of Catalunya in the north-eastern corner of Spain, is located 150 km from the French border and forms part of what has come to be known as the Mediterranean sun belt. Its favourable position and good communications have allowed Barcelona to benefit particularly from the liberalization of trade associated with the creation of a single European market. Despite a growing service sector, its employment base remains heavily influenced by manufacturing and the area has attracted considerable inward investment by multinational companies seeking a manufacturing presence in Spain.

The city of Barcelona is tightly constrained in physical terms by the sea to one side and mountains to the other. The municipality has a population of 1.6 million in a land area of a little under 100 km^2, making it one of the most densely populated European cities. However, in functional terms, the economic and social influence of Barcelona extends much further. Its metropolitan area and the more meaningful metropolitan region beyond cover a population of 3 million and 4.3 million people respectively, out of a total 6.1 million in Catalunya as a whole. Like other advanced European cities the municipality of Barcelona and its immediate metropolitan area has been losing population for the last decade or more as residents and jobs decentralize to the outer areas (Sau, 1992).

Barcelona is a highly distinctive city in architectural terms. Activity was contained within the old walled city, the *Ciutat Vella*, with a number of satellite towns located within a short distance. However, from 1860 onwards the city was allowed to expand according to the famous plan of Idefons Cerdà into the area known as the Eixample (Cerdà, 1867). The legacy of this plan is the grid structure of the central city, originally intended as a low-density system in which only two faces of each block would be developed, but ultimately transformed due to financial pressure

European Cities, Planning Systems and Property Markets Edited by James Berry and Stanley McGreal. Published in 1995 by E & FN Spon. ISBN 0419 18940 8.

and development demand into a much higher density area in which all four faces of the blocks were built up. The area provides a rich mix of commercial and industrial uses, currently housing around a quarter of a million people and 350 000 jobs within its 650 blocks (Busquets, 1992a). It contains some of the city's most important architecture by Gaudí, Domènech and other architects of the *Modernista* movement. To some extent this should be seen as a reaction to the uniformity of the Cerdà grid (Hughes, 1992) although even the more humble architecture of the Eixample is important to the visual integrity of the area.

Recent years have seen extensive change and a new dynamism in the city. Economic growth and the self-confidence generated by the Olympic Games have resulted in a wave of new development and infrastructural investment. As well as improving the environment of the city, these changes have opened up numerous underutilized and obsolete areas for new activity and have improved accessibility between the city and its hinterland.

This chapter, in considering the planning and property market, explains the administrative structure and the legal framework for urban planning and identifies some of the important initiatives which have been introduced in Barcelona during the last 20 years. The operation of the Spanish property market is considered against the background of planning constraint, with the Barcelona office market taken as a case study of recent patterns of use, investment and development.

12.1 PLANNING CONTEXT

12.1.1 The Spanish administrative and planning structure

Physical planning in Spain follows, in principle at least, a hierarchical top-down procedure in which plans drawn at one spatial level guide and constrain the contents of lower level plans (Keyes *et al.*, 1991). This hierarchy follows the governmental and administrative structure of Spain, and the distribution of planning powers provides an essential key to understanding the mechanisms of planning for a city like Barcelona.

The administrative system is currently organized in three tiers: central, regional (the autonomous communities) and local (the provinces and municipalities). This reflects a substantial decentralization of power from central to regional government following the death of Franco in 1975 and the restoration of parliamentary democracy. Under the Spanish Constitution of 1978, a democratic and autonomous tier of government was established at the regional level with the right to claim independent legislative powers in many areas of activity including land-use planning and housing provision. By 1983, 17 autonomous communities had been created, passing their own regional constitutions and claiming powers in most of the activities permitted under the Spanish Constitution. The Catalan Parliament has been among the most vigorous in taking advantage of the legislative and administrative autonomy which the Constitution allows.

The newly created autonomous communities also acquired powers from the provincial level of local government. The 50 Spanish provinces combine central and local administrative functions, being both territorial delegations of the central government and associations of municipalities. However, with the decentralization of power from central to regional government, they have lost much of their previous importance. This applies in the field of planning. While they formerly constituted the higher planning authority to the municipalities, in many cases it is the new regional governments which now supervise local planning activity and approve local plans, and this applies in Catalunya.

As the autonomous communities have claimed legislative powers over planning matters under the 1978 Constitution, the power of the central administration over land-use planning has correspondingly reduced. However, there remain many closely related activities for which central government still has responsibility. It is on the grounds of meeting these responsibilities that, after progressively transferring planning powers to the autonomous communities in the 1980s, the central Parliament has attempted to regain a greater degree of control by means of the 1992 Planning Act (*Ley del Régimen del Suelo y Ordenación Urbana*). This contains two kinds of articles; those which have to be followed by planning acts passed at the regional level and those which apply where autonomous communities have not developed their own planning legislation. Although, in practice, regional planning legislation has tended to follow closely the previous Planning Act (1976) introducing only minor changes, aspects of the 1992 Act have been seen as a threat to regional autonomy in planning matters. As a result, various articles of the new Act are being challenged by a number of autonomous communities in the Constitutional Court and a question mark hangs over their future freedom to legislate as they wish.

At the local level it is the municipalities (of which there are over 8000 in Spain and almost 1000 in Catalunya) which are the effective planning authorities, responsible for policy and development control in their areas. The more populous municipalities prepare a master plan, called the general municipal plans (*plan general municipal*), which are legally binding documents containing detailed zoning and land-use requirements for the whole of the municipality. Since these plans represent the lowest level in the hierarchy, they are required under law to conform with the guidance provided in higher level plans. However, to date this constraint has existed in theory only since no higher level plans have so far proceeded beyond the draft stage.

It is permissible under the law for a number of municipalities to co-operate in the production of a joint land-use plan and similarly possible to form administrative entities to oversee planning and related matters. This occurred in the case of Barcelona and 26 adjoining municipalities with strong economic and commuting links to the city. In 1974 they combined to form an administrative association known as the Metropolitan Corporation of Barcelona (*Corporación Metropolitana de Barcelona*), lying between the municipal and provincial levels of administration, and enjoying most of the local planning powers normally vested in the municipalities. It was for this functional area that a general land-use plan was formulated and passed in 1976. The Metropolitan Corporation was abolished by the Catalan government in 1985 for political reasons often compared with the abolition of the metropolitan counties in Britain (Busquets, 1992b). Its planning responsibilities went partly to the municipalities involved and partly to the regional government, but the metropolitan plan remains in force as the legally binding land-use plan for the area.

12.1.2   The land-use planning framework

The origins of the modern Spanish planning system stem from the 1956 Planning Act which was revised in 1975 and replaced by the consolidating Planning Act of 1976. The detailed operation of the planning system was refined through a series of central government regulations as well as by minor modifications introduced at the regional level in legislation passed by the autonomous communities. A further reform, consolidated in the Planning Act of 1992, contains some controversial measures but does not substantially affect the hierarchy of plans or the internal workings of the Spanish planning system, and in any case has not yet been fully implemented one year after approval. It is therefore the 1976 Spanish system together with the relevant modifications introduced by the Catalan Parliament which are the key to understanding the contemporary planning framework in Barcelona.

In the spatial hierarchy of the Spanish system, legal provision for the preparation of plans at the national, regional, and local levels, creates an integrated framework of physical land-use planning and guidance (Keyes *et al.*, 1991). The 1956 Planning Act envisaged a national urban planning scheme (*plan nacional de ordenación*), the principle of which has been carried into the 1976 and 1992 Planning Acts. The purpose of a plan at this level is to ensure the co-ordination of physical planning with economic and social objectives (Keyes *et al.*, 1991) and to articulate land-use principles in the national context (Bassols Coma, 1986). No such plan has so far been achieved, although an abortive attempt at an indicative economic plan was made in the early 1960s. It now looks increasingly unlikely that a national plan will ever be formulated given the extensive devolution of planning responsibilities to the regions.

The 1976 Planning Act includes provisions for the preparation of regional co-ordination plans (*planes directores territoriales de coordi-nación*) to address strategic land-use planning matters at a regional scale, including transport and communications, water supply, sites for waste disposal, provision of utilities, defence zones and conservation of areas of environmental and cultural significance. However, with regional plans not yet fully developed in Spain the implication is that under this notionally top-down system local plans are proceeding ahead of the regional plans which were intended to provide the guiding framework for the preparation of plans at the local level.

As the autonomous communities exercise their discretion, several regions have legislated to formulate regional plans in a slightly different way. In the case of Catalunya, three categories of regional plan are to be prepared; a general territorial plan (*plan general territorial*), partial territorial plans (*planes parciales territoriales*) and sectoral territorial plans (*planes sectoriales territoriales*). The Catalan Parliament issued guidelines in 1981 for the preparation of a general territorial plan to cover the whole of the autonomous community, dealing with those matters which are normally the subject of a regional co-ordination plan. Particular significance is attached to those proposals for the future distribution of population growth, emphasizing decentralization from the congested Barcelona area to other less populated sub-regions of Catalunya. A draft of the general territorial plan of Catalunya was made available for institutional enquiry (the general public could consult the plan but could not formally submit opinions) from January to July 1993. Final approval may take another two years, depending on the reaction of the different regional and local administrations to the draft.

Partial territorial plans will be prepared to deal with similar strategic planning issues but at a sub-regional level and in greater detail concerning land use. A partial territorial plan for the wider Barcelona area is already in advanced draft form although, formally, it will have to follow the requirements of the final version of the general territorial plan and must therefore wait until the latter has been passed. Similarly, sectoral territorial plans may be drawn for different key sectors of activity, such as com-munications or the protection of open spaces. These must again conform to the general territorial plan and may operate as a constraint on the content of the partial territorial plans since consistency must be ensured between them. Since there is no appropriate sub-regional administration to formulate partial and sectoral plans, all aspects of regional planning are the responsibility of the Catalan administration, with varying degrees of co-operation from the local governments concerned. Under the Planning Act, special plans (*planes especiales*) may be drawn up at the regional or sub-regional level for a given sector of activity. As such these are very similar to the Catalan sectoral territorial plans and, hierarchically, control the contents of local plans with respect to their specific subject matter.

The general plan, as the cornerstone of the Spanish local planning system, is a legally binding land-use plan formulated for the entire area of a municipality or, in some cases, a group of municipalities. The municipal government is responsible for the preparation and implementation, although final approval is required from a higher planning authority which, in the case of Catalunya and some other autonomous communities is the regional government. The content of general plans as specified in planning law must include (Keyes *et al.*, 1993):

1. a memorandum statement which sets out a brief justification of the project, analyses the key decisions involved in preparing the plan and outlines any alternatives which have been rejected, together with background complementary studies such as population projections;
2. analytical maps showing the land-use zones and lines of infrastructure;
3. planning regulations applying to each of the land-use zones;
4. a schedule of implementation covering two consecutive four-year periods, programming the development of both new and existing urban areas in line with growth forecasts;
5. a financial and economic study.

These plans are usually prepared by teams of professionals acting as consultants to the municipality although some of the larger local administrations have established their own in-house planning departments to undertake the task. In the absence of a formal town planning profession in Spain, the courts have established that planning teams must be led by graduates whose university degrees included a significant element of urban planning. In practice this means that it is normally architects or in some instances civil engineers who supervise the preparation of general plans, although the planning team will normally be interdisciplinary (Riera *et al.*, 1991).

General plans classify the territory of a municipality or municipalities into three types of land; urban (*suelo urbano*), urbanizable (*suelo urbanizable*), and non-urbanizable (*suelo no urbanizable*). Land is defined as urban where it is already largely built-up or where essential infrastructure is available to allow its immediate development. Urbanizable land, in contrast, is that which is considered suitable for new development in accordance with foreseeable needs. This is divided into programmed urbanizable land (*programado*) which is scheduled for development over two successive four-year periods and non-programmed urbanizable land (*no programado*) which is held as a reserve to meet possible further needs. The rest of the municipality's land, identified as non-urbanizable, includes protected environments where there is a strong planning reason for the prohibition of development and a residual land area which is not regarded as necessary for future development.

The general plan provides different degrees of information about land-use and development requirements. In the case of urban land the plan gives very detailed specifications for the use of each plot, specifying the volume and even the aesthetics of permissible future development, together with infrastructure requirements and social provision. No additional planning instrument is necessary to establish the legal right to develop urban land for the specified purposes, although planning permission must be granted before development may commence.

Concerning programmed urbanizable land, the general plan provides less detail. Typically, it defines zones of land use, lines of basic infrastructure, plot ratios and densities, and also specifies the value of the mean profit (*aprovechamiento medio*), an instrument designed to ensure that the benefits and costs of development are distributed equitably between landowners. However, this level of planning detail is not sufficient to allow development to go ahead. An additional planning instrument, known as a partial plan (*plan parcial*), is required to bring the planning specification of urbanizable land up to that provided in the general plan for urban land. This will include the detailed alignment of streets and other infrastructure, requirements for public facilities and precise information on the density of development. Since a partial plan must conform to the provisions of the general plan it obviously cannot be adopted before the general plan is itself approved. The power to approve partial plans normally lies with the municipal government. However in Catalunya the final decision rests with the regional government, a procedure which has been challenged in the Constitutional Court and which awaits a legal judgement.

In the case of non-programmed urbanizable land even less detail is provided in the general plan concerning its future use. A two-stage process is necessary to bring such land forward for development. First, a programme of urban action (*programa de actuación urbanística*) must be prepared to give non-programmed urbanizable land the same planning status as programmed urbanizable land. In effect, this mechanism updates the coverage of the general plan by performing the same function with respect to non-programmed urbanizable land as the general plan does with respect to programmed urbanizable land (García de Enterría and Parejo, 1979). Second, a partial plan must also be prepared in order to establish the finer detail of planning requirements in the same way as for programmed land.

General plans may be supplemented by special plans drawn up at the local level to deal with particular themes and provide additional information about allowable development. In Barcelona, much of the infrastructure associated with the 1992 Olympic Games was implemented through special plans. Another variation is the so-called special plan of internal reform (*plan especial de reforma interior*) which permits the reconsideration of existing plans in order to improve particular sites through urban regeneration policy. These have been used extensively to carry out urban renewal projects in the older areas of Barcelona (Carbonaro and D'Arcy, 1993). Furthermore, while a general plan is very specific in its provisions for future urban land use, there are many situations where implementation of specific projects raises complex problems which have not been fully anticipated by the plan. Detailed studies (*estudios de detalle*) address this complexity by dealing with matters such as street alignments, precise volumes and heights of buildings or the provision of minor infrastructure, although they cannot be used to modify substantially the land use specified by the general plan.

It is not necessary for all municipalities to produce general plans, although in Catalunya those that do account for over 87% of the population (Keyes *et al.*, 1991). In many cases the size of the municipalities and the complexity of the development issues they face does not justify the exercise. As a result there are two simpler approaches to local planning which are often adopted. First, complementary and subsidiary planning guidelines (*normas complementarias y subsidiarias de planeamiento*) are commonly used as a simplified form of general plan, being less complex, costly and time-consuming to prepare. Like general plans, they divide land into urban, urbanizable and non-urbanizable categories but do not split urbanizable land into programmed and non-programmed. Again like general plans, further detail must be specified in a partial plan before urbanizable land can be brought forward for development, and special plans and detailed studies may also be used to enhance the development specification outlined elsewhere. Just over 30% of municipalities in Catalunya, containing 8.6% of the population, employ this approach (Keyes *et al.*, 1991). Second, a municipality might employ a simple delimitation of urban land (*delimitación de suelo urbano*) as a minimal alternative to a general plan. In this case the municipality is divided between urban and non-urbanizable land. Urban land is defined less stringently than in a general plan or in complementary and subsidiary guidelines, as land where at least 50% of the area is either built upon or in possession of the basic infrastructure necessary for development to go ahead. Urban land delimitation is normally employed by the very smallest municipalities where development problems are unlikely to be highly complex. In Catalunya about 11% of municipalities adopt the measure but this affects only 1.5% of the population (Keyes *et al.*, 1991).

Regarding those municipalities without any form of local planning instrument, accounting for 30% of the municipalities but only 2.4% of the population in Catalunya (Keyes *et al.*, 1991), the Planning Act provides minimum standards to guide development. These deal with the provision of basic infrastructure, open spaces, public facilities, building densities and heights.

12.1.3   Development control

Once the relevant plans have been approved and the permissible use of each plot of land fully specified, the landowners concerned have both the right and the obligation to develop in accordance with those plans. Since it is assumed that the plan and the relevant legal requirements will anticipate all planning issues, development control is reduced to a simple administrative check on the conformity of any proposed scheme. In applying for

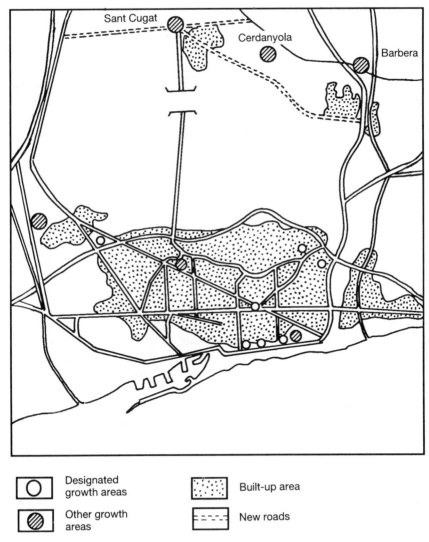

Figure 12.1   Barcelona and periphery: focus of new development
Source: Jones Lang Wootton (1992), reproduced with permission.

planning permission, the developer must first submit the proposal to the architects' professional body (*Colegio Oficial de Arquitectos*) for a certificate of approval (*visado*) stating that the drawings for the building meet the basic standards established by the relevant laws and regulations. An application must then be made to the municipality for a licence (*licencia*) to develop. There is no discretion in the system. If the proposal meets all the stated planning and legal requirements a licence must be granted but, if it does not, the licence must be refused. Appeals can therefore only occur on points of law and procedure rather than on matters of planning judgement. It also follows that appeals can be made either by the developer against the refusal of permission or by other interested parties against the grant of permission.

Where the municipality fails to deliver its judgement within a specified time there is an opportunity to refer the application to a higher planning authority and, where they also fail to meet the statutory deadline for a decision, the developer can initiate development on the assumption of positive silence (*silencio administrativo*). However, the onus to ensure the legality of such development remains with the developer and the planning authority has powers of enforcement against illegal building work. Where, in contrast, it is the developer who fails to submit an application or fails to act on a permission within a specified time limit, the 1992 Planning Act establishes that part of their development rights can be expropriated as a penalty designed to discourage the speculative with-holding of land.

In theory the Spanish planning system appears extremely inflexible. This offers the advantage of certainty to landowners and developers but the disadvantage that it may not always be able to respond rapidly to changing market conditions. In practice, however, minor modifications to a general plan may be very frequent, taking about six months on average to implement. For example, the municipality of Sabadell experienced 21 zoning modifications relating to 20% of its land area during the period 1978–89 (Riera *et al.*, 1991). A planning authority faced with an ap-plication for a large development which does not conform with the general plan will often negotiate with the applicant in order to modify the contents of the plan. Both developer and planning authority stand to gain from this procedure. The developer attempts to secure betterment from the granting of planning permission, while the municipality uses such negotiations as an opportunity to share in the betterment on behalf of the local community (Keogh, 1994). Occasionally, the negotiation of a licence is used to favour development in particular parts of the city in pursuit of new planning objectives, even where no formal modification of the general plan is involved. For example, the expectation of complementary development and public infrastructure in the surrounding area may be an important influence on the decision of real-estate investors looking at different locations for implementing a commercial scheme. Full-scale revisions of the plan are more rare. The production of a replacement plan is both expensive and time consuming. There is no legal requirement for general plans to have a time limit although the planning authority may opt to state a deadline for its validity. Many specify a period of 16 years, based on the initial eight-year development programme plus another eight years.

12.2   CONTEMPORARY PLANNING IN BARCELONA

The planning of Barcelona in the modern sense started with the Barcelona County Plan (*Plan Comarcal*) which was initiated in 1945 and approved in 1953. Since it preceded the 1956 Planning Act it had to be approved by a special act. One of the main objectives of the plan was to contain Barcelona's growth and avoid the absorption of nearby towns and settlements by urban sprawl. Following planning fashion at the time, the 1953 County Plan envisaged Barcelona and its area of immediate influence as a network of self-contained settlements around the otherwise undeveloped Collserola mountain.

The Plan was detailed in its objectives, providing for up to 39 different land-use zones to accommodate 3.2 million people in the Barcelona area and 800 000 in the rest of the county. However, it was adopted prior to the heavy pressure of inward migration which Barcelona and its surrounding area experienced from the mid 1950s to the mid 1970s and proved not to be sufficiently restrictive. The resulting population growth exceeded both the scope of the plan to secure orderly development and the ability of the undemocratic local authorities to manage it. Consequently, the County Plan experienced many modifications leading to rapid, poor quality, high-density development, creating social and environmental problems which ultimately resulted in the Plan becoming the object of strong criticism.

In 1964 a Commission was created to revise the contents of the 1953 County Plan. The first phase of its work, which was completed by 1966 but not approved until 1968, was followed by a second-phase focusing on two spatial levels, the county and the metropolitan area, the latter reflecting the wider economic and social agglomeration of which Barcelona was the centre (Busquets, 1992b). However the new Plan was not passed and, in the absence of a thorough revision of the old Plan, its continuing inadequacies led to multiple acts of illegal and unplanned development. Thus by the beginning of the 1970s there were 634 suburban settlements in Barcelona and its area of influence, mostly of poor quality and often the product of self-build, of which only one-quarter were legal (Terán, 1982).

12.2.1   The General Metropolitan Plan, 1976

In 1971, another Commission was set up to revise the 1953 County Plan and a draft was released for public hearings and comments in 1974. The draft stressed the need for regional and local infrastructure provision, the self-containment of those towns and settlements that had not yet been absorbed by urban sprawl, the preservation of green buffer areas, and the limitation of growth and intensification in urban land use. The draft attracted some 32 000 comments, mainly from landowners who were against the proposed restrictions. It was accordingly revised to take account of public reaction although, in the interim, many planning permissions were granted in line with the 1953 Plan. Finally approved in 1976, the General Metropolitan Plan (*Plan General Metropolitano*) covers Barcelona and the adjoining 26 municipalities. This area coincides with the former County Plan area rather than the wider functional metropolitan area which was previously being promoted, although the establishment of the Metropolitan Corporation of Barcelona in 1974 was regarded as an important advance in administrative terms (Busquets, 1992b).

The plan remains in force as the principal land-use planning document for the area. Obviously, over time, the nature of Barcelona's planning problems and priorities has changed considerably and some practitioners contend that operating within this historic framework is now presenting problems. However the plan broke new ground in terms of both its analytical base and the flexibility of its implementation. Busquets (1992b) argues that it has provided a vital point of reference for development activity and has proved capable of adjustment to changing conditions, even providing a coherent framework for events like the Olympics. The basic guidelines have been modified and reinterpreted by means of a range of additional planning initiatives, some of which are considered in the following sections.

12.2.2   Urban regeneration policy

From 1979, the new democratically elected municipal government started to invest more in the public spaces of Barcelona's low-income neighbourhoods, located mainly in the old city and the inner suburbs. In the early years the scale of the project was typically rather small, dealing with public squares, avenues, streets, urban parks and buildings for public facilities. This solved some of the more urgent needs, but it was not enough to attract private investment into those neighbourhoods.

The most extensive urban regeneration initiatives have occurred in the old city or *Ciutat Vella* (Ajuntament de Barcelona, 1989). Urgent action was needed to deal with the poor physical quality of property and the loss of many legitimate economic activities from the area. Designated as an area of integrated rehabilitation (*área de rehabilitación integrada*) under a joint initiative of the municipal and regional authorities, the main planning vehicle for intensive urban renewal was a series of four Special Plans of Internal Reform, formulated for the treatment of a number of key areas within the old city. The main elements of the plans are land clearance, redevelopment or refurbishment of property, creation of public open space and provision of modern urban infrastructure. Priority is also given to the maintenance of neighbourhoods and the preservation of community.

Initial progress was slow until the municipality established a public–private sector company in 1988, Promoció Ciutat Vella S A (PROCIVESA), to carry out or co-ordinate the main works envisaged in the Special Plans. PROCIVESA has a limited time horizon of 14 years and it is assumed that its direct intervention through the urban renewal programme will show a visible improvement to help retain the commitment of the established community and encourage other property owners to maintain and improve their own buildings (Carbonaro and D'Arcy, 1993). PROCIVESA works in parallel with the Oficina de Rehabilitación Ciutat Vella which has the long-term task of promoting the area by providing advice to property owners on financial, architectural and other related issues. The first five years of the initiative have seen significant progress and, with the first phase of regeneration activity largely complete, the area has secured a number of commercial, cultural and educational developments which will help to underpin confidence and generate a lively and sustainable mix of uses.

12.2.3   Areas of new centrality

In 1986 the municipality of Barcelona launched a project to establish twelve Areas of New Centrality (*Áreas de Nueva Centralidad*). The objective was to overcome the tendency of the property market to direct new development either to the congested central part of the city or outside the city, where land is cheaper and more easily available. Thus the strategy was to identify intermediate locations, away from the established core areas but not outside the city to which private-sector commercial and residential development could be directed. These new centres were chosen with the objective of revitalizing the neighbourhoods in which they are located. Four of the areas were Olympic installations, developed for 1992 but with viable leisure or commercial use after the games were over. The other eight were straightforward commercial locations to be developed as the market dictated. While the attraction of private capital is important, so too is overall co-ordination by the public sector. For example, the municipality has provided new infrastructure, making the sites more attractive in economic terms. Furthermore the strategy has benefited from the transport improvements stimulated by the requirements of the Olympic

Games. Most of the Areas of New Centrality have already succeeded in attracting substantial new development, although their commercial success has initially been limited by the economic recession of the 1990s.

12.2.4   Olympic Games infrastructure

The scale of investment projects undertaken in Barcelona increased as a result of its success in securing the 1992 Olympic Games (Acebillo, 1992). In taking advantage of the momentum generated by preparation for the Games the city took the opportunity to implement many projects which had been delayed for years and to develop new schemes. The greater availability of financial resources allowed for co-ordinated and decisive action to renew parts of the urban fabric and to correct a historic deficit in infrastructure. Several public companies were set up to prepare and implement the projects, and most of them were co-ordinated by an *ad hoc* body Holding Olímpico S.A. (HOLSA) created in 1989. Some were established as public–private sector partnerships, as in the case of Villa Olímpica S.A. (VOSA) which developed the main Olympic village.

`Within the municipality of Barcelona, four Olympic areas were designated; Montjuic, Pedralbes-Diagonal, Vall d'Hebrò and Poble Nou, with the last two including accommodation for referees and athletes respectively, making residential and commercial space available to the market following the Games. The four Olympic areas were to be connected by an inner ring road first proposed in the 1960s. This facility probably represents the most important long-term benefit of the Olympic investment by relieving congestion, providing improved access to most parts of the city and saving travel time. A standard cost-benefit study of the ring road estimated that the net social benefit was very large, generating an internal rate of return of 74% in real terms (Riera, 1993). Furthermore, the ring road was used as a device to improve the environment and quality of life in some poorer neighbourhoods. In Nou Barris, for example, the original 1968 proposal for a motorway which would divide the area in two was modified to provide a segregated ring road of which two-thirds was covered and the rest in a cutting. The covered surface was used for open space, sports facilities, public buildings and parking space (Riera, 1991).

The ring road offers particular development potential to the depressed industrial neighbourhood of Poble Nou which was an area of traditional factory premises mixed with poor-quality residential blocks. Located on the coast, to the north-east of the harbour, it is geographically very close to the centre of the city but historically has suffered from poor communications. Despite being next to the sea, a railway line prevented the neighbourhood from having access to it. This railway, the oldest in Spain, has now been removed and relocated underground, and the new ring road which follows a similar route is recessed in a cutting and covered in places to link the neighbourhood with the sea. New beaches were created and the space between the beaches and the neighbourhood has been converted to a substantial green open space with sports facilities.

In the 1960s, the renovation of Poble Nou was included in a Special Plan which was never implemented. However, considerable new development has already occurred in Poble Nou as a result of the infrastructure improvements stimulated by the Olympics and guided by the provisions of a Special Plan of Internal Reform. The Olympic village itself, temporarily used by the athletes and now available for residential and commercial use, was developed at the southern end of Poble Nou, together with a marina, a hotel, office space and a major shopping centre.

Further opportunities for development exist at the northern end of Poble Nou with the remodelling of the sea front and the extension of Avinguda Diagonal to the coast. The latter will ensure easy access to the central part of the city and is intended to act as a trigger for higher quality commercial and residential development to penetrate the area. These investments have already resulted in a major improvement in both the environmental conditions and the accessibility of the area, and these changes are reflected in the way people value the renewed area (Riera, 1993).

12.2.5   Barcelona 2000

Some municipalities or groups of municipalities have developed non-statutory strategic plans which set out basic planning objectives for the area in the medium and long run. While not mandatory, the expectation must be that any local government which initiates such a plan will be likely to follow its recommendations in the preparation of future land-use plans. However in some cases these plans may be very general, being more to do with regional promotion and image building than with physical planning issues.

In 1988, Barcelona began the preparation of an economic and social strategic plan, *Barcelona 2000*, for its region. Led by the municipality of Barcelona, ten institutions were involved in its preparation representing the views of employers, trade unions, universities and bodies responsible for the promotion of economic activity. The plan was finalized two years later, with the stated goal being to 'consolidate Barcelona as an enterprising European metropolis with influence over its macro-region and with a modern, socially balanced quality of life, deeply rooted in Mediterranean culture'. In order 'to promote Barcelona's role within the "macro-region" identified as the area containing Valencia, Majorca, Toulouse and Montpellier (with a population of 15 million)', the plan sets up three strategic objectives; 'to make Barcelona one of the key centres of the macro-region, to improve the quality of life and progress for people, and to provide support for industry and for advanced services to business' (Marshall, 1990). Each strategy is developed further, but they remain extremely general. However this lack of specificity, together with the absence of budgetary commitments and the non-mandatory character of the plan facilitates agreement among very different institutions with potentially conflicting interests.

12.3   THE OPERATION OF THE PROPERTY MARKET

Real-estate markets in general suffer a range of efficiency problems but there is reason to believe that these problems are more acute in the Spanish market than in most. The key issues concern the way in which Spanish property is held, the availability of property market information, the relative immaturity of the market and, arguably, the relationship between town planning and the property market.

12.3.1   Property rights

The predominant form of tenure in all the main property sectors is owner-occupation. While, in principle, there is no reason why owner-occupiers should be less efficient in their property market behaviour than other participants in the market, it is a form of ownership which offers protection against market discipline. For residential owner-occupiers the decision to remain in a dwelling or home is only likely to be reviewed infrequently. Householders derive a complex range of satisfactions from their ownership and use, many of which are not quantifiable in financial terms. Reluctance to sell or to move even in the face of strong financial incentives may constitute a serious barrier to the renovation, renewal or replacement of property to meet modern standards. Commercial and industrial owner-occupiers are similarly protected. Although a business in owner-occupation earns part of its returns as a property investor it is frequently the case that its decisions are driven by primary business activity rather than by land management criteria. As a consequence many businesses which would be unprofitable if their use of land and buildings were costed at current market rates remain in situ, thus preventing the upgrading of sites to modern uses and contemporary building standards.

It appears that, until recently at least, the cultural attitude to property ownership in Spain has favoured long-term ownership and the passing down of property across generations, rather than an active strategy of management to secure the maximum value and development potential from property assets. However, this perspective on the part of individual owners is often compounded by the relationship between owners. Many Spanish buildings involve multiple freehold owner-occupation, whether in residential apartment blocks, in multi-occupied business premises or in buildings which combine housing and commercial uses. The realization of potential value through refurbishment and redevelopment increases rapidly in complexity as the number of individual owners increases.

The high level of owner-occupation reflects two issues. The first is the established culture of property ownership but the second is the unfavourable legal conditions which, until 1985, governed the holding of property for investment purposes. The relationship between landlord and tenant was controlled by the 1964 Urban Lease Act (*Ley de Arrendamientos Urbanos*) which, in the interest of providing stability for business and residential occupiers, operated to the advantage of the tenant. For leases granted under the 1964 Act, the tenant enjoys a statutory right to extend the lease on the same terms as originally agreed, and this right even continues to apply after the demise of the original tenant since the lease can be passed on to heirs and successors. The lease term would generally be short, typically one or two years, but clearly this was immaterial given the extreme security of tenure. In theory, rent review conditions could be included in the lease but, where this was done, it was normal to link rents to the cost of living index. In the absence of explicit rent review provisions, the law allowed for indexation based on movements in the cost of living to be implemented every two years. In the case of leases granted prior to 1964, their previously controlled rents were first frozen at 1964 values, then adjusted according to the age of the lease, and thereafter became subject to the same provisions as post 1964 leases.

From an investor's perspective, property offered few attractions. While there were certain periods when the link between rents and consumer prices worked to the landlords' advantage, rental growth prospects were severely constrained. More seriously, however, security of tenure made it difficult to secure market rents through the eviction of unprofitable occupiers and to realize potential value through the refurbishment or redevelopment of a site. The law made provision for an owner to secure possession of a building to carry out major works, but subject to the highly limiting obligation to provide comparable space for existing tenants in the new or modernized building, or to pay substantial compensation. Under this legal regime the only course of action which could reasonably be followed was to negotiate to buy out individual occupiers. This could be time-consuming and costly given that secure tenants were often as reluctant to move as owner-occupiers. Obviously this again presented a substantial obstacle to the upgrading and renewal of all categories of real estate.

The conditions for a modern investment market in property, with its implications for both the tenanted and owner-occupied sectors, were not realized until the Boyer Law (*Real Decreto – Ley Sobre Medidas de Política Económica*) of 1985 effectively modified the 1964 legislation. Its effect was to shift the advantage firmly in favour of the landlord by abolishing the tenant's statutory right to extend the lease. Rents continue to be indexed to consumer prices, on an annual basis, but the landlord can secure a reversion to market rents on expiry of the lease. Similarly, potential development value can be realized as leases fall in. In the early years, the so-called Boyer leases were agreed for relatively short terms, typically three or five years. However this arguably provided tenants with too little security and too short a planning horizon, and deprived owners of a secure and predictable flow of income in the medium term. The trend is therefore now towards rather longer lease terms, perhaps ten years, with rents indexed annually to the retail price index but subject also to open market review every three or five years.

The effect of the Boyer reform was to open up the potential for an investment market at a time of obvious economic opportunity. Entry into the EC in 1986 and the high profile sporting and cultural events of 1992 contributed to strong growth in the economy of Spain as a whole and Catalunya in particular. As well as stimulating strong activity from domestic investors and developers, Spain started to attract the attention of foreign investment finance and development expertise. However the market continues to live with the problems created by owner-occupation and the prevalence of pre-Boyer leases, difficulties which are spatially defined. In Barcelona, as in Madrid and other Spanish cities, the ownership regime has prevented the turnover of space and the redevelopment of property in the key central locations, particularly where commercial and retail property is concerned.

In an attempt to ease these problems the central government has produced proposals to replace the provisions of the 1964 Act which would phase out the security of tenure attaching to pre-Boyer leases and bring these rents into line with market values. The proposal as it stands is to offer tenants a choice of two options (Du Passage, 1992). Option A sets a termination date at between two and seven years from the effective date of the proposed new law, such that the older the lease the shorter will be the period to termination. Option B allows for a rent review to be phased in over the five years following the date of the new law and extends the period to termination under option A by a further 13 years. It has been argued that most tenants will choose option B with the obvious consequence that the elimination of pre-Boyer terms will be a protracted process lasting up to 20 years, with little immediate impact on either investment or development. However, in the long run, the reform will stimulate movement among occupiers, creating demand in other areas of the market and freeing up many central sites for refurbishment or redevelopment. The question is whether this process will be rapid enough to maintain the status of existing prime locations? In Barcelona the prime office and retail locations are around Passeig de Gracia, parts of Avinguda Diagonal, Plaça de Catalunya and Rambla de Catalunya. However the shortage of sites for development and re-use in these zones has already seen the focus of development activity shift particularly to the Areas of New Centrality and to out-of-town locations. Thus the problem is that by the time legal changes release current prime sites for new works the value potential of these sites may have been dissipated and redistributed across the city.

12.3.2   Information in an emerging market

The legal and institutional history of the Spanish property market, and its very recent emergence as a modern investment market, has compounded the normal problems of imperfect information. Traditionally the market has been highly decentralized and informal, with information flowing through personal contact or such channels as newspaper advertisements. The involvement of property agents has been relatively minor and it is estimated that, even today, only about 20% of transactions are handled by agents. Lack of both transactions and open market rent reviews has resulted in poor information about use and investment values. However, this situation is now changing. The internationalization of investment and development has led to a similar internationalization of agency and consulting. For example, many of the major players among British surveying practices are now represented in Spain, either directly or in association with Spanish or other international firms. The pattern has generally been to establish a presence in Madrid first although most major practices now also have offices in Barcelona. While the agency role is important to these firms it is probably the demand for advisory and consulting services which has done most to encourage the spread of reliable property market information.

However, while the growing availability of information is one thing, its interpretation is another. The emerging post-Boyer market has only seen one turn of the property cycle. Strong growth conditions were experienced from the mid 1980s until 1991 when property values in all sectors stabilized. This was followed by a fairly precipitous fall in values from late 1992 into 1993, although this is based on a relatively low level of transactions. There is a sense that, in the Spanish market, prices are particularly sticky downwards. There has been strong resistance to writing down rental and capital values with many owners preferring to leave buildings empty rather than accept a loss. This may be a product of local business culture combined with the relatively low exposure to debt of many operators in the market. It is also a reflection of the learning process required to make sense of the first property crisis in Spain since 1985.

12.4   BARCELONA OFFICE MARKET: USE, INVESTMENT AND DEVELOPMENT

12.4.1   Use and investment markets

The Barcelona office market provides an interesting case study of market performance and development activity. As such it provides clues to the relationship between the property market process and planning control. Its history since 1985 is one of strong growth and increased investor and developer activity, followed by acute oversupply and a period of market stagnation.

Following a period of falling real rents in the early 1980s, user demand started to increase in 1986. This requirement for floorspace, reflecting the growth of the Catalan economy and the shifting balance in favour of service sector employment was focused on a severely restricted supply of modern office buildings and an effective regime of planning restraint in the existing central business district. Rental evidence from the longest established British property agent in Barcelona indicates average growth in prime rental values of almost 300% over the period 1986 to 1991 (Richard Ellis, various dates). After stabilizing at approximately 4500–4750 ptas/ m^2/month in 1991, rents started to fall sharply from late 1992 onwards. Estimates of current (mid 1994) rental values vary according to the source. Some suggest 2500 ptas/m^2/month while others put it as low as 1700 ptas. All market commentators agree, however, that the fall has been dramatic, returning the market to below 1988/89 values, and that very few transactions are now taking place. Naturally rents vary significantly with the location and quality of office buildings. One recent report (Richard Ellis, 1994) shows that rents may start from around 1100 ptas in the more secondary areas of the city centre and Eixample, while space can be acquired from 900 ptas upwards in out-of-town developments.

The Boyer reform and the market evidence of rental growth were quickly reflected in income yields as both domestic and foreign investors turned their attention to the Barcelona office market. Income yields on prime offices were estimated at around 9.5% at the time of the Boyer decree but fell steadily to stand at below 6.0% in early 1991 (Jones Lang Wootton, 1992), although it is important to remember that these figures tend to be based on a small number of key transactions. Since then, yields have increased to reflect the initially static and then declining levels of rental value. There is currently very little activity in the investment market, giving rise to a range of largely hypothetical estimates of current yield (Richard Ellis, 1994; Jones Lang Wootton, 1993). Once again, there is a spread of yields depending on location. While the Richard Ellis report puts prime yields at 7.5%, it indicates yields of 8.5–9.5% elsewhere in the city and 11.5% on the periphery.

To some extent the cycle in rents and yields reflects the business cycle. Spain was relatively late entering the current international recession and, as worsening global economic conditions began to be felt in the domestic economy, projections of growth were rapidly revised downwards in 1991/92. However the key to understanding the current crisis in the property market is the long-run supply response implemented by means of office development.

12.4.2 Office development

The rapid growth in user demand and the growing interest of investors came together to signal the potential for profitable development activity. This potential attracted Spanish developers and also drew in international developers, often working in collaboration with local firms. The development initiative came from property and construction companies, but also from financial institutions acting directly to generate high-quality property assets for portfolio purposes.

While it is commonly argued that tight planning control severely limits opportunities for office development in Barcelona this has only proved to be true in the established core areas of the Eixample. The designation of the ten New Areas of Centrality has identified new locations to which development activity can be directed, and the extensive infrastructure work carried out in preparation for the Olympics has ensured the accessibility of these new areas. The critical point is that not only has development land been made available but it is generally land which had not previously been used for offices and where every square metre of new floorspace would represent an equal net increase in the Barcelona office stock. To date new development within the city has focused on the extension of Avinguda Diagonal, Carrer Tarragona close to the central Sants station, the Olympic Village, the port area, the França station and the Plaça de les Glories. Future proposals for new office building include the Poble Nou area immediately to the north of the Olympic Village.

At the same time that office development was opening up new areas of the city to commercial use, development and investment interest was being turned to the potential for out-of-town office space. The concept of the business park is a fairly recent one in Spain and has still to overcome the resistance of office users and their employees to a working environment divorced from the usual facilities of the city centre. However the good accessibility of the area around Barcelona airport and of the Vallès area some 20 km inland from the city attracted the attention of developers. In the 1980s Spain's first technology park was established at Cerdanyola as a joint venture between the Consorcio de la Zona Franca and the Metropolitan Corporation of Barcelona. Two business park proposals were initiated in Sant Cugat alongside a number of purpose built office schemes promoted by owner occupiers, and building started at the Mas Blau business park adjacent to the airport. Since these developments again represent new office areas the additional floorspace directly increases the stock of offices in the Greater Barcelona area.

It has been estimated (Darby, 1993) that the total stock of office space in the Barcelona area stood at a little over 2 million m² in 1985 with a vacancy rate of approximately 5%. Over the next four years, as office market conditions became more favourable, new development added a further 500 000 m² to the stock and availability was driven down to about 0.7%. The lagged response to market signals of rising rents and falling yields means that the rates of development have accelerated since then. It was estimated that by the end of 1993 the office stock would have reached almost 3.6 million m² of which 10% would be effectively available. This tide of oversupply occurred alongside a sharp fall in take-up as the economic and property crisis took hold. Take-up reached its highest recorded level in 1991 at around 150 000 m², but evidence for 1992 suggests realized demand of only 70 000 m² indicating that, at these rates of activity, there was about 3–4 years' worth of available floorspace. The oversupply position becomes progressively worse when the existing pipeline of development is considered. New construction phased for the three years 1994–6 is expected to deliver something approaching 700 000 m² of office space, increasing total stock to almost 4.3 million m² with a predicted peak rate of vacancy of around 15%.

Relatively little of the new development is occurring in traditional or emerging prime locations. Limited refurbishment is occurring in the prime area of the Eixample and a small number of sizeable new schemes have been completed in the extended central business district at the top of Avinguda Diagonal. However, most recent and programmed development is occurring in the Areas of New Centrality where approximately 175 000 m² of new space should enter the market in the period 1993–6. While new building in the peripheral and out-of-town locations is slowing down, with some schemes being mothballed until market conditions improve, these areas are also likely to generate around 100 000 m² during the same period.

12.5   CONCLUSION

The review of the Spanish planning system reveals a hierarchical and apparently inflexible system of land-use plans which grant legal rights to develop. However an examination of contemporary planning guidance for Barcelona shows that, while the current plan is almost 20 years old and is based on many urban projects proposed in the 1960s, it has provided an approach to planning which is both robust and flexible. Modification of the plan and the use of measures like special plans have allowed the orderly implementation of a substantial wave of new development and infrastructure through the 1980s and into the 1990s.

However, there is a significant gap in strategic guidance and potential conflict between levels of government in the distribution of responsibilities for plan-making. Strategic guidance is only now in preparation at the regional level. Its implications will be significant particularly in the attempt to control and modify the distribution of population within Catalunya. In many respects the reality of Spanish land-use planning is that it is effectively bottom-up, driven by the existing patterns of development allowed for in local planning guidance. For Barcelona the strategic planning framework is important given the extensive network of functional economic and social relationships between the city and its area of influence.

In the city itself it is often argued that planning control is very restrictive and it is certainly the case that development and redevelopment has been difficult in the central area of the Eixample. However the constraints attributable to the legal system of property rights may be much more significant than those attributable to planning. Plans to open up new areas of the city with development potential, partly with the intention of creating new zones of centrality, have removed many of the land-use constraints on private-sector development activity. Some might say that the constraints have been relaxed too much. Property development has proceeded too rapidly, resulting in problems of oversupply of space, particularly in the office market. This may reflect inexperience in a property market which has only been exposed to modern forms of investment activity within the last ten years, although it is worth noting that other more mature markets have a similar tendency to oversupply (Keogh and D'Arcy, 1993). What is clear is that the planning system has not acted as any sort of counter-cyclical brake on development activity in anticipation of a downturn in the property market.

Whether for good or bad, the Barcelona property market is rapidly being transformed into a modern investment market. There is a growing tendency towards speculative development and an increase in the letting market which is accommodating the need for greater flexibility in use and income generation. Further changes in the legislation controlling tenancies will force relocation of users and bring older properties into the market for redevelopment or refurbishment. These changes will help to promote a market environment in which measures of rent and yield will provide a more meaningful expression of value than is currently the case.

REFERENCES

Acebillo, J.A. (1992) El progressiu canvi d'escala en les intervencions urbanes a Barcelona entre 1980 i 1992, in Narcís Serra *et al.*, *Barcelona Olímpica: La Ciutat Renovada*, HOLSA, Barcelona.

Ajuntament de Barcelona (1989) *Revitalització Urbana, Econòmica i*

Social, Primeres Jornades Ciutat Vella, Promoció de Ciutat Vella S A, Barcelona.

Bassols Coma, M. (1986) Town planning in Spain, in J.F. Gardiner and N.P. Gravells (eds), *Planning Law in Western Europe*, Northern Holland, Amsterdam.

Busquets, J. (1992a) Projectes Olímpics i estratègia urbanística, in Narcís Serra *et al.*, *Barcelona Olímpica: La Ciutat Renovada*, HOLSA, Barcelona.

Busquets, J. (1992b) *Barcelona*, Editorial Mapfre, Madrid.

Carbonaro, G. and D'Arcy, E. (1993) Key issues in property-led urban restructuring: a European perspective, *Journal of Property Valuation and Investment*, **11**(4), 339–53.

Cerdà, I. (1867) *Teoría General de la Urbanización, y Aplicación de sus Principios y Doctrinas a la Reforma y Ensanche de Barcelona*, Imprenta Española, Madrid, and reproduced by Instituto de Estudios Fiscales, Madrid, 1968.

Darby, R. (1993) The Barcelona Office Market since 1985, unpublished MPhil thesis, University of Reading.

Du Passage, B. (1992) Spain prepares for lease changes, *Estates Gazette*, **2939**, 3 October, 122.

García de Enterría, E. and Parejo, L. (1979) *Lecciones de Derecho Urbanístico*, vol. 1. Cívitas, Madrid.

Hughes, R. (1992) *Barcelona*, London, Harvill.

Jones Lang Wootton (1992) *The Spanish Property Market Report 1991–1992*, Jones Lang Wootton, London.

Jones Lang Wootton (1993) *Quarterly Investment Report: The European Property Market*, Winter 1992/93, Jones Lang Wootton, London.

Keogh, G. and D'Arcy, E. (1993) Market maturity and property market behaviour: a European comparison of mature and emergent markets, discussion paper in Urban and Regional Economics, series C, No. 87, University of Reading.

Keogh, G. (1994) Land law and urban planning in Spain: an economic perspective, *European Planning Studies*, in press.

Keyes, J., Munt, I. and Riera, P. (1991) *Land Use Planning and the Control of Development in Spain*, Working Papers in European Property, University of Reading.

Marshall, T. (1990) Letter from . . . Barcelona, *Planning Practice and Research*, **5**(3), 25.

Richard Ellis (various dates) *World Rental Levels: Offices*, Richard Ellis, London.

Richard Ellis (1994) *Barcelona Office Market Bulletin*, Winter 1993/4, Richard Ellis, Madrid.

Riera, P. (1991) *Barcelona's New Ring Road for the 1992 Olympic Games. An Evaluation using Contingent Valuation Analysis*, PTRC Transport, Highways and Planning Summer Annual Meeting, vol. P351, 57–79.

Riera, P. (1993) *Rentabilidad Social de las Infraestructuras: Las Rondas de Barcelona*, Cívitas, Madrid.

Riera, P., Munt, I. and Keyes, J. (1991) The practice of land use planning in Spain, *Planning Practice and Research*, **6**(2), 11–18.

Sau, E. (1992) El Creixement del Sistema Urbà de Catalunya. Del Pla Comarcal al Pla Metropolità una Anàlisi de les Propostes, MSc Dissertation, Universitat Autònoma de Barcelona.

Terán, Fernando de (1982) *Planeamiento Urbano en la España Contemporánea (1900/1980)*, Alianza, Madrid.

13

Rome

Lorenzo Bellicini
and Francesco Toso

Territorial administration in the Rome area is marked by two main reference instruments: the 'General Regulatory Plan' (PRG) of 1962 and successive variants; and the Law for Rome ('Capital of the Republic') of 15 December 1990. An analysis of these two instruments, which have profoundly different characteristics, provides a reflection on the way that the government of the city has altered through time, as well as highlighting elements of continuity which have characterized urbanization policies.

These instruments encapsulate on the one hand the main strategic objective behind the rationalization of the urban development process of the city, namely the realization of a (decentralized) tertiary area, Eastern Directional System (SDO), aimed at solving the problem of congestion in the historical core through public- and private-sector activity. On the other hand they may be considered to amount to derogated reference elements in the operation of the transformation processes in the city.

The first characteristic which emerges from the transformation processes in Rome is the fact that the city appears to have grown in an unorganized manner in comparison to the urbanistic design intended. Indeed the development of Rome followed a *macchia d'olio* (small widely spread but unconnected growth) pattern, then a period of 'radialcentric' expansion which prioritized the main road axes, and finally the filling-in of remaining spaces (Mirabelli, 1981).

This process of 'development in jumps' has left large unbuilt areas particularly in the suburbs. While in many respects this is a characteristic common to many Italian cities, in Rome it has taken on specific dimensions because of the quantity of unauthorized settlement realized in the rural area beyond the city. Although localized, the settlement nuclei proceeded without any authorization on the part of the administrative

European Cities, Planning Systems and Property Markets Edited by James Berry and Stanley McGreal. Published in 1995 by E & FN Spon. ISBN 0419 18940 8.

authorities, and despite not conforming to the regulations in force such settlements have spread over the whole local authority area especially in the last 20 years. This has led to environmental damage over a considerable area stretching beyond that blighted by the actual development (Della Seta and Della Seta, 1988).

The problem highlights the phenomenon of land consumption and the scale of unauthorized production. However it is necessary to consider that the city authorities with more than 150 000 ha of administrative territory is one of the biggest in Italy, whereas the Milan administrative area consists of only 18 000 ha. A study conducted in the second half of the 1980s quantified consumption of land in the decade 1971–81. Over this ten-year period urbanized land grew from 28 500 ha to 38 500 ha, an increase of more than 35%. Thus in 1981, 26% of the 150 000 ha which compose the administrative territory was urbanized, while in 1971 the figure was only 19%. Furthermore, of the 900 000 rooms produced in the 1970s in the Rome area, more than 50% were carried out without any building permission. This phenomenon of unauthorized development continued throughout the 1980s (Perego and Clementi, 1983; Martinelli, 1988).

13.1   ADMINISTRATIVE STRUCTURE, PLANNING INSTRUMENTS AND THE URBAN DEVELOPMENT PROCESS

The structure of the urbanistic instrumentation of Rome as represented by the PRG was conceived in the 1960s. The plan, elaborated upon at the end of the 1950s and early 1960s, was adopted by the Rome Town Council in 1962 and approved by the Ministry of Public Works in 1965. Under this, urban planning of the 1950s was changed whereby private initiative had the freedom to build large suburban areas of a monofunctional residential nature. Thus the divide became increasingly apparent between the polyfunctional urban centre and a suburban area composed largely of residential functions.

The PRG aimed at bridging this gap and re-equilibrating the city with the creation of new centres. The instrument for bringing about this philosophy, the East Directional System, was based on an infrastructural road system inside which urban structures and services were to be established. Localization in the east orientated the future expansion of the city in that direction, whereas in the 1930s development had been towards the sea. The most ambitious objective of the PRG was the creation of an alternative to the historical centre, to save it from the risks of incumbent tertiary processes and the relative congestion of the central area. This was also accompanied by the protection of the areas of archaeological interest and of the coastal zone. However, more than 30 years later none of the objectives contained in the plan has been achieved. What is more, even the forecasts of a population which should have reached 4.5 million at the beginning of the 1980s proved to be unrealistic. Indeed the population was a little less than 2.8 million and diminished further over the decade.

A more detailed analysis of the objectives (Cremaschi, 1991) and the results of the PRG include unitary setting-up acts (concessions, parcelling-out plans), which permitted building production (about 80% of those planned were carried out); the development control system was significantly disregarded, hence the unauthorized growth measured in hundreds of thousands of rooms in the past has not yet been brought to a halt, especially as regards productive activity; and none of the strategic objectives of the PRG has been fulfilled.

13.1.1 The urbanistic regression of the 1980s

Since 1962, the PRG has undergone many adjustments to its original structure with the last general change adopted by the council administration in 1974 and by the Lazio Region in 1979. Throughout the 1980s a general re-thinking of this key instrument remained outstanding.

Nevertheless planning had a very different character in the early part of the decade relative to the end of the 1980s. In the former there was a consistent effort aimed at development, even if it had difficulty in translating itself into projects and spending commitments; whereas, in the latter period, planning activity and urban development was substantially neglected, despite the guidance coming from higher institutional levels namely the Region and the State. For example the opportunity created by the setting up of territorial planning (Territorial Plan of Co-ordination of the Region) is a case in point (CRIPES, 1988).

13.1.2 The town council–region conflict

In the first five-year period the attempts of the administration to undertake revision of the instruments for urban policies experienced little success due to the intrinsic weakness of the methods used and the conflict which developed at an institutional level with the region. Rather ideas and projects matured in a debate which was not at an institutional but civil level and was substantially dissipated due to the vast number of unrealized projects. The main casualty in the general planning strategy of the 1980s relates to the revision of the regulatory plan which was articulated in segments and sectors (districts and services, suburban renewal, area plans, etc.) in the false belief of rendering more realizable a process which appeared, otherwise, long and unduly protracted.

The 1983 variant for unauthorized zones (the Plan for zone 0), which followed two successive delimitations of the compromised zones, was extended to more project phases and consecutive approvals and was articulated in a total of 72 particular plans. The operation was anything but sectorial, though its consequences were noteworthy and speedily rendered practicable. Collectively 3308 ha were subjected to executive planning, incorporating more than 310 000 inhabitants.

The outcome was not particularly good, from the point of view at least of the realization procedure and probably also (but this can only be judged *a posteriori*) concerning the methodology behind the realization of the plans. Indeed the procedure proved to be so lengthy that nine years since the setting up of the variant only one plan had been approved (plan No. 46 of Selcetta Trigoria in the XII district); seven plans had received favourable opinions from the Urbanistic Technical Commission (CTU) and five more were being examined. In only 11 of the 49 plans presented (in 1988 or in 1989) was the preliminary project found to be in the second phase of planning; eight finally were directly drawn by the technicians of the council, while the remaining ones were late for various reasons.

13.1.3 The case of PEEP (1985)

The new 'Plan for cheap popular housing' (Peep) of 1985 (the first was approved in 1964) was adopted with a certain rapidity in April 1985. As an instrument Peep was entrusted with tasks specifically of a suburban orientation. The qualitative aim of the plan was based at the level of planning choice and awareness of the critical nature of operating with modifications or variants to the general plan. Furthermore both the methodological choice and the purpose of the instrument are consciously directed at forcing the limits of the plan.

The Peep assumes as an objective the continuous redevelopment of the urban fabric suggesting, where possible, structural elements of a higher scale than the local one, to be included in the revision of the general urban plan, with particular attention to the morphology of construction, settlement principles and the availability of green spaces. This programme was added to area plan forecasts at the completion of the first Peep and of the integrating variants approved in the first years of the decade. The first Peep forecast an initial settlement capacity equal to 711 000 rooms but reduced to 674 000 with the approval of the Ministry of Public Works. Restrictions and various impediments (unauthorized edification, geological incompatibility) add up, however, to 430 000 rooms; though the successive variants have added more than 34 000 rooms.

The Peep of 1985 forecast the construction of 41 zones with a total of 192 000 rooms. Following criticisms during the formal procedure objections reduced the plan to 120 000 rooms. Following this, the region approved the plan but reduced the estimates further to 25 zones and

97 000 rooms because of restrictions, environmental impediments and contrasting provisions of territorial plans. Finally, delays of a legal nature with owners concerning expropriation led to crossed appeals to the Tar (a type of court of appeal) and the Council of State. Deliberations by the council, and the wish to achieve consensus in the realization programme, lead to the initial use of six areas with a total of 28 000 rooms; and depending upon the outcome of the legal dispute with the owners, another two areas for about 12 000 rooms.

13.1.4 The dispute with the State and other public decision-makers

During the early 1980s, strategies forwarded by the relevant urban authorities resulted in a complex set of objectives, in certain cases of a divergent nature, concerning the future scenario of the city (de Lucia, 1992). In this context at least three different criteria are of potential importance.

First, planning of the suburbs, initiated in continuity with infrastructural operations already carried out for unauthorized districts (delimitations and sanitary works), address the criterion of re-equilibrium with the city centre. Second, a policy aimed at rediscovering particular public sites, termed Roman Summer, and proposals for the forums and an Archaeological park. In 1980 a political-entrepreneurial pact was made between the town council, co-operatives, constructors and unions for the construction of houses in the suburbs reflecting in many respects the trends of the 1970s, whereas in 1990, the Law for Rome became the framework within which the role of the Eastern Directional System was again stressed. However, the same political-entrepreneurial forces which had sponsored popular housing in previous years advanced their case for the realization of the SDO although the public-sector interest is stronger due to state ownership of land in the area. In essence the problems may change, but the actors adapt themselves to different circumstances.

13.2 THE PLANNING PROCESS AND THE AUTHORIZATION OF DEVELOPMENT

In the absence of effective programming and planning, the use of land and buildings in Rome is confused and often contradictory. Therefore, not only is there unauthorized 'consumer' use of land and massive reclamation (primary and secondary urbanization works), but also there is a lack of institutional response to the problem of unresolved tertiary growth which has knock-on consequences for the city (Bellicini, 1991).

The political-administrative functions of the State have counteracted to a certain degree the difficulties arising from localization and through periodic intervention has promoted significant building programmes (de Lucia, 1992). However the city centre and adjacent areas have a privileged status due to the activities of different government departments and public agencies. In contrast the private tertiary sector has been active in essentially infill development and sites periodically offered by the market and in areas designated specifically for private services. In the case of the latter involvement in peripheral areas, particularly those close to large road networks (the Ring Road; Rome–Fiumicino motorway, Rome–Naples, Rome–Aquila) is significant. Besides the Magliana pole, commercial development has sprung up in the district of Cinecitta and the area of Anagnina, while more modest schemes characterize other zoning plans, thereby reducing the area destined for residential use.

13.2.1   The creeping counter-reformation

While the 1960s represented an era of great battles for urban reforms, with little legislative change, from 1967 onwards there was a number of small but continuous steps forward, up to the climax reached with the Ten-Year Plan. However, within a short time there was the beginning of a progressive and apparently informal erosion of the system built up in the previous ten years. This creeping counter-reformation was the outcome of various processes which were provoked at different times and by different instruments. An illustration of this is the series of sentences of the Constitutional Court which deprived the legislation of fundamental instruments and a reunion of representatives of interested bodies which had the power to examine projects and approve them. A representative of the junta of the Commune (the government of the city) overruled the decisions of the town council (those responsible for urban decisions) and the other representative groups of city-dwellers in deciding about the works which were to influence the future of the cities involved. However, the complexity of the mechanism and the conflict which it produced ultimately led to the raising of prices and substantial inefficiency in terms of output. Despite the procedures put in place only 40% of the works were implemented.

13.2.2   The 'pardon' for unauthorized building

Paralleling the procedures for deregulation (between 1982 and 1985) the government decided to utilize unauthorized activity to reduce the public debt. Thus the State permitted, with the payment of a value in proportion to the size and scale of the development, correction of the irregularity – a phenomenon which was widespread in the Rome area and in the south of Italy. One of the theses which accompanied the operation of the 'pardon' for 'abusive' works, apart from the necessity of finding resources, was that town-planning consisted of an ensemble of 'snares and traps' which halted development. Therefore unauthorized activity was argued to be an effect of planning and specifically the rigidity of the planning process. However, the practice of the 'pardon' for irregularities generated a situation of 'awareness' that with the passage of time unauthorized activity could, with modest sanctions, become legal.

13.3   LAND MANAGEMENT AND IMPACT ON URBAN DEVELOPMENT

Before the 1970s Rome was considered on a par with Naples as an emblem of urban misgovernment. However, in the 1970s new entrepreneurial realities began to emerge which operated in the areas expropriated by councils for building intervention and where sale prices were agreed with the council administration. This was the phase in which Rome was the model for a national scale incorporating the council administration and a group of private enterprises.

13.3.1   Real-estate property, earnings and profit

In the 1970s the law norm 167/1962 was abolished (article 16) which allowed owners of areas included in the Peep plans (Plans for cheap popular building) to obtain for themselves or for others the possibility to build (Storto, 1992). This situation had opened up a market in the areas to be developed on the one hand but on the other hand fostered collusion between landowners and public administrators. Once this law was abolished, it was established that the land destined for residential purposes should be acquired at prices corresponding to the compensation for the expropriation, with no priority for previous owners. In this way earnings were separated from profits, at least for large areas of the city.

This tendency altered radically in the 1980s. If before there was preventive expropriation, now owners were encouraged to permit building. The Peep restriction in a particular area no longer amounted to a penalization, but rather a prize – as town-planning of the 1970s consisted of projects in which the initiative assumed by economic groups signified one of real-estate exploitation. What is of interest is not so much the work which was carried out but rather a realization of the value difference between an area which was agricultural or industrial in nature and which was subject to a prestigious private commercial and/or public administration development. During this phase the council was influenced by decisions taken by the private sector and 'contracted town-planning' became established. However, the decision-making power, at least formally, was the task of the councils, and landowners had to 'contract' with the representatives of those bodies.

13.3.2   The land regime and compensation for expropriation

The present framework concerning expropriations for public utility has been established by the Constitutional Court provoking two distinct effects, but of an equal gravity, regarding the management of land and the development of settlement structures. The Court established that in principle compensation must be in proportion to the effective value of the property but did not provide precise indications about the mechanisms to be employed.

The first effect of the ruling was that of a net tendency towards an increase in the value of compensations, no longer referred to agricultural values but to effective market land values. Arising from this public administrations were forced to face up to financial needs which were not only elevated but above all, added unexpected financial requirements. Furthermore the ruling altered costs 'during works' which, within certain limits, had already been foreseen in various urban programmes and building development being carried out.

The outcome was, on the one hand, a net contraction of the quantity of land which was the object of expropriation processes and, on the other, to a very wide dispute about expropriation processes in operation (Coppo, 1991). Although compensation values remained very high, at the start of new development programmes, local administrations were able to make realistic forecasts. Also after an initial period of adaptation, the practice became diversified according to contractual capacity and the objectives of opposing parties.

In the second half of the 1980s certain public administrations offered compensations equal to a third or a fifth of the land value, while other administrations conceded compensations of a value equal to that of the market. Variations were determined by the characteristics and the attitude of the parties (public authorities and owners) and not by intrinsic factors concerning the nature of the land and the type of operation (Tocci, 1993). The strongest and most well prepared were able to bend the interpretation of the law to their advantage.

13.3.3   The SDO and the tertiary sector

The most significant structural element of the Roman PRG of 1962 was that which later became the Eastern Directional System (SDO). This consisted of infrastructural axes and directional zones. The SDO was intended to interrupt the *macchia d'olio* expansion and carry out a strategic reorganization function. Indeed its realization could still be useful as a solution to the three basic problems of the city viz mobility in terms of bringing about a reorganization of transport in the eastern sector by constructing a number of rail transport lines; renewal of the degraded surrounding areas; and decongestion of the city centre with the transference to the SDO of ministerial functions.

Moreover, the usefulness of the SDO is conditioned by two factors: the public acquisition of the area concerned and the programme of relocation by government departments. Regarding the first, the town council had approved that realization of the SDO should be entrusted to owners, however, by imposing the expropriation for public utility the town-planning project was entrusted to the same consortium which arose originally for direct utilization of the area. However the council administration failed to become involved in the problem to the extent that it should have done and through time there was a diffusion of tertiary functions over the whole Rome area. Of the various examples, the localation of the Health Ministry was directly contrary to policy. An analogous situation happened with the Finance Ministry which acquired two buildings (in the areas opposite those of the SDO) to set up the land office.

13.4   CHARACTERISTICS OF THE PROPERTY MARKET

In Rome the divide between policy contained in urban planning instruments and norms on the one hand and the use made of land and building patrimony on the other is the first and most important reference for any analysis of the character and the dynamics of the property market in the 1980s and the early 1990s. Recent years have been dominated by the exclusion of urban policies of conservation and a notable incapacity on the part of the municipality to guide the relationship between the localization of functions and the use of land and buildings. At least part of this inconsistency is due to the different levels responsible for urban choice, namely the city council, the region and the state. Thus, set within a scenario of notable urbanistic 'disorder', the main factors which condition and influence the behaviour of the actors who operate in the property market are, the functional uses which different parts of the city have assumed during the 1980s, the practice of landed owners and plans for council-owned land. Such factors are the basis of property dynamics, in terms of exchange and value.

There are many functional typologies which define urban space and the economy within Rome. Thus, rather than having a city organized according to recognizable parts within the administrative area that defines the council territory of Rome there are profoundly different situations (AAVV, 1986; Bellicini, 1988). On the basis of building characteristics, it is possible, and indeed reasonable to split Rome up into five different sub-cities: viz the historical city; the city of large-scale speculation built by entrepreneurs in the boom years from 1950 to 1973; the fragmented city of the 're-filling' programme which characterized the private legal production of the 1970s and 1980s and was localized in the spaces left by previous building development; the public city represented by large areas of residential building spread over the expansive suburbs; and the unauthorized city. However, such sub-division has to be subjected to further examination concerning the economic functions of the different parts of the city, in order to reflect on the dynamics of the Rome property market.

On the basis of this criteria there exists a **political and bureaucratic city**, concentrated in the historical core, in parts of the semi-central area and in some large semi-suburban locations (EUR, Magliana). This 'city' is influenced by investment decisions of the different public bodies, and by the demands of those persons living there. Similarly there is a **tertiary city of private services** which is also concentrated in the central area, but especially in certain important quarters that can be defined as semi-central. The **tourist city** is mostly that of the historical city, the **private residential city** is partly represented in the historical and semi-central areas

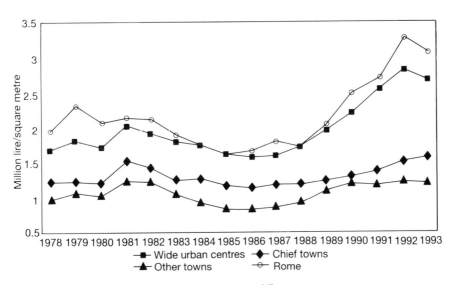

Figure 13.1 Dynamics of house prices in middle-income areas

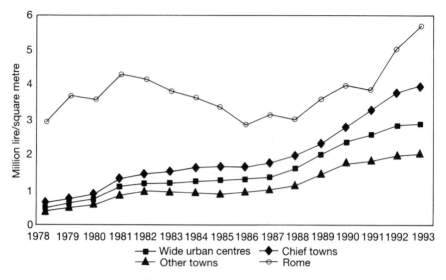

Figure 13.2   Dynamics of house prices in semi-central areas

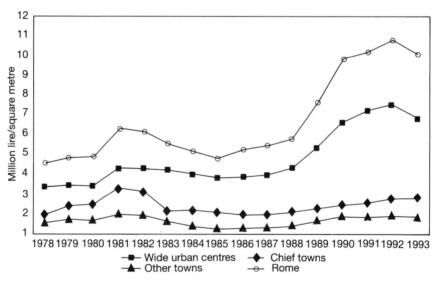

Figure 13.3   Dynamics of house prices in central up-market locations

but largely concentrated in the dense mono-functional suburbs. The remaining components are the **public residential city** and finally an **unauthorized residential city**.

Such a superimposition of functions (and sub-cities) leads to a high degree of complexity and differences of value of real-estate property in the city. Simplifying the preceding classification the city can be divided into a central area (where the mixture of functions is more sophisticated and in particular where public and private tertiary functions are added to the tourist potential); the semi-central area linked closely to the presence of private commercial activity and the suburban residential area. Information presented (Figures 13.1, 13.2 and 13.3) compares the price of housing in Rome with that of the other 15 major Italian urban centres, 74 provincial towns and with the average value of other Italian towns in terms of different locations within the city.

In 1992 the price of dwellings in the prestigious central Rome area reached 11 million lire per m^2; in the semi-central areas it was about 5 million lire per m^2; in suburban areas 3.2 million lire per m^2. The size, scale and importance of the city certainly influence the fact that prices in Rome are by far the highest at national level (together with those of Milan). It is interesting to note that the price level of the residential suburbs is substantially similar in terms of values and trends to those of the other 15 large Italian urban areas. However, the value of dwellings in the semi-central areas and in the central core of Rome is clearly the highest within the country and shows contrasting trends, compared to the other great Italian cities.

The failure of the municipality, first to provide and second to guide the expansion of some economic functions and the strong process of concentration of tertiary functions in the boom years (1987–92), produced a spontaneous growth of commercial activities in the existing city. This has led to a concentration of uses in areas already congested by residential, productive (artisan) and also public sector (for example, the political-bureaucratic) functions. The most obvious effects have been a decline of residential and artisan functions, a rapid transformation in the identity of entire quarters and an exceptional increase in property values particularly in Rome, but also apparent in all the large urban areas of Italy.

13.5 CONCLUSION

Against the development and investment activity in the private market must be placed the failure to realize certain rationalization projects for tertiary demand, like the Eastern Directional System. Arguably this is the result of property interests guided by the logic of funding revenue. The creation of a tertiary pole of high-level functions, as the SDO would be, provides an important project in a part of the city where there ought to be growth but this may have the effect of lowering property values in those central and semi-central areas which in the second half of the 1980s saw rapid growth in property values. The decentralization of tertiary functions in both the public and private sectors from the central and semi-central areas towards the SDO (given the forecast dimensions) would have acted as a counter to the established city (central and semi-central). Furthermore, the significant increase of land supply would in all probability have had an immediate lowering of price levels.

The funding and building of property in Rome has always had an exclusive position in council administration and the maintenance of privilege in the city. For example, the vast funding sources and real-estate property portfolios of a few large bodies (including the Vatican State) and the ability of these in the recent past for the guaranteeing of political favours in exchange for building permits or area concession. Although the 'real-estate bloc' has enriched itself with a new band of smaller owners it is still able to 'resist' profound change like that planned under the SDO.

REFERENCES

AAVV (1986) *Roma, Parigi, New York. Quale urbanistica per la metropoli?*, Cagemi, Reggio Calabria.

Bellicini, L. (1988) La scomposizione e i residui. Note sul processo di trasformazione e sulle esigenze di recupero in sedici grandi città italiane, in L. Bellicini (ed.), *L'Italia da recuperare.*, cit., vol. I, 27–120.

Bellicini, L. (1991) La produzione fisica della nuova città economica. Appunti sui processi di investimento in capitale fisso edilizio, sulle politiche urbane e sulle trasformazioni economiche nella città europea degli anni '80, in L. Bellicini (ed.), *La costruzione della città europea negli anni '80*, cit., vol. I, 29–97.

Coppo, M. (1991) Regime degli immobili e urbanistica, *Urbanistica Informazioni*, **118**.

Cremaschi, M. (1991) Roma: Urbanistica a 'bassa intensità', in L. Bellicini (ed.), *La costruzione della città europea*, cit., 279–334.

CRIPES (1988) *Progetto Roma Capitale e governo metropolitano. Il ruolo della regione e degli enti locali*, Roma.

Della Seta, P. and Della Seta, R. (1988) *I suoli di Roma. Uso e abuso del territorio nei cento anni della capitale*, Editori Riuniti, Roma.

de Lucia, V. (1992) *Se questa è una città*, Editori Riuniti, Roma.

Martinelli, F. (1988) *Roma nuova. Borgate spontanee e insediamenti pubblici. Dalla marginalità alla domanda di servizi*, F. Angeli, Milano.

Mirabelli, F. (1981) Roma, in L. Bellicini (ed.), L'Italia da recuperare, cit., 469–514.

Perego, F. and Clementi, A. (eds) (1983) *La metropoli spontanea*, Dedalo, Bari.

Storto, G. (1992) La legge Bucalossi: un bilancio, *Urbanistica Informazioni*, **123/124**.

Tocci, W. (1993) *Roma che ne facciamo*, Editori Riuniti, Roma.

14

Athens*

*Pavlos Delladetsima
and Lila Leontidou*

In the social geography of Athens the east–west differentiation, based upon middle- and low-income population groups respectively, is at present dissolving. Though many areas of the city are still missing basic infrastructure and services it is apparent that the traditional concentric model, incorporating an affluent inner city and poorer peripheral settlements, is currently undergoing significant change. On the northern and south–coastline of the conurbation the development of two areas with broadly similar characteristics is taking place. These areas consist of high-income housing and retailing while the main road network (Kifissias, Singrou, Vouliagmenis Avenues) leading to these areas has become the favoured zone for the location of large-scale office, retail and administration activities (Figure 14.1). However these do not imply the formation of a clearly segregated pattern; rather Athens in many respects is a mixed city and arguably this seems to be its prime characteristic.

The development process which has produced a complex mixed land-use structure (bringing residential, industrial, commercial and service sector activities in close proximity) has also been accompanied by: dramatic increases in commuting and traffic flows; extensive suburbanization trends; and the relative population decline in traditional housing areas in the centre of the city. All these to a certain extent signify that the city has been reaching certain physical, functional, traffic and environmental thresholds without, at the same time, generating any serious public awareness on the matter. Athens of the early 1990s seems to be seeking solutions to its problems once more, as in past decades, in major infrastructural works, leaving the land-use and physical development pattern untouched. In fact the construction of the Athens metro has become the

* *Special thanks are due to Professor F. Moulaert (University Lille I) for his intellectual support and fruitful comments.*

European Cities, Planning Systems and Property Markets Edited by James Berry and Stanley McGreal. Published in 1995 by E & FN Spon. ISBN 0419 18940 8.

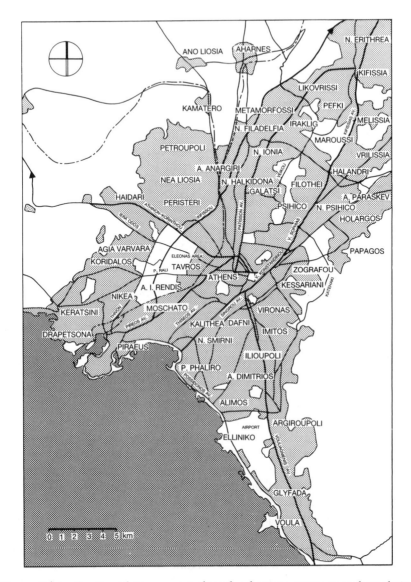

Figure 14.1 Greater Athens: municipalities/local communities; town boundaries; major road networks

major priority and is expected to act as a catalyst for solving all major problems of the metropolitan area.

Set within this apparently irregular context, an understanding of the planning system and of the operation of the property market cannot be based on the same kinds of rationale adopted for other cities in the European setting. However the resulting confusion does not imply the absence of state policy in the field as a whole. What is different in the Athens case is the objectives of state action in urban development, the mechanisms adopted and the role of landed property. All of these elements have been the outcome of a complex historical evolution primarily during the post-war period. Thus, understanding and explaining current developments in Athens requires a historical perspective. This chapter will therefore proceed by analysing the various critical periods in the development of the Athens Metropolitan Area, in relation to major legislative, institutional and policy changes, identifying the key elements from each period which have influenced long-term aspects of post-war development. All these constitute an integral part of the analysis of the contemporary situation within Athens.

14.1   INTERPLAY OF PLANNING LEGISLATION AND URBAN DEVELOPMENT DURING THE INTER-WAR PERIOD

Urban development of Athens has its structural roots in the inter-war period, especially after 1922 when 1.3 million refugees from Asia Minor arrived in Greece and the entire settlement network was reorganized. Population in Greater Athens in 1920 was 453 042 (constituting 8.9% of the total population of Greece) and in 1928, 802 000 inhabitants, or 12.93% of the total population (Table 14.1) (Polyzos, 1984; Leontidou, 1989).

It was during this period that the main legislation constituting the formal basis of state policy for spatial development in modern Greece was enacted. This was the 1923 Town Planning Act for the Cities, Towns and Villages of the Country. The Act provided for building and property boundaries systematization, compulsory expropriation and amalgamation of property and for approval practices. For the first time in Greece the concept of the city plan was introduced. Since then, the notion of property ownership inside or outside the plan boundaries has become the core element in spatial and property development.

The basic principles of the Act were conceived under the exceptional conditions experienced with the rebuilding of the city centre of Salonica following the devastating fire disaster of 1917 (Karadimou, 1985). The Act followed a logic based on limited availability of capital and thus considered the predominantly small landowner as also being a developer. Furthermore, it embodied an expansionist logic focusing on peripheral (or free) land development and excluded any notion of economic value generated by state actions in space. Economic differences, between the central state and the landowner, arising within the property boundaries systematization or expropriation procedures, were to be resolved almost exclusively by court actions (Delladetsima, 1991a).

The 1923 Act has been considerably modified and amended in the inter-war and more particularly during the post-war period. These modifications reflect pressures created by the dramatically changing urbanization trends. It has been, however, the legislative basis for the Greek planning system par excellence and only in 1979 did a major modification lead to the implementation of any substantial change to its basic principles.

In 1929, as a consequence of the implementation of the 1923 Act, the General Building Code was introduced. This became the first comprehensive building code legislation in Greece (Leontidou, 1992). Another important issue of the inter-war period, which determined the property development pattern, was the 3741/1929 Law. This provided the right to build on a single plot and then distribute ownership by floors and apartments, preserving in common use the service areas of the building. Multi-storey apartment buildings thus started appearing in the 1930s but the financing of urban development via *antiparochi* was only formalized during the post-war period (Marmaras, 1989). The system, which is based on exchange arrangements between landowner and entrepreneur and on pre-sales of apartment units for the financing of the construction process, clearly expresses the lack of capital for the financing of physical development. Other legislation of the period is the 5269/1931 Law, which provides for compensation of all land assets and 'existing elements' on expropriated or systematized through planned action properties. The inability, however, of the local authorities to obtain the necessary finance for such compensation led to a constant loss of public space in the inter-war and the post-war period.

Table 14.1   Population in Greater Athens, 1920–91

	Population in absolute nos	% of total Greek population
1920	453 042	8.19
1928	802 000	12.93
1940	1 124 109	15.30
1951	1 378 586	18.05
1955	1 621 000	20.42
1961	1 852 709	22.18
1965	2 133 000	24.89
1971	2 540 241	29.00
1975	2 860 000	31.79
1981	3 027 284	31.08
1991	3 096 775	30.19

Source: Leontidou (1990), updated with 1991 ESYE general population census.

This period also involved the adoption of the first rent control regulations which first appeared in 1917. Rent control has gradually expanded since then and in 1923, following the Asia Minor defeat, the first complete rent control legislation was enacted (Leontidou, 1992). Between 1930 and 1935 rent control regulations declined but were again intensified between 1935 and 1940. Rent control measures and property requisitions expanded enormously during the occupation of the country by the Germans. It was above all an expression of the power exerted by the occupation authorities and may have been the only mode adopted for dealing with the acute housing problems of that period (Delladetsima, 1991a).

14.2 THE PERIOD OF RECONSTRUCTION: THE CONSOLIDATION OF THE DOMINANT URBAN DEVELOPMENT PATTERN

Current developments in the planning system and property market in Athens are rooted in the immediate post-war period, the so-called period of reconstruction. This period (1944–52), comprising mostly the civil-war years (1944–9), meant Greece experienced an acute crisis during which fundamental changes with respect to the political, ideological and economic basis of state functions took place. These changes constitute an integral part of an exceptional regime created in response to specific crisis demands. Their importance clearly supersedes their contemporary time perspective, becoming determinants for the entire social (Tsoukalas, 1984) economic (Thomadakis, 1988) and political/institutional (Alivisatos, 1986) development of post-war Greece. Moreover, a new form of relationship was shaped between the state and landed property. Still, it can be considered as a formalization and consolidation of pre-war trends. This new state-landownership relationship proved to be highly critical for post-war spatial development and, in particular, for the urban agglomeration of Athens (Delladetsima, 1991a).

The reconstruction process in Greece lagged behind other European countries due to extreme socio-political conflicts and the intensity and character of reconstruction demands (Delladetsima, 1981, 1984). In other words, immediately after the war the country was faced with acute starvation problems and housing needs incomparable to any other European country. State policy in Greece during reconstruction was overwhelmed by exceptional measures of intervention in response to either the acute problems and needs created by the war, or in response to dramatic tensions arising during the period itself and especially by the civil conflict. The issues which dominated policy and in particular policy exhibiting a spatial bias were rent controls and property requisitions; regulation of property transactions during the German occupation; rebuilding incentives for destroyed properties or for property development in general; and the creation of a new administrative/planning structure to meet exceptional reconstruction demands (Delladetsima, 1991a). Other planning proposals, activities or even legislation, developed at the time, remained unimplemented or assumed a nearly Utopian character – in particular the Plan for the Reconstruction of the Capital which suggested the creation of a new-town administrative centre in the outskirts of Athens and various other minor proposals constituting local expressions of land-use planning intervention of the period.

14.2.1 Rent controls

Rent controls (*enikiostasiio*) and property requisitions could be considered as the most extensive and possibly more critical form of state policy influencing (unintentionally) urban development. Under escalating conditions of inflation the implementation of extreme rent control measures produced both direct and indirect effects on the available building stock (housing and other uses). In the long run it contributed to the consolidation of the role of the small fragmented property sector. State policy constantly expanded rent protection, either in reply to pressure by the emerging demands (war victims, civil war victims) or because of a 'purposive choice' to serve direct political/ideological legitimization and alienation needs. Therefore, the policy favoured specific social strata or professional categories, namely those directly involved in and structured by the civil war context (such as public employees, military personnel, police force). The expansion of formal rent control acted as a barrier for access to housing and shelter for a wide section of the population (migrants, other non-protected categories). This in turn was accompanied by an informal increase (that is independent from the state's intentions) of the population obtaining shelter in rent-protected properties under special agreements: viz between owners and tenants, between tenants and sub-contractors. Thus, through formal and informal processes an over-concentration of urban population took place in rent protected properties.

These population strata obviously benefited from such tenure and rent relationships and exerted significant pressure to preserve them. Housing and shelter alternatives for other categories, outside the protected sector, were found in the sphere of the small fragmented landed property. That is on the one hand new constructions and property acquisitions for the higher income groups and on the other illegal constructions in peripheral areas for the lower income groups (Roussopoulou, 1951). Taking into account that no public policy existed which was able to generate an alternative housing supply, rent control measures, in the long run, led to a drastic reduction of available building assets. This was caused by the physical deterioration of the properties under rent protection (that is by the inability to invest in repair and maintenance) and by the purposive preservation of existing rent control arrangements on behalf of the state, in order not to disturb the critical social equilibria formed around property and rent relations. The same forms of rent control were preserved throughout the 1950s; the last legislation more or less preserving the same rent control logic was the 835/1960 Royal Act (Delladetsima, 1991a).

14.2.2 Property transfer during the German occupation

The second major issue which dominated urban property development during reconstruction was the extensive property transfer during the German occupation. While this has not been researched systematically, based on information provided by a study promoted by the Ministry of Reconstruction it is argued that between October 1940 and June 1945 approximately 36 600 properties were transferred in Athens and 250 000 all over the country (Ministry of Reconstruction, 1946a,b,c; Delladetsima, 1991a).

State policy was developed in two directions. The first concerned the special taxation of all properties and profits obtained during the occupation; the second meant the cancelling of all property transactions which took place during the same period. With respect to the first direction, property taxation, 17 legislative regulations were enacted the most important of which was the 12 March 1945 Compulsory Law no. 182. The second policy direction, cancelling of property transactions, involved the enactment of 12 legislative regulations throughout the period, the most important of which being the 1323/1949 Compulsory Law.

The enormous complexity created by attempts to implement legislation in both directions produced a policy condition similar to rent control. In particular, it created an uncertainty concerning ownership rights for a vast number of properties. This in turn acted as a barrier to the use and development of such properties, contributing further to the reduction of available assets. Furthermore, a physical deterioration of such properties occurred, partly because of the inability to invest in their repair and maintenance (Delladetsima, 1991a). The legislation attempting to regulate the matter of property transfer during the German occupation lasted until the 1950s but the related repercussions at the court level lasted until the late 1960s and even longer.

14.2.3 Rebuilding policy and incentives

The acute housing problem constituted one of the main policy priorities of the first post-liberation governments. In this context, the first legislative action attempting to deal with the issue of rebuilding destroyed properties appeared in 1945 (The 261/1945 Compulsory Law). The aim was basically an attempt to regulate rent relations so that they would not obstruct possible repair or rebuilding works. In parallel with this legislation, an attempt was made to mobilize small income savings (either of the owner or the tenant), for rebuilding and repair operations. Despite the fact that such legislation was never implemented, it did form the prelude to a basic redevelopment practice which offered, as a principal rebuilding incentive, the possibility of removing any existing rent control obstacles. As a consequence on 23 August 1947, the *KH' Psifisma* (Resolution) was passed with the purpose of promoting the rebuilding of destroyed properties. This offered two kinds of incentives to the private sector namely tax allowances and exemptions; and the removal of all rent control and requisition measures in case of rebuilding. The implementation of the Psifisma with respect to its two basic provisions was specified respectively in 1947 and 1948 by two amending acts (the 22 October 1947 Royal Act and the 23 September 1948 Royal Act). All sections of the Resolution and of its amending Acts remained unaltered until 1951. In March of that year the first legislative measure was passed which severely curtailed the predicted tax allowances and exemptions. In 1953, a limited extension of the already curtailed tax allowances was given, and the possibility of removing rent control and requisition measures was preserved. A special section of the Resolution, providing for taxation on building permits, was also preserved. In 1958 the application of the section was further extended and since then, following consecutive extensions, has been maintained and still applies at present.

Thus, by definition, all basic regulations of the *KH' Psifisma* were directly related to rent and to taxation policy legislation. The Resolution however was also highly interrelated with issues such as expropriations and other planning matters. For instance, it directly influenced the creation of the Fund for the Implementation of the Athens Plan (*Tamion Efarmogis Schediou Protevousis*) by absorbing and diverting nearly all the Fund revenues to private-sector construction. Moreover, sections of the Resolution were directly combined with a 1948 Act concerning property fragmentation (1948/690 Legislative Act) which proved to be highly important in post-war development. It could be argued, however, that the *KH' Psifisma* did not constitute a comprehensive policy to stimulate rebuilding, since the taxation allowances were severely curtailed in 1951. The *KH' Psifisma* should therefore be considered as a provisional measure aiming to encourage and sustain a certain level of building activity under the extreme crisis conditions of the period. In this context, the Resolution seems to have produced certain results and in 1947 a notable increase of building activity took place within the Athens Metropolitan Area. This increase was primarily related to small-scale constructions, but it also incorporated the potential for multi-storey construction (Delladetsima, 1991a) and building activity as a consequence intensified, particularly during the 1950s.

The non-implementation of sections of the *KH' Psifisma* regarding building loans and mortgages by state agencies meant that rebuilding incentives operated in a 'financial vacuum'. Indeed the sums which were allocated for 'private rebuilding' by various banking and public institutions were of negligible importance and were not consistent with the rationale of the enacted legislation.

14.2.4   Creation of new institutions: the Ministry of Reconstruction

Finally another major issue which emerged within the reconstruction context was the creation of a new institution, the Ministry of Recons-truction. Its basic aim was to face the acute physical reconstruction demands. However, this Ministry gradually accumulated a wide spectrum of competencies and tasks, which transformed it, even though provi-sionally, into an overall planning policy institution. The creation of the Ministry of Reconstruction was the product of a combination of factors, namely the reconstruction demands and the increasing needs created by the escalating crisis; the pre-electoral climate of the 1946 elections; legitimization needs of the consecutive coalitions in government; and the presence of an important and controversial personality, the architect/planner Doxiades.

Throughout its existence, the Ministry of Reconstruction underwent various changes, determined by the political coalitions which were suc-ceeding one another in government. Thus, soon after its creation in 1945, an attempt was made to transform it into a completely autonomous plan-ning institution, but the results of the 1946 elections suspended further action in this respect. In 1947 a further attempt was made to increase its role and importance; this also failed to materialize and was followed by a gradual devaluation of its activities. In 1951, the Ministry of Reconstruction was abolished (under the 1671/1951 Compulsory Law). Its responsibilities were transferred to the Ministry of Public Health and Welfare, while in 1953 (2386 Legislative Act) all planning and development control respon-sibilities were returned to the Ministry of Public Works, thus re-introducing the pre-war administrative structure. This meant, among others, the formal reconstitution of the pre-war relationship between the state and landed property (Delladetsima, 1991a). However the re-introduced pre-war structure was severely affected by considerable distortions which initially produced a climate of uncertainty with respect to the competencies of the various state institutions responsible for reconstruction policy (Doxiades, 1950); planning and related policy (Vassiliou, 1950); expropriation policy; and also with respect to central-local administration relations (Biris, 1966). It could be argued that this uncertainty operated in favour of private landed property. This became abundantly clear in court decisions in con-tested cases between landowners and the state (Delladetsima, 1991a).

Moreover, the hyper-inflationary conditions during reconstruction cannot be ignored. Inflation in this period was basically a speculative phenomenon. According to Thomadakis (1988), practically every economic commentator from 1945 until the early 1950s focused on this phenomenon of alleged 'psychological inflation' which threatened to undermine the system at every turn. While it may be expected that property owners were part of this speculative condition and especially those who had no other constant sources of income, it is not apparent whether landownership followed any consistent response pattern with respect to inflationary developments. Publications of the period demonstrate a tendency towards land and property acquisitions which also involved public institutions (Saunatsos, 1947). In other words, inflation proved to be a key factor for the potential expansion of owner-occupation in the immediate post-war period (Delladetsima, 1991a).

The discussion indicates how exceptional reconstruction conditions contributed above all to the creation of a particular relationship between the state and landed property. To a large extent, this relationship defined the terms of future urban development. Demand generated by the acute housing and building deficit (as determined also in combination with the emerging urbanization trends) and the general need to overcome property obstacles was channelled only in the area of small fragmented ownership. State policy simply attempted to liberate properties from development obstacles, as well as mobilize small income savings. This attempt was fully expressed and systematized in the *KH' Psifisma*, which offered the possibility to free properties from existing rent control and other obstacles (e.g. regulations related to property transfer during the German occupation), but the law maintained the same structure of landed property, without any form of investment or financial policy.

Hence the basis for concessions to landed property was both intensive and extensive in character. The intensive nature of these concessions was expressed through the weakening of planning and development control policy, especially in the central areas of Athens. Lessening of controls effectively commenced in 1947 and intensified from 1950 onwards (Biris, 1966). The extensive nature of concessions included tacit acceptance and tolerance of the illegal construction phenomena which occurred in peripheral unbuilt areas. In 1955, prior to the elections, the first legalization concerning vast unauthorized built-up areas was enacted (3275/1955 Law). This is reflected by the fact that between 1940 and 1961, 6300 ha were added to the 11 600 ha of the official city area (Leontidou, 1990). Though in part easing pressure for shelter and facilitating the emerging demand for central uses, in essence such concessions meant an overwhelming concentration of building activity in the Athens Metropolitan area. Indeed the pre-war relationship to the rest of the country was reversed and by the end of the reconstruction period Athens contained, both in terms of value and volume, most of the building activity in the country. The contrast is vivid whenever pre- and post-war figures are compared. For example, in 1938 48.5% of construction works were concentrated in Athens and 51.5% in the rest of the country, whereas in 1949 investment in Athens reached the 72% and only 28% in the rest of the country. Furthermore, during the post-liberation years, in terms of the value of construction, there was an increasing bias towards Athens. Thus, in 1945 the value in construction works in Athens represented 44% of the national total, in 1946 46.5%, in 1947 67%, in 1948 the 68% and in 1949 the 72%. The average rate for this five-year period was 66% for Athens and 34% for the rest of the country.

Concessions towards small property ownership were accompanied by strong ideological biases, shaped initially by various personalities and institutions (Varvaressos, 1952) arguing in favour of the need to consolidate and expand such ownership. This was to become the dominant ideological stand of the Greek state with respect to property development. However, contrasting minority opinions argued in favour of the need to reduce property rights (Doxiades, 1977) in order to promote social and economic modernization (Delladetsima, 1991a).

In fact, the period of reconstruction in Greece led to the dismantling or even the exclusion of spatial planning as a basic form of state function. The primary cause for this exclusion was the political and social need to consolidate small landed property (which potentially embodies a vast section of population strata), which by its nature cannot be incorporated into a planning and welfare system. Contrary therefore to developments in Western Europe, Greece was not in a position to promote planning, within the terms of a Keynesian social consensus. Thus, pre-war physical regulatory relations were re-introduced for the control of urban development. Since then, non-conventional forms of state action have proved to be more critical in influencing spatial developmental trends than common planning practice expressed through physical plans. The key output of long-term importance for post-war Greece has been the creation of a dual polarized structure between landed property and state policy. This in turn has meant an expanded role of court actions in regulating all trivial situations appearing in spatial/property development. Meanwhile, state policy has tended to ignore development in the content and mechanisms of long-term spatial regulation and exceptionally resorted to interventions of a specific character only when these were necessary (Delladetsima, 1991a). Overall, since the reconstruction spatial/property development has been predominantly serving socio-political legitimation purposes and fiscal needs of the state.

14.3 THE EXPANSION OF THE MODEL IN THE 1950s–1960s

Spatial development in the 1950s and 1960s was overwhelmed by rapid urbanization trends, especially in Greater Athens. For example in 1940 the population in Greater Athens constituted 15.3% of that for the country; in 1951 18.5%; while in 1955 it reached 1 621 000 inhabitants or 20.42% of the total for Greece. The annual rate of growth for 1940–50 was 1.87% and for 1951–5, 4.13%; in subsequent years rates were in the range 2.5% to 3.0% but slowed down after 1975 (Leontidou, 1990).

State policy immediately following the reconstruction period was not to intervene in the complex ownership pattern as there was a desire not to disturb the critical socio-political equilibria created. Furthermore small ownership development acted as a substitute for the overall absence of intervention in the field of reproductive investment and in particular public housing. Spatial development thus followed the pattern shaped and consolidated during the reconstruction period (Delladetsima, 1991a). This development meant consecutive waves of concessions towards small landed property, leading to an escalating intensification of construction in central areas and to uncontrolled urban sprawl. Characteristically, by 1961 the authorized city plan area was 3/5 of the built-up area of Greater Athens, 17960 and 27130 ha respectively (Leontidou, 1990). Between 1951 and 1958 approximately 75 000 building projects were completed in the Athens Metropolitan Area, 78% of which were entirely new developments while the rest consisted of refurbishments, repairs and extensions. The majority of new buildings (84%) were relatively small in size, comprising 1–6 rooms. Taking into account demolition, new housing construction represented a 26% increase in the total number of housing units in Athens (ESYE Statistical Survey, 1962).

Overall development policy throughout the period focused on economic stabilization, the attraction of foreign investment and the promotion of infrastructural projects. However, development trends did not relate to the ambitious development programmes launched during these years, such as the five-year plan of 1960–64, the 1966–70 Programme and the two development programmes of the dictatorial regime, the 1968–72 Programme and the Development Programme 1973–84. At the same time, urban development in Athens bore little resemblance to consecutive urban, transportation and related plans (the W. Smith and Associates. Transportation Study for Athens 1964–5, the 1966 Athens Master Plan) which on the whole remained unimplemented. Private property development and the construction of new infrastructural works, especially road construction (e.g. the Athens–Sounion road, the extension and modernization of the airport and the construction of two major highways connecting Athens with the northern and the southern regions of the country), which in turn released new land for private development, were the leading factors in the development process. The 4458/1965 Act provided for the first time the legislative framework for the creation of industrial zones in Greece.

State action in the property market assumed an indirect form through development control practice and a loosening up of building regulations which encouraged private development in certain areas; through building

concessions for specific uses such as tourism; through rent control legislation which gradually reduced categories of eligible properties; and
through taxation policy. At the same time only very limited and rather
disjointed planned interventions in the urban fabric and housing projects
took place, while public housing provision was constantly reduced, despite
considerable legislative activity (for example the 1667/1951 Law For
Public Housing, the 2963/1954 Act for the creation of the Independent
Organization for Public Housing). Thus, investment in housing which in
1948–50 constituted 27.9% of public expenditure, declined to 7.7% in
1951–2 and by the end of the decade was only 2.9%.

The end of the 1960s was marked by a major constitutional upheaval.
The policy of the dictatorship and its regime (1967–74) highlighted to the
extreme the 'traditional developmental path'. Another round of unimplemented plans for Athens thus followed: revision of the previous 1966
Plan in 1969, formulation of a new plan in 1976, the Regional Plan and Programme for Athens by Doxiades and Associates, following an appointment
by the regime in 1972. State policy therefore was defined by new concessions towards landed property (building height concessions with the
395/1968 Law, building control concessions with the 625/1968 Compulsory Law and legalization of unauthorized constructions with the 410/
1968 Compulsory Law); and increased exceptional interventions particularly in relation to infrastructural projects, tourist development and major
industrial investments. An *ad-hoc* pattern of intervention was expanded
and assumed in many cases an official legislative status. Indicative of this
was the 1003/1971 Act concerning positive planning and its amending
797/1971 Act concerning expropriations (Voivoda *et al.*, 1977), which
illustrated the desire of the regime to legitimize its exceptional powers. All
these resulted in increased speculation and accelerated the deterioration
of the built environment, not only in Athens but in the entire country.
There was consequently a speculative building boom in Athens during the
dictatorship period, dominated by multi-storey apartments (Table 14.2).
At the same time illegal housing constructions were suppressed and
incorporated into the city plan, so that the urban development process
was transformed (Leontidou, 1990).

During the dictatorship, however, several legislative regulations were
introduced, some of which remained virtually inactive (such as the 1262/
1972 Act and its amending 198/1973 Act introducing for the first time at the
legislative level the notion of the Master Plan). Others proved to be highly
critical for property development, such as the 1024/1971 Legislative Act
for the Constitution of Vertical Property Development (the right to promote development involving property division of more than one construction on the same plot) and the 8/1973 Legislative Act amending the
1955 Building Code.

Thus during the 1950s and 1960s the self-financed private property

Table 14.2   New buildings in Greater Athens by number of storeys, 1961–89

	Single storey	2–3 Storey	Multi-storey	Total number	
	% number of private buildings				
1961	80.19	11.85	7.96	8 309	
1964	65.38	19.51	15.11	7 073	
1971	42.99	31.42	25.59	8 695	
1975	29.87	44.04	26.09	7 053	
1981	20.74	52.14	27.13	4 051	
1984	20.33	54.65	25.02	2 966	
1989	16.46	54.56	28.98	6 169	
	% volume of private buildings				
				1000 m^3	m^3/build.
1961	31.65	15.21	53.14	7 103	854.86
1964	20.66	16.88	62.46	9 765	1380.60
1971	13.16	20.29	66.55	17 365	1997.12
1975	11.78	30.63	57.59	12 719	1803.35
1981	16.22	39.12	44.65	7 735	1909.41
1984	15.86	38.67	45.47	5 876	1981.12
1989	11.72	40.11	48.17	12 105	1962.23

Source: Leontidou, 1990, updated for 1989 from ESYE Statistical Yearbook.

pattern was further extended. This consisted of speculative construction in housing and commercial properties relying heavily on pre-sales of dwellings (as a critical financing component) and of small housing construction for occupation by the owner. The differences to that of subsequent decades relates primarily to the composition of real estate demand and the role of the state in the financing process (Delladetsima, 1991a).

14.4   THE POST-DICTATORSHIP YEARS: MODERNIZATION ATTEMPTS OF THE 1970s

Following the overthrow of the dictatorship, attempts aimed at modernizing existing legislation and institutional structures relating to planning policy were made. This effort in its preliminary stage was expressed also in the new Constitution of 1975 (section 24). At the institutional/ administrative level, the 360/1976 Law for Planning and Environment foresaw the creation of the Supreme Council for the Environment. Soon after, the Public Corporation for Urban Development and Housing (DEPOS) was formed, substituting provisions regarding positive development of the previous 1003/1971 Law. Undoubtedly DEPOS started off with very innovative aspirations in housing and planning projects, but it has gradually lost importance. In 1976 the Ministry of Planning Housing and the Environment was created as the overall planning institution of the country, but no substantial planning policy responsibilities were conceded to local authorities.

These years were characterized again by the formulation of a series of programmes and plans, on the whole remaining unimplemented and accompanied by an extensive planning/modernization debate. To a certain extent, this debate was activated by the anticipated entry of the country to the EEC (now the European Union). At the regional level, an overall developmental policy was launched, having as a prime objective the decentralization of population from Athens and secondly the creation of a settlement system giving priority to concentrating development in six selected urban centres in the country (Centres of Intensive Developmental Programmes). This policy commonly known as 'Opponent Cities' (*Antipales Polis*), constituted a kind of a '*Metropoles d'equilibre*' experiment, but has not materialized. In 1977, the Master Plan Department of the Ministry of Public Works started a new round for the formulation of a plan for the Athens Metropolitan area. The 1977 plan remained inactive and in 1978 the government appointed five private planning offices to produce an alternative plan for five distinct areas of the conurbation. The five different plans produced for each area were then recomposed as an integral new Master Plan for Athens. In 1980 a further attempt towards drafting a Master Plan (Supreme Council Decision no. 2094) was made, structuring the city into nine districts. The study of each district was then allocated to private architectural/planning studios; the first phase of the respective studies was concluded by May 1980. However, the disjointed character of the plans and the general political and social environment did not allow for any implementation process to proceed (Leontidou, 1981).

With respect to development control policy, the existing building code was amended and modified with the 205/1974 Legislative Act. Set within the overall modernization attempt of the period, in relation to development control and physical development, legislation concerning parking spaces (960/1979 Law) and plot ratio transfer rights (880/1979 Law) was introduced. At the same time, the expanded owner-occupier sector and the reliance upon the private rented sector (in the scarcity of public housing provision) forced the Ministry of Commerce to preserve and occasionally extend rent-control regulations.

The end of this period is marked by the enactment of a new planning law: the 947/1979 Law for Housing Areas which constituted the first historical break with the 1923 Act and provided for the formulation and implementation of 'Housing Areas Projects' according to various zoning modalities. The major innovation introduced by this new law regards development in expanding and other areas. For the first time, in the creation of public spaces and infrastructure, the participation (financially and in land) of the property owner became compulsory as a general condition for all properties in a development area. The contribution in land (as a percentage of the property) was determined by the zoning modality and the financial contribution by the market value of the property. Any changes in value, potentially produced by planned action or by public investment, were not taken into consideration as an integral part of the legislative rationale. However, the law remained inactive and was later modified by new legislation reflecting also the governmental change following the 1981 elections.

On the whole, the modernization attempts of the 1970s, did not produce any radical change of the existing centralized structures, nor did they alter the basic principles governing planning and related legislation; rather ongoing developmental trends proved to be far stronger than the 'official planning rationale' which was introduced and the expressed interventionist intentions. Thus, the dominant pattern of property development in Athens has remained the same, but what has changed is the structure of demand as determined by different social/demographic groups in different geographical areas of the conurbation (Delladetsima, 1991b). The dominant process in the 1970s was one of homogenization rather than segregation, brought about by the diffusion of the multi-storey apartment building (Leontidou, 1990) and the increase of second-home ownership often in illegal constructions.

14.5   THE 1980s: A NEW RHETORIC FOR AN UNCHANGING PATTERN

This period saw changes in the existing legislation and policy setting accompanied with a strong ideological outlook, tightly linked to the rhetoric of the new PASOK government. It did not result, however, in changes of any major importance. Thus, the 1337/1983 Planning Law, while maintaining most of the sections of the previous 947/1979 Law, incorporated some significant new provisions. These relate to approval practices and new zoning modalities especially in relation to new urban development. However, the main change introduced by the new law concerns the compulsory participation of the landowner for the creation of public spaces and infrastructure. In this respect the 1337/1983 Law attempts to produce a more fair system: the level of participation of the landowner (in terms of land and finance) is determined according to plot size and to the entire number of properties owned in an area. However once more, no value notion is included. Compensation and expropriation prices are determined by an appointed committee with the law always preserving an expansionist logic, focusing primarily on private housing development on new land. Thus planning legislation, even in its more recent expression, is heavily bound by old physical deterministic conceptions proposing a segregated land-use structure similar to that of the 1960s. Implementation is perceived within a context defined by limited investment potential and by the need to respect the existing form and structure of private landownership.

Within the aforementioned legislative context, in 1983 the Ministry of Housing, Planning and Environment promoted 'Operation Urban Reconstruction' aimed at producing simultaneously land-use plans for all urban areas in Greece, including the municipalities within the Athens conurbation. It also promoted a national programme entitled 'Open Cities'. This was an attempt to structure, in a hierarchical fashion, all settlements of the country, primarily according to their population size, for the effective distribution of services and resource allocation (an ambiguous exercise in the context of Christaller's neo-classical locational theory). At a later stage, as an indication of the implementation limits of the programme, the Ministry of the Interior promoted a further policy which to a certain extent overlapped or contradicted the former. This concerned the delineation of 'development units' rather than settlements 'for the effective distribution of public investment in technical and social infrastructure, and also of productive investment of local importance' (3329 10/8/1987 Min. Decree).

The 1515/1985 Law, complementing the 1337/1983 Planning Law, enacted the Athens Master (Regulatory or Structure) Plan (*Rithmistico Schedio*). This was accompanied by the creation of the Athens Agency (*Organismos Athinas*) as the institution charged with the implementation of the plan. However the plan remained a published blueprint and the agency gradually lost importance, with its activities being determined by central government decisions and emerging demands. Complementary to the main planning law is also the 1650/1986 Environmental Law, which has remained unimplemented (no amending implementation acts have ever been enacted). Nevertheless this law is relevant to planning policy legislation due to the specific control measures and zoning modalities it embodies.

Concerning development control legislation in 1985 a new 'General Building Code' was introduced which, though preserving most of the existing regulations, strongly embodied an architectural 'free' logic. This resulted in significant confusion and cleavages at the implementation stage which were contested at the Supreme Court level. Within the development control practice, parking spaces legislation (1221/1981 Law, the 1340/1981 Act and the 1339/1981 Act), the Fire Safety Code (71/1988 Act) and the Building Safety Code (3046/304/1989 Min. Dec.) were enacted. Also restrictions on industrial activity in Greater Athens became more rigorous in the 1980s and decentralization policy, at the national level, was supplemented by legislation against environmental pollution (e.g. 84/1984 Law).

In 1982 important legislation 'For the Determination of Objective Values of Real Estate Properties' was enacted by the Ministry of Finance (1249/5/4/1982 Law, section 41), attempting for the first time to formulate a rational pattern for determination of urban land and property taxation. The law was implemented in 1984 with a Ministerial Decree (9821/187 31/12/1984). The conceptual basis of the legislation is relatively unsophisticated. Essentially it divides the urban area into value zones more or less arbitrarily according to criteria such as centrality, proximity to major arteries and other factors. Property values are determined in each zone by measurements such as a building index, plot ratio, age of the building and floor space, as well as locational criteria such as the 'business/commercial character' of the street. This process represents an attempt by the state to rationalize land-value and property patterns through an external mechanism independent from the planning process and controlled by a different institution (the Ministry of Finance) rather than by those directly involved in spatial development. The legislation was first implemented in Athens and Salonica and has gradually been expanded to all urban areas of Greece. Initially it was conceived as an auxiliary to taxation policy, however it has also impacted upon urban development. In spite of the divergence in many cases between objective and market prices, the former have become the guiding instrument for determining expropriation and compensation prices (especially by court decisions in case of contested differences) and property transactions (property contracts are effected on an objective value basis). Even more so the determination of objective values, combined with development control regulations, have been transformed into a mechanism by central government for influencing property values and generating building demand in areas within the urban setting, aimed occasionally at increasing public revenues (Delladetsima, 1991b). Objective values are revised by the Ministry of Finance every two years.

At this stage there were also various administrative reforms of minor importance, such as the amalgamation of the Ministry of Planning with the Ministry of Public Works; and the expansion of the responsibilities of the prefectures in development control and planning approval practices (1337/1983 Law, section 33 par. 1, 1512/1985 Law, 2–4/14/1985 Act, 183/1986 Act).

The end of the period is marked by an unprecedented expansion of housing mortgage policy (developed within a pre-electoral climate), which included for the first time interest rate subsidization (by one-third) for first-home acquisition. This policy led to 48 000 new mortgages with a total value of 160 billion drachmas (250 billion in current prices), channelled principally into private self-financed property development (Mandikas, 1993). Favourable mortgage policy accompanied by rising family income thus

Table 14.3 Private building activity in Greater Athens, 1985–89: construction of new buildings, number and value in million drachmas

	Number	% Total country	Value	% Total country
1985	3.581	7.8	13457.5	22.0
1986	4.798	10.0	19952.7	25.1
1987	5.167	11.4	26002.6	30.0
1988	4.685	9.8	24176.4	25.4
1989	6.169	11.5	26919.3	25.3

Source: adapted from NSSG (ESYE) Statistical Yearbook.

produced a considerable increase of construction output (Tables 14.2 and 14.3). Spatial policy therefore, in this decade became a component of the socialist rhetoric of the PASOK government. However in spite of policy initiatives and legislative output, the development pattern remained unaltered: centralism, property fragmentation, speculation, and uncontrolled urban expansion.

14.6 THE CURRENT SITUATION

Having gone through the various phases of the development of Athens in parallel with the evolution of the institutional and legislative system for spatial planning, an analysis of the current (early 1990s) situation can now be placed in context. In order to examine the impact of state action in Athens, it is necessary to take into consideration all areas of intervention which directly or indirectly influence land development. It is often the case that in a given historical context, certain forms of intervention, either independently or in interaction, could prove to be more critical than formal planning intervention. It is therefore necessary to proceed by investigating areas of state intervention such as planning policy (land-use, planning practice and development control); the institutional setting (central, local and other institutions); taxation policy; and mortgage policy. Subsequently current developmental and policy trends in Greater Athens will be examined.

14.6.1 Planning policy

Broadly planning policy, as discussed, has developed in relation to physical land-use plans (still at an early stage of development) and development control for which there is a greater level of experience though at times poorly articulated. It must be pointed out however that the dominant and highly undisputed physical/deterministic nature of planning in Greece has led not only to perceptions which tend to dissociate planning from any economic and social components but, even more, to perceptions which deal with land-use planning, planning practice and development control as independent and non-interacting procedures (Delladetsima, 1994).

Concerning plan formulation, current activities evolve around the main planning legislation of the 1923 Act, the 947/1979 Law and the 1337/1983 Law and include three levels of intervention. In particular, experience until now at the first level (master plan) is very limited and inconsistent, developed only in blueprints in Athens and Salonica.

The second level consists of physical plans which can be produced based on provisions deriving either from the 1923 Act (applied mostly in the existing urban setting) or from the recent 1337/1983 Law which by definition focuses on areas of urban expansion. This latter law provides for the formulation of General Land-Use Plans and Detailed Plans, introducing a two-tier system. The prevailing rationale of the land-use plans, based on a 1960s planning standard logic, is expansionist and on the whole tends to undermine renewal and related interventions within the urban fabric. However, to all the main planning laws there corresponds a labyrinth of amendments, modifications, exemptions and special planning laws concerning construction in pre-1923 towns; construction in towns with less than 2000 inhabitants; construction in vernacular settlements; forest area determination etc. By taking into account, therefore, such a complex legislative and operational context, planning practice and implementation becomes a highly difficult exercise.

Moreover, plan implementation is meant to be financed by a Special Fund (ETERPS) enacted in 1972 (1262/1972 Act), whcih accumulates finance from various sources such as public subsidies, public loans, incomes deriving from the exploitation of public property as well as from other sources. However, due to the inability of the central state to guarantee inflow from these sources and due to the insufficient level of finance which could be generated, the role of the Fund remains highly inefficient. Other sources of finance for plan implementation activities concern local authorities which have obtained certain planning practice and development control powers. These sources basically consist of percentage transfers on incomes generated by special taxation on building licences (imposed by the *KH' Psifisma*, 1947). On the whole, there is a marked lack of constant resources allocated to the planning process thereby critically inhibiting most implementation attempts.

Furthermore matters appear as complex or impossible for formulating and implementing a consistent land policy, and in fact no attempt of this kind has ever been registered. In particular, the various tools available through the existing legislative framework, namely compulsory expropriation; compulsory participation of the landowner for the creation of public spaces and infrastructure; preference acquisition by the public; and plot ratio transfer rights appear as an unbearably impractical set of regulations.

In contrast to all the above, development control practice proves to be a more efficient, though again highly laborious process. Procedures are now structured on the 1577/1985 General Building Code, which incorporates a vast number of sections from all previous codes, and on legislation concerning building safety, fire safety and parking spaces.

14.6.2   The institutional setting

With respect to planning institutions it is important to stress the extremely centralized character of the Greek system. The main planning institution in the country is the Ministry of Planning, Environment and Public Works (YPEHODE) which is involved in all levels of planning policy (general policy, environmental policy, regional planning and even development control), implemented by the respective planning offices at the various Prefectures. Important central institutions involved are also the Ministry of the Interior with the Prefectures (the Region of Attica includes four Prefectures).

The role of the local authorities, though not negligible, is highly restricted, especially when compared with other European countries in which, on the whole, municipalities appear as the core local development and town-planning institutions (Leontidou, 1993). The planning law system in Greece includes a vast number of scattered sections from different laws and acts which vaguely determine local authority responsibilities. These include: implementation of central government policy (Ministry or Prefecture); participation in administrative bodies and commissions concerning planning matters; initiatives for the promotion of planning actions; advisory responsibilities; responsibilities in planning and social policy; involvement in the plan-making process; planning practice and development control (Christophilopoulos, 1989). More specifically, with respect to the responsibilities related to plan formulation, planning practice and development control, these appear to be not clearly defined and disjointed.

At the first planning level (master or structure plan), local authorities have only control powers within the plan formulation and implementation processes. Only at the second (land-use plan) level have local authority powers recently evolved, particularly with respect to the plan formulation process. All main Planning Laws (17/7/1923 Act, 947/1979 Law and 1337/1983 Law), while recognizing and defining the role of local authorities in plan formulation, preserve the right for final approval to remain exclusively with the central state competencies (Ministry or Prefecture). However, with the latest Planning Law (1337/1983, section 33), local authorities for the first time have obtained certain plan approval powers (Christophilopoulos, 1989). Such powers are determined by legislation, following a request by the municipality. But there is a pre-condition that the latter is in a position to organize an appropriate 'engineering' department able to comply with the requirements for the accomplishment of specific functions (as determined in section 27, par. 1 of the 1577/1985 Building Code). Therefore it would seem that a process similar to the one developed in the UK in the late 1930s and 1940s, concerning the City Engineer's and City Architect's department and the consecutive introduction of the planning department is not even in its early stages in the Greek local administrative structure.

In addition development control practice on the whole remains a central government matter. With the 947/1979 Law, however, local authorities have obtained the right to acquire certain development control powers (such as the granting of building permits, building code control) with the pre-condition that the local authority which requests to obtain such powers is in a position to organize the appropriate 'engineering' department. Thus, though local authorities dispose certain planning practice and development control powers (not accompanied however by the necessary finance) in relation to procedures of the 1923 Act, the 947/1979 Law and the 1337/1983 Law, these powers have been conceded disjointly and without shaping any consistent rationale within the planning process.

Moreover besides the Ministry of Planning (YPEHODE), the Ministry of the Interior, the Prefectures and the municipalities, there are other bodies whose actions impinge upon spatial development. Some of these bodies include the Organization of Athens, the Public Agency for Housing and Planning (DEPOS); the Organization of Public Transport in the Agglomeration of Athens (OAS); the Ministry of Industry, Research and Technology (responsible for granting industrial location permits and for the implementation of industrial policy in general); the Ministry of Agriculture (especially the Forestry Department); the Ministry of Transport and Communications; the Ministry of Education and the Agency for School Building Development (OSK); the Ministry of Health and Social Welfare; the National Electricity Board (DEI); the Mortgage Bank of Greece (EKTE, the principal mortgage institution in the country, which is also involved in development projects); the Industrial Development Bank (ETVA, responsible for the creation and organization of industrial zones); the Independent Organization for Public Housing (AOEK); the National Board for Tourism (development and location permits for tourist activities); the Ministry of Defence and many others. In addition the indirect influence of decisions and policies of the Ministry of National Economy (mostly responsible for development grants and incentives policy); the Ministry of Finance (taxation policy and determination of objective values) and the Ministry of Commerce (rent policy for residential and commercial uses) must also be considered. This mere reference to the array of institutions involved with spatial planning reveals the confusing, overlapping and conflicting decision-making and policy context.

14.6.3 Taxation

Similar complexity and irregularity arises in the examination of land and property taxation. On the whole, this consists of taxation on incomes deriving from the properties (taxation on rents), taxation on property capital (property tax, property transfer tax, hereditary property tax, parental property transfer tax) and other fees and contributions (participation in money according to the modalities of the planning law, local authority service provision fees, construction permit fee, imposition of VAT on construction) (Velides, 1993). The actual interrelationship of the taxation system with planning as a mechanism and in the context of resource transfer is very limited, though a recent development has been the creation of the property fee which will be directly transferred to the local authorities. The property fee is defined by a local authority decision as a per thousand on the objective value of the property (0.25–0.35%) (Emmanuel, 1993). However no provision is included to relate such local authority income to planning activities.

Other issues of importance include the fact that taxation policy vaguely differentiates between ownership in land and in buildings (Papamichos and Skouras, 1981); central government occasionally imposes property taxes to meet exceptional fiscal needs, as has been the case of a recently imposed property tax; and that there is a potential condition towards taxing construction rather than landownership. Moreover, tax regulations introduced in various periods tend to target a specific population and housing categories.

14.6.4 Mortgage policy and financing

Two important chacteristics of the real estate market must be stressed when analysing housing and commercial property acquisition in Greece and Athens in particular. The first concerns the overwhelmingly extended role of family income savings and property transfers as the core financing mechanism. Indeed 50% of the households in the major urban areas of Greece have acquired properties in the owner occupation sector through family assistance (DEPOS, 1989; Emmanuel, 1993). It should be pointed out that during the last 30 years investment in housing and commercial property has also constituted an important family income mechanism highly competitive with bank savings (Kotsambopoulos, 1991). Only recently has this mechanism lost in importance in relation to other investments such as government bonds. In fact rent yield on properties in the free market in 1991 amounted to 8–10%; it currently amounts to 6.0%

and 3.5% in the rent-controlled sector (Kotsambopoulos, 1991; Mandikas, 1993). The second characteristic concerns the limited role of public and banking institutions in the real estate market. During the last decade for instance mortgage policy covered only 20–25% of new owner-occupiers (DEPOS, 1989; Emmanuel, 1993). Until the mid 1980s, mortgage policy consisted of low interest rate lending to various categories of beneficiaries deriving from centrally controlled capital assets and according to annual programmes determined by the fiscal authorities (Mandikas, 1993). The 1988 reforms in this sector included interest rate subsidization for first home acquisition; loan increases amounting from 50% to 75% of the property value; and the introduction of an incomes saving/mortgage policy. However the reforms introduced remain structured on the self-financed private property development model.

In relation to commercial property development, the role of public or banking finance is limited. Concerning construction output, public and other private financing covers only 15% of the total in this sector in Greece (Emmanuel, 1993). In the case of major retail, industrial and tourist investments, financing has been related to a certain extent to the various development incentives laws (such as the 1078/1971 Act, the 1312/1972 Act, the 849/1978 Law, the 1262/1982 Law, the 1892/1990 Law); however, these do not seem to have impacted to any appreciable extent on urban development particularly in Athens.

Thus within such a legislative and policy context it could be argued that real-estate operation is the outcome of considerable market freedom as determined by general economic conditions, household incomes, financing policy on behalf of the state, investment potential of major economic public and private agents, and locational advantages (Delladetsima, 1994). On the whole the operation of state action in the field is rather intrinsic.

With respect to real-estate transactions, these have been constantly increasing both in number and value. The total number was 242 300 in 1985 and 350 000 in 1989, corresponding to a value of 253.4 billion drachmas and 715.4 billion respectively. Increases in value have been 43% between 1987 and 1988 and 45.5% between 1988 and 1989. The real level of property transactions, however, was estimated to be 2.5–3 times higher than the one officially registered and thus the value of property transfers in 1990 was between 2.7–3.2 trillion drachmas. Differences occur due to objective values being much lower than real values and also where ob- jective values are not determined, transactions are registered at a lower rate than the real level (Kotsambopoulos, 1991).

According to census data 52.2% of the total number of transfers has been effected in the region of Attica (Kotsambopoulos, 1991). Between 1980 and 1990 land prices in Greece have increased 10 to 12 fold. In parallel, during the same period, real-estate prices (housing, office, retail) have increased by a factor of 9–10 with the greatest increase occurring after 1987. In the case of Athens high property values occur in certain areas of the centre, in the high income suburbs and in locationally advantaged sites along certain major arteries. Demand in general seems to be concentrating on high income housing, second home ownership and in new retail and office uses, particularly retail centres (Delladetsima, 1991b).

Current conditions (1993), with the public sector affected by an austere policy aimed at reducing expenditure and the private construction sector seriously struck by recession, have led to a stabilization or a reduction of values. Therefore expectations and forecasts of the late 1980s have not materialized. This is also evident in the determination of objective values. In 1991 objective values were increased by the Ministry by 80–90% on average (which according to estimates of real market prices have been 30–40% higher). The most recent revision of objective values, accompanied also by the introduction of a new more practical and realistic mode of calculation (Ministerial Decree 21/1/1993), has led to their reduction in 245 zones of Athens and to an increase in only 9 zones. The largest decreases are most marked in properties of the high-income northern (19 to 38%) and coastal suburbs (20%), while objective value increases were introduced in certain areas of the centre (10–25%) and in linear zones along major arteries (10–18%). It would seem that these new regulations constitute an attempt by central government to readjust objective values due to the wide divergences identified with market values, especially in the high-income suburbs and possibly encourage or at least not obstruct demand in other areas of the conurbation (by facilitating property transfer). Nevertheless differences between objective and market values remain high and tend to converge in few areas of Greater Athens.

In housing development, in spite of the current crisis and the changes in the modes of financing and central state participation in mortgage policy, the dominant private property development pattern continues to persist. Also new forms of office and retail development again comply with the existing pattern; indeed the selection of sites for the location of new retail and office building is based on short term, conjunctural criteria. Financing mechanisms do not derive from new investment policies on behalf of banking or other financial institutions, rather investment in the construction of such projects is based on capital provided by the builder/developer and therefore relies heavily on pre-sales. In recent years, however, there has been a marked interest on the part of banks, insurance and retail companies in new construction and several real estate/speculative developments are evident (Delladetsima, 1991b). Such activities, however, though potentially important, do not yet form a precise investment trend.

It could be argued that despite some potentially important indications of change in Athens, there are indeed limited major capital investment initiatives (both public and private) in the existing urban fabric (Delladetsima, 1994). This condition has been reciprocally shaped by planning and related legislation. The 947/1979 Law, for instance, provided for the participation of private capital in 'positive planning' (renewal) programmes. This provision was abolished by the 1337/1983 Law without allowing other institutions, such as the local authorities, to assume this task. The possibility therefore of any renewal policy remains virtually stagnant (Christophilopoulos, 1989). Under the circumstances, assets of the existing fabric assume a very limited role in real estate development. For instance, from the entire number of property transfers which occurred in the major urban centres of the country, the overwhelming majority related to new construction and only 26% to the existing stock (DEPOS, 1989; Emmanuel, 1993).

Changes in planning legislation and policy introduced by the Conservative government, which came to power in 1990 (though defeated in the election of autumn 1993), are too early to evaluate. However, on the one hand the central state proves to be, as in the past, highly efficient when dealing with exceptional major infrastructural works. The elaborate and integrated rationale of the Athens Metro legislation (1955/1991 Law), resulting in turn in a rather efficient implementation process, would have been ideal if extended also to planning legislation of a more general character. On the other hand, other enacted legislation tended to introduce a liberalizing doctrine, as an incentive to capital investment initiatives, involving attempts to lessen and abolish rent control regulations on both housing and commercial properties.

It appears, however, that even such a doctrine proves to be weak and therefore becomes distorted when applied to the Athens or Greek context. The 1947/1991 Law and the complementary 2052/1992 Act, allowing for the privatization of public landed assets and for 'private urbanization works' have been watered down in their implementation. The initial precondition for 'private urbanization' of a minimum property size of 100 ha has been subsequently curtailed to 50 ha, under the pressure of wider social and economic interests. The creation of a Controlled Development Zone (ZEA), designed specifically for the Elonas area (an industrial area adjacent to the centre of Athens), constitutes an attempt to create an ad hoc planning and development control zone of an independent statute from the surrounding urban context. However, the investment logic, the forms of spatial regulation and building incentives do not at all differentiate it from the dominant pattern in the Athens region. The measures have not been accompanied or have not generated any new forms of public or private investment. It therefore seems that the liberalizing attempt has resulted only in introducing a deregulation policy into an already deregulated urban setting (Delladetsima, 1994). But in the end, what still determines the urban development process is the self-financed private property pattern and the expansionist logic deriving from it. In essence it results again in new waves of legalization and the incorporation of further peripheral areas within city plan boundaries. The most recent governmental change is meant to bring new policies but this remains to be seen.

14.7 CONCLUSION

The period of post-war reconstruction has led to the exclusion of planning as a basic form of state intervention and to the creation of a dual polarized structure between landed property and state policy, consolidating pre-war trends. The 1950s and 1960s were characterized by the intensification and geographical expansion of the private property development model. Modernization attempts of the post-dictatorship years and the subsequent 'new' policy of the 1980s have not led to any changes in the dominant model despite the marked difference in the structure of demand in Greater Athens.

Thus, the current situation (early 1990s) is characterized by a highly centralized administrative planning system; a weak local government structure with disjointed and loosely defined responsibilities; an immense number of public and other institutions which directly or indirectly influence through their actions spatial development; an infinite number of new and past legislative regulations for which no attempt has ever been made towards codification and rationalization; a planning policy that has evolved primarily from development control measures and only recently has addressed land-use plans; the lack of financial resources and of any rational resource allocation mechanism for planning policy. All these in combination define a 'non-planning situation', which predominantly serves a long-standing informal consensus between the state, landownership and the social and economic actors (developers/engineers, professional chambers) concerning the structuring of the land development model in Greece and Athens in particular. By contrast no consensus has ever been structured around planning (involving different agents), as has been the case in most countries in Europe.

Past and present forms of demand in land and property are bound to comply with the dominant private property development model. The state intervenes in the process not through planning and the related expropriation policies, but mostly through development control (building height, plot ratio definition); through the definition of new plan or town boundaries; and through mortgage and taxation policy, assisted more recently by the determination of objective values. The inability to restructure the existing fabric and further intensification of the central areas still leads to a constant and extensive geographical expansion of the self-financed private property development model in the entire region.

REFERENCES

Alivisatos, N. (1986) *Political Institutions in Crisis (1922–1974): Facets of the Greek Experience* (in Greek), Themelio, Athens.

Biris, K. (1966) *Athens from the 19th to the 20th Century* (in Greek), Planning and History of Athens Foundation, Athens.

Christophilopoulos, D. (1989) The role of local government in regional and urban planning (in Greek), in EETAA (ed.), *New Local Government Institutions*, EETAA, Athens, 147–53.

Delladetsima, P.M. (1981) *Urban Disasters Land and State Policy: The Post-War Reconstruction of European Cities (Coventry-Rotterdam-Piraeus)*, MPhil thesis, Univ. College London.

Delladetsima, P.M. (1984) *The Post-War Reconstruction in Europe: State Policy and the Land Development System*, BISS Proceedings, Venice.

Delladetsima, P.M. (1991a) *Forms of State Intervention for the Removal of Property Barriers: The Case of Greece 1944–1952* (in Greek), PhD thesis, NTUA, Athens.

Delladetsima, P.M. (1991b) *New Forms of Land and Property Demand in Greece: Major Retail Centres* (in Greek), NTUA Research Programme, Athens.

Delladetsima, P.M. (1994) Recent developmental trends in Athens: investment changes, state policy and the role of the small landed property, paper presented at the IFRESI/PIRVILLES/CNRS, International Conference, *Cities, Enterprises and Society at the Eve of the XXIst Century*, Lille, March 1994.

DEPOS (Public Agency for Planning and Housing) (1989–1990) *Conditions and Trends in the Housing Market of the Major Urban Centres: Research Programme 1988* (in Greek), Vols I–II, DEPOS, Athens.

Doxiades, C.A. (1950) *To Vima*, series of articles, August.

Doxiades, C.A. (1977) Ekistic policy for the reconstruction of Greece and a twenty year plan, *Ekistics*, **260**.

Emmanuel, D. (1993) in S. Velides, D. Emmanuel, P. Karga, D. Makris and S. Tachos, *Taxation Burden and Financing Cost of Building and Housing in Greece* (in Greek), Parts 1 and 2, TEE, Athens.

ESYE (National Statistical Service of Greece) (1962) *Construction and Development in Urban Areas: 1958 Sample Survey*, Athens.

Karadimou, A. (1985) *The Rebuilding of Thessaloniki Following the 1917 Fire Disaster* (in Greek), Municipality of Thessaloniki Edition, Thessaloniki.

Kotsambopoulos, A. (1991) *Feasibility Study for the Creation of a Real Estate Company* (in Greek), Athens, 14–19.

Leontidou, L. (1981) Master Plans for Greater Athens, 1950–1980: their political functions and social origins (in Greek), *Architecture in Greece*, **14**, 70–8.

Leontidou, L. (1989) *Cities of Silence: Working-Class Colonization of Urban Space in Athens and Piraeus, 1909–1940* (in Greek), Athens, ETVA Foundation and Themelio.

Leontidou, L. (1990) *The Mediterranean City in Transition: Social Change and Urban Development*, Cambridge, Cambridge University Press.

Leontidou, L. (1992) Greece, in C. Pooley (ed.), *Housing Strategies in Europe, 1880–1930*, European Science Foundation and Pinter Publishers, 297–324.

Leontidou, L. (1993) Informal means of unemployment relief in Greek cities: the relevance of family, locality and housing, *European Planning Studies*, **1**(1), 43–68.

Mandikas (1993) It is possible to implement an exceptional 5 year housing programme (in Greek), *Kerdos*, 14 July, 8.

Marmaras, E. (1989) The privately built multi-storey apartment building: the case of inter-war Athens, *Planning Perspectives*, 4, 45–78.

Ministry of Reconstruction (1946a) Ekistic analysis (C.A. Doxiades) (in Greek), *Athens Reconstruction Series*, **1**.

Ministry of Reconstruction (1946b) Building policy for reconstruction (C.A. Doxiades), *Athens Reconstruction Series*, **3**.

Ministry of Reconstruction (1946c) The sacrifices of Greece during World War II (C.A. Doxiades), *Athens Reconstruction Series*, **9**.

Papamichos, N. and Skouras, P. (1981) Land taxation in Greece (in Greek), *TEE Journal*, 1–2.

Polyzos, I. (1984) *The Installation of the 1922 Refugees: An Extreme Urbanization Case* (in Greek), NTUA, Athens.

Roussopoulou, A. (1950) Luxury apartment buildings or public housing? (in Greek), *I Nea Ikonomia*, **9**/45, September.

Roussopoulou, A. (1951) The unauthorized constructions (in Greek), *I Nea Ikonomia*, **10**/58, October.

Saunatsos, I. (1947) Comments, *I Nea Ikonmia*, **9**, July.

Thomadakis, S. (1988) *Stabilization Development and Government Economic Authority: Greece in the 1940s*, revised version of the paper presented at the Vilvorde Conference on the Greek Civil War, Copenhagen 1987, unpublished.

Tsoukalas, C. (1984) The ideological impact of the Civil War, in *Greece in the 1940 and 1950s*, Themelio, Athens.

Varvaressos, K. (1952) *Report on the Economic Problem of Greece* (in Greek), Athens.

Vassiliou, D. (1950) The structure of ministries and public departments (in Greek), *Technica Chronica*, **318**, December.

Velides, S. (1993) in S. Velides, D. Emmanuel, P. Karga, D. Makris and S. Tachos, *Taxation Burden and Financing Cost of Building and Housing in Greece* (in Greek), Parts 1 and 2, TEE, Athens.

Voivoda, A., Kisilou, V., Kloutsinioti, R., Kondaratos, S. and Pirgiotis G. (1977) City and regional planning in Greece (in Greek), *Architecture in Greece*, **11**.

PART FOUR ———

EASTERN EUROPE

15

Budapest

Barry Redding
and Ali R. Ghanbari Parsa

Budapest dominates any discussion of the social and economic systems of Hungary. It is the one major city in the country and with a population of 2.1 million accounts for more than a fifth of the country's total population. The next largest urban settlement has a population of only 200 000. The settlements immediately surrounding the capital within what may be referred to as the metropolitan area continue to attract new migrants and serve only to underscore the influence and significance of Budapest. The historic radial pattern of transport routes, with principal roads and the railways, focusing upon central Budapest, reinforce the nodal position of the capital.

In common with most Central and Eastern European cities, the planning and development processes in Budapest have been undergoing major transformation. Indeed, this is a continuing process. The new economic and political order has touched upon most aspects of life in Hungary, not least the administration and development of urban planning policy.

An evaluation of planning in Budapest and the development of an indigenous property market cannot be divorced from a consideration of the emergence of Hungary from the post-war socialist era. This chapter, therefore, starts by examining recent socio-political developments before considering the evolution of planning policy since 1949 and the legacies of that period for urban development and the environment. Planning and development in Budapest has to be set in the context of this new realignment between districts and the municipal authority, the programme of privatization and a city that is coming to terms with a more open-market economy.

European Cities, Planning Systems and Property Markets Edited by James Berry and Stanley McGreal. Published in 1995 by E & FN Spon. ISBN 0419 18940 8.

15.1   RECENT SOCIO-POLITICAL DEVELOPMENTS

Hungary's reforming process from the 'classical' socialist political economy modelled on the Soviet Union started with the introduction of the 'new economic mechanism' by Janos Kadar in 1968. Though government still prepared plans it ceased to issue centrally produced directives and devolved greater power and decision-making to state enterprises. The following decade proved difficult for Hungary's economy and its deteriorating current account position, debt, and structural problems led the leadership to reappraise priorities (Revesz, 1990).

Another spate of economic reforms were introduced in 1978 designed to attune Hungary's economy more with world markets. Economic indicators showed encouraging signs of improvement: rising GDP, falling domestic consumption, exports increasing and stabilizing imports. However by 1984 circumstances had turned and in the following years GDP stagnated, domestic consumption grew, exports fell, imports increased and national debt rose significantly. Throughout this circular process reforms continued.

The extension of private small businesses was encouraged by government, through, for example, the establishment of enterprise business work partnership (EBWP). Workers were permitted to set up EBWPs frequently using equipment and premises rented from their regular employer. These businesses have often made an essential contribution to the work of state enterprises; furthermore they provide second jobs and a source of extra income for their members. Thus a dual economy was evolving: on the one hand there was the dominant large state and co-operative enterprises subject to strong regulatory controls; on the other, a large sector of small organizations operating in a less regulated market. Indeed as observed by Revesz (1990) the introduction of new types of small businesses has given 500 000 people second jobs, and was the underlying reason behind the growth in real income and personal consumption between 1978 and 1986 despite a drop in real wages. However working and living within such a dual economy, adopting one set of values when working for the state and another set when working for themselves in a second job can lead to people experiencing a form of schizophrenia and an increasing loss of faith in the political direction of the ruling party (Swain, 1992).

This mood, and dissatisfaction with the continued stagnation of the economy, led to substantial changes among the political leadership of the ruling Hungarian Socialist Workers Party (HSWP). The period 1988–90 was one of considerable political change and economic reforms. Indeed the HSWP was replaced by the Hungarian Socialist Party which itself declined in power and influence while several opposition parties grew into well-organized political parties in preparation for the free elections in March 1990. Throughout this period (1987–90) economic reform continued apace. Price controls and quantitative controls were being replaced;

the banking sector became independent (1988), new company laws (1988), personal income tax (1987) and VAT were introduced (1990). By the end of 1988 the principle of property reform (privatization) had been accepted by the governing party. The selling of state-owned flats was politically encouraged from 1988. Also preparations were made for the decentralization of government and the transfer of state assets to the newly elected self-governing local authorities.

The government elected in 1990 is a right-of-centre coalition of the Hungarian Democratic Forum (HDF) and the Alliance of Free Democrats under the prime minister Josef Antall. Throughout their period of government the real value of GDP has been falling, industrial production declining and inflation has been high (1992 year end 20–25%). While in 1993 there are signs of domestic recovery, albeit weak, with unemployment levelling off at 13%, bankruptcies declining and interest rates falling (EIU, 1993), doubts are nevertheless being expressed about the prospects of the current coalition remaining in power after the general election in spring, 1994 (Tamas, 1993). Indeed the results of the 1994 election saw the re-emergence of The Hungarian Socialist Party.

15.2   EVOLUTION OF PLANNING POLICY SINCE 1949

In the immediate post-war years Hungarian traditions of urban planning and design dominated in the preparation by the Commission of Public Works of an urban development plan for the wider metropolitan area of Budapest. The plan was to cover outlying areas beyond the then boundary of the city. Planning was influenced by Western-European theories which were addressing social tensions in spatial terms and encouraging processes of decentralization.

These plans and the processes established to effect them were abandoned with the establishment of a socialist state in 1949. The Commission for Public Works was abolished and the legal and financial means of planning were taken away from local municipalities. Effectively local planning was eliminated and central authority subordinated the processes of planning to its own ideological and economic interests with urban development interpreted as a sector of the national plan (Enyedi and Szirmai, 1992). Such ideological and economic interests emphasized the acceleration of industrial development, particularly in terms of heavy industry. The development of and investment in urban infrastructure in general and in housing and community facilities were subordinated to the overall goal of achieving an autonomous national economy. In particular the centralist state control over the processes of urban planning and development within Budapest was particularly evident in the programmes of housing estate development.

Funds for planning and development became diverted from local communities, and local 'ownership' of and support for policies dissipated. As Enyedi and Szirmai (1992) observed

> urban planning was no longer based even on a limited consensus between the decision makers and the inhabitants: the public conflicts of interest – between entrepreneurs, property owners and tenants – had ceased. Decisions on issues of urban development were made within the internal bargaining processes of state institutions, independent of the inhabitants, socially interested groups or the public.

In the early 1950s the Budapest municipal council was directed to prepare a Master Plan for the metropolitan area to promote the development of a greater Budapest. It was finally approved by government in 1960, at a time when central government 'planners' were embracing 'growth pole' principles of economic and physical development. Promoting the decentralization of development from the capital to the regions supported the theory. Within the Budapest metropolitan sub-region, the plan proposed the development of a ring of eight large villages and small towns. The capital needed cheap labour to support its industrial development programme. Hence the plan sought to identify opportunities to expand housing provision while avoiding the development of 'middle-class' satellite towns, with associated expensive social and physical infrastructure investments, which were becoming a feature of the planning for many Western metropolitan regions.

The struggle for limited resources, however, both between the capital and the regions, and between the capital and the Pest county council surrounding Budapest, became the backcloth for the reconsideration of this decentralization policy. In addition, the councils within the metropolitan area of Budapest, but beyond the formal administrative area of the municipality, were mistrustful of the motives of both the central government and the Budapest council having seen the swallowing up of numerous settlements in the expansion of the Budapest municipal area in 1950 (Elter and Baros, 1993).

During this decade, with practically no new development taking place within the capital, housing conditions began to deteriorate. The policy of decentralization halted in the early 1960s but not before many immigrants settled in these outer areas. Houses often self-built and owner-occupied provided good standards of internal space accommodation but social facilities and utility services were poor. By 1960 government had recognized that there existed a serious housing shortage and a programme was established to build one million new flats by 1975 by a combination of state development and building by individuals for their own occupation. Six hundred thousand flats were to be built, mostly in the capital. The location of this new development was influenced by the need to keep the costs of providing public amenities and transport services as low as possible. New estates were built on the borders of the inner parts of the city, the periphery of the pre-1950 administrative area of Budapest, along existing transport networks and near old industrial zones.

This early development phase did little to address the chronic housing shortages among Budapest's working population. Its location, convenience to city centre services, good standards of accommodation (although in later years the limited floorspace for the flats would attract criticism) encouraged an allocation process distorted by political patronage which was to result in some degree of social segregation. The elderly and other marginalized social groups were left living in the crumbling, high-density pre-war tenement housing of the inner city while the estates built during the first wave of development became the residences of the highly qualified leading and professional layers of the society, and of young families with several children (Enyedi and Szirmai, 1992).

The Budapest Master Plan of 1970 formalized the development criterion which had evolved during the previous decade. There was to be limited territorial expansion of the built area and new development would concentrate along existing transport corridors within which a network of fast transport routes would be established. The construction of 410 000 housing units was envisaged between 1970 and 2000. The objective of this programme of housing development was to be achieved through development of housing estates located in the outer areas of the capital and the redevelopment at higher density of the older, inner housing areas and the encouragement of 'private' family housing in the environs of the city. However the redevelopment of inner areas did not materialize though the development of large state-owned housing estates did occur, particularly in the northern area of the capital.

The large-scale development of housing estates, first at the inner fringe and later in the outer areas of the city provided spectacular and very 'visible' evidence that the ruling socialist ideology was working, i.e. providing a better life and a house for all citizens. It also housed at the lowest cost the labour needed to sustain the rapid industrialization programme that was underway. Thus the allocation of flats provided a significant means of furthering the political and economic interests of the state while the allocation system for the second, outer ring of estates reflected the need to provide access for the 'working class'; 70% of these flats were to be occupied by manual workers.

These estates were designed and built, with quantity the criterion rather than quality. Rapid construction techniques, incorporating pre-fabrication processes from the Soviet Union, and a lack of attention regarding maintenance of the properties, have left a legacy of structural problems and disrepair for the new local governments. Many of these estates were poorly provided with community facilities and shopping, and with difficult access to inner-city public and community services, the estates have developed an increasing sense of isolation among their residents with associated social problems.

The 1970 Plan proposed the establishment of a hierarchy of sub-centres to provide local and neighbourhood functions; in essence an expression of the concepts of central place theory. This was to be achieved by reinforcing the significance of traditional district centres and developing six new sub-centres in the new housing areas, thereby utilizing existing infrastructure and transport links. A recurring theme of lack of resources to implement the policies and proposals within the plan diminished the impact of the suburban centres. Furthermore the poor quality or total absence of infrastructure in many outer areas precluded significant development in advance of investment by the state to raise the quality of utility services, telecommunications and the transport network.

The 1980 Master Plan continued to be underpinned by the concept of the state housing programme, largely to be achieved through the development of a belt of housing estates encircling the capital. The thrust for new development in the 1980s was to be northwards along the Danube and in southern areas of the capital. Building rates were planned to slow down after 1990 with a switch of resources being made towards redevelopment of inner area properties. Thus while the number of flats constructed in Hungary fell throughout the 1980s Budapest continued to attract the greatest share of resources to deploy towards the development of flats.

Throughout the 1970s and 1980s, the 'green spaces' within the city were swallowed up by the wave of new state housing. However in the 1980s increasing political freedoms were reflected in the housing market, indeed some state developments in inner areas near the Danube comprised large flats destined for sale. Higher income groups, managerial, professional and white-collar employees sought the more attractive and less polluted environment of the Buda side of the Danube, contributing to the continued erosion of the woodlands which cover the hills. While the provision of 'public' housing was subordinated to the interests of state housing, it is clear that without a private housing market the state's flat construction programme would have been a marked failure (Enyedi and Szirmai, 1992).

The 1988 Master Plan outlined the development concept of Budapest for the following 15 years and sought to establish the network for the principal infrastructure for a 30-year period. It restated earlier policies for a decentralized spatial and functional structure with an increased role for suburban centres. Rehabilitation of inner-city housing was to be given emphasis and environmental issues were becoming more significant considerations. However, the plan for the City continued to reflect the former politically centralized public-sector philosophy. Based on general zoning principles, the plan has rapidly become out of date in the changing political climate occurring since 1990 and the enthusiastic push towards a more open market economy.

In particular the 1988 Plan did not reflect the implications of the decentralization of planning functions to district local authorities within the capital provided for in the Local Government Act of 1990. Also it did not recognize that 'local plans' might be prepared by districts (notwithstanding the ambiguity within the legislation). Nor did it consider the proposals for the Expo 1996; though five years on, progress on the Expo scheme appears minimal so in hindsight, this omission may not have been significant.

The response of the Municipal council has been to embark on the formulation of a Master Plan for the city (due to be completed in 1993). The plan places the future planning and development of the city within its regional setting, pointing specifically to its relationships with surrounding settlements. It defines the principal land-use zoning categories, the strategic road and infrastructure developments, and important environmental and heritage issues and policies. It attempts to address strategic issues confronting the city, focusing upon those matters which require agreement among two or more district councils. In doing so, there is an expectation that the local autonomy of individual districts will be more clearly delineated in respect of those matters which will affect only individual districts.

In the interim before completion of the new plan for Budapest the municipal planners published a policy statement which outlines their priority medium-term development objectives (Schneller, 1992). It identifies the most important development projects to which the limited resources available to them should be directed. These projects, while separate, are presented as part of interdependent area developments. Together they seek two principal objectives, namely, to relieve the pressure on the present city central area, and to open up the shores of the Danube to the city. The priority area development projects identified in the statement include the following:

1. The completion of the Hungaria Ring Road (the grand boulevard) and the construction of a new bridge (the Lagymanyos Bridge) over the Danube. The road and bridge are intended to syphon off through traffic from the inner road network and provide a distributing function to the radial main roads and motorways. It is also intended to open up Southern Pest and revitalize valuable yet under-utilized territories in the area of the ring road (Schneller, 1992).

2. The rehabilitation of the South Buda Danube shore embraces proposals for the extension of the existing university campus, the rehabilitation and development of existing industrial areas, the reclamation of part of Lagymanyos Bay and the development of a water sports and recreation

centre. These improvements would be supported by transport works including the new bridge, the completion of the new Route 6 main road, connections to the Motorway network (M1, M7 and M0) and the construction of the first stage of the new Metro line.

3. The rehabilitation of the South Pest Danube shore which embraces the reconstruction of the Market Hall (nearing completion at the end of 1993) and the redevelopment of the railyard along the banks of the river.

4. It is hoped that the completion of the Hungaria ring road will reduce the volume of through traffic using the Kiskorut (the small boulevard). Once this is achieved it is intended to develop the corridor along this inner ring road and thereby enhance the priority given to and the environmental quality enjoyed by the pedestrians.

Two significant development proposals are not detailed in the document, namely the 1996 World Expo and the construction of the new Metro-line. If they were implemented both would have considerable impact upon the development of the city 'pulling' the city centre in a southern direction. Their absence is a significant omission in the policy statement as it ought to have contained an assessment of the sensitivity of the proposed area projects to whether or not either or both the Expo and the new Metro-line were implemented.

Expo is planned for the South Buda site designated for the extension of the university campus; however, there is considerable scepticism surrounding the ability of Expo to be ready in time. Physical works for it have hardly commenced (summer 1993) and no other previous Expo has carried out the amount of building works needed in the number of months remaining. The redevelopment of the railway yard along the South Pest Danube shoreline was targeted as a source of much needed finance for the Expo development. Earlier in 1993 tenders were invited for the purchase of 15 plots delineated within the railway yard. A total of 14 responses were received, none of which met the basic conditions which included provision of financial guarantees. It is understood that subsequent negotiations may see three of the plots sold (one for a petrol filling station), but this lack of interest from the private investment and development sector exposes a major weakness in the economic basis of the Expo development. It looks increasingly likely that the government will need to underwrite costs by further calls upon taxation, or reduce the scale of the exhibition still further or cancel it entirely.

15.3   ENVIRONMENTAL CONDITIONS

Many of the environmental difficulties faced by Budapest are typically associated with the modern urban developments experienced by West

European and American cities. In Western cities, however, democratic institutions, consumer movements and financial resources are available to ensure that the environmental conflicts could be mitigated. However in Hungary the socialist economy could not afford to allocate resources for such purposes. Indeed such considerations were contrary to the prevailing political and ideological values which emphasized the development of energy-consuming heavy industry throughout the 1950s and 1960s. The 1970s saw the introduction of environmental legislation; the most notable being the Protection of the Human Environment Act 1976. A set of national regulations to effect implementation of the Act were approved by the Council of Ministers in 1980. This set off a process of elaboration of the regulations at ministerial level and then downwards through the hierarchy of councils. The City Council for Budapest approved in 1982 its concept for environmental protection to the year 2000. However as discussed by Enyedi and Szirmai (1992) no significant changes have taken place despite new legislation and indeed environmental hazards have increased over the past decade. Part of the reason for the lack of action resides with the local councils, which in theory were empowered to enforce the law, but at the same time are partly dependent for their finances on the polluting industrial plants.

The establishment of democratic institutions at local government and the greater freedom to organize 'interest' movements to advocate ecological and environmental agendas will bring such criteria to the decision-making process. The Danube Circle, the first non-government environmental group in Hungary, successfully generated opposition to the proposed Nagymaros Dam development scheme with Slovakia. Furthermore there are indications that a more positive relationship is developing between the Ministry of Environment and Regional Policy and environmental advisory groups. New regulations have been introduced (hazardous wastes) and new environmental legislation is under discussion (Fisher, 1992). The emergence of a stronger middle-class within the capital which is responsive to the values of an environmentally aware lifestyle will add weight to the evolution of a broad consensus on the environment. Nevertheless key questions remain. The public budget is limited and difficult compromises will have to be faced by local governments. The difficulties surrounding local government finance emphasized by Enyedi and Szirmai (1992) are exacerbated in the post-socialist period by the effects of central government policies to redress the country's economic problems. The ability and willingness of the population to pay for environmental improvements is an unknown factor as recent polls suggest that most Hungarians believe economic improvement takes priority over environmental problems (Picard, 1993).

Budapest experiences some of the highest levels of pollution to be found in European cities affecting its air, land and water. Air pollution is of particular concern with concentrations of sulphur dioxide, nitrogen dioxide and carbon monoxide caused by outdated industrial plant and heating systems, and vehicles. Concentrations of air, and indeed noise pollution in the inner-city area and the older industrial zones are exacerbated by the radial patterns of the road and rail network which funnels local, regional and international traffic into central Budapest. The explosion of the ownership and use of private vehicles appears to represent another expression of the new political freedoms. For example in 1970, only 70 000 cars were privately owned, however by 1990 this figure had reached 500 000 (Enyedi and Szirmai, 1992). Moreover, the Working Air Action Group of Budapest predicts that cars in the capital will number approximately two million by the year 2000 (Picard, 1993).

Until the early 1980s the collection and treatment of industrial and hazardous waste was largely ignored. Materials were frequently burnt or illegally dumped with consequences for the pollution of the atmosphere and water courses. A government scheme in the 1980s for the development of a national network of waste disposal achieved little. Restrictions on government spending inevitably had an effect but so did the protests of local communities and the conflicting interests of the county councils. Also central government was finding it less easy to impose 'solutions' on local government during this period of political change.

The least developed part of the capital's public utility infrastructure is the water supply, sewerage collection and treatment. In many parts of the outer districts, other than in the state developed housing estates, the utility services are lacking; in inner areas they need upgrading to cope with the demands made by the modern city. Furthermore water quality of the Danube is poor before it reaches Budapest and becomes worse as it passes through. The replacement or improvement of elements of the sewer and the water supply trunk network is proposed as part of the planned road building or widening set out in a planning policy statement issued by the Municipal Authority in 1992 (Schneller et al., 1992). However the difficulties in obtaining agreement among the district authorities on the location of a new sewage treatment plant should not be underestimated (case study 1). Also the quality of existing utility services available to a prospective development site will always be an important consideration. In the majority of development situations the 'developer' should expect to contribute to the cost of necessary improvements to utility services to and on the development site, though in the contract to sell a development site the local government of District 22 agreed to use half of the proceeds of the sale for the provision of utility services to the site (case study 2).

15.4   NATIONAL AND LOCAL FRAMEWORK FOR PLANNING

Following the establishment of the socialist state in 1949 the first act of 1950 provided for the setting up of local councils for each community. The council for Budapest was given special administrative status as befitting its position as the capital city. The primacy of state control over local government broke with the tradition of Hungarian public administration. Each council comprised a large number of members organized in a range of professional committees though the importance of the bureaucratic-political dimension was stronger than the representative function. The influence of national ministries, technical institutes approved by government, and the communist party via party committees established at each level of government provided the bureaucratic and political direction, thereby subordinating the independence of the 'elected' council.

The administrative system was adapted in 1954 and again in 1971 to provide greater hierarchical subordination of community councils to county councils rather than a direct relationship to central government. Financial dependence on central government remained, perpetuating a strong control on the general steer of policies and on the local budget and economic management.

From 1971 changes took place in the representation of the electorate with the introduction of the possibility of multiple candidacy. It was not until the local elections of 1985 that this was to become obligatory thereby providing electors with some choice. However local councils conformed to a vertical structure and at each level of the system a council was directed by the level directly above it. In Budapest 22 local councils nestled beneath a central municipal council for the city as a whole which could control and override decisions made by the smaller local councils. Thus the important decisions were made centrally and, as Horvath (1991a) discusses, financial resources were re-distributed by autocratic decisions.

The necessary legal conditions required to establish a reformed local government system were provided by a series of legislative measures between May 1989 and May 1990. The principles on which the new system of local self-government was established include: the separation of the local government and the state bureaucracy; multi-party elections; decentralization to and independence of local government; local governments of equal status; and relationships between local authorities based on free negotiation and co-ordination.

At central government level the Ministry of Interior is responsible for public administration and is actively supporting the decentralization of processes to regional and local levels and countering the efforts of sectoral ministries to retain power. The Ministry of Environment and Regional Policy has responsibility for urban planning, the environment and regional planning. However at present the scope of the Ministry's responsibility is under discussion and it is probable that new legislation defining its future role will be considered by Parliament by the end of 1993. This is likely to have a supervisory and consultative emphasis with further legislation expected on urban planning and on the environment (Takas, 1991).

In Budapest the 22 districts are considered to be local self-governments while the Municipal or City council is regarded as a 'special local self-government'. The district authorities have a number of obligatory functions which include elementary education, basic social and health services, water supply and the maintenance of streets and cemeteries. Public rented housing has been transferred to them from the state, together with the responsibility to develop policy appropriate to the locality concerning rents, privatization (market value discounts), and maintenance programmes. Districts have become the 'local planning authority'. The Municipal authority has additional responsibilities appropriate to its position as a form of county authority, particularly in respect of the Master Plan, utility services, and transportation. The relationship depends upon co-ordination between the Municipal council for Budapest and the 22 districts as there are no subordinate positions. However, given the number of district councils involved and the decentralization of power and authority, co-ordination by the Municipality of strategic planning for the city as a whole is particularly difficult.

A 'representative body' is at the centre of power within the local government. In the Budapest municipality it comprises 88 members, 66 of whom are elected by the population of the city from the lists of 'candidates' drawn up by the political parties, and 22 members are delegated by the districts within the city. However the internal relationship between the local 'power bases' within the municipality is taking time to stabilize.

15.4.1   Development plans and control

The land-use planning system introduced in the mid-1980s during the period of social and economic reform needed to adapt to the changes in the local government administrative system. The plans have consisted of the general zoning plan (the *Altalanos Rendezesi Terv*, ART) and the detailed plan (the *Reszletes Rendezesi Terv*, RRT). The ART delineates zones in which specified land uses are permitted. Land-use classification is provided for in a national code (1986 Act) which distinguishes nine principal classes and within the residential class there are sub-classifications, each of which may be subject to more specific regulations.

Since 1990 (Ministry of Environment Protection and Construction, Decree 1) a range of uses has been permitted within residential zones. These are generally those uses which provide essential services for the local community. Some evidence suggests that local councils may have been exerting inadequate control over the establishment of non-residential uses within residential areas and thus the prospect of 'bad neighbour' types of use being introduced to the detriment of the local environment (Baar, 1992). In contrast there have been little if any guidelines concerning the uses within non-residential zones. This is not surprising; indeed the lack of specific regulation of non-residential uses is consistent with the fact that in 1989 non-residential construction was almost solely a state activity with little regulatory control (Baar, 1992).

The detailed RRT plan is concerned with control over the site planning of individual plots. It requires that the owner or developer conforms to the specified buildings on the plot. This type of plan epitomizes the approach towards town planning through development control by regulation and is in marked contrast to the administrative negotiation style of local planning which has been a feature of post-war Britain. Detailed site plans (RRT) were a product of the centrally planned approach in that they were formulated by the relevant public agency, often by an architect appointed for the purpose, because the state was both the 'planning agency' and the investor/developer. On the basis of the detailed plan a builder was sought to implement the scheme. Decisions concerning RRTs were made by the appropriate building official.

In the evolving market economy the continued relevance of these publicly prepared detailed plans is being questioned. Since 1991 decisions on these have been transferred from officials to the councils, thereby setting them within the local democratic process. The state is withdrawing from the investor/developer role in urban development, and construction projects are increasingly dependent upon the decisions of developers to bring forward proposals for specific sites. In such circumstances the impetus for preparing detailed plot plans might sensibly rest with the developer rather than the public authority. Notwithstanding this debate, some district councils have continued to appoint an independent architect to provide specific site plans (RRT) without consulting potential investors with an interest in the sites or their architects.

The Municipal Council for Budapest has the power to adopt and amend the general zoning plan (ART) for the city while the district councils have the power to prepare and adopt the more plot specific plans (RRT). Beyond this statement there appears to be an ambiguous relationship between municipal and district councils in respect of preparation and adoption of 'development plans'. There is further uncertainty as to the scope and relative detail of provisions which each type of plan may contain, as districts vie with the municipal authority for effective power over policy development and authority over the control of new development. The legislation (1991, Law No. 22) is unclear on which types of plan must be approved by the municipal council as well as the districts. It is possible for the municipal council to seek to frustrate the power of the district by refusing to record zoning changes adopted by the districts (Baar, 1992).

The preparation of the city-wide plan is largely an act of faith. The municipal council cannot exercise any strategic authority to ensure that the policies within the plan are heeded or proposals implemented. Implementation depends upon the views and decisions of each district council, with the municipal council pursuing an influencing and a co-ordinating function.

15.4.2 Planning and building control

The procedures for obtaining building permits are set down in a national government decree of 1986 (Ministry of Construction and Settlement Development 1986, Decree No. 12). Prior to making an application a builder or developer is required to obtain technical permits from the appropriate utility and infrastructure authorities. The nature of such permits and the detailed information required to secure them means that the proposed scheme will have to be prepared to a more detailed technical design and specification, at an earlier stage, than would normally be the case in Britain. Notwithstanding the published guidance (1986, Decree No. 12), it is advisable to consult the chief architect of the relevant council on the technical permits required to support the application for a building permit for the particular development.

In Budapest applications for building permits are made to the district council. Decisions on applications must be made within 30 days of their submission. Decisions may be delegated from the assembly of the district council to 'planning' committees and from the relevant committee to the chief architect and building officers. There does not appear to be any guidance on the extent and implementation of such delegation and considerable variation can be expected among district councils in Budapest. Since 1990 the district council may appoint an architectural review committee (if they have the resources to so do) to consider applications for building permits and advise officers on their merits. An alternative, attractive to many councils having to wrestle with local budget deficits, is to engage an 'expert' (usually an architect) to critique major projects.

In the event of the application for a building permit being refused or no decision being made within the 30-day period, an appeal may be made within 15 days after the (non) decision to the Commissioner of the Republic. The Commissioner is expected to rule on the appeal within 30 days. An appeal to court may be made within 30 days after the decision by the Commissioner. Typically such appeals are heard within four to five months though the scope of such appeals is limited to technical code issues (Baar, 1992). It is interesting to note that the owner of the relevant plot and owners of adjacent plots may appeal against decisions of the district council. Furthermore, such appeal may be against the grant or the refusal of a permit.

In determining the application for a building permit the district council are required (by Ministry of Environment and Construction 1990, Decree No. 1) to ensure that there is adequate provision of water supply, drainage (sewage and rain water) and electricity; hence the technical permits which have to accompany the application (case study 3). The national code also requires that new building meets general environmental standards, where appropriate historic monuments are preserved, and public views safeguarded.

Proposals are assessed for conformity with the general zoning plan (ART) and with the detailed building plan (RRT). The latter may well embody elements of a national building code. However, there exists the potential for conflicting requirements within the zoning and building plans on detailed matters of site planning. While it appears that for many proposals the application for a building permit will be determined within the 30-day period, research by Baar (1992) has indicated that it is common 'in cases involving medium sized or large projects, building officials will require an RRT or a revision of the existing RRT even if the proposal is consistent with the current RRT in order to avoid exposure to criticism for approving a project'.

15.4.3 Case studies

1. Sewerage works proposals for Csebel Island: conflict between the Municipal and District Councils

Csebel Island comprises the northern tip of District 21, bounded on three sides by the River Danube, and on the fourth side by redundant docks. The area is largely in agricultural use. The Master Plan proposes that Csebel Island is the best place to construct a new sewerage treatment plant for the City. However the Council of District 21 disagree and view this tract of land, which is the closest point of District 21 to the centre of Budapest and in close proximity to the proposed Expo 96 site, as having greater commercial value. The realism of such a view is clearly questionable given the location of the site and the general nature of the property market in Budapest. Consequently the District has suggested an alternative location for the sewage treatment on redundant industrial land further south; but this would cost an additional HFt 10 bn. Under present administrative arrangements the municipal council could obtain a court approval to acquire compulsorily the land needed for the plant, but the District could still frustrate the proposal by refusing to grant the necessary building permits.

The proposal has stirred emotions within the District such that the council is considering a referendum to leave the Budapest group of councils. However such a change in the status of a district may not take place within the 12 months immediately prior to a Parliamentary election and as this was due in 1994, a period of inaction resulted. The Commissioner of the Republic whose function is to 'supervise the operation and practice of the local government' (Horvath, 1991b) is very much 'the main of the central government' and as such has not been viewed by either the Municipality or the District as an appropriate mediator. Also difference in the political control of Parliament and local government further increased the reluctance of the local authorities to invite the Commissioner to be involved.

2. Shopping Centre Development in District 22: entrepreneurial activity of local authority

District 22, in the south-western edge of the Budapest Municipal area, is a largely residential suburban area with a population of 50 000. The majority of dwellings are small family homes but there are three comparatively small multi-storey housing estates built by the state in the 1960s. District 22 is typical of districts outside of inner Budapest in that the provision of utility services is limited due to lack of investment prior to 1990. Drainage and sewage are of particular concern in District 22; there is a limited network of piped water and electricity.

In drafting its budget for 1993, District 22 identified that planned expenditure of HFt2500 m exceeded expected income by HFt500 m. Cursory review of their assets in the form of vacant land revealed that much of this would be unattractive to the private market as it lacked essential utility services and other infrastructure. Thus the District was in a 'catch 22 position', namely the need to exploit vacant and under-used property assets in order to fund the annual budget deficit and invest in improvements to the District's infrastructure; but, in order to do so, the infrastructure improvements had to be provided.

One prime site was perceived as a key to initiating development improvements for the district. Located in the south of the district, the 18 ha plot of land between the upgraded E73 road and the railway is largely empty, also the intersection with the motorway M0 is nearby which provides access to the M7 and M1 motorways. The Zoning Plan (1989) reserved the area for public services and entertainment facilities, for example swimming pools, and 'forest' uses. In essence the character of the area was intended to be low-density land use.

In 1991 the district promoted its outline ideas for the commercial development of this tract of land. Among the foreign investors to approach the district was a consortium of German banks, led by the Hippo Bank, with proposals for a mixed development comprising a shopping centre, hotel and offices. After more than 18 months of negotiation, agreement was reached whereby the Consortium are to pay to the District Council HFt1500 m for the land. However, commencement of the development is dependent on the District providing utility services (including electricity, water and sewage) to the site. The contract, signed in June 1993, requires the Council to spend half of the receipts of the sale (HFt750 m) on the provision of this infrastructure.

3.   BKD Building: obtaining a building permit

The BKD Bank is a joint venture development between Hungarian, German and French banks. The development proposal is to provide a new headquarters building situated along Honved utca in District V, requiring the refurbishment and part demolition of an existing building with the addition of a new wing. The building and land had been purchased from a timber trading company; a transaction facilitated by the State Property Agency.

Building permits were required for both the refurbishment and new build elements of the project. Approximately 20 technical or infrastructural consultations or permits were required to accompany the applications. They covered such matters as fire protection; proposals in respect to mechanical engineering, electrical, catering service, garbage disposal elements; demolition approval; specialist consultations on structural calculations, soil mechanics, geotechnical survey and service elements etc. In addition car parking was a major consideration. Presently this is an important issue in Budapest and the current car parking requirement of one space per sq m is being reviewed so as to provide fewer parking spaces with the expectation that this might apply a restraint on car use within the city. Meanwhile, the application of current ratios continues. In tight sites, and most in central Budapest are, the total number of spaces cannot be provided on site, and financial contributions are expected to be made (currently at HFt 1 m per space) to the District Council so as to fund a car-park facility to be built some time in the future. This liability, inflation-linked, is a charge on the land and will be called in by the district council when the car parking is built. The car-parking permit for the BKD development required a total of 105 spaces of which only 30 could be provided on site without incurring expensive underground provision.

The design team engaged a Hungarian architect to advise on technical permits, assist in preliminary discussions with the Chief Architect of the District Council and to collect the required permits. Each regulatory body was visited in person to obtain the necessary opinions or permits. This took two months but was considered to be a far more effective approach than relying on postal applications. Furthermore, use of an experienced Hungarian Architect is important and pays dividends, but will not totally prevent the application being referred back by the District Council for additional approvals.

The granting of this building permit took six months. The design team decided against appealing because of the additional uncertainty that course of action would involve. Indeed the experience of overseas companies seeking a permit is that the process is more problematic than for Hungarian firms. Also it is important to maintain regular and frequent contact with the Chief Architect's Office to ensure that the application is not 'sidelined'.

The design team made two presentations of their proposals, the first of which took place prior to the application being submitted to a City Architectural Jury organized by the Ministry of the Environment. This consisted of about 30 architects, town planners and heritage specialists. The Jury considered the impact of the proposals on the local environment, given that the site is located within a 'preservation area'. It may, in practice, consider any project which is of such size or character as to make a significant impact on the city environment; however this body only performs a purely advisory function. The second presentation of the scheme was to local residents at a public meeting at which the principal fear voiced concerned possible damage to properties during construction. In the event, the building permit was granted subject to several conditions safeguarding the interests of neighbouring residents.

15.5 MUNICIPALITIES AND THE MARKET

The ability of local government to enjoy the increased local autonomy and to be effective in policy-making depends greatly upon the economic resources at their command. In 1991 the largest part of local revenue was accounted for by government grants which altogether stood at approximately 68% (Min. of Finance cited in Peteri, 1991). Personal income tax is essentially a centrally determined tax: to date it has been normal for one-half of tax revenue to be remitted back to local councils but in 1993 this has been reduced to 30% reflecting the tighter national budget. This shared element constituted approximately 13% of local revenue in 1991. Local councils have increasingly become freer of central government directives on how it may be used. The remaining source of fiscal revenue is local taxation. While the proportion of local revenue which this represents is low, 17% in 1991, it can be an important component in local policy-making, particularly in respect of 'income redistribution'. Most councils are having to make priority judgements among services deciding which to maintain and which to cut. The 'objects' of local taxation (property, community and business) and the maximum rates of tax are specified by central government; an 'object' can be rated by only one local tax at a time. The principal bases for local taxation are businesses and tourism.

The majority of the government grant is distributed by objective criteria (e.g. on a per capita basis); the remainder is subject to competition between councils for specific projects or programmes. Government grants to local councils have been decreasing each year since 1987 as part of government policy of fiscal austerity to address the national economic problems. This period has also seen a combination of high and consistent inflation and significant decreases in the proportion of local council budgets being devoted to capital expenditure; the latter being less than 20% in 1990 (even lower in Budapest). Councils are thus finding themselves in a paradoxical position of having greater freedom to formulate and decide policy but in circumstances of greatly reduced resources. Hence most councils are having to make priority judgements among services, deciding which to maintain and which to cut.

In the context of decreasing budget contribution from the central government local councils may consider levying local taxes. However, in District 22, the authors were advised that the council was reluctant either to raise the local income tax further as households were too poor, or increase the local business tax. The latter was viewed as a realistic option only in the more central districts where businesses might be able to absorb increased local tax on top of the current VAT, at 25%. Also local 'politicians are reluctant to increase tax rates since most wish to avoid conflicts with their electors' (Horvath, 1991b). Such sensitivity is particularly significant in this first period of office of new local governments. The impact of grasping this nettle is unlikely to make a dramatic contribution to balancing the local budget as local taxes are, and are likely to continue to be, a small proportion of total local revenue. Councils will need to look at how best to exploit their property assets if they are to improve their economic and fiscal base.

Since the Local Government Act 1990 and the local elections of that year the opportunity for entrepreneurial activity has become an important urban policy consideration. The following assets were transferred to the local government by the 1990 Act: state land within the settlement (excluding land owned by state companies); public works including the water and sewage system, roads and public parks; public institutions such as schools and hospitals; public enterprises (for example stores, small shops, garages); and state (social) flats and public buildings.

Councils, however, need to develop a strategy for gaining maximum budgetary benefit from their newly transferred property assets. One option is to choose to adopt a more 'market-oriented' approach towards the management or leasing of properties, thereby generating an income flow and a contribution to the Council's revenue account; or alternatively to realize capital by selling-off parcels of property to the private sector. Only half of the receipts realized from the privatization (disposal) of companies (public enterprises) established before 1990 can be retained by the local councils. The remainder is remitted to central government as a contribution to reducing the national budget deficit and the huge foreign debt (Peteri, 1991).

The diversity of approaches in policy-making and the relationship between the local councils and the market can be illustrated by considering the evolving housing policy among districts in Budapest. Thus Horvath (1991a) points to the fact that the varying policy surrounding house sales in differing districts of Budapest is independent of political affinity. Furthermore Hegedus et al. (1993) consider that careful privatization close to market price, together with housing allowances, rent increase and institutional changes in housing management, can constitute a new model for the rental sector and one that does not cause further financial loss for the local government. However, such a policy involves the cross-subsidization of the retained poorer stock of rented units with revenues, rental income or cash receipts, from the better stock. Also it presupposes that districts are capable of developing, financing and administrating the housing allowance system and assumes that there will be sufficient better stock to 'fund' the programme. One potential problem lies in the fact that districts may be too small to act alone and, given the present autonomy between districts, the policy may merely exacerbate existing social and economic differences between them.

15.6 PROPERTY LAW AND PRIVATIZATION

The right to own private property in Hungary was never totally removed by the state. The majority of privately owned housing was excluded from the nationalization programme of the 1950s and throughout the following years this stock was added to by individuals building their own homes. The result is that the proportion of private ownership of residential property is comparable to that of most cities across Europe (DTZ, 1991).

The move towards a market economy has been facilitated by the programme of privatization of state-owned enterprises and the establishment of a more liberalized regime to encourage foreign investment and ownership of land. The basic principles of real property law, however, remain unchanged; the law in Hungary relies upon a codified system rather than case law precedent. The basis of the real property law is the principles prevalent in the Austrian/German civil code; however, many of these basic principles were repealed or amended during the period of socialist control (Aisbett, 1991).

Land generally may be owned by private individuals or companies, as well as state companies and co-operatives. A foreign person may acquire land through a Hungarian subsidiary company, which itself may be up to 100% foreign owned, for the purpose of its business. This requirement may preclude the prospect of more speculative land acquisitions by foreign developers. The three main forms of title to property are *Tulajdon*

Jog – full ownership right; *Kezelo Jog* – handling rights; and *Berleti Jog* – rented right.

The transfer of rights over land is guided by the principles within the civil code dealing with the formation of contracts for sale. The concept of a lease is distinct from English law as it does not take effect as an interest in land but is rather a contract of tenancy giving a right to occupy or use the premises upon agreed terms and conditions. Leases, therefore, may not always be registered in the Land Registry. Given that this civil code largely dates from the socialist period it may prove inappropriate for commercial lettings in the developing property market. Hence a variety of styles of lease are being introduced as foreign traders and investors use the forms of lease common in their home market (Aisbett, 1991).

Transfers of freehold interests in former state-owned properties in Budapest to local authorities of the capital will also lead to changes in the market. The adoption of an entrepreneurial approach by local authorities (case study 2) will see them seeking higher rent, nearer the market level, from the user of the property. This will in time reduce the traditional profit rent element of the *Berleti Jog* which had been previously enjoyed on account of the artificially low rents paid by users to the IKV (the local property handling enterprise).

Real property is subject to a system of land registration. All titles must be registered with the Land Registry maintained by local authorities. There are three parts to the register, namely: the description of the property, permitted lease, etc.; the register of title showing previous transfers, current and past owners, actual title held; and, a schedule of charges, mortgages and other registerable matters affecting title (Healey & Baker/ RICS, 1991).

The privatization programme is a central plank of government policy in the transformation of the national economy. In 1990 the State Property Agency (SPA) was established to guide and oversee the privatization of state-owned companies. The initial role of the SPA was primarily reactive, its task being to approve privatization proposals coming from enterprises wishing to be privatized. In doing so the Agency had a duty to ensure that the maximum benefit accrued to the state from the privatization.

In addition to these so called 'spontaneous' privatizations it is possible for investors (Hungarian or overseas) to make a bid for a state company in whole, or in part. Approval by the SPA follows a similar process to that for companies which had been offered for sale by the Agency, but the onus placed upon the bidder to obtain and verify information about the business and its assets is greater. Furthermore the SPA has rapidly moved towards a more active privatization programme, the aims of which are to provide the government with a more active role in the process of privatization, improve competition in economic markets, expand the capital and stock markets, create proceeds for government, encourage small investors in Hungary and facilitate the growth, profitability and efficiency of the privatized companies (Denyer and Eaton, 1991).

The privatization programme has been organized in a series of rounds, each comprising a group of companies, not necessarily related, to be sold. For each company to be sold, a legal and financial adviser is appointed (selected by tender) to provide guidance on restructuring the organization of the company and its management, and ensuring the most efficient means of privatization so as to achieve not only the best value for the state company, but also to secure its long-term business viability. Before the enterprise is offered for sale it goes through a transformation process. This is the formal change in the status and corporate identity of the enterprise to a public limited company from one directly linked to the state. This process is managed by the SPA and the transformed status is registered with the courts; the company is also valued at the same time. If transformation is not completed within six months of the valuation a new valuation is required. A common feature of early privatization is that initial valuations have been too high and ultimately most enterprises were sold for a figure lower than the initial valuation.

Valuation, as an exercise, poses a number of challenges for the SPA. For the past 40 years there has been no need for valuations particularly in the industrial and commercial sectors. Ideologically land belonged to the community and was therefore not tradable. It has therefore been held at zero value in the accounts of companies. There is a widely held perception among Hungarian 'owners' that market price is established by the vendor and influenced by the notion of depreciated replacement cost. Notions of 'value' and concepts of 'risk' and 'return', particularly in respect of real estate transactions, are part of the new business vocabulary to which Hungarians are having to adjust.

The SPA has its own valuation team but also engages the independent valuation services of professional consulting firms, Hungarian and overseas. Three methods of valuation are commonly used: asset valuation, business valuation, and liquidation valuation. Most Hungarian 'valuers' have an empathy for the assets approach as it stems from a history of strong accountancy practice. Information is derived from the company books and other records. The approach gives rise to a number of problems; namely, land and buildings are held at zero rent in the books; capital assets (buildings, plant and machinery) are recorded at historic cost which are unrealistic in the context of recent levels of inflation. In addition former state companies often held unrealistically large stocks of materials and semi-processed goods which were not reflected in the book valuation; also most companies are operating at levels well below full capacity of the assets employed.

Viewing a former state company as a 'business' is a comparatively new valuation phenomenon. Discounted cash flow approaches are beginning to be employed. The determination of appropriate discount rates to be used is problematic due to the uncertainties of the privatization process itself and the continuing high level of inflation. Furthermore projecting the income generation of the business beyond a few months ahead appears to be difficult as business plans if prepared frequently are statements of hope rather than well researched planning documents. In addition for many state enterprises future business prospects are poor and the SPA have to consider valuation for liquidation purposes. In this context prospective purchasers of companies have been assessing 'breakup value' as part of possible down-sizing or relocation strategies.

Individuals who consider that they can establish their ownership of assets, real property or business, prior to the communist period may seek compensation for their loss. However an application for compensation was required to be filed before the end of 1993; by June 1993 400 000 applications had been received and compensation granted with up to another million applications expected before the end of 1993. However no restitution of the actual asset is available; nor will the compensation comprise money. Instead compensation is by way of 'voucher' or 'warrants' to a maximum value in any single case of HFt5 million. The vouchers enable their holders to participate in the property market and in the privatization process. The vouchers can be used to purchase land or state-owned flats, or acquiring assets such as machinery and buildings belonging to state companies being privatized. They can also be used to invest in the shares of state-owned companies being privatized.

Besides addressing the issue of compensation for past injustices, the voucher system was thought to be a good means of achieving a policy of providing a wider base of share ownership among the population and increasing private property ownership. Moreover, it would go some way to avoid the accusation being levelled at the government that they were 'selling the country's assets abroad'. The reality is less encouraging, indeed many who receive vouchers are generally uncertain of how to use them; several are elderly, suspicious of the new institutions established, and need money for daily living rather than 'investments'. By June 1993 vouchers to a face value of HFt50 billion had been granted, of these about HFt 5 billion had been returned to the state in exchange for assets. They are also tradable and vouchers to a face value of HFt 30 billion are on the Budapest Stock Exchange.

The government are promoting the use of vouchers as an investment through educational and advertising campaigns. The vouchers can be used in employee share ownership schemes. All Hungarians over 18 years of age are eligible to access credit up to HFt100,000 to purchase vouchers which can be used to 'buy' shares in privatized companies. However, there remains considerable uncertainty in the operation of the voucher system. Originally it was expected that all the vouchers would be returned to the state within three years. Clearly this is optimistic and the scheme is destined to be in operation for an additional three years at least. While vouchers remain in circulation the SPA will be obliged to retain a pool of assets against which the vouchers may be redeemed.

15.7   THE PROPERTY MARKET

There has yet to be established a mature commercial property market in Hungary. The absence of a stable and widespread leasing market for office and industrial premises gives rise to a poor property investment market and with the exception of premium office space (and residential accommodation) there is propensity towards property being offered for sale rather than for lease. This orientation is encouraged by businesses reacting to a short-term requirement for cash to remain liquid; thereby disposing of real property assets to stave off bankruptcy. Many Hungarian companies occupy too much space for their business needs and on privatization some have attempted to realize their assets in a programme of 'down-sizing'. If the premises occupied are located in one of the central districts, and the business does not benefit from such a location, relocation to a fringe area so as to release the central site to a Western company can be a sound business strategy. The termination of state subsidies may precipitate businesses going into liquidation with the prospect of the forced sale of property assets. The SPA continues to emphasize the selling of properties to ensure a flow of capital from the privatization programme to contribute to the repayment of the national debt.

The consequence of these separate but interrelated decision areas is a mismatch between the demand and supply of space, in the Budapest market. The short-term business and 'political' policies outlined above have emphasized the selling market in the 'older' premises. Also the increased number of premises coming on the market have acted to depress prices. Of the large supply of existing office space, little matches the specifications expected by most Western companies. Many of these entering the Hungarian market for the first time will typically want to lease premises rather than buy so as to limit their exposure to risk from capital expenditure. Hence Western companies have been the principal targets for developers of new premium office space available for rent.

Standard conventions have yet to be established for the measurement of floor areas and the consistent use of gross/net areas in published documents. This makes information from different firms of consultants difficult to compare with, for example, data published in a special office building survey in the *Budapest Business Journal*.

The total stock of 'modern' office floorspace at the end of 1992 was approximately 170 000 sq m. The development of new office space increased from 1989 with significant additions of space taking place in 1991 and 1992.

Five schemes were completed in 1991 to provide a total of 32 000 sq m, of which half of the floorspace was accounted for by the East West Business Centre. Development activity increased again in 1992 with 16 schemes providing a total of 64 500 sq m of office space; and is due to expand further in 1993, with 19 schemes bringing forward 71 000 sq m. More than 100 000 sq m are planned to be completed in eight schemes in 1994–95. The average size of schemes has been increasing throughout this period (Price Waterhouse, 1993); market studies by DTZ suggest that the average size of planned schemes is almost three times larger, at 11 990 sq m, than those developments recently completed or presently under construction. Currently the greatest demand is for office suites of up to 500 sq m. Once business activity is firmly established, space needs are expected to expand and additional demand is anticipated to come from companies located in poor accommodation in the capital (DTZ, 1991).

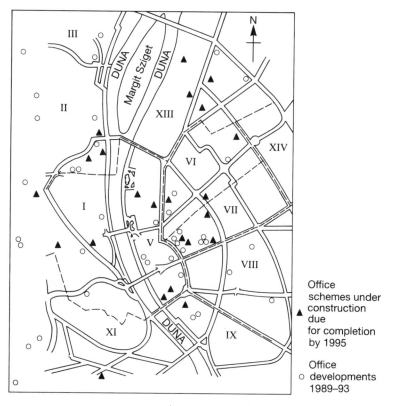

Figure 15.1   Budapest: central area office development since 1989
Source: drawn by Mahtab Akhavan Farshchi.

The main office districts are on the Pest side of the River Danube within the outer Boulevard (Robert Karoly–Hungaria Korut ring road). At the core of this area is district V which is the focus for central government and municipal government offices, banking and commercial administration. The building stock is comparatively well maintained. Much of this district is conserved under heritage regulations and plots are densely built up with little ground-level space for car parking.

Approximately 53% of Budapest's office floorspace is located within the inner-boulevard (Szt Istvan–Terez–Erzsebet Krt–Joseph Krt) comprising the district V and the inner parts of districts VI, VII, VIII and IX (the 'inner fringe'). There has been considerable building activity within this inner fringe area since 1989, with several important schemes due for completion by 1995 (Figure 15.1).

Since the 'opening up' of Hungary to the interests of international business office rentals have increased considerably. The DTZ Hungary Office Index shows a 250% rise since 1987 from a level of 22 DM per sq m per month to current (mid 1991) levels of 55 DM per sq m per month (DTZ, 1991). In 1992 rentals peaked at 60 DM per sq m per month for best quality office space but have since stabilized. As yet, the office areas have not evolved sufficiently to develop clear differentiation between rental levels in each area; for example, rental levels in district V and the inner fringe areas are comparable. Discounts on space is minimal in the outer fringe areas between the inner and outer boulevards. However as the office space currently being constructed and planned space come on to the market the distinction between prime and secondary office areas will become more marked. Nevertheless secondary locations may be compensated by good car parking provision and adequate telecommunication (telephone and fax) facilities – key business requirements which act as capacity constraints to the development or refurbishment of building plots in the central area. The Buda side of the Danube is traditionally a residential area, suffering less traffic congestion, easier car parking, and lower levels of pollution. Hence interest has increased among occupiers in locating business on this side of the river and several new office developments ensure that the area will have a commercial role.

There is no formal structure to the retail real-estate market. Despite considerable growth in the number of privately operated and managed shops during the 1980s, the sector was still dominated by state-owned and collective enterprises. At the end of 1989, 126 state companies controlled over 16 000 shops across Hungary, accounting for 53% of national retail sales. These outlets were not co-ordinated nor integrated in the way expected of Western chain stores.

Budapest has a relatively large share of private shops, many of which offer specialized services. The capital has three of the four large supermarkets owned by the Skala-Co-op, and 14 of the 32 state-owned Centrum

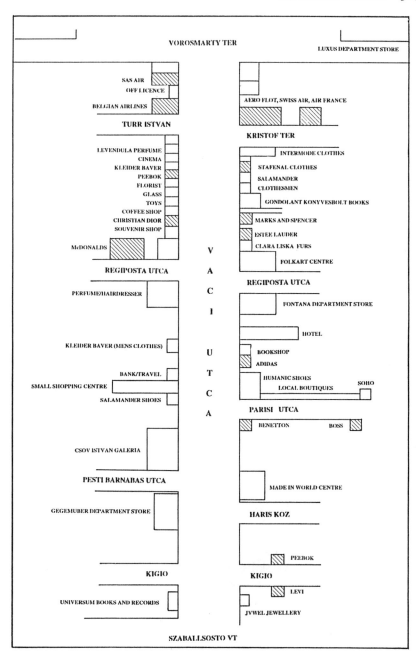

Figure 15.2 Budapest: Vaci Utca Street and its Western retailers
Source: drawn by Mahtab Akhavan Farshchi.

department stores. Budapest has a developed retail area located within the area bounded by the Szt Istvan Krt–Joseph Krt ring road. It has traditionally been the focus for shopping for residents in Budapest and continues to draw shoppers from some distance. The retail sales per capita in Budapest is higher than elsewhere in Hungary whereas the sales ratio in Pest county, surrounding Budapest, is the lowest in the country (EIU, 1991).

A few international retailers have expanded into Hungary and have located within the inner-city core area along the Vaci Ut. and adjoining streets (Figure 15.2). This area is increasingly serving a recreation, tourist and higher income service function. Budapest does not at present have any 'out of town' retail centres. The traditional patterns of shopping behaviour militates against such development, as does the poor infrastructure but with the influence of Western capital both may accommodate change in the coming years. Indeed this change has recently manifested itself in the growing number of edge of town warehousing and distribution schemes, the most notable being the IKEA development. The focus of such development activity is at the major junctions of the emerging motorways network around Budapest, particularly on M1 or along the Budapest–Vienna corridor.

15.8 CONCLUSION

It has been a feature of urban planning in Budapest that most of the policies and proposals which were not directly related to the state goal of industrial development (and associated housing for the workers) were frustrated by lack of resources. The political and administrative contexts may have changed but the budgetary constraints remain and will continue to frustrate the implementation of policies for local governments. The political realities of new freedoms for district authorities embrace a diminishing revenue base from central government, an as-yet undeveloped local taxation system, and deteriorating standards of living among the city residents. The economic and political costs of applying and enforcing environmental policy will be high.

Local governments, politicians and their planning and financial staff are needing to master new skills in negotiation, valuation and appraisal techniques when dealing with private developers and foreign investors. Indeed there exists a missing generation of Hungarian planners and real-estate valuers with experience of working in a market economy. The greater involvement of foreign investors and developers will hasten the adoption of more appropriate valuation methods and other requirements of a mature property investment and development market, not least reliable sources of market information.

The transformation of ownership through land becoming owned by private individuals, private companies and by local government is reshaping relationships. This is particularly so for local government (districts in Budapest) exercising their planning functions and needing to balance these objectives with the attraction of adopting an entrepreneurial approach to the use of local authority property assets.

There are numerous pressures for change to the social structure of Budapest. Revitalization of the historic centre combined with growing tourism will contribute to continuing changes to the nature of shops and services in central Budapest. Provision for speciality goods and luxury items, and the presence of outlets of overseas companies may give rise to increasing mismatch with the retail needs of local households. Also increasing competition for central space from new hotels, office and other central area commercial uses will begin to squeeze out residential activities.

The ambiguous relationship between the municipal authority and the districts has left a vacuum in strategic policy and increased uncertainty in decision-making. District authorities can act as autonomous governments and there is potential for city-wide goals to be frustrated by the parochial interests of individual districts. Hence there is the real fear that existing social and economic differences between districts may be increased. Furthermore the district councils have to deal with the legacy of the communist period, including a poorly maintained housing stock, particularly in the inner districts, and the soulless environment of much of the factory-built outer housing estates; unacceptable levels of air, water and soil pollution; lack of infrastructure and essential utility services in the outer areas of Budapest and wider metropolitan area; and the random distribution of office building which, due to the irrelevancy of location as an economic variable in the socialist era, meant that there was little incentive to invest in the centre of Budapest.

In the short term a new style of 'urban management' is required of the municipal authority acting as a co-ordinating body to persuade the districts to develop a city-wide perspective to their policies and actions. It is evident that in several policy areas, for example, housing, transport, and the utility services, there is need for guidelines or a central framework to foster consistency among local districts. This could be provided by the muncipal government. In the longer term there may be a compelling case to consider the reorganization of local government for Budapest; having larger district authorities within an extended territory of a metropolitan authority.

REFERENCES

Aisbett, A. (1991) European Property: Property Law in Hungary and Czechoslovakia, in *The Estates Gazette*, issue 9130 (3 August), 36–7.

Baar, K. (1992) Hungarian Land Use Policy in the Transition to a Market

Economy with Democratic Controls, unpublished paper, September.

Denyer, S. and Eaton, R. (1991) Privatisation in Hungary. The vital role of the State Property Agency, in *Euromoney*, May, 33–6.

DTZ (1991) *The Budapest Property Market*, DTZ, Hungary, October, 10.

DTZ (1992) *Budapest Property Statistics: A Pictorial Overview*, DTZ, Hungary, December, 12.

EIU (1991) Retailing and Wholesaling in Hungary, *Economic Intelligence Unit*.

EIU (1993) Country Report Series, *Economic Intelligence Unit*.

Elter, I. and Baros, P. (1993) City profile: Budapest, *Cities*, **10**(3), August, 189–97.

Enyedi, G. and Szirmai, V. (1992) *Budapest: A Central European Capital*, Belhaven Press, London.

Fisher, D. (1992) *Paradise Deferred: Environmental Policy Making in Central and Eastern Europe*, Royal Institute of International Affairs, London.

Healey & Baker/RICS (1991) *Real Estate Guide: Hungary*, Healey & Baker/RICS, March 1991.

Hegedus, J. *et al.* (1993) Local options for transforming the public rental sector, *Cities*, **10**(3), August 1993, 257–71.

Horvath, M.T. (1991a) The structure of the Hungarian local government, *The Reform of the Public Administration*, Hungarian Institute of Public Administration, Budapest, 81–90.

Horvath, M.T. (1991b) Emergence of policy making, *The Reform of the Public Administration*, Hungarian Institute of Public Administration, Budapest, 163–70.

Peteri, G. (1991) Market: 'pressure or possibility', *The Reform of the Public Administration*, Hungarian Institute of Public Administration, Budapest.

Picard, N.L. (1993) Eco-tourism still green and growing, *Budapest Week*, 24/30 June, 10.

Price Waterhouse (1993) Office Developments since 1989 in Budapest, Unpublished statistics, Price Waterhouse, Hungary.

Revesz, G. (1990) *Perestroika in Eastern Europe, Hungary's Economic Transformation 1945–1988*, Westview Press.

Schneller, I. (1992) *Most Important Middle Term, Development Objectives of Budapest*, Budapest, Municipal Authorities, February.

Swain, N. (1992) *Hungary – The Rise and Fall of Feasible Socialism*, Verso.

Takas, K. (ed.) (1991) *The Reform of Hungarian Public Administration*, Hungarian Institute of Public Administration, Budapest.

Tamas, G.M.L. (1993) Ugly faces are popular again, *The European*, 30 September–30 October, 7.

16

Prague

Luděk Sýkora

This chapter provides an analysis of recent changes in urban planning practice in Prague, in the context of transition from a totalitarian to a democratic political system and from a command to a market-led economy. Special attention is devoted to the emerging tensions between political goals, planning strategies and market forces. The main tasks for contemporary urban planning and politics in Prague are to keep planning regulations in operation and defend the legitimacy of the planning system; to preserve the spirit of the historical core of the city and reconcile it with new commercial, mainly tourist-oriented, development; to designate areas for new commercial and office development close to the centre, attract foreign investments and stimulate progressive economic activities; to anticipate potential social tensions based on growing polarization, especially in connection with accessibility to housing; and to find a solution to the city transportation system.

In understanding present urban development in the city of Prague and the planning response, it is necessary to establish a basic framework, which consists of an appreciation of the city's historical development, encompasses an overview of basic 'socialist' urban economic principles and outlines the transition from totalitarian urban economy managerialism to a liberalized real-estate market. The planning system and its response to market forces will be analysed including the traditions, rules and institutional background to planning in Prague. Three contemporary planning activities, a new Master Plan, transportation proposals, and preservation strategies for the historical core of the city are considered.

16.1 HISTORICAL DEVELOPMENT OF PRAGUE'S URBAN STRUCTURE

The foundation of Prague coincided with the arrival of Slavic tribes into the Bohemian Basin. At the end of the ninth century Prague Castle was

European Cities, Planning Systems and Property Markets Edited by James Berry and Stanley McGreal. Published in 1995 by E & FN Spon. ISBN 0419 18940 8.

founded in a strategic position controlling a merchant path on the Vltava river. At that time Prague was the seat of the Přemyslid princes which gradually came to dominate the entire territory of Bohemia and Moravia. Prague's second castle, Vyšehrad, was built in the tenth century and an extensive settlement grew up between Prague's castles on both river banks linked in the twelfth century by a stone bridge.

The medieval development of Prague culminated with the planned foundation of a New Town by Charles IV in 1348. Prague's four towns (Hradčany, Malá Strana, Staré Město and Nové Město) were encircled by new ramparts. However, the politically independent towns resisted administrative unification. At that time Prague had its own university and archbishop, and the Charles Bridge was constructed. The city covered a total area of more than 800 ha, and with an estimated 40–50 000 inhabitants ranked among the largest European cities of that time. The dimensions of the New Town development surpassed anything that was planned in the Middle Ages. More importantly, half of the area remained unbuilt and so accommodated city development until the beginning of the nineteenth century.

From the fifteenth to nineteenth centuries, periods of city decline alternated with times of economic expansion, cultural revival and population increase. Prague became a provincial town and due to a peaceful development it preserved not only a medieval (Romanesque and Gothic) street network, but also the scale, character and appearance of the medieval town. Although the Renaissance and Baroque Period did not bring great urban planning ideas, many of the city's architectural jewels date from this era. In particular Prague's historical core was based on a succession of building styles, which created an exceptional array of urban architecture. In 1784 the four historical parts of Prague were unified and in 1850 a fifth element (Josefov) was added. Altogether with Vyšehrad, annexed in 1883, they form the historical core of the city. In the middle of the nineteenth century the central city core contained 120 000 inhabitants, twice that of today.

The development of the city in the nineteenth century was influenced considerably by the industrial revolution. First, manufacturing workshops emerged beyond the city ramparts followed by expanding suburbs. In 1817 the suburb of Karlín was developed in a planned fashion (Hrůza, 1992) and gradually, further suburban districts expanded in all directions initially unplanned and later, in the second half of the century, on the basis of planned layouts. As the population of the historical core stagnated, adjoining areas developed quickly, ultimately achieving the status of independent towns. At the end of the nineteenth century these towns were inhabited by twice the population of the historical core. The suburbs and the core, in morphological terms, formed one urban unit with the total population of more than half a million. Late in the nineteenth century and early twentieth century the process of urban renewal based on the concept of Hausmann's renewal in Paris changed the face of Prague's historical core. The picturesque Jewish ghetto (Josefov) was demolished and replaced by a residential neighbourhood built in the *art nouveau* style. Urban structures dating from the Middle Ages were replaced by a new street network with a wide central boulevard.

After the First World War and the proclamation of the independent Czechoslovak Republic in 1918, Prague became the capital city. Its new geopolitical position brought rapid development to the urban area. In 1922 Greater Prague was formed by amalgamation of 37 municipalities. The city area expanded more than eight times to 198 km² with 677 000 inhabitants. New public-sector buildings were erected in the inner city, their shape affected by conservative regulations, which, in the context of the old urban structure, did not allow for major alteration in height or volume. Urban growth was especially concentrated in the suburbs and garden districts. Some of these garden towns were developed to planned

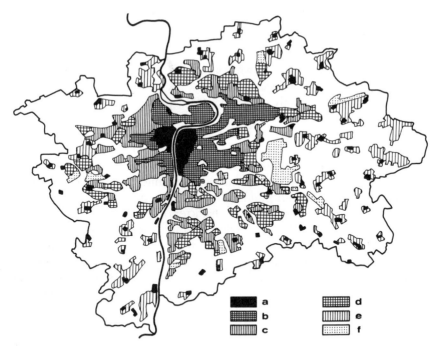

Figure 16.1 Prague's urban structure: (a) historical core and cores of formerly independent municipalities; (b) compactly built-up area of inner city; (c) villas, single family houses, garden towns; (d) residential areas built since 1945; (e) urbanized villages on city outskirts; (f) industrial zones
Source: redrawn from ÚHA (1992b) *Územní plán hlavního města Prahy (druhé čtení): plán využití ploch – stabilizovaná území.*

layouts and today still rank among the most attractive residential districts. Suburbanization processes also became clearly visible in Prague's
metropolitan area (Grime and Kára, 1990). The population of the city rose
to nearly one million in 1940 but as a result of the Second World War the
pre-war population size was only re-established in 1957 (Sýkora and
Štěpánek, 1992).

The Communist coup in 1948 started a new historical epoch of building
a socialist society. All urban land was nationalized, land ownership was
replaced by the so-called personal use right (Michalovic, 1992). Most
houses (with the exception of small single-family houses) were also
nationalized and the state took over responsibilities for the management of
the housing stock as well as for a new construction. In the 1950s housing
construction in Prague almost ceased, strongly influenced by the political
goal to level out differences between urban and rural life. One consequence
was an emerging housing shortage which the government responded to
by starting an ambitious programme to build large residential units at the
periphery requiring expansion of the city territory. Accordingly 51 surrounding municipalities were incorporated in two steps (Kára, 1992),
the first in 1968 and the second in 1974. Consequently the city now
covers approximately 496 sq km and according to the March 1991 census
1 212 010 inhabitants. During the 1970s and the 1980s the so-called
North, South and Southwest Towns (large housing estates, each consisting
of approximately 100 000 people) created a characteristic picture of the
Prague outer city. Currently (1993) 830 000 people live in housing estates
erected during the Communist period.

From a planning perspective the city has developed more or less
in concentric zones (Figure 16.1). Around the historic core are predominantly residential suburbs dating from the nineteenth century and
early twentieth century. Both the core and the inner city are characterized
by compact buildings; with building space totally filled by 1930s development. The adjoining zone retained its character of relatively separate suburbs
and garden towns consisting mostly of family houses. Socialist housing
estates from the 1950s were located in these areas, however a massive
building programme based on the construction of large housing estates
shifted development activity to the outer city. Beyond this zone, but within
the city's administrative boundary, individual villages form an interface with
the rural hinterland.

16.2   FROM TOTALITARIAN MANAGERIALISM TO
A LIBERALIZED URBAN PROPERTY MARKET

The Prague urban environment has gone through tremendous restructuring
since the collapse of Communism in November 1989. Such urban restruc-

turing has to be seen in the broader context of societal transformation of which a fundamental part is the transition from a command to a market economy. However, before considering contemporary developments, an outline of basic features of the 'socialist' city and the implications for an urban real-estate market is necessary.

16.2.1 The 'socialist' urban economics and its consequences

Socialism, according to Smith (1989) is defined as a social-economic-political system in which the capacity to produce and deliver goods and services is substantially within state ownership and control. In the Czech Republic, the basic features of 'socialist' economics were established following the Communist coup in 1948 and these influenced the development of Prague's built environment for four decades. The socialist urban economy in Prague was characterized by the state ownership of urban land together with most of the housing stock; the public management of state properties and intervention of the state to other sectors (private and co-operative) as a decisive means for allocation of scarce resources; centrally regulated prices and rent controls. The crucial feature of the socialist political economy, which explicitly influenced the city development, was the priority given to production factors, grounded in collective needs and working-class interests, over the consumption requirements of individual citizens.

The subordination of consumption to production requirements led to the dictate of large state enterprises concerning building activities. Large-scale projects proved to be more profitable than reconstruction and rehabilitation of old housing stock and infrastructure. Physical planning tools were subordinated to national economic planning goals and only elaborated on principles set by the needs of the production sector. These determined an estimation of citizens' objective needs and set standardized norms for an individual civic life. Consequently, an extensive amount of homogeneous dwellings in 'grey' housing estates at the city outskirts emerged while, at the same time, the maintenance of inner-city housing stock was totally neglected. The latter was further influenced by other factors, for example the extremely low rental incomes of the Housing Services Corporations which were extracted from residential as well as non-residential premises. The rent amounted to, on average, 5% of total family income (Musil, 1968; Carter, 1979). In 1989 only one-third of the revenue of the Housing Services Corporations came from rental income (Sýkora and Šimoníčková, 1993). Scarce financial resources did not allow for basic maintenance of houses, and even less so for capital investment programmes for rehabilitation and improvement of older and sub-standard housing stock. Thus gradual physical deterioration of houses in the inner city followed, with the result that many dwellings were declared as unhabitable.

In impact terms the socialist urban economy therefore produced homogeneity in the socio-spatial structure of the city and underutilization of the housing stock in the inner city (Sýkora, 1993). It is obvious that the first issue is contradictory to the basic outcomes of the capitalist urban economy, and does not accord with the contemporary developments of most inner cities in developed capitalist countries. These disparities can create potential for possible economic development as well as contributing to the emergence of social tensions.

16.2.2   Transition to the market: system transformation

Contemporary urban restructuring is primarily influenced by processes deliberately directed by central government actions. The institutionalization of liberal democracy in Czech politics at the beginning of 1990 and the stabilization confirmed by the parliamentary elections 1992 (Jehlička *et al.*, 1993) created the necessary preconditions for a governed transition to the market economy. The scenario for rapid economic change was approved by parliament in 1990, and since that time a succession of partial reforms have transformed fundamental features of the Czech economy, which has influenced the restructuring of society as a whole and the urban areas in particular. The principal goal of economic reform is to make the Czech economy healthier and more compatible with Western standards as quickly as possible. The decisive factor is the decentralization from a publicly, centrally planned, system to the market allocation of resources. Measures are based on the economic liberalism of neo-conservatism, which exists at the top of post-communist politics in the Czech Republic.

Three general transformations can be conceptualized. First, the deregulation of public management of resource allocation to actors in the marketplace. This is, of course, tightly bound to the reduction of indirect public influence through the dominance of state ownership and the regulation of exchange processes, and is reflected in the second and third transformation which are designed to create an environment in which market forces become a main allocator. In this context the privatization process breaks down the dominance of state ownership into a more fragmented structure, creating a broad and complex set of individual subjects which can undertake exchange. Furthermore, the liberalization of prices installs a market environment in its narrowest sense, by deregulating public involvement in exchange measures (prices, rent), thus permitting relatively free action of individual agents in market exchange.

At the urban level these three general spheres of transformation are being realized. In public management deregulation, attention is being directed at the reduction of local government competencies to influence the allocation of resources, for example by releasing non-residential premises for particular users and functions. With the privatization of public services, the Housing Services Corporations which were responsible for the public housing stock are being replaced by private real estate agencies. Another very important factor is the general antagonism directed towards public activities and to planning regulations in particular.

Ownership structures are transformed by several mechanisms. In urban areas the most important are restitution, small privatization and large privatization. While the first two processes have been active in transforming the Prague urban environment, large-scale privatization is still in its early stages. Concerning the first of these mechanisms, restitution is a process whereby previous owners, or their heirs, are given back properties that were confiscated by the Communists in the period after 1948. Changes in ownership structure declared by restitution is one of the most important aspects affecting the contemporary restructuring process in the inner city of Prague. For example, in Prague 1 (constituting two-thirds of the historical core) nearly 70% of housing stock has been restituted. In the other two inner city neighbourhoods (Prague 3 and 5) restitution has affected about 50–60% of housing stock (Sýkora and Šimoníčková, 1993).

The second mechanism, small-scale privatization, commenced in Prague in January 1991 and terminated at the end of 1993. The aim was to sell, by means of public auction, small state-owned businesses (shops, restaurants, smaller enterprises) to the private sector. There are two ways in which properties were sold. Whole properties, often including land, where the premises were located in free-standing buildings accounted for 20% of all auctions and applied particularly to shopping or service centres built during the Communist era. Facilities, furnishings or machinery were sold at the remaining auctions. Where property was bought in an auction, a five-year lease was guaranteed to a new owner by law, indeed in the centre of Prague only leaseholds were sold. In spite of the huge number of buildings in restitution, 2528 shops, restaurants or smaller enterprises found new owners or lessors in the small privatization auctions during 1991–3.

Sale prices under the small privatization scheme represented the first comprehensive indicators of market value in Prague. The extreme differences which exist between the price paid for one square metre in the centre compared to the outskirts of the city illustrate the value of location within the urban market. The prices indicate general trends in the development of a rent or price surface, indicating buyers expectations of a future profit differential across Prague's urban space. The emerging price surface is very similar to the neoclassical rent curve with peaking in the centre and decreasing values towards the edge of the city (Sýkora, 1993).

This spatial trend is also confirmed by land prices and rents in the non-residential sector. In 1992 the market prices for one square metre of urban

Table 16.1   Rent in non-residential sector (1992, in DM/m^2)

Urban zones	Offices	Retail
CBD	50–70	80–140
Historical core	25–50	40–80
Inner city	15–30	20–40
Suburbs	5–20	10–25

Note: Based on data obtained from real estate companies První Vinohradská, Royal – pražská realitní kancelář, Jendrusch & Partner and Ryden Intl. Consultants.
Source: Sýkora and Šimoníčková, 1993.

land ranged from 700 Kč (Czech Crown; 1 GBP = 44 Kč) at the city outskirts to 70 000 Kč in the CBD (Sýkora and Šimoníčková, 1993). In the 1980s, there was one administratively set price for urban land within Prague's territory; this amounted to only 20 Kč/m^2. The land was then sold at 'shadow' prices up to 350 Kč/m^2 in the best locations (Kramplová, 1989).

In the immediate aftermath of the revolution a new system of rent regulation/deregulation was introduced. Local authorities were allowed to mark zones that are not subjected to any rent regulation. In the case of a lease contract with a foreigner or a company with a major share of foreign capital the rent is negotiated without any restriction. These developments split a deregulated segment of the rental sector, defined by the involvement of foreign subjects, from the domestic segment. The market performance of foreign/deregulated sector, where the rent was and still is negotiated in hard currency, particularly in German marks (DM), has mirrored the dynamics of real-estate market constitution in the city of Prague.

The rent for office and commercial space leased to foreign subjects in central locations increased rapidly up to 70 DM/m^2 in the first half of 1990 (Sýkora and Štěpánek, 1992). The boom of prices within the deregulated segment continued during 1990 due to demand exceeding the supply of required premises, with the result that realized leases fetched an extremely high rent of 150 DM for one square metre of office space. In the first quarter of 1991 rents decreased to 90 DM/m^2, caused by a growing supply of restituted houses and in the middle of 1991 further decreased to 60 DM/m^2 stabilizing in autumn 1991 at 40 DM/m^2 (ÚHA and SÚRPMO, 1991), a level which matched the domestic segment of the rental sector. Contemporary rent levels for office and commercial space within particular urban zones in Prague are shown in Table 16.1.

16.2.3   The constitution of the real estate market and new development projects

The restitution process and the privatization of state properties created a new distribution of resources amongst private owners. The combination of price and rent deregulation as well as decentralization of decision-making from public authorities to individuals creates opportunities for private capital in the emerging real-estate market. Once property has been restituted or privatized it can be freely marketed, although some restrictions are placed on free exchange. The most important of these concerns is the control of foreign subjects entering the Czech real estate market. Under these circumstances the purchase of real property in the Czech republic is restricted to those persons or entities meeting the following qualifications (Kirke, 1993):

1. A Czech national holding a current passport and having a permanent residence in the Czech lands.
2. A foreigner who can prove biological Czech parentage (father or mother) and subsequently obtain a permanent residency permit. The person is then treated as a Czech citizen for tax and currency purposes and can purchase property without restriction. After five years Czech citizenship becomes available.
3. A person who obtains a long-stay residency permit, renewable annually. After eight years a permanent residency becomes available. This has been the usual permit granted to foreigners who have formed either limited liability companies (private companies requiring 100 000 Kč start-up capital) or joint stock companies (public companies requiring 1 000 000 Kč start-up capital) or one of the other varieties of companies through which it is possible to purchase property. There is no necessity for Czech participation in these companies.

Prior to the sale of any land or property, a current official valuation has to be obtained. Despite the fact that this rarely corresponds with the market value, tax and dues are levied against the valuation. In the case of foreign purchase through a company, the buying contract has to be forwarded to the Ministry of Finance, which undertakes a valuation of the property to assess its value in terms of what similar property in other European capitals would fetch. The valuation is paid for, normally by the purchaser, and can be appealed. Once agreed, the price is placed on the buying agreement and sent for registration, a process which can take up to four months (Kirke, 1993).

In Prague there are now hundreds of inner-city properties for sale, most of which are fully or nearly fully tenanted. The rental income from Czechs living in the buildings is generally negligible. However, it is possible to relocate the tenants, renovate the properties and relet them at substantially higher rents, often for hard currency. Demand is high for apartments in Prague, and rent from foreigners is fully deregulated. A two-bedroom flat can be obtained from 400 to 600 DM per month, though in the city centre or some of the more attractive parts of the inner-city rents are much higher. A property which includes shops on the ground floor or contains office space greatly increases its attractiveness, due to the strong demand for retail space and the fact that rents in the non-residential sector are more or less deregulated. Although many of these properties frequently appear to be in poor condition, they are generally structurally sound with concrete stairs, floors, sound roofs and massively thick walls.

Considerable opportunities exist for private-sector-led rehabilitation of some individual properties, blocks of houses or small neighbourhoods. The possibilities for redevelopment are being recognized by real-estate agencies which have recently entered the Prague market. Currently (1993) there are about 50 foreign companies and circa three times as many Czech firms involved in a real-estate business. The activities of the property market can be seen not only on the displays of properties on offer, but also from the increase in the process of gentrication. Nevertheless, the revitalization process has touched only a rather small fragment of the total housing stock and hence has a selective spatial impact.

As far as foreign developers are concerned, major interest is devoted to large projects such as hotels, commercial and business centres. However, there are limited possibilities to squeeze such developments into the most attractive parts of the historical core, where the demand is extremely high. Particularly attractive is the Vltava river waterfront, where some developments have already started and a few others are planned. The first of these the Charles Bridge Centre, a 4000 m² complex in the 'best location' includes offices, restaurants, shops and business apartments, is due for completion in early 1994 and is based on the rehabilitation of old buildings. However new construction projects stand a better chance of obtaining approval outside the historic core, and indeed several hotels have been built since 1989. One of them, the Atrium, is located immediately behind the historical core and in the middle of 1993 an International Business Centre, the biggest office development in Prague with about 26 000 m² of total floor space, was completed on an adjacent site.

16.3 CONSEQUENCES OF TRANSITION TO THE MARKET AND CONTEMPORARY URBAN PLANNING PRIORITIES

The contemporary transformation of Czech society is aimed at incorporating the basic features of capitalism. Establishment of a competitive market environment is based on a highly uneven redistribution of resources and power among private firms, public agencies and individual households. It is aimed at stimulating and speeding-up economic restructuring, thus creating conditions for future growth. However this strategy is likely to produce social disparities which can have some undesirable effects if they are not regulated by consistency in public policy. In the city of Prague the most urgent problem in a social context is the tremendous shortage of housing. Public housing programmes terminated in 1993 and new private-sector construction has been delayed by reforms in local administration and changes in legislation.

Private developers and speculators are focusing on the housing demands of the higher income groups, with the result that the revitalization process is displacing lower income households from attractive inner-city neighbourhoods. Many newly built houses or apartments are beyond the means of even middle-income households. Thus the regeneration process and new construction programmes are socially and spatially very selective. Most of Prague's inhabitants are trapped in deteriorating inner-city housing stock or 'grey' housing estates. Yet, they are better-off compared with younger households, those starting in housing market or tenants who are being pushed out from central locations due to rising economic costs. While the housing demand created by foreigners and wealthy Czech citizens can be meet by the market, the solution to the desperate housing shortage requires a consistent public policy approach to co-ordinate national, urban and local housing programmes.

In the context of growing international competition between European city regions new economic strategies at the local political and planning level are of paramount importance. The selling of the city as a location for activity depends heavily upon the creation of an attractive urban image. Cities are therefore offering opportunities to encourage the inward movement of enterprises and capital through various economic means (infrastructure provision and financial incentives), by marketing their operational and organizational traditions (skilled and well-educated labour force), by offering cultural and historical values of the built environment as well as the natural environment. The challenge facing Prague is whether it has the potential to attract foreign investment and the commitment of the city planning authority to pursue market-orientated strategies for economic growth.

The Czech public authorities have a double-edged task. On the one hand, they have to create a competitive market environment and attract foreign investment, and on the other hand they have to solve an array of problems inherited from forty years of Communism, for example, the need to resolve the housing shortage, as well as to control and regulate undesirable consequences of market operations, and at the same time to preserve the cultural values of the historical core. Thus there are many priorities for urban planning.

First, it is considered necessary that the historical core is protected against large-scale commercial development. Preservation and sensitive rehabilitation of the historical core, including Prague's picturesque inner city environment needs to be secured. Furthermore environmental improvement along the axis of the Vltava river is to be encouraged by creating an area of tourism and leisure, with an increase in hospitality facilities and services.

Second, the consolidation and partial renovation of inner-city neighbourhoods which can be undertaken with a greater degree of aesthetic freedom than in the historical city. Most of these neighbourhoods will be neglected by private developers and hence the involvement of public-sector agencies will be necessary to stimulate the upgrading of housing standards. While the socialist towns will never compensate for the quality of urban life that is to be found in a city, which mixes functions, and offers space with identity, Baše (1993) nevertheless argues that these entities have to be considered in the overall context of city structure and there is a lot of small-scaled work which could be undertaken in these areas. Programmes for the humanization of their living environment have already been launched, but Prague's new towns need, above all, to complement residential functions with service provision and job opportunities.

Land and infrastructure provision for commercial and industrial development constitutes the third of these requirements, in particular in relation to the recovery of old industrial areas. Furthermore areas used as a railway freight zone located in the inner city offer opportunities for new office and commercial uses. Development of these zones could extend the city core area and thus secure the historical reserve from unfavourable building projects. The creation of an international trade centre in Holešovice, the office and services centre at the Main/Wilson Railway Station, and the residential and commercial centre at Smíchov are all located in close proximity to the contemporary city core. The realization of a technology park, in conjunction with university, research and production facilities to promote development of industries capable of competing with the corporations from Western Europe is intended in the outer city. Additional areas suited for administrative offices and facilities will also be developed in the outer zone.

Fourth, the transport strategy for the city, which is to be based on expansion of the public transportation system, combines programmes for the further development of urban subway lines to supplement the newly submitted system of regional railway transport. Nevertheless, the most sensitive issue is the realization of the city ring road to connect national highways and to channel both the city and transit (mostly international truck) traffic, thus easing pressure on the inner-city road network.

Finally a growing ecological awareness is focusing attention on approving established parks, promoting green space quality, and developing a system of ecological stability. The latter is to become a compulsory part of planning policy.

16.4   URBAN PLANNING IN PRAGUE

This section considers how priorities are being translated into political and planning practice. Attention is devoted specifically to three main projects which are currently central to city planning viz a new master plan, proposed transport network solutions and preservation of the historical core. However this section initially starts with a brief outline of planning traditions and the specification of the basic rules of Czech territorial planning.

16.4.1   Traditions, rules and institutions in city planning

Urban planning in Prague has a long tradition. The planned foundation of the New Town dates back to the fourteenth century and the first suburb Karlín, to the early nineteenth century. The renewal of the old Jewish ghetto, Josefov, ranks among those activities which had considerable inpact upon city development. However it was not until the 1920s that the State Regulation Board was set up to promote a plan for Greater Prague. This body was given the task of working out town-planning schemes for individual sectors of the city which then served as a basis for the overall development plan, completed in 1929 (Borovička and Hrůza, 1983) but not officially approved until the late 1930s. Consequently, during the inter-war period urban development took place independently of city planning concepts.

The first post-war city planning scheme for Prague was completed in 1948 and although this plan was not approved it did influence the foundation of the Town Planning Office in 1951. The Master Plan was completed in 1961 at which stage the Chief Architect's Office for Prague was set up. The plan approved by the Czech government in 1964 provided the strategy for the development of the city with the central focus of planning policy concentrating on the design of the traffic network and solving the severe housing shortage in the city. In 1967 the government took the decision to build an underground system and approved the annexation of the municipalities surrounding Prague. Further annexation followed in 1974, permitting the implementation of a strategy to build large residential housing estates. This gave new impetus to city planning activities. In terms of political acceptance a General Plan of the Capital City of Prague was granted approval in 1975, about the same time as the Master Plan for the City and the Regional Plan for the Prague Agglomeration (the latter being prepared by TERPLAN – the State Institute for Territorial Planning). These aimed to co-ordinate the urban development process at both a regional and the city level, and to concentrate activities in urban agglomerations. The most recent version of the Master Plan dates from 1986.

The regulations governing territorial planning in the Czech Republic are provided in the Territorial Planning and Building Act (1976). New laws such as the Space Planning Act and the Building Codex which reflect changing societal conditions are under preparation. At the present time there are three basic tools of territorial planning: territorial planning working papers, territorial planning documentation and territorial decisions. The purpose of the territorial planning working papers is to collect basic data and evaluate proposed developments. Territorial planning documentation include real urban and regional plans, which differ according to time horizons (prognosis, plan, project) and spatial scales (regional, urban, zone). The territorial decision is an executive decision of state administration and deals with changes in land use, localization of new construction, declaration of a protected area or construction closure of a particular area.

The relevant authority responsible for procurement of territorial planning documentation is at the municipal level. In the case of Prague it is the central city authority – Prague's Magistrate Office. The city has recently been divided into 57 parts (Kára, 1992) of differing size; 13 which consist of approximately 35 000 to 145 000 inhabitants, 32 with a population of less than 5000 while the four smallest parts contain fewer than 300 people. Each has its own local government, which is significantly different in terms of financial and political power. The division of responsibility between the capital city and its respective parts is set out in the Charter, a document which has been rewritten several times and is constantly the topic of political debate.

The Capital City of Prague Act delegates exclusive authority, in the field of territorial development, to the Chief Architect's Office (ÚHA). The office performs two functions. First it is charged with state responsibility for the administration of building (territorial decision) and second takes part in the governance of the city with regard to urban planning. Concerning state administration (delegated authority) ÚHA is independent of elected city politicians. The Territorial Planning and Building Act gives ÚHA the authority to organize the procedures for a territorial decision. The department of state administration issues permits for all important development projects in Prague (excluding small activities such as repairs of family housing) and ÚHA checks if particular items are designed in accordance with the Master Plan and the requirements of state institutions (departments of central government, departments of city administration, technical and transport services, institute of hygienic, national defence). It also seeks to reach a compromise among different opinions on a development proposal. When a territorial decision is issued, the permit is valid for a two-year period. The document comprising approximately 30 pages contains detailed regulations and instruction on dealing with a project. Some 700 territorial decisions are made annually and all appeals must be addressed to the city administration. Furthermore Environmental Impact Assessments were introduced in 1992 as an integral part of the planning process for trade and storage complexes with a development area exceeding 3000 sq m.

Urban concepts for the city are designed in accordance with the Master Plan which has status in law. The procedure for its preparation is financed by the Capital City of Prague, whilst planning activity is controlled by city deputies, particularly by the secretary for building and transport. During the preparation of the Master Plan, ÚHA undertakes negotiations with public authorities viz city and local governments, department of central government, protection of historical monuments, transport authorities, institutions of education and social services, national defence and also with civic movements, social and environmental pressure groups. Once the Master Plan is approved, detailed plans of particular urban zones are then worked out and usually private planning agencies are invited to take part in an open contest organized by ÚHA. The result of the competition has to be agreed by both ÚHA and the local authority from the area in question in order to anticipate future tension between the central and local levels of city government.

16.4.2 New Master Plan

A new Master Plan is currently (1993) under preparation which will reflect political and economic processes at the local level. The city central government and indeed local government within the city both favour investment with short-term returns. Furthermore, there is the perception of a growing need for independence in decision-making processes, due to suspicion and distrust of vertical structures of the territorial administration.

The first reading of the new Master Plan of the Capital City of Prague (ÚHA, 1991b), provided an indication of future trends. Its main purpose was to initiate discussion on the future development of the city and the main message taken from the first reading was the need for a change in planning principles, particularly the transformation from monofunctional to multifunctional zoning regulations. The second reading consisted of two parts: the 'stabilized areas' (ÚHA, 1992b), and the 'variants of development' (ÚHA, 1992c). According to the Territorial Planning and Building Act (1976) the Master Plan of the Capital City of Prague (1986) is still the legally valid document for state administration in the field of territorial decision-making. Nevertheless, basic principles of this plan, especially monofunctional zoning, and declared developments in some city areas, for instance the further construction of large housing estates, have been seriously challenged by new developments in Czech society since 1989.

In the context of transition there is a strong need for a new Master Plan, but its elaboration will take some time. However to use the old Master

Plan until the new one is ready would result either in permitting new construction according to rejected principles or in the slowing down of building activities. Given the contemporary situation of strong investment pressures it is necessary to create and approve a document, upon which state administration in the field of territorial planning could be undertaken, at least in areas with an agreed urban concept. Therefore documentation on the 'stabilized areas' has been prepared for the city areas with relatively fixed urban structures and where major functional changes are not expected.

The stabilized areas encompass the historical core, inner-city neighbourhoods and the new housing estates as well as green space. In total the stabilized areas cover more than half of Prague's territory. Therefore any new revolutionary urban concepts of city development can be discounted. Construction activity, such as the rehabilitation of old housing stock or new constructions on empty plots of land in stabilized areas must respect the contemporary architectural and functional character though more radical changes of planning regulations can be expected in 'white spots' of currently non-stabilized areas. The Stabilized Areas is an important planning document, which has recently been negotiated with the local administrations within the city and is to be approved by the Czech government as an alteration to the Master Plan of 1986. However this document will be valid only for the stabilized areas, while all decisions relating to new developments in 'white areas' will require new detailed planning documentation. Consequently, there will be a situation of 'double governance' in planning the territory of Prague.

The newly applied principle of mixed zoning regulation is used in the document as a means of prospective planning of functional land use in city areas. It does not determine the utilization of particular plots of land or buildings, but new developments or reconstructions have to be in accordance with functions set up by the land-use regulation. The territory of the city is divided into multi- and monofunctional zones. Four basic types of the multifunctional zones include: residential areas, mixed areas (Table 16.2), production areas, and specific areas (leisure and sport areas, fairs and congress complexes, research parks and universities). There are three kinds of functions defined in each multifunctional zone viz dominant, appropriate and exceptionally permissible. Monofunctional zones are designated by their functional homogeneity such as areas of public amenities; transport areas; areas of technical infrastructure; areas of agricultural production; arable land; areas of mining activities and for waste disposal; areas of water surface and green space.

In the document referred to as the Variants of Development the issue relates to the need for new development areas, their number, extension and location. Territorial development outside of the stabilized areas is prohibited. There are four proposed variants of the future development of

Table 16.2 Land-use zone 2.2 – generally mixed area

2.2 Generally mixed area

(A) general land use
residential area mixed with services and small production, which are not hostile to residential function

(B) functional use
• appropriate
    1. residential buildings
    2. office and commercial buildings
    3. retail, lodging and board services
    4. other services and small production
    5. administration, church, cultural, social and health services, sport and education establishments
    6. parking lots and garages
    7. areas of necessary technical infrastructure
    8. transport communication
    9. green space
    10. gas stations as a part of parking places
• exceptionally permissible
    1. separate gas stations
    2. entertainment facilities
    3. horticulture

(C) additional regulations
there can be given a limit to number of floors for individual buildings, whole territory or its part

Source: ÚHA (1992b), Územní plán hlavního města Prahy (druhé čtení): plán využití ploch – stabilizovaná území, [The Master Plan of the Capital City of Prague (second reading): land-use plan – stabilized areas].

the city, each of them deals with the city territory as well as with Prague's hinterland. Two variants called 'urban' are significant in the strategy to build a compact city whilst the other two are 'regional' variants based on the idea of spatial decentralization of new construction to settlement centres in Prague's metropolitan region and zones along main transport lines. There are variants for either a moderate or rapid pace of development within both categories. For every variant the need of development areas is estimated (Table 16.3).

There are also three categories of new development areas selected according to costs of new investment into infrastructure. In the highest status A category there are 1619 ha, in the B category 1336 ha and in C 997 ha. There is a total of 103 localities (of all categories) within the city administrative boundary (Figure 16.2) and 152 in the whole metropolitan region. The areas of potential urban rehabilitation, which relate to stabilized areas, are not considered here. Also there are large underdeveloped or

Table 16.3 The extent of development areas (in hectares) for four variants: (1) urban variant/moderate development; (2) urban variant/rapid development; (3) regional variant/moderate development; (4) regional variant/rapid development

Variants of city development	1	2	3	4
Development areas within city	1150	2500	900	2000
Development areas within region	250	700	500	1200
Total development area	1400	3200	1400	3200

Source: ÚHA (1992c), Územní plán hlavního města Prahy (druhé čtení): varianty rozvoje [The Master Plan of the Capital City of Prague (second reading): the variants of development].

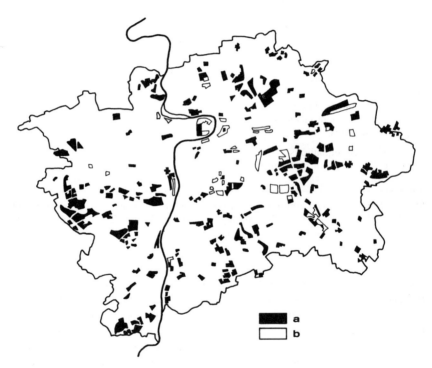

Figure 16.2 Development areas within Prague's territory, all three categories: (a) new developments; (b) rebuilding activities
Source: redrawn from ÚHA (1992b) *Územní plán hlavního města Prahy (druhé čtení): varianty rozvoje.*

underutilized areas in close proximity to the historical core, which are selected as development land in all four variants. New, mostly commercial, development is being accommodated on free land which has been until recently used by Czech railways as a staging area for trains. In this way three railway stations, Holešovice-Bubny, Main/Wilson Railway Station and Smíchov, are to be developed as a World Trade Centre, an office centre and a commercial centre respectively. Political and planning priorities are being given to these developments which are attracting considerable foreign capital. City planners are also making a strong effort to channel new developments into these areas outside the historical core and saving its historical value from a threat of profit-led redevelopments.

16.4.3   Transport networks

The specification of transport solutions, particularly the design of a road network, has been the most important determinant of city planning policies. The public transportation strategy based on an underground system (metro) with car traffic channelled through a grid of main roads was launched in the 1960s. Since then three lines of metro have been built which carry about 40% of public transport passengers. The remainder of the public transportation network is operated by trams in the inner city and buses which serve outer areas. In the context of both the expected rapid growth of individual car traffic and the contemporary strategy of city planning, increasing attention is being given to the role of public transport. Further extension of the underground network is aimed to satisfy internal journeys within the city, trams and buses providing a supporting role to the underground system.

Attention is also being devoted to the Prague's metropolitan regional transport and its link with the city transportation network. New terminals for regional bus lines are to be developed, to ease pressure on the city terminal (Florenc) for national and international bus connections. International and national express trains will be channelled to Main/Wilson Railway Station, regional trains to Masaryk Railway Station, both next to Florenc which is in an area of new commercial and office development. The most important development relates to the regional railway system. High-speed tracks are to be built, with priority given to the destination at Prague's airport Ruzyně, and at Kladno, a city with population of 72 000 inhabitants located west of Prague. Furthermore the new development of the airport at Ruzyně will allow an increase in annual passenger traffic from 2 million to 5 million in the year 2005.

During the past 30 years the concept of a road network has undergone considerable change and has not been finalized yet. The grid system was transformed by a ring-road system in 1971, based on the Moscow model while a radial system was approved in 1975 and has more or less remained unaltered since. However, this has not been fully realized particularly as the north–south link brings heavy traffic from highways directly to the city centre. The proposed express ring road aims to redistribute the internal city car traffic as well as to connect national highways outside of the built area. At the present time there are heated debates about the design route of the ring road. Several studies have been conducted since 1990 which have attempted to modify the ZÁKOS (basic communication system), renamed HUS (main road network) in 1991. The Prague's Chief Architect Office (ÚHA), the Prague's Institute of Transport Engineering (PÚDIS), the State Institute of Territorial Planning (TERPLAN), the Association for Urbanism and Territorial Planning and various private agencies have produced their own proposals. The general feature of all these studies is a differentiation of the ring road according to expected traffic intensity in a particular segment. The strong antagonism of local political representations as well as some environmentalist pressure groups against the express ring road is adding to the ongoing debate.

16.4.4   Prague's Historic Reserve

One of the most important questions in contemporary city planning is how to reconcile new developments with the preservation of Prague's cultural/historical heritage. Fortunately, Prague was spared from extensive damage and destruction during both world wars and at the present time it presents a picture of an evolution of building eras which are absolutely exceptional for an area north of the Alps. It extends from the Middle Ages to Renaissance and Baroque, to the period of Classicism and the early Modern era (ÚHA, 1991a). While there are some possibilities to direct new investments into development areas in the close vicinity of the historic core this will not satisfy the considerable pressure to use historical buildings for commercial purposes. The new and progressive development cannot be curtailed but will have to be regulated so that the city's 'genius loci' (Kratochvíl, 1992) is preserved.

There is a tradition of wide public interest in the preservation of historic monuments. Indeed in 1900 the Club for Old Prague was established to defend cultural and historical monuments. The first concept for the protection of historical urban areas was formulated after the Second World War. In 1950 the Czechoslovak government designated historical cores in 30 Bohemian and Moravian towns and in 10 Slovakian towns as protected urban areas. In 1956 the Institute for Reconstruction of Urban Historic Reserves and Monuments (SÚRPMO) was founded and a systematic investigation of historical cores started. In 1960 the set of national monuments was declared; a high number of them belong to Prague's historical core.

The Czechoslovak government in August 1971 proclaimed the entire historical core of Prague an urban historic reserve protected by law. The reserve encompassed that area where the development of the city was concentrated until the nineteenth century, an area containing 13 national cultural monuments, 1400 protected architectural monuments, and about 10 000 protected works of art and artifacts. Also 36% of the housing stock is protected (Figure 16.3) in an area where only 5.6% of all houses were built since 1945. In 1981 the protective zone of the historical reserve was declared. All new developments, all modernization and all changes even outside the preserved area, which impact on the urban environment are checked. In 1993 Prague's historical reserve was put on the list of UNESCO's world cultural monuments.

Prague's Historic Reserve fulfils its city centre function with regional, national and international institutions located within it. The area covers 1.5% of the whole city territory (866 ha), it houses only 5% of city's inhabitants (60 000 people), but includes one-third of all jobs (210 000).

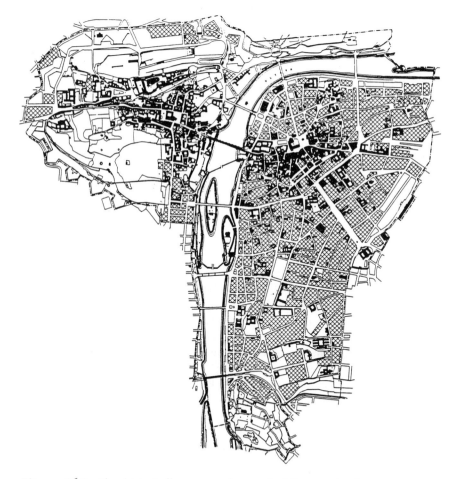

Figure 16.3 The historically protected area: buildings and other monuments protected are marked in black
Source: ÚHA (1992a) Prague: Metropolitan Area Report.

It is estimated that 460 000 persons come into this area daily (ÚHA and SÚRPMO, 1991). Clearly the contemporary transition to a market economy is bringing a more intensive commercial utilization to the historical core which could cause a further concentration of jobs, a decrease in residential function, further environmental degradation and damage cultural and aesthetic values. It is therefore necessary to reconcile new developments with the preservation of historical and cultural values.

In 1991 the capital city government charged ÚHA and SÚRPMO to undertake an urban study of Prague's historical reserve. The main conclusions of the study are to stabilize or even decrease the number of jobs within the area, to stabilize the number of inhabitants to 50 000, and to shift all major commercial and office developments to areas in close proximity of the historical core.

16.5   CONCLUSION

At the present time Czech local politicians and planners are learning, after forty years of totalitarianism, how to play their roles in a new political and economic environment. Planning activities are replaced by inconsistent and often chaotic political goals, though hopefully more comprehensible policies and planning strategies will be adopted to influence the future development of the city.

An important attempt to consolidate the control of the city territorial development is the new Master Plan. Unfortunately, the document is being prepared in an old-fashioned spirit of physical planning. There are no urban policy mechanisms effectively geared to the instant problems which are emerging during the transition. In particular, there is only a very limited knowledge on how to use economic tools to encourage urban development, and, consequently, economic incentives are not currently being used. Also no explicit link is made between city planning and contemporary real estate market performance. The application of such measures will require new knowledge transferred from 'Western' experience and closer co-operation between politicians and planners, between political bodies at various governmental levels, and between the public and private sectors.

The most important tasks to be solved by new mechanisms in the near future are concentrated in two issues. First, the necessity to create a friendly economic environment which will attract foreign investment and in this context the possibility of using financial incentives and establishing urban development corporations in some city areas have been discussed. Second, there is a necessity to solve an urgent housing shortage. Public housing projects have already been terminated and newly built houses or rehabilitated inner city apartments are affordable only for high income groups. One suggested solution has been to subsidize a transfer of municipal rental flats to private ownership (ÚHA, 1992c), in an attempt to stabilize the domestic middle class. Nevertheless, affordable flats should also be accessible to young middle- and lower- income households. Any solution of this problem will not be offered by market mechanisms, but depends on actions of public policies.

REFERENCES

Baše, M. (1993) Plány rozvoje sídlišť [Plans of housing estates development]. *Architect*, **4**, February.
Borovička, B. and Hrůza, J. (1983) *Praha: 1000 let stavby města [Prague: One Thousand Years of Urban Development]*, Panorama, Praha.
Carter, F.W. (1979) Prague and Sofia: an analysis of their changing internal city structure, in R.A. French and F.A.I. Hamilton (eds), *The Socialist City: Spatial Structure and Urban Policy*, John Wiley & Sons, Chichester–New York–Brisbane–Toronto, 425–59.
Grime, K. and Kára, J. (1990) The metropolitan region of Prague: spatial structure and population change. Paper presented to the *IV World Congress of Soviet and East European Studies*, 21–6, July, Harrogate, England.
Hrůza, J. (1992) Urban concept of Prague, *Sborník ČGS*, **97**(2), 75–87.
Jehlička, P., Kostelecký, T. and Sýkora, L. (1993) The Czechoslovak parliamentary elections in 1990: old patterns, new trends, and lots of surprises, in J. O'Loughlin and H.H. van der Wusten (eds), *The New Political Geography of Eastern Europe*, Belhaven Press, London, 235–54.
Kára, J. (1992) The capital of Prague: city growth and its administration, in P. Dostál, M. Illner, J. Kára and M. Barlow (eds), *Changing Territorial Administration in Czechoslovakia: International Viewpoints*, Universiteit van Amsterdam, Instituut voor Sociale Geografie, Amsterdam, 33–8.
Kirke, N.M. (1993) Where to begin: investigating your options in Prague real estate. *Prognosis*, 2–15 April, A special advertising supplement to Prognosis: Real estate in Czech Republic.
Kramplová, L. (1989) Vývoj cen pozemků v Praze do současnosti [The development of land prices in Prague], PhD. dissertation, Vysoké učení technické v Brně, Ústav soudního inženýrství.
Kratochvíl, P. (1992) Point de vue philosophique sur l'héritage sauvegardé de Prague, in A. Novotná-Galard and P. Kratochvíl (eds), *Prague: Avenir d'une ville historique capitale*, Éditions de l'Aube, Association pour la Communauté Culturelle Européenne, Paris, 15–29.
Michalovic, P. (1992) Housing in Czechoslovakia: Past and present problems, in B. Turner, J. Hegedüs and I. Tosics (eds), *The Reform of*

Housing in Eastern Europe and the Soviet Union, Routledge, London, 46–61.

Musil, J. (1968) The development of Prague's ecological structure, in R.E. Pahl (ed.), *Readings in Urban Sociology*, Pergamon Press, Oxford, 232–59.

Smith, D.M. (1989) *Urban Inequality Under Socialism: Case Studies from Eastern Europe and the Soviet Union*, Cambridge University Press, Cambridge.

Sýkora, L. (1993) City in transition: the role of rent gaps in Prague's revitalization, *Tijdschrift voor Economische en Sociale Geografie*, **84**(4), 281–93.

Sýkora, L. and Štěpánek, V. (1992) Prague. *Cities*, **9**(2), 91–100.

Sýkora, L. and Šimoníčková, I. (1993) From totalitarian urban economy managerialism to liberalized urban property market: Prague's transformations in early 1990s. Paper presented at the *International Workshop on Problems of Development and Administration of Prague*, Prague, Central European University Foundation, 26–27 April 1993.

ÚHA (1991a) *Workshop Prague '91: Strategy of the Future Development of Prague*.

ÚHA (1991b) *Územní plán hlavního města Prahy (první čtení)*, [The Master Plan of the Capital City of Prague (first reading)].

ÚHA (1992a) *Prague: Metropolitan Area Report*.

ÚHA (1992b) *Územní plán hlavního města Prahy (druhé čtení): plán využití ploch – stabilizovaná území*, [The Master Plan of the Capital City of Prague (second reading): land-use plan – stabilized areas].

ÚHA (1992c) *Územní plán hlavního města Prahy (druhé čtení): varianty rozvoje*, [The Master Plan of the Capital City of Prague (second reading): the variants of development].

ÚHA and SÚRPMO (1991) *Pražská památková rezervace. Urbanistická studie – koncept*, [Prague's Historic Reserve. Urban planning study – a concept].

17

Warsaw

Eamonn Judge

The radical change which Eastern Europe is now experiencing (1993) impacts visibly upon the major cities with each city struggling to reposition itself in its own context, and in the context of others. Arguably in this respect Warsaw presents a distinctly different case in comparison to other first-ranking East European cities. While the Warsaw of 1939 is remembered fondly, and perhaps with exaggeration, by old Polish expatriates in the West as 'the Paris of the East', after 1945 the image in the West is of the city wantonly destroyed and then rebuilt. Unlike, say, Prague or Budapest, where preservation from wartime destruction means that the historical base constrains the possibilities for change, the largely post-war inheritance of Warsaw is pregnant with such possibilities. Perhaps more reflective of its current situation is the view that it is a city for the visionary (Roskelly, 1993). The latter refers mainly to its prospects for the developer, but perhaps it should apply generally to all those who have a role in shaping the future of the city.

This chapter which is in nine parts commences with a background to the city as it is now. The second sets out the city's historical context, and the third discusses its post-war reconstruction as the capital of socialist Poland. The fourth considers the problems of planning in the socialist city, constituting, in a sense, the inheritance of the new era. The fifth considers the problems of adjustment which the transition to a market economy poses for the urban system. The sixth part assesses the nature of the property market as it has developed over the last four years of this adjustment process. The seventh considers the effect of change in the property market on the planning system generally, and the eighth part discusses the development of the planning framework under market conditions in Warsaw itself, especially the new Master Plan. Finally the concluding section emphasizes the need for a visionary prognosis in assessing future investment prospects in Warsaw.

European Cities, Planning Systems and Property Markets Edited by James Berry and Stanley McGreal. Published in 1995 by E & FN Spon. ISBN 0419 18940 8.

17.1   WARSAW'S CURRENT SITUATION

Warsaw, the Polish capital, lies on the River Vistula, about 520 km east of Berlin, and about 160 km from the nearest point of the former USSR (now Belarus). The Baltic is about 270 km to the north. It is situated at the junction of East–West and North–South trade routes, which brought much development to the city, and, from time to time, war and destruction (Jankowski, 1990). The current population (1990) is 1 650 000, with 2 422 000 overall including those in the Warsaw *voivodship*, or administrative region. Warsaw city within its extended post-war boundaries has an area of 485.3 sq km and a population density of 3400 persons per sq km (Wilski, 1993). It is divided into eight independent communes, though there is a city-wide administrative system which is discussed later. The population is currently declining at a rate of 2.6 per 1000 per annum, compared with growth rates of 7.2 in the 1960s and 3.2 in the 1980s. As a consequence of the Second World War, most of the city has been constructed since 1945 which presents both problems and opportunities in the current transitional situation. However despite the newness of the built fabric, the pre-war character of the city has exerted a strong influence, and a short account of this will be valuable to understanding the current situation.

17.2   WARSAW IN HISTORICAL PERSPECTIVE

Warsaw is about 700 years old, though it has been the capital of Poland only since 1596. The previous capital was Kraków in the south. Once Warsaw became the capital it grew rapidly, though its growth was punctuated by national misfortunes. It is not well known in the West that by 1600 Poland was, as the dominant partner of the Polish-Lithuanian Commonwealth, one of the most powerful nations in Europe, extending at its peak from the Baltic to the Black Sea, and from Poznan in the west to east of Smolensk (Ostrowski, 1966).

However despite its greatness, an unstable political system and the absence of defensible frontiers left the country prey to its neighbours. By 1792 Warsaw had reached a population of 120 000, but two years later partition and war precipitated decline and by 1800 the city had only 63 500 inhabitants. With Poland divided among Prussia, Russia and Austria, Warsaw became capital of the puppet Congress Kingdom of Poland within the Russian Empire. This period was nevertheless associated with renewed economic growth, punctuated by unsuccessful risings in 1831 and 1863 which again slowed growth. The second half of the nineteenth century saw rapid industrial and population expansion. In 1914 the city had a population of 885 000, compared to 223 000 in 1864. Dropping to 700 000 during the German occupation, it grew rapidly again after Poland

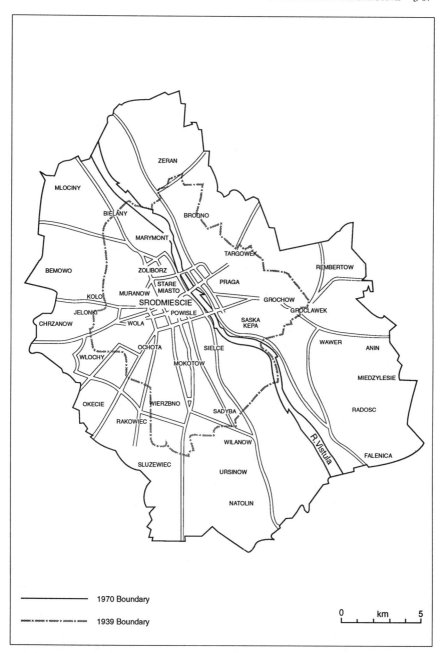

ZERAN

MLOCINY

BIELANY

BRODNO

MARYMONT

TARGOWEK

BEMOWO

ZOLIBORZ

REMBERTOW

STARE
MIASTO

PRAGA

KOLO

MURANOW

SRODMIESCIE

JELONKI

POWISLE

GROCHOW

GROCLAWEK

CHRZANOW

WOLA

SASKA
KEPA

WAWER

ANIN

OCHOTA

SIELCE

WLOCHY

MOKOTOW

MIEDZYLESIE

OKECIE

WIERZBNO

RADOSC

RAKOWIEC

SADYBA

WILANOW

R. Vistula

FALENICA

SLUZEWIEC

URSINOW

NATOLIN

———————   1970 Boundary

xxxxxx x xxxxxx   1939 Boundary

0   km   5

Figure 17.1   Main areas of Warsaw
Source: based on French and Hamilton, 1979.

regained its independence in 1918. By 1921 it had 937 000 inhabitants, and almost 1 300 000 in 1939 (Jankowski and Ciborowski, 1978).

In 1939 Warsaw was the eighth largest city in Europe, covered an area of 141 sq km, had a perimeter of 55 km, and north-south and east-west dimensions of about 12.5 km (Kasprzycki, 1984). It was a major industrial, commercial, educational, and cultural centre though having its fair share of drab industrial and tenement buildings. In 1939 70% of apartments were two rooms or less, and 46% of dwellings had no sewerage (Dziewulski, 1966). However Warsaw also had its beautiful Stare Miasto (Old Town), elegant avenues, squares, palaces, public buildings and residential areas (Jeżewskiego, 1960). Hence the epithet, justified or not, referred to Warsaw as 'The Paris of the East'. This was due to both the inheritance of nineteenth century and earlier development, and also of interwar development which included many internationally known schemes (the new East Bank residential area of Saska Kępa was exhibited at the 1926 International Housing Exhibition in Vienna (Faryna-Paszkiewicz, 1989)). The location of a number of districts of the city which are mentioned in this discussion and the pre-war and post-war boundaries are presented in Figure 17.1

The history of Warsaw from 1939 is well known abroad, but in addition, both this and its pre-war history are germaine to an understanding of its current development situation and potential. After the outbreak of war in 1939, the city fell after a three week siege. About 12% of buildings were destroyed, with 60 000 civilian casualties. The occupation was a severe trial, culminating first in the destruction of the Jewish Ghetto of about 4 sq km just west of the city centre in April/May 1943, then in the 63 day Warsaw Uprising beginning on 1 August 1944 in which approximately 150 000 civilians died. The remaining population was expelled, and those buildings not already destroyed were systematically demolished, especially historic ones. Figures are both difficult to give or comprehend, but it is estimated that 800 000 of the pre-war population of 1 300 000 perished, with total destruction of 85% of the city.

17.3   WARSAW AS A SOCIALIST CITY

Reconstruction activity in Warsaw began immediately after liberation in January 1945. An early decree in October 1945 considerably eased the reconstruction process, but had particular consequences for the current planning and development situation in the city. Namely, this decree effectively nationalized all land within the pre-war city boundaries. Buildings still belonged to the previous owners, though this had little significance as 90% of buildings had been destroyed. It meant that the planners could effectively start afresh without worrying about ownership rights. The disruption of the time meant that there was probably little practical alternative, while it gave 'something which most town planners can only dream of: complete freedom in disposing and arranging the whole area for modern urban development' (Ciborowski, 1969). While communalization of land has consequences now (1990s) as owners reclaim their property, or seek compensation, in the short term the fact that land belonged to the city gave freedom to plan, but also made planners think that land was free (Ciborowski, 1956). It took some time for them to realize that communalizing land did not eliminate the meaning of land value (Jankowski, 1990).

The first reconstruction plan was prepared as early as March 1945, with a final version in September 1946. Despite the freedom given to planners through the communalization of land, there were still some fundamental restrictions, principally although buildings were destroyed, the basic street network and underground installations were largely intact. This was however not a problem with the Stare Miasto, which was to be reconstructed in accordance with its historical context. This, and the Krakowskie Przedmiescie Street (well known in Canaletto's paintings) and the early nineteenth-century Nowy Swiat Street were completed by the mid 1950s. Outside the historic core, while the network of water and sewerage mains were followed as far as possible, the opportunity was taken to rebuild and improve the street system to provide wider streets suitable for a modern city, and provide fast through routes and access to the suburbs (Jankowski, 1990). As a result, the reconstructed centre is generally well spaced out. Thus many pre-war streets have disappeared (Kasprzycki, 1984). While the effect of ideology was less evident in the historic core reconstruction, the development of the rest of Warsaw was required to show evidence of the new Socialist era.

Thus outside the Stare Miasto and surrounding areas, the reconstruction of pre-war Warsaw was in a more modern and often 'socialist realism' style. The epitomy of this is the Palac Kultury (Palace of Culture) on the Marszalkowska completed in 1955. Said to be a gift from the USSR, it is a multi-purpose complex with congress and conference facilities, theatres and cinemas, scientific institutions and exhibition facilities. Built on what was initially part of the Ghetto, it occupies a large area of the city centre, and with its 'wedding cake' style is an alien element quite out of place and proportion, not only in the city centre, but in the city as a whole. Strangely enough, in the period of transition its presence possibly underlines the radical changes taking place. Occupied by Western companies such as Coca Cola, and surrounded by temporary shops, stalls and funfairs, the site has been the subject of competitions to decide on its possible redevelopment.

In the context of time the reconstruction of pre-war Warsaw took place remarkably quickly. Indeed the pre-war area was substantially completed by the mid-1960s. However, because the planners could plan freely, densities were much lower (ground plan comparisons with 1939 are quite marked, with the virtual disappearance of the characteristic pre-war courtyard tenement style (Luba and Stępinski, 1965)). The corollary of redesign of the pre-war core was substantial outward/peripheral development with the result that the population of the inner core was perhaps only a fifth of the pre-war total (Ciborowski, 1969).

As the reconstruction of the pre-war city took place, a sequence of master plans for the long-term development of the larger city within extended boundaries progressed simultaneously. It was these plans, together with the early physical realization of the reconstruction process which focused world attention on Polish planning. Indeed in the 1960s and 1970s many British planners thought there was much to be learnt from the Polish school of urban planning. The early master plans for Warsaw from 1945 to 1956 (six in all) focused on the immediate reconstruction. In terms of the long-term development of the city, the 1961 plan is usually taken to be the fundamental exposition (this and the 1964 revision are described by Ciborowski and Wilski (1965)). Subsequent plans in 1964, 1969, 1979, and 1982 all adopted the spatial directions laid down in the 1961 plan, although each introduced many detailed changes (Niemczyk and Romiszewski, 1990).

These plans saw the pre-war population size being reached and then exceeded in housing areas which extended out in radial 'belts' of lower density development from the pre-war urban core where housing densities were also significantly reduced. These belts were separated by green wedges, which also extended along the Vistula river to protect the low riverside escarpment from development (which was the only significant physical feature in the otherwise flat city area). The belts were the ecological basis of the plan, allowing the city to 'breathe'. Despite the destruction of Warsaw, the belt concept was very much influenced by the development possibilities suggested by the pre-war structure of the Warsaw region, with the development of relatively unharmed satellite towns extending out along the lines of the radial rail routes from the city (Dziewulski, 1966). Incorporated into the belts were a number of industrial areas, seven in all, thus establishing a very clear separation between housing and industry. The city centre of Warsaw was to provide the higher level retail and service functions, and in the rest of the planned area a hierarchy of service centres providing lower order retail requirements. The housing and industrial areas would be served by an efficient and cheap public transport system of buses and trams, with ultimately a metro system (Figure 17.2). High-rise development was to predominate with the exception of private developments, and pre-existing older housing mainly on the relatively less damaged east bank (Wilski, 1990).

In a sense, given the limited constraints, implementation of such a master plan might be considered a large, but relatively straightforward

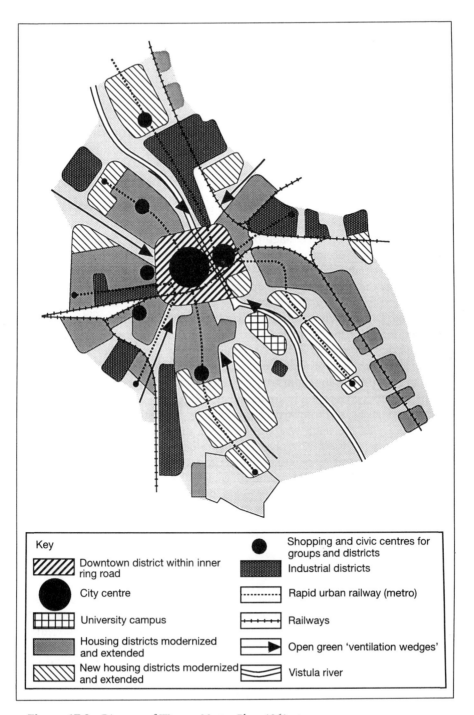

Figure 17.2 Diagram of Warsaw Master Plan, 1961 *et seq.*
Source: based on Wilski, 1990.

undertaking. However there were obvious difficulties that could be fore-seen. The blue print approach implies that the whole concept must be in place for it to operate effectively. For example the radial belts depend on the transport system, resulting in a relatively more dispersed city, with a rigid separation between work and residence location, and the service centres need to be implemented to avoid extra pressure on the city centre. The concept was clearly land-intensive and unlike a typical Western city growing on a more incremental basis, there was much less scope for adjustment if parts of the plan were not implemented.

17.4 PROBLEMS OF SOCIALIST URBAN PLANNING

The development of Warsaw took place within a socialist economy, and quite apart from the early attempts to create a visually 'socialist' city, the *modus operandi* of such an economy and society impacted at an urban level. The socialist economy was centrally planned, with rapid industri-alization as the main objective. Master plans were intended to integrate with national and regional economic plans. However, the latter were driven by the industrial ministries who tended to implement their plans independently of the municipalities. This frequently caused plan changes as ministries implemented developments not envisaged in the plan (Ryder, 1992). The allocation of resources tended to operate by a bidding process, with the ministries and industrial combines having more power than the municipalities: consequently industrial development got priority, whereas housing, social and infrastructural services received a lower priority. Imbalance was inevitable and furthermore there were problems in the planning process itself. The process of producing master plans consumed inordinate time and resources, while more short-term urban management problems were ignored. Also when it suited the politicians, the plan was simply ignored. On top of these were the inefficiencies in the socialist economy which impacted on the urban planning and development process in Warsaw.

17.4.1 Housing

High-rise housing was not unusual in pre-war Poland and in the 1950s and 1960s there were many good examples of housing development. However, as time went on, and quantity became more important than quality, the relative concentration on high-rise development produced monotonous development patterns (Judge, 1990). Using industrialized building tech-niques, the role of site planning was subordinated to the operational requirements of plant and machinery. Development became increasingly space intensive suiting the demands of the large construction companies which favoured the development of green field sites and resulted in extensive peripheral expansion. The lack of services provision and adequate transport facilities in outer suburban areas caused them to be described by the eminent Polish planner, Chmielewski as 'areas of forced residence' (Wilski, 1990). Low-rise development undertaken by private initiative produced another type of urban sprawl which took place beyond the official master plan area.

17.4.2   Transport

While a visitor might have considered public transport in the urban core both cheap and efficient, the Warsaw inhabitants tend to be more critical. Despite the fact that the tram system has almost complete coverage outside the city centre, it was not the intention to have trams (and buses to a lesser extent) bear the brunt of the public transport demand. Whereas the rail system brings in commuters from the outlying towns, it makes very little contribution to moving people around within the city. The earliest versions of the master plans envisaged a metro system which would 'eliminate tramways from mid-town Warsaw' (Ciborowski, 1969) but its development was dogged in the early years due to unfavourable geological conditions. By the 1950s it was felt these difficulties had been overcome sufficiently to enable the opening of the first underground line before 1960 (Ciborowski, 1956). However writing in 1969, Ciborowski described the non-completion of the metro as 'the most dramatic town-planning failure of the post-war reconstruction period'. According to Ciborowski tramway lines had to be laid out along the new, modern thoroughfares in the centre of Warsaw. Latterly the problems became more economic, especially during the stagnation of the 1980s. In 1993 the metro is still not open, though one line from Kabaty in the Mokotów district to the centre near Warsaw Polytechnic is almost complete. Some observers question if the line is in the right place, given other more recent changes that have taken place, while the possible impact of the line on development trends would appear not to have been sufficiently considered (Ryder, 1992).

Furthermore the post-war trend of creating separate industrial areas, often on the periphery, separated from housing, has created a demand for travel particularly cross-commuting. Lijewski (1987) argues that Warsaw's population requires a great deal of transport because most people did not freely chose their place of residence but were forced to take an allocated flat due to a scarcity of residential properties. Changing residence was extremely difficult and in consequence most people live at distances from their workplaces or places of interest. Also problems were compounded by failures in the service sector, particularly as a considerable amount of land reserved for suburban service centres was never utilized. Apart from leaving large gaps around the city, residents lacked services which could only be obtained by travelling to the centre or elsewhere on an inadequate public transport system.

Unauthorized development under the socialist regime in Warsaw meant that development outside of the plan frequently took place. This may have been due to the cumulative effect of individuals ignoring regulations, or more importantly, as a result of the ministries for different economic sectors pushing through plans irrespective of the contents of the master plan. An example of this in Warsaw concerns the Huta Warszawa Steel Works in the north of the city built to proletarianize the employment structure of the city, but contrary to the master plan was constructed between a residential area and a national park. In addition there are other examples of unplanned development viz the scattered development of individual houses on large plots on the urban periphery, 'temporary' houses on allotments within urban areas, and summer houses in the countryside (Mezga, 1993). Whether temporary developments built with permission, or permanent developments without permission, all look likely to remain, and promise to pose a serious problem in years to come (Judge, 1992).

17.4.3   Urban conservation

The massive efforts to rebuild historic areas has overshadowed the failure to preserve existing buildings. This is due to a number of reasons such as the lack of resources, rent controls, the absence of a role for land values and poor property management. Combined with pollution which is also a major problem and low maintenance standards many fine nineteenth-century buildings have consequently deteriorated badly.

17.5   THE IMPACT OF ECONOMIC AND POLITICAL CHANGE

The constraints of the master plan system were merely a reflection of the problems in the economy and society generally. As the economy stagnated in the early 1980s, and with Solidarity banned and martial law declared, it became apparent as the decade progressed that radical change in the management of the economy was necessary which would ultimately have an impact on the planning system. Before the collapse of the old order, Regulski and Wawrynski (1989) argued that without fundamental reorientation, the Polish planning system would clearly disintegrate.

Once the decision was made to move quickly towards a market economy under the 'shock therapy' of the Balcerowicz plan from January 1990, the problems of the old system clearly stood out (Sachs, 1993). Although the socialist system may not have created a socialist city as such (French and Hamilton, 1979), it created a city which reflected many of the short-comings of the socialist economy. In comparison with a Western market economy the socialist economy was both unbalanced and underdeveloped, with the same argument applying to the socialist city (Ryder, 1992). Over-endowed with inefficient heavy industry, Warsaw lacked the services and modern infrastructure of a Western city. Office and retail space was both in short supply and of poor quality. However in an emerging market economy, these problems are also opportunities and the property sector is one where changes are likely to be most apparent.

17.6 THE PROPERTY MARKET

While Prague and Budapest have initially seemed more promising property markets, with private investors finding less political uncertainty and less bureaucracy, the fundamental features and strengths of Warsaw are now emerging more clearly. Namely it is the capital of a much larger country than its two competitors, and thus has more growth potential. Also, in physical terms the aftermath of the last war has created ample development space in central Warsaw (Jones, 1993).

Thus two major sites have been the focus of much attention (Figure 17.3). The first concerns the Palace of Culture which stands in the centre of an enormous site (20 ha gross) which is only partially occupied by the building itself, and represents a major development possibility for modern Warsaw (Wyporek, 1993b). The commercial potential along with the desire to change the character of the area in the new era led to the initiation of a design competition in May 1991. An entry from Brussels by Bielyszew and Skopinski won the competition with an imaginative design which evoked comparisons with New York (Pakalski, 1993). However the fundamental issue of financing the proposed development scheme is yet to be resolved. The second site although smaller has also enormous potential. The Plac Teatralny which for a variety of reasons was not particularly well developed, occupies an area of historical and cultural significance in Warsaw. The scheme, involving 60 000 sq m of development, has been put out to overseas tender (Matyjaszkiewicz, 1993).

17.6.1 The hotel sector

Since 1989, the tourism and business travel sector has grown rapidly in Eastern Europe (at rates of 50% per annum). This has highlighted the deficiencies in the hotel and tourism industry, but also the opportunities for future development. In contrast to Prague and Budapest, Warsaw has low provision of hotel bedspaces. Budapest has about 100 bedspaces per 10 000 inhabitants, Prague about 90, and Warsaw has less than 50. The

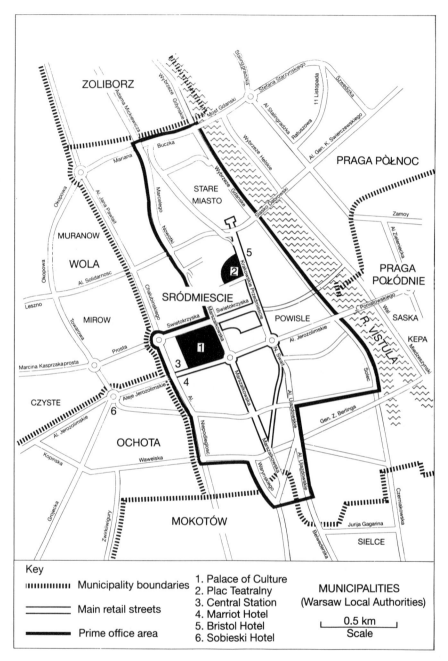

Figure 17.3 The Central District of Warsaw
Source: redrawn from original base maps.

overall deficit is revealed by comparison with Vienna, which has about 330 bedspaces per 10 000 inhabitants (Hudson, 1993).

The pressure in some parts of the market is reflected in hotel rates. In July 1991, 3–5 star hotels in Warsaw varied between $60–$175 per night, and in December 1992 the range had extended to $50–$210 per night. Thus there is a shortage of high quality hotels: in 1990 only 52 out of 480 hotels in the whole of Poland were four star or above, although several new developments have been completed, with others in the pipeline. A recent addition is the refurbished Hotel Bristol on the edge of the Stare Miasto which was completed in December 1992 at a cost of $50 million, and represents the first true five-star hotel in Poland. The four star Sobieski was completed in 1991 and the Mercure in 1993.

17.6.2   The office sector

In Warsaw there is a shortage of good-quality office space with rents among the highest of the Eastern Europe cities. Indeed rents are considerably in excess of several Western European cities, for example rents in Warsaw are double those in Brussels, though half those in London (Hudson, 1993). Although there is ample development space in central Warsaw, a recognized central business core does not yet exist and speculation continues regarding where it will ultimately emerge, if at all (Grzesik, 1992). This gives rise to some degree of uncertainty concerning where is ultimately the best location for development. Furthermore the fragmentation of local authority control among the districts of Warsaw (Figure 17.3) means, that there is an element of competition between them for development. Getting development off the ground is also slowed by bureaucratic procedures, and especially where there is a dearth of basic infrastructure such as the shortage of telephone lines and the non-completion of the metro system.

In spite of the constraints, a considerable volume of construction is currently (1993) being achieved, some having recently been completed. This is urgently required, as only 7.4% of the office space in the city is available in multi-user buildings suitable for commercial tenants. The rest (92.6% of 1 347 000 m^2) is occupied by state enterprises and central and local government administration. This accounts for the stopgap appearance of converted flats and hotel rooms being used as office accommodation. Demand for high-quality office space from overseas companies requiring representative accommodation up to 300 m^2 is high. It is estimated that the city needs over 25 000 m^2 of space per annum for some years to come, to meet the growing demand of the 17 000 Polish and Western companies which are registered and is increasing at the rate of 500 companies per month (Anisfeld and Hudson, 1993). International comparisons suggest that Warsaw will experience a high growth in office space demand for several years to come (Bellman, 1992).

Rents are currently at levels of $45–$55 per m^2 per month for modern centrally located space, with a 30–40% discount on this for out of centre locations. It is anticipated that supply will grow from 2300 m^2 in 1992 to 8600 m^2 in 1993, to 33 000–67 000 m^2 in 1996 and to 17 000–31 000 m^2 per annum from 1997 to 2002, while demand remains consistently above the rate of input. Thus, it seem likely that rentals will remain high over the foreseeable future.

17.6.3 The retail sector

Prior to 1989 shops in Warsaw were, by and large, dingy, drab, and half empty of goods, with queues ubiquitous. The retail sector has progressed rapidly from on-street trading, to stalls, to wooden cabins, and finally to the privatization of state shop units. While in 1988 only 13% of shops were privately owned, the current (1993) figure represents 80% (Anisfeld and Hudson, 1993). In fact the city is beginning to attract new shopping centres and superstores (which in relation to total space still remains a rarity). Despite the increase in private ownership, the retail sector is as yet underdeveloped. It is estimated that Warsaw alone needs 200 000–300 000 m^2 of extra retail space by 1995. More generally, Poland had less retail space per head of population than even the former USSR, less than 2000 m^2 per 10 000 population, while the UK has about 8500 m^2 (Hudson, 1993). Although the under-provision of retail space has been marginally compensated by the doubling in the number of shops between 1989 and 1991 (Rostowski, 1993), major retail outlets are required to meet demand.

Even though there are numerous retail developments in the pipeline, there is a considerable distance to go before the retail sector in Warsaw approaches the mass consumer image of Western European cities. The first supermarkets with extensive carparking provision and electronic scanning checkouts were opened by the Austrian group Billa in Warsaw in September 1992, but the first out of town shopping mall may yet be some time in the future. Rentals for retail floor space still remain attractive for investors, running at $70–$100 per m^2 per annum in prime central area locations (though data from local informants in December 1993 suggest that values are higher at $200–$300 per m^2 for the best sites), $30–$50 on the periphery of the central area, and $5–$20 in the Warsaw suburbs. Outside of Warsaw these prices would be 20% less in the larger cities (Anisfeld and Hudson, 1993).

17.6.4 The residential property sector

Currently (1993) real incomes are low, inflation is high, public housing expenditure is very restricted as indeed are the opportunities to borrow

Table 17.1 Apartment prices by size band, Warsaw 1993 (prices for 1, 2, 3 and 4 room flats in million złoty per square metre)

Rental range	5 m zł & <7 m	7 m zł & <9 m	9 m zł & <11 m	11 m zł & <13 m	13 m zł & over	Row total
Area <40 sq m	4	14	5	1	1	25
40 sq m & <70	6	29	13	5	2	55
70 sq m & <100	3	4	2	1	1	11
Over 100 sq m	1	0	1	0	0	2
Col Total	14	47	21	7	4	93

Source: Zycie Warszawy, 30 June 1993.

for housing finance. Hence, the market for the main output of the development industry (high-rise blocks of flats) is very sluggish. At the start of 1993, the Ministry of Physical Development and Construction reported that 12 000 new apartments stood empty, a statistic which is likely to increase to 30 000. Simultaneously 1.6 million families wait to be housed (Pietura, 1993a). Of course, a high proportion of the housing stock is still publicly owned in some form or other, though patterns and categories of ownership are complex. Owner occupation in Poland in 1990 was about 40%, but in the cities this was much lower. Generally, Poland's housing stock still continues to function for the most part under conditions imposed by a socialist, non-market economy (Herbst and Muziol-Weclawowicz, 1993).

Nevertheless, where there are those who own and wish to sell, and those with money to buy, there is an active market with property pricing now apparent in a way which would not have existed prior to 1989. As far as flats are concerned, prices continue to vary radically among Warsaw districts (Pietura, 1993a). The most sought after flats are around 30–40 m² in size, fetching prices of 6.2–7.8 million złoty per m² (a million złoty being about £40 in June 1993). Though property price data tends to be fragmentary, and difficult to compare between sources, Table 17.1 compiled for 93 flats in the Zycie Warszawy for 30 June 1993 provides data consistent with Pietura's figures. The overall average price is about 8.5 million złoty per m².

The variation in prices of course reflects not merely distance from the centre, but the presence of preferred and less preferred areas. Prices in desirable areas are 5 to 6 million złoty per m² higher in the Sródmiescie (centre), Mokotów, and Ursynów than in Praga, Bemowo and Tarchomin. Prices in Warsaw are significantly above those in other Polish cities. In Poznan, for example, the average is about 4.5 million złoty per m², and in Bydgoszcz about 3.7 million per m² (Pietura, 1992a). Generally, prices in large cities outside Warsaw are 20% lower.

As regards housing provision, there is a generally slow market, although single family houses and villas in attractive suburban towns attract market interest. Houses of $200-250\,m^2$ in attractive towns near Warsaw (Wilanów, Komorowo, Pyry and Międzylesic) cost on average 1.5 to 2 billion złoty (Pietura, 1992a). Within Warsaw, prices vary according to area: the most expensive is a house in the centre or Zoliborz (respectively 25 and 23 million złoty per square metre), Saska Kępa and Mokotów are medium price (14 and 12 million złoty per square metre respectively), Wola and Ochota are least preferred (7 and 6.2 million złoty per square metre) (Anisfeld and Hudson, 1993). Though mass market housing is largely unattractive as a development possibility, there nevertheless seems to be potentially profitable business from expatriates and the local well-to-do.

Self-build housing is one means of entering into home ownership. This may start as a summer house, and the usual first step is to obtain or purchase a plot. For many years scattered housing development has taken place around Warsaw and other major cities (Mezga, 1993), and is ubiquitous for $15-25\,km$ out of Warsaw in any direction. This development is often subject to limited, or no planning control and with increasing motorization could assume much greater significance as a problem area (Judge, 1992). As a reflection of the current economic difficulties, building plots near Warsaw fell 50% in price during 1992 from $10-$15 to $5-$7 per square metre (Pietura, 1993b).

Despite the glum view of the market, there are nevertheless encouraging changes taking place. Official estimates consider that $59 billion needs to be invested in Polish housing to the year 2000 which would tend to indicate enormous demand providing a satisfactory financial framework exists. Since November 1991 local authorities have been free to dispose of land and building, and as they own 80% of Polish real estate (Anisfeld and Hudson, 1993) this is seen as a significant first step. Laws are now required to allow restitution of property, and to provide a suitable framework for housing finance. The latter is progressing slowly, though a number of schemes are in operation which are supported by the World Bank and the US Government. Though limited in scale, they should provide a precedent for the development of housing finance schemes.

17.6.5 The industrial sector

In relative terms, industry is possibly the sector which has experienced the least amount of change. Given the rapid development of external trade, the need for warehousing and manufacturing space, and the unsuitability and poor condition of buildings vacated by the closure of inefficient state industries, this would tend to suggest that there ought to be a greater amount of development in the industrial sector. However, this has not been the case to date. While recognizing some of the obstacles to development, such as problems of title, planning and finance, Łozinski (1993) also stresses the difficulties associated with the immense lack of infrastructure which can particularly affect sites which would otherwise appear suitable for industrial development. For instance, most of Warsaw south of the residential district of Mokotów is not connected to the district sewage and drainage system. Often indeed for development to proceed it is necessary for the developer to provide infrastructure as well, and recoup the costs later.

In Warsaw, the most popular areas for new industrial/warehouse development are in Ochota near the airport, at the Katowice/Kraków motorway junctions in south Warsaw, and at Raszyn and Janki. These are high-quality serviced facilities with rental levels of $12–15 per m^2 per month (with capital values estimated at $1000–1300 per m^2). It is estimated that for the next two years the supply of new space in the Warsaw area will be about 80 000 m^2, but demand is 300–500 000 m^2. Consequently considerable potential exists if the obstacles can be overcome: but the property market, especially in Warsaw, has been obsessed with office developments and has failed to recognize the opportunities on offer from the industrial sector (Łozinski, 1993).

17.6.6 The construction industry

The changes taking place in the various property sectors also impact on the construction industry. As in the case of most industries in socialist economies, the Polish construction industry was composed of large combines, and consequently the multitude of small to medium-sized building firms so ubiquitous in Western European economies are not present in Poland to the same extent (European Construction Research, 1993). Industry based on large combines is best suited to the undertaking of large development projects, for example those commissioned by government ministries and where there is less emphasis on building costs. This impacted on the built environment, as did the deterioration of the Polish economy in the 1970s and 1980s, which resulted in declining investment, low-quality standards and low productivity in the construction industry. Nevertheless, in the context of Eastern Europe the Polish construction industry is considered to be one of the most efficient (Anisfeld and Hudson, 1993), and indeed some of its enterprises, such as Budimex, have a high reputation abroad. It is predicted that the Polish construction industry will undergo a transition to a profile which is more typical of Western Europe and away from gigantic projects and large state-owned companies (European Construction Research, 1993).

17.7 THE IMPACT OF CHANGE IN THE PROPERTY MARKET ON PLANNING

The transition to a market economy since 1989 has produced rapid change in the property market. It has also become apparent that changes to the planning system are necessary. The early post-war reconstruction period was one of apparent success in which the planning system was oriented to the physical realization of goals which were contained in national and regional economic plans. The success of this period led to the emergence of the 'Polish school of urban planning' (Wyporek, 1993a). The legislative process which produced the systems of master plans in Warsaw was the 1961 Physical Planning Act. This, and various environmental and building laws, plus the final version of the Act on Spatial Planning (1984), formed the legal basis of planning in 1989 which continues to be the case pending the passing of new legislation. The emphasis of the system was on the preparation of long-term regional and local development plans (i.e. master plans). The regional plans were approved by the Voivodship Council (i.e. the regional authority), while master plans and detailed urban plans were approved by the City Council (neither of which were truly independent local authorities). In theory, this represented a very favourable planning model but in reality the strict hierarchical system proved to be too rigid to be workable and effective (Wyporek, 1993a). Furthermore, the socialist legal framework was extremely confusing, and this has been at the root of many present urban conflicts and problems (Dekker *et al.*, 1992).

Given these deficiencies within the system, the planning framework was inappropriate for the operations of a market economy. The former system of rigid land use allocations was incompatible with the sort of planning instrument required in an economy where most resources come from the private sector, and where the priority of the planning system is to control development in the public interest on the one hand and to encourage private-sector investment and development on the other. In a market economy the planning system has a key role to play facilitating public and private sector partnership in the development process.

The drafting of a new law to reflect the changing conditions was carried out from early 1990 onwards, and went through many versions (there were said to have been 16). Producing the new law was a controversial process: indeed there were many who wished to go for a free market approach with a minimum of planning involvement. Arguably planning was associated too closely in the public mind with the previous regime, and it was difficult to communicate the necessity and role of a different type of planning in a different system. Kowalewski, the then Deputy Minister, summed up the situation and its urgency when he said in 1992:

> this reform will be very complicated and will face many obstacles
> and thresholds. Nevertheless, this reform is, for many reasons, ex-

tremely urgent. The environmental pollution is permanently increasing in Poland and the uncontrolled urban development has become a common feature of our country. (Kowalewski, 1992)

In 1992 the Building Code Bill and the Physical Planning Bill came before Parliament for ratification. The former was adopted in March 1993 by the Lower Chamber of Parliament, but the Physical Planning Bill (Sejm, 1993) was still awaiting the same procedure when Parliament was dissolved by President Wałesa earlier in 1993 in preparation for the September election. One might have expected a reappraisal with the new government, but in fact the Bill has already (November 1993) been sent to the Sejm.

As far as the current proposal for the new Physical Planning Bill is concerned, a change from the old system specifies that the only level of administration for which a legally binding development plan can be prepared is the lowest level, or commune (gmina). Higher level plans at the voivodship (or, in the case of Warsaw, which is divided into seven communes, the city level) are not legally required, and if prepared will have only an advisory role. However, a commune does not have to prepare a plan if it so decides, though in this case any land-use decisions which are made may be overseen by the voivodship authority (an unelected body responsible to central government). As is appropriate to the new era, the Physical Planning Bill enshrines the legal protection of private property ownership. It also incorporates measures to strengthen public particip-ation, and to extend the openness of the planning process (Wyporek, 1993a). Plans formulated under the legislation would have to indicate areas where development would be allowed, and to specify where land was reserved for infrastructure and other public uses. In the case of the latter owners of the reserved land would be compensated at full market value. The provisions contained in the legislation seem not unusual in the context of market planning frameworks, though Polish planners, while welcoming the legislation seem pessimistic about the Bill, especially with regard to the lack of a regional planning framework, and the optional requirement for plan preparation. It remains to be seen what changes the new government will introduce, but first indications are that very few of the outstanding bills will be passed in the form they were in before the election.

17.8 THE DEVELOPMENT OF THE PLANNING FRAMEWORK IN WARSAW

Although a new planning law in its final form is still awaited, the election of independent local governments in May 1990 changed the position vis à vis the plans produced under the old system. The new authorities 'main-tained a considerable reserve towards draft plans of physical development for districts prepared in a different political, social and economic situation'

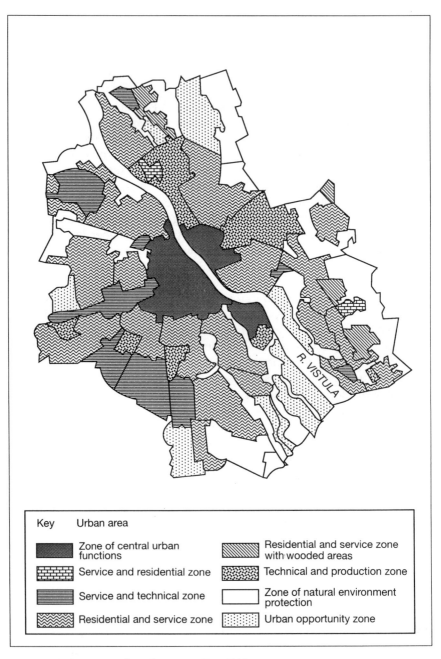

Figure 17.4 Master Plan of Warsaw City, 1992
Source: redrawn from Rosciszewski, 1993.

(Niemczyk, 1993). The existing Master Plan of Warsaw, and of the central area, were considered too rigid, detailed and unreal, and very wasteful in terms of land use.

Accordingly, a new plan was prepared and approved in September 1992 by Warsaw City Council. The new plan departed from the former practice of master plans of specifying detailed land-use allocations for specific investments. Instead it is based on the use of functional zoning and although not employed before, such an approach is not contrary to the currently effective 1984 Planning Act (Rościszewski, 1993). Functional zoning is based on dividing the city into zones characterized by dominant land use types (Figure 17.4). These zones were based on analyses of existing programmes and solutions derived from the 1982 plan, subsequent planning studies up to 1991, plus the applications and proposals of the new Warsaw local authorities, social organizations, private citizens and other private bodies. In the case of those zones where the dominant functions could only be determined in more detailed local plans prepared by individual municipalities these were recorded as urban opportunity zones.

The Plan has three functions: first to act as a co-ordinating mechanism between the local plans of each local authority; second to ensure a city wide framework for environmental and ecological protection; and third to provide an information base. The Plan indicates for each zone a series of preferences, allowances and exclusions which 'define the area of acceptable leeway in the selection of locations for new investments during the location process, as well as defining the sphere of maintaining and modernising or liquidating existing investments' (Rościszewski, 1993). The Plan no longer sets out a comprehensive physical development programme, but does include public investment programmes for transport and technical infrastructure, and public facilities such as schools and hospitals (Niemczyk, 1993).

The Plan clearly will be implemented over time and although it is perhaps too early to comment on its operational aspects, a number of problems have already been raised in relation to it. First, local government organization in Warsaw is a potential problem in that Warsaw City Council is an indirectly elected body, consisting of members elected from and by the elected councillors of the individual communes of the city. At its best, the process of preparing a Master Plan which is acceptable to all communes must involve compromise: Niemczyk (1993) refers to the 'new negotiating function' which is necessary between the various parties, private and public, involved in the development of Warsaw. At its worst, the words of Letowski (1993) may be appropriate: 'This city is dying before our eyes. It is not only the victim of the general collapse of the country, but also of the labyrinthine division of the city into independent communes. Above the communes is a mayor who is virtually powerless...' (Letowski, 1993).

This is perhaps an aspect of what Poles themselves mention frequently, and what the Pope described as the national vice: 'an exaggerated individualism which leads to the fragmentation and division of the socio-political scene. Its forte lies in opposition, and not in the constructive proposals that lead to successful government' (Gawronski, 1993). While these opinions may appear severe, most Poles would be more moderate in their criticism of the local authority structure in Warsaw.

A second problem concerns land ownership within the 1939 Warsaw boundary which was communalized in 1945. While it is the declared intention of government to return lands to former owners, and invitations to register claims have been made, the practical measures to allow restitution have not been finalized, let alone submitted to Parliament. No matter how appropriate the master plan is, if ownership structures remain unclear development will be held back. There are at present 70 000 unsettled claims for Warsaw alone (Anisfeld and Hudson, 1993), and concerning the problem of clear title, Losinski considers this to be a developer's nightmare and is of the opinion that dealing effectively with the restitution of property should be one of the main priorities of government (Losinski, 1993). In the case of Warsaw, restitution is less likely than some type of compensation, though this has not yet been determined (Herbst and Muziol-Weclawowicz, 1993). Thus, property regulations in Warsaw are complex (Niespodziewańska, 1992).

A third problem which may impact on investment and development is difficulty in getting planning permission. Developers still see this process as inordinately bureaucratic and time-consuming. It is not uncommon for the planning of a commercial development to take more than two years to reach the construction stage, and indeed the District of Wola, for example, expects this (Losinski, 1993). This is a significant criticism especially, as Wola District is reputed to be one of the more entrepreneurial of the Warsaw local authorities (and they are all now publicizing development opportunities extensively), though inspection of its procedures for granting planning permission indicates a period rather more like 15–18 months, which may nevertheless be regarded as too long (Buczek, 1992). Michonski argues that Poland is loaded with regulations, and this is unlikely to change in the near future (Michonski, 1992). All of these factors create a complex and difficult climate for the development process, which is emphasized by the fact that despite the large number of developments proposed in Warsaw, speculation continues over how many will actually by completed.

17.9 CONCLUSION

Though some writers (Walker, 1993) are pessimistic about the prospects of non-capital cities in Eastern Europe, there seems, in spite of the problems associated with planning systems and property markets, overall optimism about the prospects of the capital cities (Hall, 1993). In this context Warsaw seems to generate more optimism than most of its competitors (Musil, 1993). Nevertheless, this chapter has revealed a complex framework against which to judge its future prospects. The Warsaw municipalities are scrambling to be more entrepreneurial, looking actively for international investors to develop prime sites and the property press is replete with advertisements. The city planners have produced a new master plan more suited to market conditions despite still working within the framework of the old socialist legislation. Although the inherent economic prospects of the economy appear encouraging downside aspects include: the poor state of infrastructure and the general built environment, a difficult business climate for overseas investors, a slow bureaucracy, fragmented local government, and uncertainties over land titles.

Thus, Warsaw is not a city for the faint-hearted investor looking for quick returns. The 'up-front' costs are considerable, and it is necessary to take a long view. Over the longer term perspective observers are more optimistic. Thus, for so many reasons, it is no ordinary city, but as Roskelly would put it, it is a city for visionaries (Roskelly, 1993), those who can make the subtle balance between current known problems and future uncertain gains. There are few such visionaries, but those there are will profit handsomely.

Finally given the city's history, the politicians and the planning and property professionals shaping its future also need to be visionaries. As the city approaches its 400th anniversary as capital in 1996, the visionary approach must go further than recognizing the need to encourage imaginitive conceptions of physical form and image for the city. Much more important will be vision in bringing together all the conditions – political, legal, financial and administrative – which will form the basis for securing investment and development opportunity in a market economy.

Acknowledgements

The author wishes to acknowledge the assistance received from colleagues in Warsaw and in particular Dr M. Niemczyk, Dr B. Wyporek and Grzegorz Buczek for providing comments on the text and to Phillipa Boyce for reproduction of graphics. The chapter benefited from work carried out by the author during 1993 on an EC Research Fellowship based at the Foundation in Support of Democracy, Warsaw and supported by EC DG X11 (Co-operation in Science and Technology).

REFERENCES

Anisfeld, L. and Hudson, P. (eds) (1993) *Real Estate Development in Poland*, Interforum Publications, London, 3rd Edition.

Bellman, T. (1992) The demand for office accommodation in Warsaw, *Estates News*, **12**(16) December, 5–6.

Buczek, G. (1992) Communal land development. Wola: a case study, *Estates Times*, **8**(11), June, 13–16.

Ciborowski, A. (1956) *Town Planning in Poland, 1945–1955*, Polonia, Warsaw.

Ciborowski, A. and Wilski, J. (eds) (1965) *Plan Generalny Warszawy* (General Plan of Warsaw), Wydawnictwo PRN m.st. Warszawy.

Ciborowski, A. (1969) *Warsaw, A city Destroyed and Rebuilt*, Interpress Publishers, Warsaw.

Dekker, A., Goverde, H., Markowski, T. and Ptaszynska-Woloczkowicz, M. (1992) *Conflict in Urban Development: A Comparison Between East and West Europe*, Ashgate, Aldershot.

Dziewulski, S. (1966) Development of the General Plan of Warsaw, in J.C. Fisher (ed.), *City and Regional Planning in Poland*, Cornell University Press, Ithaca, 85–106.

European Construction Research (1993) *Construction and Property in Poland*, ECR, Copenhagen, February.

Faryna-Paszkiewicz, H. (1989) *Saska Kępa 1918–1939, Architektura i Urbanistyka*, Wydawnictwo Polskiej Akademii Nauk, Wrocław.

French, R.A. and Hamilton, F.E.I. (eds) (1979) *The Socialist City: Spatial Structure and Urban Policy*, John Wiley & Sons, Chichester.

Gawronski, J. (1993) States of savagery, seeds of good, *Guardian*, 2 November, 11.

Grzesik, K. (1992) Warsaw office supply – an alternative view, *Estates News*, **12**(15), December, 7–8.

Hall, P. (1993) Forces shaping Urban Europe, *Urban Studies*, **30**(6), 883–98.

Herbst, I. and Muziol-Weclawowicz, A. (1993) Housing in Poland: problems and reforms, *Cities*, **10**(3), 246–56.

Hudson, P. (1993) Scope for and funding of urban regeneration in eastern Europe, in J. Berry, S. McGreal and B. Deddis (eds), *Urban Regeneration: Property Investment and Development*, E & F Spon, London, 77–94.

Jankowski, S. and Ciborowski, A. (1978) *Warsaw: 1945, Today and Tomorrow*, Interpress, Warsaw.

Jankowski, J. (1990) Warsaw: destruction, secret town planning, 1939–44, and postwar reconstruction, in J.M. Diefendorf (ed.), *Rebuilding Europe's Bombed Cities*, Macmillan, London, 77–93.

Jeżewskiego, A. (1960) *Warszawa na Starej Fotografii* (Warsaw in Old Photographs), Wydawnictwo Artystyczno-Graficzne, Warsaw.

Jones, A. (1993) Polish realty, *Central European Business Weekly* (Realty Supplement), June.

Judge, E. (1990) Going to market: the Polish planning system meets the free economy, *Planning*, No. 893, 2 November, Ambit Publications, Gloucester.

Judge, E. (1992) Energy, environment, transport and land use: an Anglo-Polish comparison, *Conference of Association of European Environmental and Resource Economists*, Kraków, June.

Kasprzycki, J. (1984) *Warszawa Jak Było: Oryginalne mapy Stolicy sprzed 1939 i z 1945 roku* (Warsaw as It Was: Original City Maps before 1939 and in 1945), Wydawnictwa ALFA, Warsaw.

Kowalewski, A. (1992) *Ministerial Statement* (mimeo), Ministry of Physical Planning and Construction, Warsaw, February.

Letowski, J. (1993) Polish public administration between crisis and renewal, *Public Administration*, **70** (Spring/Summer), 1–12.

Lijewski, T. (1987) Transport in Warsaw, *Transport Reviews*, **7**(2), 95–118.

Losinski, J. (1993) Warsaw: commercial space supply, *Estates Times*, **1** (17), January 5–6.

Łozinski, J.A. (1993) Industrial property market, *Estates Times*, **10**(26), October, 14.

Luba, J. and Stępiński (1965) Sródmieście (The City Centre), in A. Ciborowski and J. Wilski (eds), *Plan Generalny Warszawy* (General Plan of Warsaw), Wydawnictwo PRN m.st. Warszawy.

Matyjaszkiewicz, J. (1993) Teatralny Square in Warsaw, in *Raport, Planowanie i Rozwój Przestrzenny-Wyzwania i Alternatywy dla Europe Srodkoweji Wschodniej w Latach 90.* (Report: Challenges and Choices in Physical Planning and Development – Central and Eastern Europe in the Nineties), Międzynarodowy Kongres TUP (International Congress of Polish Society of Town Planners), Warsaw, June 1993, 84–7.

Mezga, D. (1993) Polish para-urbanisation: residential sprawl within the urban-rural fringe, *Town Planning Review*, **64**(1), 23–35.

Michonski, D.M. (1992) The Warsaw environment for office space supply, *Estates News*, **11**(15), November, 6–8.

Musil, J. (1993) Changing urban systems in post-communist societies in Central Europe: analysis and prediction, *Urban Studies*, **30**(6), 899–905.

Niemczyk, M. and Romiszewski, A. (1990) Planning works 1916–1988 – a brief overview of the planning history of Warsaw, in J. Cierpinski *et al.* (eds), *Plany Urbanistyczne Warszawy*, Towarzystwo Urbanistów Polskich, Warsaw.

Niemczyk, M. (1993) Master Plans, in J. Wilski, (ed.), *Warszawa Rozwój Przestrzenny*, Oddział Warszawski Towarzystwa Urbanistów Polskich.

Niespodziewańska, U. (1992) Real estate development in Warsaw – the present and the future, *Estates News*, **10**(14), October, 9–11.

Ostrowski, W. (1966) History of urban development and planning, in J.C. Fisher (ed.), *City and Regional Planning in Poland*, Cornell University Press, Ithaca.

Pakalski, Z. (1993) Manhattan wokół pałacu, *Zycie Warszawy*, 14 June.

Pietura, E. (1992a) Property exchange, *Estates Times*, **8**(11), August, 4.

Pietura, E. (1992b) Property exchange, *Estates Times*, **12**(15), December, 4.

Pietura, E. (1993a) Property exchange, *Estates Times*, **1**(18), January, 4.

Pietura, E. (1993b) Property exchange, *Estates Times*, **2**(19), February, 4.

Regulski, J. and Wawrynski, J. (1989) Polish planning in transition, *Town Planning Review*, **60**(3), 247–69.

Rościszewski, J. (1993) New Master Plan for the City of Warsaw, in *Raport, Planowanie i Rozwój Przestrzenny-Wyzwania i Alternatywy dla Europy Srodkoweji Wschodniej w Latach 90*, Międzynarodowy Kongres TUP, Warsaw, June, 49–53.

Roskelly, M. (1993) Financing dreams in the Warsaw office market, *Estates News*, **9**(25), September.

Rostowski, J. (1993) *The Implications of Rapid Private Sector Growth in Poland*, Discussion Paper No. 159, Centre for Economic Performance, London School of Economics.

Ryder, A. (1992) Urban planning in post war Poland with reference to Cracow, *Cities*, **9**(3), August 1992, 205–19.

Sachs, J. (1993) *Poland's Jump to the Market Economy*, MIT Press.

Sejm (1993) *Ustawa o zagospodarowaniu przestrzennym* (Spatial Development Bill), 5 May.

Walker, A. (1993) Łódz: the problems associated with restructuring the urban economy of Poland's textile metropolis in the 1990s, *Urban Studies*, **30**(6), 1065–80.

Wilski, J. (1990) A critical evaluation of spatial development plans of Warsaw, in J. Cierpinski *et al.* (eds), *Plany Urbanistyczne Warszawy*, Towarzystwo Urbanistów Polskich, Warsaw.

Wilski, J. (ed.) (1993) *Warszawa Rozwój Przestrzenny* (Warsaw Physical Development), Oddział Warszawski Towarzystwa Urbanistów Polskich (Warsaw Chapter of Polish Society of Town Planners).

Wyporek, B. (1993a) Changes of the physical planning system in Poland, in *Raport, Planowanie i Rozwój Przestrzenny-Wyzwania i Alternatywy dla Europy Srodkoweji Wschodniej w Latach 90*, Międzynarodowy Kongres TUP, Warsaw, June, 54–6.

Wyporek, B. (1993b) Warsaw City Core, in *Raport, Planowanie i Rozwój Przestrzenny-Wyzwania i Alternatywy dla Europy Srodkoweji Wschodniej w Latach 90*, Międzynarodowy Kongres TUP, Warsaw, June, 80–3.

18

Berlin

James Berry
and Stanley McGreal

With the re-unification of Germany in October 1990, the city of Berlin became in population terms by far the largest city within the newly created state. Occupying an area of 883 sq km the city has a population of circa 3.43 million while the next largest cities within Germany, Hamburg and Munich have populations of 1.65 and 1.3 million respectively. In this context the decision to transfer the capital functions for Germany from Bonn has created certain fears that Berlin may become increasingly dominant and ultimately destabilize or at least lead to a rearrangement of the German system of cities (Krätke, 1992; Dangschat, 1993).

However Berlin is presently a capital without the established national (federal) administration. Furthermore, despite experiencing an unprecedented period of change following the dismantlement of the Wall in 1989, the city still remains very much an 'island'. While the relevance of this description to the former West Berlin has disappeared with the momentous political developments within Germany during 1989–90, the reconstituted city nevertheless finds itself completely surrounded by the new Länd of Brandenburg. Under the decentralized federal system of government within Germany with considerable devolution of functions the separation of Berlin and Brandenburg, each as individual länder, poses major questions concerning the planning process and has implications in terms of development and investment activity.

18.1 HISTORICAL DEVELOPMENT

While the history of Berlin is explicitly tied up with major world events of the twentieth century it is important to note that the origins of the city go back nearly 800 years. The city is believed to have been founded circa 1230 on the banks of the River Spree with the first written documentation

European Cities, Planning Systems and Property Markets Edited by James Berry and Stanley McGreal. Published in 1995 by E & FN Spon. ISBN 0419 18940 8.

dating from 1237. Initially the settlement was in two parts, Berlin and Colln, on opposite banks of the river, corresponding to the present-day district of Mitte. Due to economic growth based upon trading activity and the migration of Germanic people into the Slav lands the settlement continued to develop. In the seventeenth and eighteenth centuries considerable expansion and extension of the city was related to the growing influence of Prussia as a European power. It was at this stage that some of the great public buildings of Berlin particularly those on the Unter den Linden were constructed. Also the city of Charlottenburg was established in 1706. However the growth of Berlin postdates that of both Paris and London, with Berlin's population increasing from 170 000 inhabitants in the early 1800s to about 500 000 by the mid nineteenth century.

The latter part of the nineteenth century and the founding of the German Empire in 1871, with Berlin as its capital, provided the momentum for major expansion. At this stage (1862) under the Hobrecht Plan the city was expanded to include Charlottenburg and early signs of a bi-centric structure emerged. This plan, designed to accommodate a population of up to 4 million, guided the development of Berlin for about fifty years up to the start of the First World War. During this period economic growth was accompanied by major industrial development and the construction of the S-Bahn railway ring which arguably demarcates the inner central core of today's city (the inner 10% or 87 sq km).

In 1920 a central administration was established and Berlin was expanded to cover an area that is broadly equivalent to its present size but one which was composed of a highly fragmented internal structure. At this stage Berlin's population was circa 4 million peaking at 4.5 million in 1942, a figure which was to decline to 2.8 million at the end of the Second World War. The 1920s–1930s extensions to the city included primarily social housing provision. However, of greater significance was the development of the A-10, Berliner Ring. Also during the 1930s while the bi-polar structure of the city centre was starting to become more apparent (Figure 18.1), the core of the city remained clearly fixed in Stadt Mitte and in particular locations such as Unter den Linden and Potsdamer Platz.

The development of the Berlin conurbation during the period 1880–1940 was very much influenced by the pattern of rail networks. Indeed Frick (1991) equates the shape of Berlin to that of a star with radial lines of development interposed with green wedges. The fact that this morphology still exists is, to a large extent, a function of the post-war division of the city (1949–89). Frick observes how a common outcome of separate development within both the western and eastern sectors has been the limited degree of suburbanization and urban sprawl. A further outcome of the division was the inclusion of the former administrative centre of Berlin in the Russian sector of the occupying allied powers and ultimately in the territory of the German Democratic Republic (GDR).

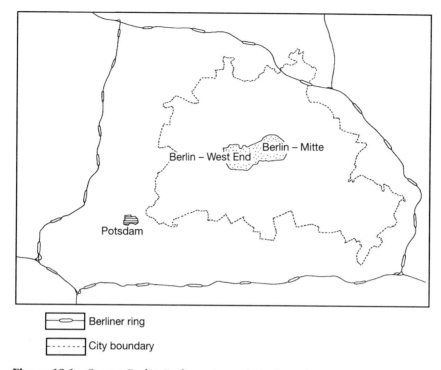

Berliner ring

City boundary

Figure 18.1 Greater Berlin: Berliner ring and City boundary

The consequences of forty years of separation has been enormous with West Berlin in essence a highly subsidized island while East Berlin was developed as the administrative, cultural and academic centre of the former GDR (Frick, 1991). Indeed East Berlin was given special status with a concentration of infrastructure development, technical/scientific/communicative, in a bid to elevate the image of the eastern sector as a major international centre (Krätke, 1992; Bremm and Ache, 1993).

In considering the impacts of the division of the city, Dangschat (1993) considers that West Berlin was forced to become independent of the public utility system of both East Berlin and the surrounding GDR. Furthermore the disruption of transportation links which historically had been east–west within Berlin led instead to the development of north–south systems within what Dangschat refers to as the 'half-city'. Frick (1991) in discussing the consequences of differences in the technical infrastructure between the two parts of the city notes that while the superior utilities in the former western sector could provide a positive contribution to the development of the entire conurbation, first- and second-class territories may result. It should be stressed however that while east–west linkages were cut the physical structures remained intact thereby enabling, for example, the renewal of public transportation systems between the two sectors. However this process particularly in relation to the roads infrastructure is not without problems.

Further consequences which arose from the division of the city include the transferral of political functions from West Berlin to Bonn, the loss of industrial jobs and population decline in the western sector until the mid 1980s, the need for subsidization and in particular the separate development of the commercial cores of the two cities. As the original heart of Berlin was centred around the Unter den Linden (Mitte District) there thus became the need to create within the western sector a city core. This commercial core of retail and office activity but lacking administrative and government functions emerged several kilometres to the west of the former centre in the Kurfürstendamm (Charlottenburg) which developed as the prime retail location in Berlin (Healey & Baker, 1993). In contrast the centre of East Berlin was dominated by governmental, administrative and trade functions (Dangschat, 1993). Thus the bi-polarity of the two centred city was formed, separated by the Tiergarten (Figure 18.2), with

The inner city of Berlin

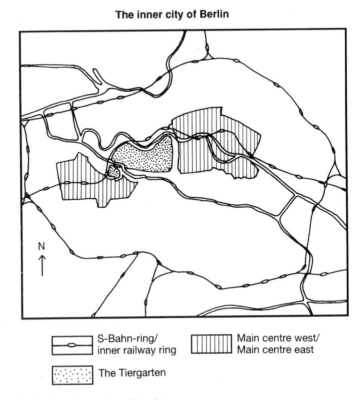

| S-Bahn-ring/ inner railway ring | Main centre west/ Main centre east |
| The Tiergarten | |

Figure 18.2 The Inner City of Berlin

the western core expanding westwards and the eastern core in a reciprocal fashion. Indeed this inherited pattern will continue to have considerable influence upon city planning, development and the future operation of property markets within the re-united city.

18.2 ADMINISTRATIVE STRUCTURES

Germany as a federal state is divided into several tiers of government (Dieterich *et al.*, 1993). There are essentially three autonomous layers: the federal government (Bund), the state government (Länder) and municipal governments (Städte und Gemeinden). At the upper level of the hierarchy the federal ministry with specific responsibility for land and property is the Ministry for Spatial Development, Building and Town Planning (Bundesministerium für Raumordnung, Bauwesen und Städtebau). Unlike the United Kingdom there is considerable devolution of powers to successive levels of government, thus each of the Länder is able to exercise control over a considerable range of issues including matters relevant to planning, property, the development process and investment activity.

Following unification the structure of government and administration which applied throughout the Federal Republic of Germany (FRG) was adopted for the entire state. The former GDR was divided into five new länder. In the context of Berlin the most relevant of these is Brandenburg which completely surrounds the city. Furthermore the administrative authorities for Länd Brandenburg are located at Potsdam, immediately to the south-west of Berlin (Figure 18.3). Regarding Berlin, the city, in common with Hamburg and Bremen, has the status of a länd bestowing upon it a direct relation to the federal government. Thus Berlin in essence has a double identity, as a municipal authority and as a länd, but one administrative structure. Due to its status, the city can pass its own laws with the Senate being both the government of the länd as well as providing the administration for the city.

Within this administrative structure there are eight departments each of which is headed by a senator or minister. Several of these departments are either directly involved in the planning process or impact upon it, in particular the Department of Urban Development and Environmental Protection (Senatsverwaltung für Stadtentwicklung und Umweltschutz) and the Department for Construction and Housing (Senat für Bau- und Wohnungswesen). The lead role belongs to the former with key areas of consideration including planning for the new Capital Berlin, regional coordination of transportation planning and the preparation of the statutory land-use plan, the Flächennutzungsplan.

Below the level of the Senate, Berlin is divided into 23 administrative districts or *bezirks* (Figure 18.4) each of which has its own level of administration and competencies. In essence the structure of government

Figure 18.3   Berlin and the surrounding Länd Brandenburg

is modelled upon that previously existing for West Berlin in terms of the differing levels at which power is exercised. Concerning planning, detailed matters are handled at this second level of administration, with each *bezirk* having its own urban planning department. Specific matters include the preparation of detailed local building plans or *Bebauungsplans*. Each *bezirk* is headed by an elected mayor and is influenced by local coalitions of political parties. While in terms of democratic principles there are strong reasons for such a system, the fragmentation of local authorities and their varying political composition has adverse consequences for the efficiency of the planning system in Berlin.

The planning process is also fractured at an upper level by the separate systems of administration that exist between Berlin and Brandenberg. Both are separate länder and can therefore develop their own distinctive planning policies to suit particular needs. While both länder are willing to co-operate on programmes relating to development activity in essence no

Figure 18.4 Administrative districts within Berlin

regional development plan exists for what might be considered to be the Greater Berlin area. Under these circumstances conflict situations can arise between the two authorities. For example, currently there is considerable development pressures arising to the south of Berlin due to economic linkages with and the growth potential of Leipzig and Dresden. Länd Berlin which does not have any powers to act beyond its spatial boundaries (in reality the area covered by the city) favours development in the area between the Stadt boundary and the A-10 Berliner Ring whereas Länd Brandenburg suggests development to the south of the Ring. The situation is made even more complex by the fact that certain local authorities within Länd Brandenburg, particularly those to the south of Berlin who are anxious to reap the rewards of development within their areas, have been willing to grant planning permissions for industrial/office parks (*Gewerbeparks*) and residential development. The lack of co-ordination which runs at differing levels may only be ultimately resolved by the merger between the two länder. While discussions have been taking place it is unlikely that there will be a rapid resolution of this issue.

A further area of uncertainty which is currently (1993) impacting upon the property sector within Berlin surrounds the decision to move the capital functions and some of the federal departments from Bonn to Berlin. While the commitment to achieve this has been given, the pace of trans-ferral of various ministries is causing concern and has acted, with other factors, as a break on development and investment activity. More recently a timetable for the relocation of government offices covering the period 1998–2003 has been established with Berlin receiving most of the key ministries, for example Foreign Affairs, Justice, Finance and Economics (Weatherall Green & Smith, 1992). Clearly the establishment of such a timetable should go a long way to retain private-sector investment con-fidence in Berlin. It is estimated that 530 000 sq m of usable office space will be required to accommodate the anticipated number of new work spaces though a counter-flow of other administrative offices out of Berlin, some of which will be back to Bonn, will reduce the net increase of jobs in the public sector to about 3500. It is also estimated that investment volume will reach 10 billion DM in the period 1994–8 (DTZ Zadelhoff, 1993).

18.3   THE PLANNING SYSTEM

In Berlin the planning and development process is regulated at various administrative levels within the government hierarchy, viz Länd Berlin and the municipalities which constitute the city (Figure 18.4). Urban devel-opment and planning is governed by the Federal Building Act (BauGB) and the Ordnance on the Use of Buildings (BauNVO). In the states of the former GDR (Neue Länder) parts of the Ordnance on the Permission of Construction (BauZVO) will continue to apply until 31 December 1997 in order to facilitate construction, investment and ensure orderly urban de-velopment (Schneider, 1991).

The utilization of land for building purposes is dictated by local devel-opment plans (*Bauleitpläne*) consisting of the land-use plan or structure plan (*Flächennutzungsplan* or F-Plan) which is a preliminary devel-opment plan; and the detailed local development plan (*Bebauungsplan* or B-Plan). The latter is more specific and based on the policies and proposals contained in the land-use plan.

A *Flächennutzungsplan* is drawn up for each municipality and in general shows how the land within the local authority's jurisdiction is to be used. The main purpose of the plan is to zone land for urban development in accordance with a proposed use but it does not contain any compulsory provisions governing the use of individual plots, though it does set the framework for the preparation of the detailed local plan (B-Plan). As a comprehensive planning instrument the F-Plan has to take into account all demands for different land uses, and not just demand for new building land (Dieterich *et al.*, 1993). Any construction which is in conflict with the land-use allocations in the plan are deemed to be against the public interest and will consequently preclude against the granting of building permission (*Baugenehmigung*).

Within the context of the F-Plan, the detailed local development plans or B-Plans are prepared. These establish compulsory guidelines on the development and use of land in accordance with statutory regulations (BauGB). The Ordnance on the Use of Buildings (BauNVO) regulates the application of these provisions (Schneider, 1991). The B-Plan only becomes legally effective after explicit or tacit approval by the Senate.

In terms of function, the plan determines not only the land uses but also establishes several building parameters with regard to the development process such as the position and dimension of buildings; the total floor area to plot area; the density of development; the number of floors; the area for traffic and social infrastructure; and the area for public and private open space (Dieterich *et al.*, 1993). The legality of a project cannot be disputed if the proposed development is in accordance with the criteria laid down in the B-Plan. Conversely, however landowners are not obliged to implement the plan and if a proposed development departs from the provisions contained in the document, exceptions can be applied (*Ausnahme*) but these must be included in a written statement within the B-Plan. It is also possible for a developer to apply for dispensation (*Befreiung*) from the regulations of the B-Plan, for example to develop a greater amount of floorspace than would be generally permitted. Dispensations are usually possible only if the public benefit and the interests of neighbours are not materially affected by the proposed development. In circumstances where the proposed development land is not covered by a B-Plan, the developer may seek approval under the provisions of article 34 of the Federal Building Act. This article states that such a development will be permissible if its proposed use, construction and building density display the same characteristics as other buildings in the immediate vicinity; and if public service provision has been assured.

In Berlin, the Project and Development Plan (*Vorhaben – und Erschließungsplan* or V & E Plan) is an instrument which has been increasingly used with considerable effect to speed up the plan making process, and thus facilitate investment and development. Under section 55 BauZVO approval may be granted for building projects which cannot in principle be approved without a development plan being prepared, but which are urgently needed to secure or generate jobs, to meet housing needs or to develop necessary infrastructure. Such approval may be given if the developer or investor planning the project is willing and able to carry out the project and development work on the basis of a submitted plan. In these circumstances, the developer/investor must give an undertaking to implement the project within a specified period (Schneider, 1991).

The approval of the V & E Plan, is granted under contract between the local authority and the developer, and therefore becomes the personal responsibility of the latter with regard to the financing, phasing and development of the project. Consequently the developer becomes liable for the proposed development in accordance with the contractual obligations. It is however possible to convert a V & E Plan into a B-Plan in which case the project and development plan becomes the detailed local development plan for the area. This conversion process may be utilized in circumstances where the developer finds it difficult to complete the project in its totality, or where the market circumstances have changed, or where the developer wants to withdraw from the contractual obligations. From the local authority's perspective the V & E Plan can be advantageous on administrative grounds. First by facilitating the planning and development process through speedier preparation and adoption, and second the developer or investor incurs the costs for its preparation. The V & E Plan assumes the same legal status as a B-Plan.

Within the context of the development plan framework, control over development operations is regulated by building permission. The procedure for obtaining building permission is laid down in the Building Code (Bauordnung) which contains technical regulations (fire precautions, environmental protection). Building permission consists of two stages involving firstly, a preliminary application (Bauvoranfrage) which establishes in principle whether it is possible to build; and second an official building application (Bauantrag) which specifies the details of the proposed development such as type and intensity of land use, technical safety standards of construction and design. Construction can only begin on receipt of written permission and can take six months or longer to process. A building permit is granted once all those authorities with a vested interest have been consulted (planning department, police authorities, public health department, traffic department) and provided no justifiable objections are raised concerning the project.

In Germany the planning system is considered to be bureaucratic, protracted and complex in nature and directly impacts on development opportunity. The rules and instruments followed by the various government departments tightly regulate the allocative functions of land supply, controls urban development and influences the distribution of property and ownership. In Berlin, the magnitude of the problem in regenerating the city requires a flexible, coherent and market-led approach, but instead is frustrated by the inefficiency of the planning system and the convoluted nature of the decision-making process. Recognition of this, together with the overwhelming need to attract serious investment and create regeneration has stimulated the increasing use of the development-led V & E Plan. Since it would take a considerable period of time to prepare development plans particularly for the new länder and the eastern part of Berlin, the

Unification Treaty provides for this simplified procedure to the planning process.

Reconciling investor interest, the policies of the Berlin Senate and the current real estate situation within the city, which has been argued by Krätke (1992) to be one of the driving forces behind Berlin's metropolitan transition, has necessitated specialist responsibilities being concentrated and vested in the Coordination Committee for Inner City Investment (KOAI). Managed by the Department for Construction and Housing the KOAI is a forum where inter-departmental decisions are expedited and action taken in circumstances where planning interests are concerned; investment is expected to have significant economic repercussions; property owned by Länd Berlin is affected; or a number of different developments are involved in a proposed scheme.

18.3.1 The *Flächennutzungsplan* for Berlin

The reunification of Berlin, the imbalances in the existing urban structure and the anticipated increases in growth have imposed a new set of requirements and perspectives for the urban and regional planning of the city. Previous planning concepts were totally inadequate to deal with the pressure emanating from these changes. For the eastern part of the city there was no zoning plan while the one for West Berlin, dating from 1988, was never adopted. Consequently in the autumn of 1990 the Department of Urban Development and Environmental Protection commenced preparation on an integrated Land Use Plan (F-Plan) for the whole of Berlin. The draft plan has proceeded through the public participation stages and is expected to be ratified in May 1994 (Senatsverwaltung für Stadtentwicklung and Umweltschutz, 1993).

The spatial structure concept embodied within the draft plan presents an overall picture of the development of Berlin to the year 2010 and provides scope for growth of up to 300 000 additional inhabitants and at least an equal number of new jobs in the city. The main objectives of the plan are to build upon Berlin's characteristic qualities; to give shape to the new roles of the capital city, seat of government and European metropolis; to encourage internal development through better use of existing space; to develop the polycentric structure of the city; to retain the character of a green city; to absorb an appropriate proportion of the regional population growth of approximately 1 million within the city boundary; to provide new employment opportunities in the service sector and processing industry; to create a balanced mix of urban land uses; and to develop transportation networks without producing urban, environmental and social diseconomies.

Given the need to develop the service sector of the economy and the new capital city functions, the plan concept recognizes the importance of

the inner city (area within the S-Bahn ring) to the future development of
Berlin (Figure 18.2). The development of the inner city is to be closely
determined by the existing urban fabric. Opportunities are to be targeted
along the S-Bahn ring, by the River Spree and in the wastelands along the
former border. The core areas of the inner city centred near the Zoological
Gardens (Tiergarten) and Alexanderplatz are to be developed in accordance with scientific, cultural, political, economic, trade and service
facilities. Parliament and government functions will be placed in central
Berlin near the Reichstag, in the historic core around Kronprinzenpalais
and on Spree Island, at Leipziger Strasse and between Tiergarten and
Alexanderplatz. The district of Mitte will become a diversified centre
combining government, cultural, education, services, retail and housing.

Retailing is envisaged as a growth sector of the economy particularly
because of the imbalance in the eastern part of the city and Berlin's
increasing importance in regional terms. Even if the population remained
at its present level a demand for additional retail space of the order of
1.35 million sq m is anticipated. With an expected population increase of
300 000 inhabitants within the city the demand for retailing space could
increase by a further 320 000 sq m. Consequently the plan is working on
the assumption of 1.6 to 1.7 million sq m of retailing space by the year
2010.

Concerning the service sector, the plan envisages that Berlin employment levels will come into line with those of other leading German cities.
With the anticipated population increase this would mean that Berlin will
require a further 11 million sq m of gross floor space. Although Berlin
would like to continue the tradition of being an industrial centre and
service city at the same time, the emphasis is expected to shift in favour of
the latter.

Key city centre locations including Friedrichstrasse, Unter den Linden
and the Kurfürstendamm will be utilized more effectively for commercial
and service sector activity which have specialized requirements with regard to accessibility and prestige value. Additional sites for service industries are to be developed as parts of existing nuclei in the inner city
mixed with retailing and housing. However an excessive increase in density
could create problems in the inner city with weaker uses; particularly
housing being forced out, together with the integration of large building
masses in urban development terms and traffic generation. In view of these
problems it is envisaged that increasing use will be made of the development potential along the periphery of the inner city. New commercial
space is planned in the north of Berlin in Buch, Buchholz and Blanken-
burg; in the east in the Mahlsdorf area; and in Bohnsdorf in the south-east.
However the attractiveness, accessibility and commercial viability of these
sites have yet to be established.

The residential function in the inner city is to be retained and strengthened in a bid to prevent gentrification of these districts and change of use will be resisted by designating sufficient sites for the development of offices. Furthermore on central sites targeted for new service-sector development at least 20% of the new floorspace is to be reserved for housing, a ratio which increases depending upon location and existing land use composition. Policies concerning the integration of planning and housing are critical as it is estimated that 400 000 additional residential units will be required in Berlin to the year 2010 to meet the needs of both the existing residents and the envisaged population growth projections for the city.

The combination of pent-up demand, increased importance and the expansion of various functions will produce a major redefinition of structural development in Berlin. The requirements for space necessitates a supply-orientated planning approach to the redevelopment process. Demand will be stimulated by an active and co-ordinated policy in terms of infrastructure provision and urban development.

18.4   RESTITUTION AND PRIVATIZATION OF PROPERTY

The transformation of the former GDR from a centrally planned system to a capitalist economy has been somewhat problematic as far as land and property is concerned. The Unification Treaty of 31 August 1990 combined the legal systems of the two countries under the overall principle that the existing legal system of the FRG was to apply to the five new länder. There are however exceptions to the principle, which take into account the vast differences existing between East and West Germany with respect to property title and privatization matters.

18.4.1   The restitution process

The law relating to restitution has been changed a number of times since unification. In 1990 the Unification Treaty made reference to the Joint Declaration of the Governments of the Federal Republic of Germany and the German Democratic Republic on the Settlement of Unresolved Property Claims (Duckworth, 1993). This declaration became an integral part of the Treaty which established that expropriated owners of property shall have a right to restitution of title, except in certain cases in which they shall only have the right to compensation. Consequently all land and property which was nationalized illegally by the socialist authorities was to be returned to former owners on application; and restitution of property rights was to have precedence over privatization and sale. This resulted in a massive backlog of claims totalling more than 100 000, each of which must be thoroughly investigated by the government and the courts.

In compliance with this declaration the then existing East German

Government enacted the Regulation on the Restitution of Property Claims which provides for the registration of claims for restitution of property. The legal basis for claims is contained in the Act on Unresolved Property Claims (Restitution Act) which was ratified in conjunction with the Unification Treaty (Volhard *et al.*, 1991; Duckworth, 1993). The Restitution Act applies to enterprises, shares in companies, real estate and other properties and covers all expropriations by the Nazis for religious and political reasons between 1933 and 1945; and all expropriations by the East German state between 1949 and 1990. Expropriations carried out between 1945 and 1949 under Soviet military occupation were excluded from the Restitution Act. The terms of the Act has proved to be somewhat restrictive with regard to the property market and the development process in that if a restitution claim to property was filed within a specified time period, the formal owner was no longer entitled to dispose of the property without the consent of the former owner. Recognizing the constraints which the terms of the Act imposed and the urgent need to attract investment into the regeneration process the government revised the laws of precedence of restitution over investment in relation to property claims (Duckworth, 1993).

Under the Investment Priority Act (1992) consideration is now given to whether the restitution claimant has undertaken to make the same or similar investments as a third-party investor claiming priority to the property. If this is not the case (i.e. the restitution claimant cannot or will not match the third-party investment plan) then priority is given to the third-party investor, even against the will of the party entitled to possession of the property. Provided that the restitution claimant offers to make such a special investment, an investment priority ruling is granted which gives protection against the claims asserted by other parties filing for restitution or by any third party. Thus from the restitution claimants' point of view, there is a clear need to provide an investment plan to accompany a restitution claim to regain title to an expropriated property asset. The intention of the legislation is that investment in land and property is to receive priority and to ensure that investors can make use of real estate without those claiming ownership rights blocking economically productive investments. If real estate is sold the purchaser will receive an entry in the land register. This means that those registering ownership rights cannot assert any claims to the return of the real-estate asset, although they will receive the right to compensation to the amount of the current market value at the time of the sale. Also from a legal perspective a restitution claimant must submit a competing/counter proposal within a specified time period.

18.4.2 Privatization of state-controlled property

In 1990 GDR set up the Truehandanstalt (THA) in Berlin as a state-controlled body with the task of privatizing companies in East Germany. The aims of the THA were to sell 100% of the previously nationalized property to private investors; to promote the reconstruction of East German companies where possible and necessary to facilitate their privatization; and to split up the former combines, not only for the purpose of privatization but also to create an efficient and competitive economic structure (Duckworth, 1993). Within the scope of the privatization order, the THA realized that in addition to the necessary privatization of enterprises, non-operational necessary real estate required management and utilization. Consequently in order to concentrate the real-estate management and competence within the THA, the real-estate arm, the Truehand Liegenschaftsgesellschaft mbH (TLG) was established in 1991. The TLG acts by order of the THA with responsibilities to maintain an inventory of land and property, to value and manage assets and to return property to its former owners on the basis of an application for restitution or transfer it to public authorities (länder and municipalities) or to sell to private investors (TLG, 1992).

The THA takes responsibility for collecting data preparatory to sale (data on buildings, abstracts of title, site plan, cadastral extracts) whereas the TLG relies on the data available to value property and estimate possible risk. The procedure includes data from current contracts (current use), cadastre (size), land register (servitudes and mortgages), construction plans (possible use) and expert opinion (environmental damage). The TLG is supported by an 'expert advisory council for valuation' composed of nationally approved experts on property valuation. The council's main task is to develop principles to determine market value and to investigate available appraisals and valuations of property (TLG, 1993).

The TLG also utilizes the 'Berliner Model' which is based on conferences at which a binding decision is taken on the future use of the property. The purpose of the model is to provide guidance and security to buyers in what could otherwise be an uncertain acquisition. Before the public invitation to bid is issued a steering committee discusses the use and its acceptability which are embodied in the specifications included in the offer for sale. The steering committee, consisting of members from the various public authorities (town planning, construction and housing, finance), submits its proposals to the Truehandanstalt decision-making body. It is important to note that the public agencies involved at this stage are those which are later responsible for granting building permission.

Non-operationally necessary real estate forms the majority of the TLG inventory. It includes some of the property of the former nationalized industries which can create liquidity for the enterprises themselves but only if fully utilized. In other cases jobs can be saved or created through better use of available buildings or partial sale of business sites. Thus, the sale of the non-operationally necessary real estate can be the start of new and positive developments. However the greatest problem hindering property sales is legal ownership. Restitution, utilization and sale of property depends upon reconveyance claims having been clarified, although the Law on Priority of Investment (1992) now provides the basis for accelerated privatization whereby investors who offer a promising business concept, viz ensuring or creating jobs and guaranteeing development, are granted investment rights over former owners who are not able or prepared to invest. The THA is responsible for decisions on investment preference while the TLG conduct necessary investigations, enquiries and decides on utilization procedures. Official reconveyance and determination of restitution claims are not the responsibility of either the THA or the TLG although the latter works in close co-operation with the responsible authorities (TLG, 1993).

The TLG has sold some 5000 properties to investors for a total of DM 4 billion (September 1992), with estimated investment amounting to DM 17 billion and 130 000 jobs saved or created (TLG, 1992). However the reconstruction process has inevitably lead to considerable unemployment throughout East Berlin especially as the former state-controlled companies were trading at vast losses due to over-manning, low investment and productivity, and technical inefficiency. Efforts are nevertheless increasingly being made to attract foreign investment into economic ventures as well as real-estate investment and development.

18.5   FINANCIAL AND TAXATION INCENTIVES

In striving to restore its position as a major European city, Berlin has embarked on a major reconstruction and revitalization programme to modernize its infrastructural base, to overcome the negative growth effects of socio-spatial polarization, to restructure the productive capacity of the urban economy and to facilitate investment in residential, commercial and industrial property. Government and administration interpret their role as one of combining planning and finance, thus developing the city of Berlin as a partnership in conjunction with domestic and foreign real-estate investors. From the foreign investors perspective, it can be advantageous not to acquire property directly but to act through a separate entity, usually a corporation established specially to hold property assets. These real-estate holding companies (*Objektgesellschaften*) finance property investments by way of a loan from rental income generated by the property (von Schenck, 1991).

The Berlin investment market to date (1993) has been largely domestically orientated. This is primarily due to the taxation advantages which have led to the market being dominated by individual investors and closed-end property funds, although open-end property funds, insurance companies and pension funds are also investing (Jones Lang Wootton, 1993). As argued by von Schenck (1991) the relatively high yield obtained after the deduction of taxes has encouraged many investors to participate in closed-end funds which are usually in the form of a limited partnership. Likewise open-ended funds can offer investors some tax benefits although they cannot compete with the tax efficiency of closed funds. In a 1990 amendment of the Investment Company Act, an investment company may establish a special fund, provided it has no more than ten investors which are not individuals, and that the certificates issued to the investors are not transferred without its consent. This permits the creation of tailor-made real-estate funds for single or small groups of investors who will be able to influence the investment policy of their special fund by placing represen-tatives on its investment committee.

In Berlin there are other taxation incentives specifically geared to lever private investment into the property market. Since 1991 it has been possible for investors in both parts of Berlin to claim special depreciation rates for certain purchases entailed in the construction, extension and modernization of property. These benefits are applicable for both the residential and commercial property sectors. Depreciation rates amount to 50% of the purchase or production cost and can be claimed against taxable income in a lump sum in year one when the investment was made or spread over a maximum of five years. However the building must be either purchased or constructed during the period 1991 and 1996. These taxation incentives are additional to the usual straight-line and residual depreciation possibilities.

Compared to other large cities in Germany, Berlin has a limited supply of office and commercial space. Consequently, the government of Berlin offers a range of incentives particularly to those willing to invest in the eastern part of the city. As part of the national task of improving the regional economic structure investment subsidies of up to 23% of invest-ment costs may be granted for business investments in East Berlin.

18.6 PROPERTY MARKETS

In considering the property market in Berlin a number of factors are of significance. First, the operation of the market was constrained under the formerly divided status of Berlin. Thus in the western sector, although in theory part of the market economy of the Federal Republic, heavy sub-sidization of the overall economy and property-related functions was necessary. In the eastern sector the principles of a command-based economy meant in essence that land had no value, it was state-controlled and hence no market existed. The unification of Germany and in particular the city of Berlin thus brought together two formerly contrary philosophies, the divisions between which are no more sharply apparent than in the land and property sector. The subsequent performance of different sectors of the Berlin market since 1989 must be set in this overall context, together with the efficiency of the planning system to facilitate the development and investment process, uncertainty over land ownership and the need for taxation incentives to stimulate and drive market activity. Indeed as market performance indicates, substantive differences between the former eastern and western sectors are likely to characterize the market and development/investment activity over the rest of this decade.

Second, the euphoria created in Berlin with the fall of the Wall in 1989 also found expression in the property market with a scramble to be represented in Berlin. The outcome was the existence of a highly speculative market over the period 1989–91 with rapid increases in land prices and rental values. Concerning the former, land values in the GDR were notionally worthless and were set at a nominal rate of 600 GDR marks in 1989–90. However to provide a bench mark against which increase can be judged a more realistic value for prime locations in 1990 is 6000 DM/sq m. This had risen to between 10 000 and 15 000 DM/sq m by 1991 and to 25 000 DM/sq m in 1992 for sites in the prime location of Friedrichstrasse. Indeed this 18–24 month period is frequently likened to the 'Gold Rush' mentality subsequent to which the market in the various property sectors has fallen back, thus permitting investment decisions to be made in a more stable environment (little evidence exists of changes in land values since 1992). There is however a fear that the scale of speculative activity may produce an over-supplied market notably in the office sector, a factor which in turn is influencing current (1993) market rents.

A third factor having profound impact upon current market activity centres around the movement of the federal government from Bonn. While government as an owner-occupier will not have any significant impact upon direct demand for office accommodation, the spin-off from other institutions and private-sector enterprises is likely to generate the need for additional floor space on a large scale.

18.6.1   Offices

The office market is likely to be the sector offering greatest interest to investment funds and institutions, but equally it possesses the greatest risks. Part of the difficulties in assessing the future direction of the office market lies in the fact that up until 1990 in effect no office market of significance existed in Berlin; any development activity which occurred in the western sector was primarily for owner-occupation. Thus there is relatively little data upon which to base performance measurement and when coupled with the scale of speculation which prevailed in 1989–91 comparison becomes increasingly difficult and of little value.

There is unanimous agreement that the restructuring of the Berlin economy from its former industrial base to the service sector will necessitate a major growth in office provision. Attempts to quantify this has led to comparisons with other German cities. For example DTZ Zadelhoff (1993) have utilized Frankfurt/Main as a comparable region and based projected floor-area deficits upon indicators such as the development of employment, particularly the proportion in the office sector and the office space requirements per person. Such projections and utilization of forecasts on population growth suggests a requirement for 24 million sq m of office space in Berlin by the year 2010, corresponding to a gross deficit of 11 million sq m (current stock estimated to be 13 million sq m). However, it is considered that much of the existing stock is poor by international standards (Weatherall Green & Smith, 1992) and allowing for a 20% replacement of existing space, DTZ Zadelhoff compute an annual floor area requirement of 710 000 sq m. Similar projections by Jones Lang Wootton (1992) estimates the office requirement for Berlin to be between 6 to 10 million sq m, with an annual requirement of between 600 000 and 1 million sq m.

Regarding supply the inability of the existing office stock in Berlin to meet the demand arising from unification promoted the securing of sites by both German and foreign investors to develop office buildings. However the pace of development activity up to 1993 is perceived to have been slow for a number of reasons namely: inefficiencies in town planning, time-consuming development competitions, questions of land ownership, macroeconomic factors and the financing policy of the banks. Nevertheless it is estimated that the level of supply could rise to in excess of 500 000 sq m by 1995 (Weatherall Green & Smith, 1993). Presently (1993) the best office location within Berlin is in the City West based on the Kurfürstendamm with the first newly developed speculative schemes being achieved in this location. However from 1995 onwards the development balance between City West and City East is likely to tilt in favour of the latter as a number of major schemes are completed, for example the redevelopment of Potsdamer Platz and several schemes in Friedrichstrasse. Clearly the Mitte district, the pre-war centre of Berlin and the location for most of the returning government departments, is attracting the greatest investor interest.

Although there are high predicted requirement levels for office property in Berlin, market evidence in 1993 suggests a slackening of demand coinciding with the completion of the first wave of speculative developments. This has been reflected in prime rentals achieved during 1993 namely 60–5 DM/sq m/month compared to circa 90–5 DM/sq m/month during 1991 (pre-unification rents circa 20–5 DM/sq m/month). Furthermore there is little evidence of any substantial difference in office rents between City West and City East. With approximately 13 million sq m of projected office space in the supply pipeline over the next 10–15 years concerns regarding potential oversupply at least in the short-term are now starting to arise. In this respect the synchronization of the planning, construction and letting phases are important and as von Einem (1993) observes the amount of office space in the planning or construction stage has left demand, although rising, lagging behind with possibly 1995–6 being a critical stage. However it is recognized that constraints arising from bank lending and the possible 4–5 year period which may be required to achieve planning permission and establish ownership rights on some sites may curtail supply side inputs.

Concerning investment, Berlin although not a mature investment market is considered to offer good opportunities. However with the high percentage of owner-occupation, a characteristic which is likely to continue, and a current lack of well let investment property the market is difficult to evaluate. Furthermore taxation regulations with potential to distort the market distinctly favour the German investor and closed-end property funds. The outcome being that investment funds are targeting the most significant purchases whereas domestic purchasers frequently acquire property in less recognized locations (Healey and Baker, 1992). However the stabilization of the market and indeed rents during 1993, with yields easing out to circa 6%, has increased the attractiveness of Berlin to the long-term institutional investor where the building is let with secure tenants.

18.6.2 Retail

A fundamental characteristic of planning policy, which is also articulated through the F-Plan, is the desire to achieve mixed use development, rather than purely monostructural development such as zones dedicated to office activity. Thus schemes may be required to include elements of retail or housing or indeed other uses. Indeed several of the major development schemes in City East, for example at Potsdamer Platz and Friedrichstrasse, are mixed-use developments containing substantial retail components. The expectations are to create a prime retail zone with apartment stores in the former heart of city. In this context the decision of Galeries Lafayette to develop on the Friedrichstrasse is considered to be highly significant.

However the current prime retail area in Berlin is situated in City West in the Kurfürstendamm where following the boom in retail activity stimulated by re-unification rents peaked in 1992 at about 300 DM/sq m/ month. Currently (1993) peak rentals are circa 200 DM/sq m/month. In City East retail rents are considered to be more difficult to judge, possibly reaching 200 DM/sq m/month in top locations but most are considered to be within the range 60–100 DM/sq m/month (Weatherall Green & Smith, 1992). Furthermore rental growth in the short to medium term is considered unlikely, with future prospects firmly connected to the growth of expenditure power in the former east. Although some quality occupiers have already taken up premises, certain scepticism is apparent concerning the ability to attract high-quality tenants at good rents into schemes in the former eastern sector (Weatherall Green & Smith, 1993). Indeed the principal subsidiary centres for retailing are mainly in suburban areas (part of Berlin's polycentric structure) in the former western sector for example Schloßstrasse in Steglitz where rentals are within the range 150–200 DM/sq m/month.

The investment market into retail property is limited due to the high level of owner-occupation and the apartment store domination. Furthermore retail warehousing is strictly controlled and out-of-town centres fail to get planning approval.

18.6.3   Industrial

Traditionally Berlin is an industrial city with a high concentration of manufacturing premises within the inner city. However many of the industrial plants in the former eastern sector were technologically inefficient and major polluters. Consequently since unification there has been a dramatic loss in employment within this sector. Economic restructuring is also placing emphasis upon the service sector rather than industrial activity. Also in terms of market activity little industrial property is traded due to the high tendency towards owner-occupation.

However one sector of growth has been the concept of Gewerbeparks (business parks). In essence this is a new phenomenon to Berlin post re-unification and has focused upon the development or proposed development of sites on the A-10 Berliner ring to the south of the city with rapid access to both of Berlin's principal airports viz Schönefeld and Tegel. The focus of activity in these parks is on the sale of serviced sites for light industrial, low-tech and distributive businesses rather than for office activity.

The location of Gewerbeparks on the A-10 is interesting from a planning perspective in that Länd Berlin under present administrative structures (1993) has no control over the number of planning permissions granted, rather authority lies with the appropriate administrative districts within Länd Brandenburg. The potential consequences of such planning permissions upon the economy of Berlin are apparent in the likely relocation of activities, but until such time as there is either unification of the two länder or the preparation of a regional plan, Berlin can have little influence beyond the city boundary. Indeed Jones Lang Wootton (1992) estimate that 50% of building land scheduled for industrial purposes lies outside of

Berlin and while there is a spate of planning applications for the development of businesses parks, with the risk of future oversupply, it is considered that those fulfilling locational, transport and site development criteria are likely to achieve good investment returns.

18.6.4 Housing

Berlin is considered to have a housing shortage pre-dating re-unification, a situation which has the potential to become more acute as Berlin attracts new residents from the former GDR and government employees as a result of the decision to relocate the functions of the capital to Berlin. Recognition of the need to promote housing development is one of the principal reasons underlying the taxation incentives available to investors, either individuals or closed-end property funds. Initially incentives were targeted towards commercial property development but increasingly are being utilized in the residential sector.

Such incentives have been shown to be extremely lucrative in providing a taxation shelter for both individuals and companies and while rules may change, present regulations will apply until 1996. The incentives are applicable to both newly developed property as well as existing premises which are to be converted into residential use. Regarding new build activity several schemes (for example at Mahlow) are being concentrated in the area immediately south of the city boundary, in pro-development administrative districts within Länd Brandenburg. Again in these circumstances the need for regional planning becomes apparent in terms of regulating residential development and related infrastructure. Furthermore taxation incentives to investors are reinforcing rental as the dominant tenure type in the residential sector, with owner-occupation only accounting for 15% of the Berlin market. Rental levels achieved are however highly variable and dependent upon location and scheme, for example prices of between 15 to 30 DM/sq m/month are common.

18.7 CONCLUSION

There is little doubt that Berlin will emerge as one of the key European cities of the twenty-first century. Indeed if projections of population growth are fulfilled Berlin could emerge as the third European metropole after London and Paris (Dangschat, 1993). However given the fact that many Western European cities and indeed cities in the former FRG have established niches (for example Frankfurt, Düsseldorf, Cologne, Hanover, Hamburg), Berlin is likely to develop not in competition to existing centres but as a major player in Central and Eastern Europe. Indeed Berlin arguably could become the dominant service centre in this geographical sphere, particularly for the former command economies of the eastern bloc. In this context Krätke (1992) argues that Berlin is likely to become a significant entrepreneurial co-ordinating point between Western and Eastern Europe.

However, against this, Berlin is facing a number of challenges stemming from the merger of two separate parts with two different economic perspectives. In this context fundamental issues arise particularly in relation to land ownership, the efficiency of economic and production systems and problems of integrating infrastructure. The boom scenario which followed the dismantlement of the Wall and Germany's re-unification has stabilized to one of greater pragmatism, notably in relation to land and property values. In particular the restitution issue and inefficiencies within the planning process, augmented by differing political coalitions in the various administrative areas that constitute Berlin, has helped to slow down the pace of development activity. Indeed there is certain evidence of international investors becoming disenchanted with Berlin and instead turning their attention to other cities in Eastern Europe, for example Warsaw, Prague and Budapest.

Further uncertainty has been created by the delay in relocating federal government departments to Berlin, the presence of which is considered vital in portraying the new image of the city to potential investors. Politically, matters are made more complex by the separate administrations and planning authorities for both Berlin and Brandenburg and the lack of a regional plan for Greater Berlin. Thus while Berlin has the potential to become a major European city there are currently (1993) several factors inhibiting development and investment which are causing enough uncertainty to stall, but not de-rail the process.

Acknowledgement

The authors wish to acknowledge all those persons who assisted in the preparation of this chapter. In particular we wish to thank Mark and Binte Fidler of DTZ Zadelhoff, Berlin, for their comments on the text.

REFERENCES

Bremm, H.-J. and Ache, P. (1993) International changes and the Single European Market: impacts on the spatial structure of Germany, *Urban Studies*, **30**(6), 991–1007.

Dangschat, J.S. (1993) Berlin and the German systems of cities, *Urban Studies*, **30**(6), 1025–51.

Dieterich, H., Dransfeld, E. and Vos, W. (1993) *Urban Land and Property Markets in Germany*, UCL Press Ltd, London.

DTZ Zadelhoff (1993) *The Office Markets in Berlin*, Zadelhoff Deutschland Gmbh, Berlin, 41.

Duckworth, G. (1993) The Berlin office market and the technical process of restitution in a unified Germany, *Journal of Property Finance*, **4**(1), 35–42, MCB University Press.

Frick, D. (1991) City development and planning in the Berlin conurbation: current situation and future perspectives, *Town Planning Review*, **62**(1), 37–49.

Healey & Baker (1992) *Berlin Office Market Report*, Healey & Baker, Berlin, 28.

Healey & Baker (1993) *The Retail Market in Germany*, Healey & Baker, Germany, 51.

Jones Lang Wootton (1992) *City Report Berlin 1992*, Jones Lang Wootton GmbH, Frankfurt/Main, 40.

Jones Lang Wootton (1993) *City Report Berlin*, Jones Lang Wootton GmbH, Berlin, 5.

Krätke, S. (1992) Berlin: the rise of a new metropolis in a post-Fordist landscape, in M. Dunford and G. Kafkalas (eds), *Cities and Regions in the New Europe*, 213–38, Belhaven Press, London.

Schneider, H.J. (1991) Planning and building law, public services, in R. Volhard, D. Weber and W. Usinger (eds), *Real Property in Germany, Legal and Taxation Aspects of Development and Investment*, 4th edn, Verlag Fitz Knapp GmbH, Frankfurt am Main.

Senatsverwaltung für Stadtentwicklung and Umweltschutz (1993) *Flächennutzungsplan Berlin*, Berlin.

TLG (1992) *Working Together for a Bright Future*, Liegenschaftsgesellschaft der Treuhandanstalt mbH, Berlin.

TLG (1993) *Questions and Answers concerning the Treuhandanstalt's Real Estate Company*, Berlin..

Volhard, R., Weber, D. and Usinger, W. (eds) (1991) *Real Property in Germany, Legal and Tax Aspects of Development and Investment*, 4th edn, Verlag Fitz Knapp GmbH, Frankfurt am Main.

von Einem, E. (1993) *Germany's Housing and Office Market*, Conference paper, Institut D'Etudes Politiques de Paris, October 1993.

von Schenck, K. (1991) Financing, in R. Volhard, D. Weber and W. Usinger (eds), *Real Property in Germany, Legal and Taxation Aspects of Development and Investment*, 4th edn, Verlag, Fitz Knapp GmbH, Frankfurt am Main.

Weatherall Green & Smith (1992) *Berlin Metropolitan Area, Market Profiles*, Urban Land Institute, Washington, 205–11.

Weatherall Green & Smith (1993) *Berlin Market Update*, Weatherall Green & Smith, Berlin, 3.

19

Property, planning and European progress

————————— Duncan Maclennan

The vast bulk of applied real-estate research examines specific sectors and places. This emphasis is, of course, appropriate given the inherent characteristics of property which generate spatial and sectoral submarkets. Local supply conditions and constraints, localized components of demand and limitations on cross-market arbitrage mean that 'national' property markets are often only a statistical artefact. Within national economic spaces rents and prices (quality adjusted) for residential and commercial property differ across cities, and of course inter-urban disparities are marked across the European countries. Property price change rates also differ.

Property prices, availability and investment are not solely the outcome of unfettered market forces. In most countries there are legal, fiscal, regulatory and expenditure policies pursued by governments which impact upon not only property demand but the essential functional nature of the property market. Contrast, for example, the relative importance of 'planning' in land-market functioning and outcomes in the former Soviet bloc and the Mediterranean countries. Once again, within national economies, the 'subsidiarity' arrangements are such that state/market sectors may play quite different roles in shaping property markets. For instance in Britain there is an obvious contrast between Glasgow, with its large-scale municipal ownership of land and housing, and Bristol, with a much greater market orientation.

European Cities, Planning Systems and Property Markets Edited by James Berry and Stanley McGreal. Published in 1995 by E & FN Spon. ISBN 0419 18940 8.

19.1 LOCALITIES IN CONTEXT

A detailed analysis of property and progress requires a clear understanding of local markets and policies. However it is equally important to stress that local economies and property markets are partly open systems – they are part of wider national and international economic systems. This point is widely recognized in the sense that net migration is known to impact on the derived demand for residential units and land; and the export base capacity of a city is critical in generating derived demands for all kinds of commercial property.

The openness of local property systems also raises two other important considerations which analysis often overlooks. First, property markets are related to the wider economy not solely through demand driving mechanisms. Property prices, inflation rates and availability may shape the migration of households and firms. Changing prices influence the wealth of home-owners and property shareholders alike and can influence consumption, savings and economic growth. Recent experience in some European residential property markets has also demonstrated that such property to economy feedback effects may contribute to regional and national economic instability – Finland, Denmark, Britain and, more recently, metropolitan France are clear examples (Maclennan and Meen, 1993).

Top-level discussion of key international economic processes in the 1990s has stressed the importance of labour market flexibility (Fitoussi et al., 1993). These arguments about international competitiveness are important. However there is a parallel validity in questioning whether property markets are flexible, in a non-inflationary fashion, in the face of economic change. Indeed, have not property market price and activity cycles had a causal destabilizing role in many national economies over the last decade? Furthermore the booms of the 1980s and the busts of the early 1990s have had property causes and/or reinforcers. Land prices in Japan and the USA, residential property prices in the countries cited above and commercial real-estate fluctuations in Britain, the USA and Japan (for example) all appear to have had a role in fuelling booms and prolonging downswings (Maclennan and Meen, 1993). The output or income elasticity of demand and inelasticity of supply (in the medium term) for property, combined with the significance of property in the wealth of households have, until recently, attracted little attention in macroeconomic thinking.

The second neglected aspect of property system openness lies in the sphere of policy. Local, and national policies are not unchanging, nor immune to external influences. Policy innovation (planning agreements, multi-sector partnerships, 'holistic' perspectives, environmental measures) may stem from national and international dissemination of best-practice ideas. But policy change may also be induced via the mechanism of institutional competition. Where international competition in the market for goods and finance is speeding up, competitive responses need not be limited to making labour markets more flexible. The role of housing, land and planning policies may play a critical role in shaping which places, even nations, adjust successfully to the new international economic order.

Some cities have recognized the importance of property market flexibility. In this sense flexibility means restructuring existing land-use patterns and facilitating an orderly, strategic provision of new property to meet emerging demands. Flexibility also implies encouraging land and property supply with minimal increases in rents and prices – that is, shifting the property industry on to the lowest attainable point on the long-run supply curve. The notion requires foresight, willingness to adapt and the removal of scarcity rents whenever possible.

Few nations have emulated wiser cities. The UK, for instance, shows little interest in or foresight about patterns of urban and regional evolution and the congestion and infrastructure issues which emerge. Thinking in this regard has moved back, not to basics but banalities, since the Barlow Report of 1944. A critical question remains regarding the extent to which national economic progress in the post-war period has been frittered away in rising land and housing costs. Cramped stores and higher shop prices, small homes and rising prices (over the long term) are adverse micro-consequences which Evans (1988) has drawn attention to. But equally effects on deflation, inflation and the exchange rate should not be lightly dismissed.

Over the last decade the economic integration of Europe proceeded slowly, with a new impetus in the late 1980s and the creation of the Single Market during 1992. To date (1993) this has had minor indirect effects on property: finance systems have remained strongly national as has construction activity. Further, deliberations in and about Europe have focused on creating 'single markets' in relation to mobile factors of production, labour and capital, and the market for goods. The impacts and incidence of these changes are shaped by and manifested in local property markets. 'Hot' and 'sluggish' property markets will reflect, and capture some of, the gains and losses from European integration. But, perhaps daunted by the complexity of property law and taxation, there is an ominous silence from Brussels on the ultimate 'fixed' factor, i.e. land and property markets. The European Union has no clear view on Europe's terra firma.

This omission is, perhaps, understandable in the early post-Maastricht era when different conceptions of the European Union towards the year 2000 exist. And there is no doubting the 'local' element in property policy – but how is this to be reconciled with European environmental/social objectives and external competitive pressures emanating from North America and the Pacific Rim?

In the remainder of this chapter the aim is to examine at successive spatial scales (the city, the nation, Europe) key challenges for property and planning if economic progress is to be facilitated. These are examined as related, nested levels of geographic aggregation rather than merely detailed foci. The next section sets out an analysis of urban scale approaches followed, in a further section, by a consideration of the national economic perspective. The penultimate section examines European change, integration in the West and transformation in the East.

19.2   URBAN IMBALANCES AND CHANGE

The process of urban growth is usually neither ubiquitous nor even; more often it is 'unbalanced' favouring some locations and not others. The normal historical pattern of European national growth comprised a range of positive growth rates for major metropolitan areas – some grew faster than others. Since the 1970s there has been a new awareness that some metropolitan regions in older industrial and peripheral regions of the EC are declining in scale as others grow rapidly. Further within metropolitan areas it is commonplace for social and economic change to be associated with quite different trajectories for different neighbourhoods. Decline in population, employment or income is evident at the neighbourhood scale, even within growing cities.

Change and imbalance create constant challenges for land markets and planning systems. Localized growth may mean rising property costs and new demands on the natural environment as well as accentuating stress, congestion, noise and pollution. Decline creates a different set of problems. Where localized demands for urban space are falling owners of property may sharply reduce maintenance, the public sector may not renew infrastructure even where it is not fiscally constrained, derelict land and space may emerge and assume even more negative attributes as they become the locus for vandalism and petty-crime. Abandoned then demolished industrial premises may leave behind an inheritance of contaminated land.

The patterns of growth, and decline, of cities and their neighbourhoods appear to differ markedly across EU countries. In general cities which are capitals or are located in core Europe or have a recent industrial/service base have higher growth rates than other metropolitan areas of older industrial Europe, though other cities which market their skills and images and compete hard for events and mobile capital and labour may still prosper outside the growth 'banana' (Lever, 1993). Within most European cities the processes of decentralization of population and employment from core to suburbs in the period since 1950 have been well documented. Deindustrialization, since the 1970s, has reinforced these patterns of suburban growth and core decline with inner-city decay.

However, this view of the pattern of urban change in Europe is too crude and simplistic. Some inner-city neighbourhoods, in northern and southern Europe, have remained high quality as residents attached symbolic importance to their areas, especially where city cores have a long history and even cultural meaning. Expansion of service industries in the central business districts of many cities since the 1970s has helped to retain vitality in such areas. A second consideration, of growing importance since 1980, is that unemployment has particularly impacted on social sector residents – and these now declining neighbourhoods may lie in the central city, at the periphery of core cities or in post 1960s settlements well into the suburban fringe. In the market sector not all suburbs are monofunctional dormitories, but some contain employment zones, major regional shopping centres and leisure facilities which generate serious suburban congestion, noise and environmental damage.

The core decline-suburban growth model is of questionable relevance in much of southern Europe. There the core area population of cities, in Greece and Spain and Portugal, often continued to increase into the 1980s with suburbs also growing. More recently major southern cities have had static or declining core populations but with household size decreasing and service employment rising there are few signs of property abandonment and vacant land. With extensive suburban commuting to work and intensive use of city centre leisure and shopping facilities the key issue facing many southern cities is not how to stimulate older areas but how to improve residential and environmental quality by reducing activity demands upon them. And in the suburban areas of towns in Greece, Portugal and southern Italy, in analogous fashion to rundown social housing in northern Europe, there are large areas of illegal settlement which house the poor with inadequate supportive infrastructure. Legal, illegal; market, non-market; core and suburban, the mosaic of neighbourhoods in the framework of European cities presents a variety of growth-decline scenarios with different environmental consequences, and land-use possibilities.

However, in all European countries, and most cities, there are low-quality neighbourhoods in which the poorest households have come to live in the worst urban conditions. Over the last decade, at least, international economic competition has meant that while average national income grew the real wages or benefit levels of the poorest quarter (some say a third) of the population have stagnated. Disrupted job careers have been paralleled by breakdown in family cycles with more young poor leaving parental homes in their teens, divorce and separation generating increased numbers of single parent families and so on. Likewise migration and ethnic diversity have increased.

Most of Europe's poor-quality neighbourhoods are now home to a mix, varying by country and city, of the unemployed and a new poor of elderly, single parents, ethnic minorities and single young persons. In many of these neighbourhoods suicides rates run high, mental illness is extensive, and alcohol and drug dependency is high and growing. From time to time the externalities of riot and disorder and, with a growing persistency, rising crime impact on citizens as a whole.

For many of these households lives are not sustainable now and there is a focus on current, personal survival rather than a concern with global, future issues. For the European poor, sustainability, like charity, must begin at home. Flexibility in land and housing systems will be a critical route for reducing tensions in the tradeoffs between competitive economic growth and rising environmental quality.

In this difficult context of increasing inequality, income separation, growth-decline patchwork and emerging environmental difficulty, there is much to be gained from re-examining the adequacy of local land markets and planning systems. Much of the remainder of this section emphasizes the need to address planning failures. But it must also be recognized that land markets appear to have inherent failures. Land supply sluggishness (not all due to planners) may restrict supply adjustment for decades; landowners may, sometimes, earn extensive economic rents; land-use decisions have important public good/externality effects. For instance, a pure market solution could generate socially sub-optimal cities. But how much is known, systematically, about land market failures in European cities? Very little, and it might be wise for urban governments to take a closer look at what happens now.

But then urban governments should take a close look at themselves and how they relate planning to the property market. The quality of planners and planning naturally varies from place to place. However a recent review (Maclennan, 1992a) suggested a number of deficiencies in land market planning. Of course not all of the criticisms apply to all planners in all places. The key criticisms were:

- large-scale planning, often involving major state investment, was based on a very incomplete conceptual understanding of how cities grow and develop;
- relatively little effort has been made, on a recurrent basis, to establish the social, economic and environmental geographies of cities being planned;
- plans disregarded uncertainty, most major events or trends were regarded as forecastable and plannable;
- planning, and planning professionals, had a technical and social rather than economic orientation and training and in consequence paid little attention to market signals and had a negative view of markets and developers;
- few plans were subjected to cost-benefit or cost-effectiveness analysis and the wider economic consequences of planning decisions and systems were rarely researched or considered;

- land-use planning, like government policy, was sectorally structured and selective;
- even where environmental aspects were emphasized in the planning process integrated analysis and control of pollution was a rarity;
- key methods of planning, such as Green Belt policies or demolition-clearance approaches to urban renewal were often continued in the face of public criticism;
- the style of planning was one of control;
- ever-more complex and sometimes contradictory regulations meant that few citizens understood the planning system and even fewer the resources to make expensive legal challenges to it;
- complex regulations often meant costly bureaucratic delays;
- developers and others spent a great deal of time and money in 'rent seeking' activities and occasionally in corrupting officials and politicians;
- rigid controls fuelled land price speculation and meant that developers concentrated their expertise on securing and financing land and ignored design and quality issues without penalty as consumers struggled to find space;
- planners ignored market-based consumer preference signals;
- community participation in planning was non-existent or token in form.

There was also a stream of comment which was directed at the context, set by national governments, in which plans were formed. For instance, in some countries cadastral systems were seriously incomplete, property rights unclear and the structure of urban government areas unrelated to functional urban systems.

Against this background of inadequacies, at least in some cities, planning systems are now confronted with new tasks and constraints. Local economic development policies, which ensure city competition and have grown to replace de-emphasized national regional policies, have planning requirements and implications. Area-based regeneration policies, focusing multi-sector action in parts of conurbations, pose new strategic and co-ordination tasks for planners. Planning is now also confronted with the task of imparting a new environmental impetus to city actions.

19.2.1 Changing Cities

Recent international reviews of appropriate urban policies have emphasized the importance of 'holistic', 'multi-sectoral' and 'partnership' approaches (Maclennan, 1992b). These conclusions have been reached in relation to economic development, housing, land and environmental policies. In essence they are growing out of new forms of urban governance and they are seeking a new style for market-oriented/sensitive planning.

The key elements of the approach involve

- the development of a purposive, agreed vision for a city and its neighbourhoods;
- the articulation of medium-term strategies with clear objectives and measurable targets consistent with the vision;
- the development of action plans which are 'directional' rather than 'tablets-of-stone';
- the introduction of continuous monitoring and evaluation to adapt plans in the light of learned experience;
- the formation of new partnerships of multiple government departments and agencies along with citizens, communities and the private sector;
- the convergence of goals within partnerships for the different parties and the sharing of expertise and information contribute to a more holistic approach;
- the need to recognize consumer preferences and community participation;
- the increased reliance on joint public/private funding of urban infrastructure and the use of planning gain as a bargaining tool.

A new style of urban planning is clearly emerging in the 1990s. However it is not just bureaucrats who have to change but the property industry is faced with new challenges. It too will have to develop longer-term perspectives, new ways of working with agencies and communities and new ways of establishing risk and return. For it is the cities in which the common purpose between the state and industry is best defined and most actively pursued that are likely to cope best with external change. These cities are also most likely to create purposive internal change. In a world in which raw materials and transfer costs are evening-out, economic attractiveness, city quality and social integration are increasingly complementary objectives. Crucially, cities must examine how their land and property can be best used or re-structured to meet these pressing objectives.

19.3   THE NATIONAL SCALE

National governments can facilitate urban level change in a number of ways. For example, better cadastral and land registration systems are required in many countries; contrast, for instance, effective Danish with sluggish Mediterranean systems. Central governments could also encourage more integrated thinking within and between functional departments, as has developed in France. The national to local framework for land planning could be greatly improved in much of Europe, with the Netherlands as a reference point. The role and powers of local government may require strengthening to ensure effective 'enabling' roles. Land and property taxation systems may need to be re-assessed.

In this section the 'urban policy' concerns of national governments are, for simplicity, set aside and focus is placed upon the key challenges now being confronted on the macro-economic and social agenda. For example, the UK economy, after the long boom of the 1980s in real incomes and property values, is only now emerging from a long and damaging recession. Recovery has been facilitated by the UK's departure from the ERM, in autumn 1992 allowing successive reductions in interest rates throughout 1993. Although unemployment remains high at just over 10% (with the 1989–93 recession disproportionately damaging southern Britain) GDP growth is now positive.

The residential property market is displaying stable nominal house prices for the first time since 1990 and turnover and investment levels are increasing. In the commercial property market (where values fell by 40% between 1992 and 1993) price stability is also appearing and investment has increased markedly since early 1993. Essentially, as rents have fallen less rapidly than values, commercial property yields now lie above those of gilt-edged securities. In both residential and non-residential sectors alike there is a view that, with more emphasis on borrower/tenant security and a more cautious approach by banks, the property market is now set for stable, considered recovery.

This belief is important. For there is little doubt that the housing market both boosted the 1980s boom, with new deregulated financial arrange-ments facilitating equity withdrawal from housing, and then prolonged the recovery as high interest rates then falling house prices impacted on debt exposed buyers. The UK housing system with a small rental market (at a fiscal disadvantage to owning), favours home-ownership and with land supply restrictions, is relatively unstable by European standards. Moreover variable rate mortgages (in contrast to the common fixed rate form in France and Germany) meant that the sector was particularly exposed in the downswing – thus exacerbating the recession, especially in the south.

Although some households and financial institutions with growing default rates may have learned much about the down-side of property investment, most households have survived intact. However, memories are short and the UK cannot rely on individuals and institutions to create a more stable housing system. There is still a strong case for further reducing MIRAS, with tax breaks redirected to lower income owners and the provision of a more sizeable rental market. Arguably, commercial and institutional investment in private rental housing would provide Britain with a more flexible housing system and more stable home-ownership.

There is a strong case for government, in its macro-economic planning, to take a more critical look at property investment in general. A period of booming activity in all sectors (from 1984 to 1989) in both prices and output equally fuelled the inflationary boom of the late 1980s. Subsequent collapse in profits, firm closures and a 15% vacancy rate in central city offices (4th quarter 1993) may provide room for inflation-free growth but the damage to the UK economy from 1990 to 1993 has been considerable.

There are obvious areas for enhancing 'flexibility' – 25 year leases with upwards only rent revision are hardly a beneficial arrangement for UK competitiveness. But there are also other key areas for government to examine. For example, government must also have its 'vision' for Britain and reduce uncertainties about the location, and scale for property investment. What does the UK government want London, for instance, to be by 2010? This is not a call for old-style regional planning or policy, but merely an observation that property investment is more effective where some broad, long-term uncertainties are reduced.

A further critical consideration, not least where the 1993 budget deficit is close to £50 billion, is the public/private funding of infrastructure. Across a whole range of public investment, but most notably transport and social housing, the 'rules' of the UK Treasury appear unduly restrictive by European and North American standards. Government is now looking at this issue – let us hope that the correct economic conclusion is drawn so that public subsidy rather than public spending becomes the key criterion. If so there would be direct benefits to developers, through an increased flow of work, as well as the breaking of infrastructure bottlenecks which invariably push up economic rents in the better served locations.

The juxtaposition of property market deflation and growing fiscal deficits is the norm rather than the exception in Western Europe at the start of the 1990s. Rents and capital values of prime office space have reduced by a quarter from their peak in early 1991 with the fall continuing throughout 1992–3. Jones Lang Wootton single out Barcelona as the most spectacular example of downturn; there office rents have fallen by 46% since 1991 and capital values by 61%. Vacancy rates have crept above 5% in Frankfurt, Paris and Brussels with Madrid edging up to 10%.

The combined effects of ageing, growing social programmes and recession have seen fiscal deficits in European Union countries grow markedly since 1990. With OECD emphasizing that a significant share of deficits reflect structural as well as recession components countries are faced with a real dilemma of how to undertake structural reform amidst recession.

Until a decade ago recession and unemployment would have encouraged governments to increase housing and infrastructure capital spending. Now deficit concerns are more likely to lead to efficiency/competition enhancing policy changes. There is already growing downward pressure on housing budgets. Planning and fiscal arrangements for land and other property sectors are unlikely to escape the scrutiny of governments. Institutional change and policy reform is likely to emerge, not just in Britain, but in

Europe as a whole as it faces the sustained competitive pressures of Eastern Pacific economies.

19.4   THE EUROPEAN DIMENSION

The 1990s started with two themes running through discussions of the future of the continent. First, there was a growing sense that, building beyond the completion of the single market, further economic integration through monetary union was a near certainty and that growing political union would follow. Second, the emergence of the Soviet bloc from the grip of centrally planned, communist rule offered long-term prospects of growth, trade and investment opportunities. Indeed, it was quickly recognized that a strong EC could transfer know-how and financial resources to newly emerging market-oriented economies, though the tight political structures of the European Union would require a long period of mutual adjustment before large-scale geographic expansion of the Union.

In brief, while 'market' provision became the clear winner in 'institutional' competition in both East and West, there were clearly different emphases on 'integration' and 'disintegration' in relation to linked economic blocs. Much has changed since the end of 1991 and the Maastricht treaty. The convergence criteria set as the preconditions for eventual monetary union were much closer to being fulfilled then than now. Further throughout 1993 the ERM of the EMS was ravaged as countries could not singly cope with international speculation and a rising D-Mark consequent to tight German monetary policy – even in the face of deepening EC recession.

The British departure from the ERM, without which the domestic property sector and wider economy would have been ravaged, set a new form of 'institutional' competition. In the absence of a truly European monetary policy (as opposed to German policy operating through the D-Mark) countries have watched with interest as British recovery has gone ahead of other European economies. The British view of Europe as a looser club, with more members and more national sovereignty commands more interest now than two years ago. With record levels of unemployment, large structural deficits and burgeoning social welfare programmes only Germany, France, Netherlands and Belgium now seem to lie close to a real commitment to imminent monetary union. However the apparent correlation of unemployment and nationalism in the two former countries may place domestic political constraints on full monetary union.

Ideas are also changing in Eastern Europe. There are, at least, two scenarios for evolution. In the first, growing trade and investment will raise living standards. Structural adjustment, with an essentially well trained labour force, largely through privatization will see beneficial 'spread' effects from West to East. The other view is that with slow change in the East, aggressive competition from the West to raise domestic employment (not least in the recession), will lead to an outflow of capital and skilled labour from East to West. The major cities of the East, such as Warsaw, Prague and Budapest will almost certainly grow and prosper as they reclaim lost positions in the European urban hierarchy but the fate of smaller cities and older industrial regions is less optimistic. That is, there may be 'backwash' effects in the East.

If the 1990s dawned with an optimistic 'Western Integration – Eastern Spread' scenario a 'Looser West-Eastern "backwash"' model may be more appropriate for the foreseeable future. Exports from East to West have fallen in the last two years, and although GDP growth has been impressive in Hungary, Slovenia and the Czech Republic progress elsewhere has been less impressive with potentially disastrous scenarios emerging in Russia and already a reality in the former Yugoslavia.

Regardless of which scenarios prevail in West and East governments will have to pay closer attention to the efficiency consequences of housing, land and property arrangements. Planning and property issues were alluded to above. Housing policy arrangements also illustrate the point, though some systems such as Germany are more flexible and stable than, for instance, the UK. Arguably rental markets (7% of homes in the UK and 13% in the Netherlands, versus 40% in the former FRG) could play a larger role. Pricing and investment in social housing requires a reappraisal, and the costs of housing allowances are rising rapidly. Sweden, poised to enter the European Union, is already embarking on a planned massive reduction in housing subsidies. These are, in the 1990s, falling in the UK and the Dutch government is also reducing assistance.

Unless there is a massive re-targeting of housing support (and public investment) the West European total of 2 million plus homeless will rise and the problems of rundown areas will grow. The obvious escape route is to find mechanisms which reduce market housing and land costs and improve the efficiency of these markets. The future role of housing policy, if in a less obvious fashion, is as much open to challenge and change in the West as the East. At the margin monetary union will exacerbate these problems, as system inflexibilities will have cost effects reflected in investment and employment consequences rather than currency depreciation.

In the East, understandably, it is widely accepted that a transfer of housing from stable to market sectors will lead to a more effective use of the housing stock and more appropriate investment patterns. The house types and geographic patterns of socialist housing systems have, in the long term, lead to choice distortions and households/stock mismatches on a massive scale (though such distortions are by no means unique to the East (Maclennan, 1993).

American, rather than West European, advice, expertise and approaches have been most widely available to national governments in the East. But as the essential message of the market, in jobs as well as property, is taken up the key questions for property policies, particularly at the city level, change. Eastern mayors, even ardent pro-marketeers, are faced with questions about the limits to market efficiency and the acceptability of market outcomes with changing income distributions. Once these questions are asked the pace of change is likely to slow and the costs of housing policies to increase. The real dilemma for urban housing policy managers in the East is that economically they cannot afford West European policies; politically they cannot afford the consequences of urban segregation, decay and disorder which have emerged in post-war America.

The key lesson for the East, and indeed the lagging parts of the West, may lie in the early post-war recovery phase. Then in Germany, France and the Netherlands and Denmark (for instance) a decade of putting economic restoration ahead of market housing costs was required. The East like the West faces the critical issue of containing housing costs to secure economic progress. Perhaps a new phase of East-West co-operation is now required, not involving more market missionaries but concentrating on the exchange of planners and bureaucrats who have successfully managed the market-state interface in the West. Real experience exchange rather than fast consultancy may be helpful.

19.5 CONCLUSION

From the urban to the national and international scale Europe, East and West, needs a new appreciation of the role of property in economic development. The inadequacy, in terms of vision, strategy and specific policy design of present approaches in many places is all too apparent. Rising land and housing costs may signal fundamental market scarcities and lead to efficient resource allocation. But experience suggests that too often inflation, instability and needless government expense stem from lack of insight and even political will to change.

Western governments are beginning, in a long recession, to shift housing policies as a consequence of budgetary pressures. Few countries have a clearly articulated strategy for change as in Sweden. Such strategies are now vital at urban and national scales. Indeed the European Union, though not necessarily increasing its competence in property and housing, badly needs a clearer view of how the areas which it can influence impact on property markets. If European countries and the European Union do not react purposively to these issues their share of world exports will continue to fall. Economic flexibility will not be enhanced and European cities will lose their civilized tone.

Acknowledgement

This paper is based upon research funded by the Economic and Social Research Council.

REFERENCES

Evans, A.W. (1988) *No Room! No Room!: The Costs of the British Town and Country Planning System*, Occasional Paper 79, Institute of Economic Affairs, London.

Fitoussi, J.-P., Atkinson, A.B., Blanchard, O.E., Flemming, J.S., Malinvaud, E., Phelps, E.S. and Solow, R.M. (1993) *Competitive Disinflation*, Oxford University Press, Oxford.

Lever, W.F. (1993) Competition within the European urban system, *Urban Studies*, **30**(6), 935–48.

Maclennan, D. (1992a) Planning for the market: sustainability, feasibility and flexibility in urban Europe, in D. Maclennan and V. Mega (eds), *Land Use Management and Environmental Improvement in Cities*, European Foundation for Living and Working Conditions, Dublin.

Maclennan, D. (1992b) *Assessing Partnerships*, paper presented at OECD/ Scottish Office Conference, Edinburgh, October 1992.

Maclennan, D. (1993) Decentralisation and residential choices in European cities: the roles of state and market, in A.A. Summers, P.C. Cheshire and L. Sen (eds), *Urban Change in the United States and Western Europe*, The Urban Institute Press, Washington DC.

Maclennan, D. and Meen, G. (1993) *Housing Markets and National Economic Performance in OECD Countries*, Briefing Paper Number 3, Joseph Rowntree Foundation, York.

Index

Page references in **bold** represent figures and those in *italic* represent tables

OTHER TITLES FROM E & FN SPON

Urban Regeneration
Property investment and development
Edited by J. Berry, S. McGreal and B. Deddis

The Multilingual Dictionary of Real Estate
A guide for the property professional in the Single European Market
Edited by L. Van Breugel, R.H. Williams and B. Wood

UK Directory of Property Developers, Investors and Financiers
Seventh edition
Building Economics Bureau

European Directory of Property Developers, Investors and Financiers
Second edition
Building Economics Bureau

Rebuilding the City
Property-led urban regeneration
P. Healey, S. Davoudi, M.O. Toole, S. Tavsanoglu and D. Usher

Industrial Property Markets in Western Europe
Edited by B. Wood and R. Williams

Property Development
Third Edition
D. Cadman and L. Austin-Crowe
Edited by R. Topping and M. Avis

Industrial and Business Space Development
Implementation and urban renewal
S. Morley, C. Marsh, A. McIntosh and H. Martinos

International Real Estate Valuation, Investment and Development
V.J. Nurcombe

Property Investment and the Capital Markets
G.R. Brown

Property Investment Decisions
A quantitative approach
S. Hargitay and M. Yu

National Taxation for Property Management and Valuation
A. MacLeary

Risk, Uncertainty and Decision-making in Property Development
P.J. Byrne and D. Cadman

Property Valuation
The five methods
D. Scarrett

Microcomputers in Property
A surveyor's guide to Lotus 1-2-3 and dBASE IV
T.J. Dixon, O. Bevan and S. Hargitay

Effective Writing
Improving scientific, technical and business communication
Second edition
C. Turk and J. Kirkman

Good Style
Writing for science and technology
J. Kirkman

Effective Speaking
Communicating in speech
C. Turk

Journals

Journal of Property Research (Formerly Land Development Studies)
Editors: B.D. MacGregor, D. Hartzell and M. Miles

Planning Perspectives
An international journal of planning, history and the environment
Editors: G. Cherry and A. Sutcliffe

For more information on these and other titles please contact:
The Promotion Department, E & FN Spon, 2–6 Boundary Row,
London SE1 8HN   Telephone 071 865 0066

Learning Resources
Centre